Women's work and the family economy in historical perspective

Women's work and the family economy in historical perspective

Edited by Pat Hudson and W.R. Lee

MANCHESTER
UNIVERSITY PRESS
Manchester and New York

Distributed exclusively in the USA and Canada
by ST. MARTIN'S PRESS

Published by Manchester University Press
Oxford Road, Manchester M13 9PL, UK
and Room 400, 175 Fifth Avenue,
New York, NY 10010, USA

Distributed exclusively in the USA and Canada
by St. Martin's Press, Inc.,
175 Fifth Avenue, New York, NY 10010, USA

British Library cataloguing in publication data

Women's work and the family economy in historical
    perspective
    1. Women. Employment, history
    I. Hudson, Pat, *1948–*   II. Lee, W.R. (William Robert),
    1946–
    331.409

Library of Congress cataloging in publication data applied for

ISBN 0 7190 23777 *hardback*

Printed in Great Britain
by Biddles Ltd, Guildford and King's Lynn

CONTENTS

Contents

FIGURES

TABLES

CONTRIBUTORS

Pat Ayers currently works on the Docklands History Project at the University of Liverpool. She is completing her Ph.D. on 'The household economies of dockland Liverpool in the interwar period'. Her publications include *The Liverpool Docklands: Life and Work in Atholl Street* (1987) and *Women at War: Liverpool Women, 1939–1945* (Liverpool, 1988).

Ida Blom is Professor of Women's History at the University of Bergen. Her research covers aspects of political, social and demographic history of the nineteenth and twentieth centuries. Apart from numerous articles her major publications have been *Synd eller sunn fornuft? Barnebegrensning i Norge ca. 1890 – ca. 1940* (Bergen, 1980) (on the history of family planning in Norway), and *Den haarde Dyst. Fødsler og fødselshjelp gjennom 150 år* (Oslo, 1988) (on 150 years of change in Norwegian childbirth routines).

Clare Evans is in the final stages of completing her doctorate on 'The separation of work and home? The case of the Lancashire textile industry, c. 1830–1865', at the University of Manchester. Her current interest is in developing feminist approaches to studying household data using computers. A brief outline of this is included in *Proceedings of the First International Conference on the Application of Transputers, University of Liverpool, 1989* and further results are shortly to appear in *Gender and History*.

Linda Grant is currently a researcher at the West Yorkshire Centre for Research on Women (WYCROW), University of Bradford. She is working on women's part-time employment in West Yorkshire and results will be published shortly by WYCROW. Research she has undertaken over the past twelve years in Liverpool, Coventry and West Yorkshire has been mainly concerned with women's employment, social history and, particularly, women's history.

Catherine Hall teaches cultural history in the Department of Cultural Studies, Polytechnic of East London. She is the co-author with Leonore Davidoff of *Family Fortunes: Men and Women of the English Middle Class, 1780–1850* (London, 1987). She is now working on race, ethnicity and the English middle class.

Pat Hudson teaches in the Department of Economic and Social History, University of Liverpool. Her main research interests are household manufacturing, the finance of industry and the economic and social history of British regions before and during the innovation of factory production. Her books include *The Genesis of Industrial Capital* (1986) and an edited collection: *Regions and Industries: a perspective on the Industrial Revolution in Britain* (Cambridge, 1989).

W. R. Lee is Professor of Economic and Social History at the University of Liverpool. His research concentrates on the demographic, economic and social history of Central European regions and port cities since the nineteenth century. His publications include *Urban Population Development in Western Europe from the Late Eighteenth to the Early Twentieth Century* (1989), coedited with Richard Lawton, and *The State and Social Change in Germany, 1880–1980* (1990), coedited with Eve Rosenhaft.

Anne Meyering teaches modern French and European history at Michigan State University in East Lansing. In connection with the 1989 bicentennial, she organised a symposium, wrote an article on François Furet's interpretation of the French Revolution and spent the autumn in Paris teaching American university students about the history of the French Revolution. Her main research interest is the transformation of French society and politics by industrialisation in the nineteenth century as seen through the example of the town of Montluçon.

Jane McDermid teaches contemporary European history at La Sainte Union College, Southampton. Her Glasgow University Ph.D. was on the evolution of Soviet attitudes towards women and the family and recent articles in this field have appeared in *Scottish Slavonic Review* and *Irish Slavic Studies*. She is currently working on a comparison of women in the French and Russian revolutions, and on nationality, class and gender in nineteenth-century Scottish and English education.

Sheilagh Ogilvie is a Fellow of Trinity College, Cambridge. She works on the economic and social history of German-speaking Central Europe from the sixteenth to the nineteenth centuries, with a special interest in the state, corporate institutions, and the family. Her book on proto-industrialisation will be published by Cambridge University Press in 1991.

Richard Whipp is Professor of Human Resource Management at Cardiff Business School. He has published widely on the themes of industrial and social change. Results have appeared in *Past and Present, Sociological Review* and are fully reported in his books *Innovation and the Auto Industry* (1986) and *Patterns of Labour: Work in Social and Historical Perspective* (1990).

ACKNOWLEDGEMENTS

This book started life as a series of seminars given at the University of Liverpool, Department of Economic and Social history in 1986. The papers raised a spectrum of interrelated issues about economic development, personal life and ideological structures which provoked stimulating discussion among audiences drawn from across the arts and social sciences creating sufficient enthusiasm on the part of the organisers to seek a publisher.

The chapters by Ogilvie, Hall, Blom, Whipp, Evans and Ayers were all initially a part of the seminar series whilst those by Lee, Meyering, McDermid and Grant were specially commissioned for the volume to create a more broadly-based temporal and geographical perspective. The editors owe a considerable debt to all the contributors particularly for their responsiveness to suggestions and for their patience with the delays which inevitably occured during the production of the manuscript. We also thank the other participants in the seminar series especially those who gave papers not included in this volume. Finally, a large number of colleagues at Liverpool and elsewhere have been major sources of encouragement and stimulus particularly in writing chapter 1. We owe them a debt and hope that we have produced something of the sort of useful and wide ranging volume which they had in mind.

Robert Lee and Pat Hudson   University of Liverpool
                                             September 1989

INTRODUCTION

Chapter One

Women's work and the family economy in historical perspective

PAT HUDSON and W. R. LEE

Much of the history of women's work has been written from a male perspective. This has resulted in a preoccupation with the ways in which women have 'participated' in social processes, including work, which are defined in terms of male experience. For example there has been a concentration of study surrounding changing female participation rates in the formal economy of paid work undertaken mainly outside of the home.[1] Yet we know that much of women's work throughout different historical periods has been concentrated outside of this formal economy in the vast range of tasks surrounding home and hearth and in irregular low-status employments which do not readily enter historical record.[2] This volume seeks to avoid the male perspective first by emphasising when, why and with what result women have laboured inside and outside of the home in paid and unpaid employment and secondly by emphasising the need to integrate women's history into the major debates of economic and social history more generally. The various contributions pose questions about the role of women's work in the creation of social and political identity, its importance in the maintenance of family incomes and living standards, its impact on fertility and mortality and its foundation within the wider perspective of gender relations and attitudes both inside and outside of the household and family. This chapter provides a historiographical and thematic context for those which follow by outlining some important issues concerning women's work and the family economy in Europe since medieval times.

Key themes

Five overlapping issues recur in the literature on women's work and in the contributions to this book: the role of ideology; the impact of law and of state policy; continuity and change in the sexual division of labour; changes in the technology and organisation of work and, finally, the importance of the family economy.

The ideals and beliefs of the medieval church and of the feudal elites of Europe left an embedded ideological view of women which was a mixture of misogyny, fear, mystique and subordination.[3] It became enshrined in law and literature and influenced the attitudes of all social classes. Celibate clerics, so important in promulgating the Christian view of women, inherited their contradictory ideas from Pauline teaching: woman was the instrument of the devil and the supreme temptress as well as enshrining the (unattainable) virtues of the virgin mother. Among the feudal elite women were seen first as ornamental assets strictly subordinate to the interests of transmission and preservation of the landed estate and the aristocratic ideal of women was one of fidelity and subjection within marriage tempered only a little by the notion of courtly love.[4] The seventeenth century witchcraze and the rise of Newtonian science with its stress on the 'mastery' of nature, and the foolishness of (female) superstition and intuition only exacerbated the ideological view of women as the inferior and dangerous sex.[5] Their assumed physical frailty and mental instability remained fundamental to intellectual views of women and to definitions of their appropriate work roles and capabilities. The emphasis on strenuous effort in defining gender limited an appreciation of the labour which women were able to carry out and the assumed centrality of women's reproductive function served to confine her legitimate activity, at least in theory, to the home and an 'easy life'. Within the household, ideas surrounding menstruation further contributed to customary restrictions on her activity.[6]

For the mass of the population the social position of women in medieval and early modern society was never a simple one of inferiority and subjection because economic necessity made women indispensable partners in the work of household, farm and workshop as well as vital contributors to family incomes. But ideological meanings endowed different types of work with status implications which were far from objective: although women undertook a wide range of complex and demanding activities these were primarily viewed as the social obligations of a wife or daughter rather than as the 'occupation' of a married or single woman.[7] Moreover, as Davis has said of French women in the sixteenth century, their productive energies were available to be shifted into all sorts of different work if circumstances demanded it. Their occupational identity was thin and the social status attached to specialised male work and to male crafts was absent.[8] Thus, despite their central role in a wide range of agricultural and craft work, women's social identity was defined overwhelmingly through their fathers or husbands and through their domestic and reproductive roles.

Industrial capitalism created new tensions in male–female relationships which caused some reworking of notions about skill, gender and the family. The ideal of the wife and mother at home and of the male bread-winner wage was the most powerful factor restricting women's access to the broad spectrum of paid work during the nineteenth and early twentieth centuries.[9] Gender ideology was also reinforced by the increasingly pervasive notions of correct education for girls which placed stress on traditional female domestic and craft skills important for running a home and raising a family.[10] It was believed that the mental evolution of women had been arrested earlier than men to conserve their energies for pregnancy and childbirth; women therefore had to be protected from school examinations and confined to the home.[11]

Variations in law and custom were and remain vital in creating or restricting women's employment prospects. Women in medieval and early modern Europe were constrained by a mass of legal regulations but these were often contradictory. Canon law functioned alongside common law and city or borough regulations to provide a framework of rules regarding inheritance and contracts. These gave women some rights whilst undeniably placing them in a position inferior to men.[12] The multiplicity of statutes in the early modern period provided loopholes in the regulations surrounding women's economic functions which allowed them a degree of latitude for involvement in business that they appear to have lost in the more clearly defined legal circumstances of the nineteenth century.[13] However, in the high-status trades, corporate customs which reserved political activity exclusively for men were important in excluding women from those guilds involved in municipal government.[14]

Law and custom regarding inheritance and property rights also impinged on women's economic role. For example, the right of widows to 'free bench' in England gave them between one-third and one-half of their husband's land for their lifetime but this was usually conditional upon their not remarrying or entering other liaisons. There was a variety of controls over a husband's rights in his wife's land but as land declined as a form of property women's material rights suffered.[15] A wife's personal property, stock, bonds, cash as well as her income belonged legally to her husband. This must have severely discouraged independent economic activity and contributed to women's self-perception that their income-earning roles were for family and not for individual gain.

Increased female employment in centralised factory-based production, in mining and in heavy industry in the early nineteenth century was in direct conflict with the domestic ideal. This forced government intervention in the field of protective labour legislation which was designed ostensibly to protect the position of women in the labour force and to solve the social problems (illegitimacy, bad mothering) associated with women's work beyond the household. Regulation served to reinforce the belief that a woman's role should be restricted to the domestic environment but had the effect of expanding women's labour in the sweated unregulated sector and in the informal economy carried on both inside and outside of the home.[16]

How did ideology and the framework of law influence the mental boundaries between male and female labour and to what extent did these boundaries vary with economic development and from one region to another? Spinning, sewing, millinery, silkworking, laundering, nursing and petty retailing as well as dairywork, much food and drink preparation and low-status fieldwork seem to have been predominantly in female hands over many centuries even though the structure of the economy and the market environment had changed dramatically.[17] This cannot be conveniently explained by the need for women's work to be fitted in around household and maternal responsibilities or by being physically undemanding.[18] At the same time elements of the sexual division of labour have proved mutable over cycles of labour surplus or labour shortage, or have responded to wider changes in the importance of the family as a unit of production, the extent of proletarianisation, technological change and other major variables of this kind. It is important therefore to examine the factors which influenced and determined the configuration of the sexual division of labour over an extended historical time period.

Perhaps the most important influence affecting women's access to skilled and high-status work was the changing nature of the family economy, whether through proto-industrialisation, proletarianisation or urbanisation. As long as the household remained a major unit of production, the family remained the main instrument of recruitment to work and most women worked as members of a family production unit. It is thus not surprising that their access to this work may have waxed and wained with the importance of the family as a site of production for the market in both urban and rural crafts.[19] As the family production unit declined, particularly from the nineteenth century, the opportunities for married women in regular waged work appear to have been severely curtailed outside of the sweated trades.[20] Young unmarried women and children did, on the other hand, become important potential earners in the late eighteenth and early nineteenth centuries and teenage girls in some sectors and regions were a pillar of the workforce for the following century, which had major implications for the life cycle of family earnings, the domestic relationships arising from it and for local political attitudes and structures.[21] The fact that women's rates of pay have always been inferior to men's even for comparable work is an issue of related importance. It implied a lower opportunity cost for women than for men in undertaking the major responsibility for housework and child-rearing. This served to bolster other justifications, material and ideological, for the particular immutability of women's domestic priorities and the idea of women's work being supplemental to household income and subordinate to the other functions of the household and family.

Demographic conditions of high mortality, the tendency towards an unbalanced sex ratio and low rates of marriage in some countries over long periods always ensured that there were many widows and spinsters responsible for both the income and reproduction needs of households. Outside of the conventional family economy, such women in different periods found it very difficult to earn a living in areas other than the traditional low-status tasks of the informal economy. The route of access to higher-status work in craft production or larger-scale commercial trading was via their deceased husbands or through their fathers. But as the possibilities of inheriting businesses in this way declined with changes in business structure, the problem of widows and spinsters became acute and was exacerbated by the nineteenth-century ideal of the middle-class lady of leisure. The limitations placed upon the earning and status potential of the female-headed household in the nineteenth and twentieth centuries with the emergence of the male breadwinner wage norm and its surrounding ideology helps to explain why single-parent families are accorded such low status and low welfare rights in both past and present societies.[22]

In theory one might expect that technological change would increase the opportunities for women to work on a greater parity with men. By removing or lightening tasks requiring great physical strength, more efficient tools and mechanisation might have changed that aspect of the sexual division of labour grounded in or at least justified by the notion of female physical inferiority. Deskilling, implicit in many forms of mechanisation, together with organisational changes such as those which sought to cheapen and discipline labour, may be expected to have created more openings for women's work in sectors previously dominated by male monopolies. Industrial capitalism did indeed bring some widening of the sphere of women's work outside the home, but it was accompanied by a significant redefinition and reworking of the sexual division of labour as well as by the emergence of new ideological and social constraints. Together these severely limited the levelling or liberating potential of technological and organisational change. For example, the shift of women into the male-dominated field of weaving following the removal of spinning from the home to factories in many of the textile trades was seldom accompanied by assimilation of women into the same spheres of work and work status as men. Usually women only entered into the weaving of cloths associated with lower skill, dexterity and rates of pay. Once associated with women, the social perception of low skill requirement and the low status of, and remuneration for, such work became entrenched even where market forces should have provoked upward pressure on wages and the demand for such labour.[23] At the same time, mechanised spinning, although at first associated with female labour, quickly became a high-status male preserve jealously and powerfully guarded by the male spinners' union. Once a new male monopoly was established the transmission of female craft skills from one generation to the next was lost. Mechanisation thereby reinforced the exclusion of women from many trades for long periods of time.[24] Occupations and professions *exclusively* reserved for one sex may have declined in Britain (and elsewhere) in the nineteenth and twentieth centuries, but occupational concentration and job segregation hardly altered at all.[25]

The advance of technology and the centralisation of work in the nineteenth and twentieth centuries created new supervisory hierarchies in the workplace such that even in trades where women found employment they were generally supervised by men as well as being dependent on male mechanics for the efficient running of their machines. The extent to which workplace supervision and hierarchy replicated and was endorsed by the power structures of the family and the household remains a vital question in unravelling the complex interplay of society and economy, of capitalism and patriarchy.[26] Recent research on women's work and the family economy sheds much light on this subject. We here examine the historiography dealing in turn with the primary sector, the urban trades, proto-industrialisation and industrial capitalism.

Agriculture and the peasant household

Women have always played an indispensable role in subsistence agriculture and they remained prominent in the workforce of commercialising agriculture. There were close links between non-market gender roles and those which emerged with the development of commercial farming, but commercialisation also produced patterns of restructuring of the sex-specific division of labour which varied from one region to another depending on the sorts of commercial crops, labour supply conditions and the availability of alternative work for women and for men.[27] In medieval times the sexual division of labour in agriculture remained very flexible, partly because the prevalence of peasant landholding precluded extensive occupational specialisation among the mass of the labouring population.[28] Furthermore, periodic dearth and distress also brought crises of mortality which left many women to carry on peasant agriculture and labour services. Labour shortage following the Black Death, for example, may have resulted in greater parity between the sexes both in the sort of work done and in pay rates.[29]

Over much of Western Europe before the spread of commercial agriculture and extensive rural proletarianisation, women could be found undertaking most agricultural tasks, but the household and kitchen garden were particularly their domain together with the dairy (milking, the making of butter and cheese) and the tending of pigs and poultry. In addition women made and sold ale and wine, were active as midwives and healers and some were involved in trading and moneylending. They also played a vital part in fieldwork despite the fact that this, together with stock-herding, was considered largely a male preserve. Women commonly carried out weeding and hoeing and the sowing of pulses; they also worked in harvesting, especially of hay, wheat, rye and other crops where the lighter sickle was used in preference to the scythe. The seasonal peak of labour demand in agriculture appears always to have led to greater blurring of gender roles but, despite this, scything was specifically reserved for men and only very rarely done by women from Roman times until the major changes in technology of the twentieth century.[30]

With the increasing commercialisation of farming from the sixteenth and seventeenth centuries, greater occupational specialisation occurred among agricultural workers, but enhancement of individual occupational identity was predominantly confined to men. Not only were women often excluded from new opportunities, but their status became more marginalised also because the remaining non-specialist farm work became more routine and monotonous. This was less the case in regions where there was significant demand for male labour outside of agriculture or where new cultures like root crops increased the demand for labour intensive farm work.[31]

The history of women's involvement in harvest work is illustrative of continuities and changes taking place in women's work roles and of the regional variations in such changes. The widespread and persistent exclusion of women from mowing was important because as more corn and other cereals came to be mown with the scythe rather than reaped women became concentrated in the expanding ancillary tasks such as raking and stacking.[32] Snell has stressed that the marked decline in female participation in harvest labour in the south-east of England in the late eighteenth and early nineteenth centuries was associated with the innovation of mowing across a range of cereals and marked a major shift away from a high degree of sexually shared labour. Certainly, there seems to have been a decline in female waged work in some commercial grain-growing areas of England from the late eighteenth century. Moreover, in conditions of plentiful labour supply, it became more economical to employ workers on a casual basis than to bear the costs of round-the-year hiring. So living-in service for both women and men declined. But proletarian hiring made males very vulnerable to seasonal unemployment and to avoid the burden of poor families on the rates the inferior 'female' agricultural tasks, such as dung spreading and threshing, were increasingly offered to men, reducing still more the possibilities of remunerative work for women.[33] The decline of the commons with continuing enclosure in the eighteenth and early nineteenth centuries further exacerbated female unemployment, as grazing and gathering activities had frequently been associated with women.[34] The faltering and relocation of domestic industries in the face of increasing factory competition also took its toll on female income-earning potential and on the living standards of the mass of agricultural labourers' families in the south and east of England by the early nineteenth century.[35]

These sorts of factors were common in altering women's work in many regions of commercial grain farming in Europe by the nineteenth century but we should be wary, as Lee's chapter shows, of generalising about their incidence and effects. There were marked regional variations depending on the suitability of mowing for different crop mixes, conflicting requirements of speed and care in cutting, climate (wet or dry cutting), the type of farm unit and the size of the available workforce which could influence the speed of innovation and determine whether innovation was capital or labour intensive.[36]

Away from regions of commercial grain growing, increasing production for the market brought even more varied responses in terms of female involvement in outdoor labour. Women's work frequently increased with the extension of production for the market, especially in types of agriculture which were initially labour intensive: mixed farming regimes, root crops, market gardening, dairying. This was certainly the case in Germany and in the north and west pastoral districts of England there was no counterpart to the decline in living-in female service which occurred in the south.[37] Furthermore, low agricultural incomes for men were in some areas met with a great deal of resourcefulness in finding supplementary activities for women and children:

> the trapping of wheatears on the Sussex coast to be sold as delicacies in Tunbridge Wells, the production of asses' milk for the delicate stomachs of Canterbury and London citizens, the collecting of osiers and reeds for the making of barrel hoops and baskets in the Somerset fens, the production of fish in old hammer ponds in Sussex, and the fattening of pigs on distillers' and starch makers' waste grain in town suburbs.[38]

The continued involvement of women in many regions across a broad spectrum of field tasks, including the most arduous, certainly eliminates the notion that female roles in agriculture were determined by either biological character or maternal function. The pulling up of crops such as sugar-beet and turnips and potato digging were most frequently done by women from Scotland and Ireland across to Eastern Europe. In Germany, for example, around All Saints' Day all root crops were pulled and cut mostly by women, which required a triple work shift. In livestock areas the hay harvest needed all the available labour, female and child as well as male, to ensure the best use of dry weather within a concentrated period. Winter feeding of cattle and the dung spreading characteristic of mixed rotations also increased the amount of outdoor labour in which women were commonly involved.[39] A general societal attitude which deplored heavy work for women was conveniently forgotten in areas where female labour remained vital. For example in the north-east of England in the late nineteenth century, whilst men were increasingly absorbed in heavy industry, women workers known as bondagers were employed in fieldwork gangs.[40] Thus there was much regional variation in the extent to which increased commercialisation of agriculture in the eighteenth and nineteenth centuries affected both the volume and the type of waged work available for women. This is especially important because it may well be that a large part of the European variation in rural incomes and in rates of maternal and infant mortality can be attributed to these differences.[41]

Substantial contraction in the relative size of the primary sector and the growth of large-scale production in the course of the twentieth century has inevitably impinged on women's rural work roles. But despite the much-vaunted demise of the peasantry, the fragmentation of rural labour-markets and the development of new structures of production, including workers' co-operatives, there is evidence of marked continuities in gender roles.[42] Family-centred farming on small acreages has maintained a fairly strict sexual division of work and certain rural communities in France, specialising in viticulture, retain communal proscriptions on the sexual division of work, with women expected to engage solely in the production of use-value in the domestic sphere.[43] Inevitably, many village communities throughout Europe have lost their older structures through increasing migration and economic marginalisation, but it is clear that this did not necessarily imply a uniform or fundamental readjustment in the traditional configuration of male and female work roles.

Women's work in urban production

The varying labour experiences of women in agrarian society were matched by similar differences between individual towns and cities as a result of the changing labour demands of their dominant sectors, the nature of their markets, local traditions concerning women's roles and institutional and political policies which varied from one region/nation state of Europe to another.[44] But despite this, the urban working experiences of women throughout Europe seem to have had remarkable similarities both in nature and in the impact of long- and short-term variations emanating from changing institutional structures, production methods, domestic ideologies and labour supply conditions.

In medieval towns most women worked of necessity either to supplement household earnings or to support a household independently as a widow or *femme sole*. Most women's employment, as later, centred around the home and utilised domestic skills. Women worked mainly in casual and intermittent trades of street selling, food and drink production, laundering, in service, nursing or as lodging housekeepers or prostitutes. Often women did many sorts of work over their life cycle depending on family pressures and constraints. Whereas men specialised from an early age, through formal apprenticeship with guild membership an obvious goal, women had less access to apprenticeships save through training by their parents. As supplemental earners, they most often comprised a mobile reserve, moving in and out of trades or involved in two or more simultaneously where (necessarily) craft guilds and monopolies were not evident.[45] This flexibility together with the primary commitment of women to domestic responsibilities and to domestic work regimes incompatible with the regular effort required of craft work have been used to explain the under-representation of women in the high-status market-oriented crafts and their guilds. More importantly, however, variation and change in the importance of the family work unit restricted the role of women in the crafts of the medieval urban economy, influenced their differing role from one city to another and served to reduce women's access to such work as the centuries progressed.[46]

Evidence overwhelmingly suggests that high-status work in both manufacturing and in trade was more open to women in medieval towns than it was to become by the sixteenth, seventeenth and eighteenth centuries. In fact, some high-status commercial manufactures were largely regarded as female occupations.[47] However, guild regulations, royal decrees and legal or taxation records are often misleading instruments with which to guage women's real participation and status in these labour-markets. For example, as late as 1772 borough laws of London allowed women to trade and work for their own account in the City, but other evidence suggests that by then they were no longer found in a wide range of high-status occupations.[48] It is difficult to assess the disparity between sources like the formal rules of guilds and borough regulations (often not strictly enforced or obeyed) and the reality of women's working lives. Does the admittance of widows to guilds indicate that they commonly took up their husband's trades without disadvantage? To carry on the work of her husband a widow needed tools, workplace and a labour force and these were passed on to widows less frequently than might be expected.[49] Furthermore, widows were often forbidden by guilds to take on male apprentices for training and the status of widows and *femmes soles* within guilds remains unclear, as they often had only social membership and not full participating rights.[50] Surviving evidence of female participation in particular industries and their membership of guilds also tells us little about the sexual division of labour in practice within the craft workshop.

The right of a craftsman to train his wife and daughters appears to have been generally recognised, but they were seldom allowed access to guild membership during his lifetime. In some towns, especially in weaving and spinning centres, married women and spinsters are recorded as guild members and in some countries, though not in England, there were guilds composed exclusively of women although many, such as those in Paris, were under close male supervision.[51] Women throughout Europe seem to have played a prominent role in the social and religious fraternities which were often attached to guilds and to have enjoyed the same entitlements to welfare and aid from them.[52] But in the guilds themselves their activities were hedged around with restrictions. Some guilds were completely closed to women whilst in others it was prohibited to employ women for wages and even craftsmen's widows faced severe restrictions. The daughters of leather beltmakers of Paris for example were allowed to work as independent craftswomen even if they married but were not allowed to teach the craft to apprentices or to their husbands.[53]

Thus we know that women's work in the medieval urban economy was widespread and varied yet circumscribed in important ways. Female workers were recognised in industry and trading independently of their role as wife, mother or daughter. Their legal independence (the right to sue or be sued as an individual regardless of marital status) was established in all medieval European towns. But they by no means participated in the trades on equal terms with men. What were the ideological and practical foundations of these restrictions? The literature of the period played down the economic role of women in towns emphasising instead their duties towards their husbands and their sexual chastity. The need for sexual modesty was used as an argument for the prohibition of women from employing male apprentices and definitions of femininity were used to justify exclusion from trades described as too dangerous or dirty for women. But the principle was not consistently applied and many dirty and arduous tasks were exclusively reserved for women and were never a matter of comment.[54]

Objections to and restrictions on female labour were most marked where the work competed with that of men. One can thus observe a close connection between the restrictiveness of guild and other ordinances concerning women's work and labour-market conditions. In Bristol in 1461, for example, when weavers were threatened by an influx of foreigners, men were forbidden to give work to their wives and daughters. In London female participation in the guilds apparently increased after the Black Death, but declined again with population pressure during the sixteenth century. Similarly in Salisbury in that century the trades had become less open to women than previously, but in early-sixteenth-century York, where the numbers of freemen and the population generally were in decline, females were still positively encouraged.[55]

Demographic and labour-market pressures help to explain changes in the imposition of restrictions on women's work over time but to understand the longer-term trends and marked regional variations in women's formal participation in the high-status urban trades it is useful to consider the impact of male attitudes to female work which brought women independence or access to forms of social and political power. Of critical importance was the extent to which the crafts could be confined and controlled within the patriarchal household–workshop. This perhaps explains why the vast bulk of women in the trades and guilds found access only through their husbands and fathers which seldom conferred independent status or prestige. There appears to be no record of women members of the great retail merchants' guilds, perhaps because they were governing municipal institutions. Women were denied access to such political bodies and to civic life generally and for this reason the right of women to hand on membership of merchants' guilds to husbands or sons seems only to have been recognised in towns where the guild did not form the municipal authority. There thus seems to have been an inverse association between the political status of a trade and women's place in it.[56]

By the seventeenth and eighteenth centuries fewer and fewer women feature in guild records and many guilds and companies adopted a deliberately exclusionist policy. This trend appears to be related to the changing role of both the family workshop economy and the guilds.[57] Guilds in early modern Europe often became increasingly political institutions associated with municipal government and the lobbying of central government. This was accompanied by a decline in the family production unit, hastened in many towns by the spread of craft status to a wider range of trades which brought a host of rules and regulations about working hours and regimes which were incompatible with women's domestic roles and household responsibilities. Women's participation in high-status work survived longest in jobs associated with sectors where the family production unit persisted and where the degree of craft organisation remained low. In these sectors it was still possible to gain access to trades through fathers and husbands and women's working lives here did not conflict with powerful ideologies which denied women a political existence or an independent life outside of domestic priorities and constraints. Hall and Davidoff rightly show that women continued to play a fundamentally important role in English middle-class businesses as wives and widows during the eighteenth century. At this level in the economy family firms remained dominant and women's direct participation remained crucial.[58]

As the urban family workshop economy declined women's work was increasingly restricted to the casual and inferior sectors which had long been the mainstay of female earning potential. But even here, especially in marketing and in general retailing, changes in market practices and institutions began to limit female roles.[59] In England in the eighteenth century, for example, economic changes were undermining many female sidelines which had been important elements of the family economy. Enclosure of the commons restricted petty trade in fruits, fish, rabbits, firewood and other commodities and the commercialisation of agriculture generally increased the scale of transactions in foodstuffs so that they now needed more capital and credit and thus became the preserve of large mercantile concerns rather than regraters and hucksters. There was a shift away from open markets to the male social world of the inn and urban growth encouraged large-scale trade in traditional 'female' items such as butter, cheese and fruit. The exclusion of women from such trades was further exacerbated by new regulations concerning weights and measures which were decided in the interests of the larger traders.[60]

The eighteenth century also witnessed a growing professionalisation of occupations and their restriction to men who had a monopoly of access to formal training. Medical professionalisation, for example, saw the decline of surgeonesses and midwives as well as wisewomen. Surgeonesses were banned from the fifteenth century in France and Italy and many of their functions as local practitioners were taken over by male apothecaries. Undertakers, tailors, pawnbrokers and others were soon to develop similarly as largely male monopolies.[61]

Women did not, of course, disappear from the urban economy of the eighteenth and nineteenth centuries, but their function was increasingly confined to spheres of activity separate from and generally much inferior in terms of pay and status to that of men. But to confine our analysis solely to the extent to which women participated in male activities is to underplay their contribution to the urban economy in their own right and in ways not well recorded in documentary sources. Their role in maintaining households, in organising household budgets, in forming women's networks (which were of economic as well as social importance), in the casual trades, in services, in separate industries (often carried on informally in the home): these activities underpinned the urban economy in vital ways and often made the difference to a family between starvation and subsistence or between profitability and bankruptcy.[62]

Proto-industrialisation

It has been argued that proto-industry (the extension of rural domestic manufacturing for distant markets from the seventeenth century or so) helped to transform the division of labour between the sexes by widening the possibilities of home-based female waged employment. Medick cites German examples of women cutlers and nailmakers, male spinners and lace workers and emphasises a much quoted contemporary description of Von Schwerz, 'men cook, sweep and milk the cows in order never to disturb the good diligent wife in her work'.[63] New value placed on female waged work is argued to have brought greater parity between partners in emotional and sexual life within marriage as well as in decision-making regarding housework, production and consumption.[64] In certain Swiss cantons the implications of the spread of proto-industry were apparently considerable. Daughters were more prized than sons because of their earning capacity as spinners, marriage was increasingly a reciprocal commitment between two individuals, changes were occurring in courtship, sexual behaviour and gender relations generally, whilst women's earning potential gave them a new confidence and independence manifested in their smoking in the street and entering public houses.[65] This squares with McKendrick's view of the new role which both women and children played in consumption from the later part of the eighteenth century in England as a result of their ability to earn an independent wage.[66] Such interpretations, however, suppose that women's contributions to the proto-industrial household were accorded higher status and importance than their contribution to the peasant household or the urban crafts. They ignore the possibility that there was a sexual hierarchy of labour within trades and processes which may have endorsed female subordination rather than emancipation. They also suppose that a woman's earnings in proto-industry were reasonably high and were regarded as her own to dispose of.

There is no doubt that the rapid spread of proto-industry in many regions and sectors created an unprecedented demand for the cheap labour of females and children in particular. It may well be, as Saito and Berg have recently argued, that the early industrial revolution saw the use of female and child labour in market-orientated production on a uniquely large scale compared with previous or subsequent developments.[67] Whether in lace-making in Bedfordshire, the Flanders linen industry or cotton spinning in Auffay, activity rates for women in the late eighteenth century appear very high and female workforces exceeded male by ratios of four and even eight to one.[68] But it is debatable whether women's work became more vital to the households of proto-industrial regions than it was in peasant households.[69] Much depended on the the availability of employment for men. For example, in Auffay, as in the woollen areas around the Moray Firth in Scotland and in the lace, straw-plaiting and glovemaking areas of the south-east of England, male agricultural work was available.[70] Furthermore, although proto-industry may have enhanced women's commercial employment opportunities, there is little evidence that it enhanced their job status or prestige. Nor did it commonly result in high earning levels for women. The highest paid female workers of the eighteenth century in England were probably those girls and unmarried women who worked outside the home in early factories and workshops.[71] Proto-industry largely soaked up cheap underemployed and unemployed labour. The work of women and children

15

proliferated in proto-industry because it was cheap. Furthermore, it remained cheap even when there was great pressure on labour supplies, as in cotton and wool spinning, because women's work, regardless of real skill content, was seen as low status, and supplemental in household income. According to Pinchbeck, it was during the proto-industrial period that the association of women's industrial work with low wages really became entrenched.[72]

Some historians have argued that the high participation rates of women in proto-industry occurred because, located in the home, work was compatible with family responsibilities and domestic labour, especially with the constraints imposed by child-rearing and breast feeding. This is an argument also used to explain the proliferation of female labour in the household sweated trades of the nineteenth and twentieth centuries, but it is far from convincing. There is plenty of evidence to suggest that the burdens of women's labour in the home could severely impinge on levels of childcare with serious results.[73] Also, as domestic manufacturing became dependent upon fluctuating markets, bringing periods of intense demand followed by layoffs, it became more difficult to integrate manufacturing with the demands of housework and infant care.[74] Furthermore, the extent to which domestic industry could be conveniently meshed with women's household or other responsibilities varied enormously from one sector or region of proto-industry to the next and over time depending on products, processes, markets and industrial organisation.

Although information about male and female roles and about family life in rural manufacturing is sparse, we do know that women were an important source of labour in practically every sector but especially in textiles. Within this sector, as in others, female and children's roles varied from one sort of product to another, from one region to another and in response to long-run technological and organisational changes. Yarn spinning and preparation by hand seems everywhere to have been a female task, with child assistance, as was lacemaking and many of the processes involved in the manufacture of silk. In the linen industry women sometimes harvested the flax as well as spinning and winding it and in some regions at certain times they were important in knitting and in hand weaving.[75] Women were sometimes employed directly in these tasks by putting out employers, or they were subcontracted (technically) by their husbands or fathers. In other cases they worked as part of a household production unit or small business usually under the control of the male household head. Differing organisational structures were important in determining the extent to which increased female work in commercial manufacturing translated itself into independent female incomes, new status or freedoms for women. In the Yorkshire textile industry, for example, female worsted spinners were employed independently by putting-out employers, whereas spinners in the woollen trade most usually worked within the artisan household alongside their husbands or fathers.[76] Worsted spinners had the possibility of financial independence, but in practice their wages were usually too low for this. Furthermore, we do not know what motivated such women to work. In many cases it was the dire necessity of ensuring a family subsistence income rather than to gain economic independence. Female lacemakers were known to stay longer in the parental home despite their earning potential which indicates that they were encouraged to regard their work not individualistically but as part of family labour.[77] However, there is evidence that female incomes from domestic industries could and did contribute to the viability of female-headed households. In Auffay in 1796, 16 per cent of households were headed by female spinners, though whether this proportion of female heads was much above the norm in other populations without significant sources of female proto-industry is unclear.[78] In northern Ireland groups of female spinners commonly lived together.[79] But there is also evidence that attempts at social independence and alternative lifestyles were the subject of ridicule and condemnation which must have placed strict limits on proto-industrial earnings as an avenue to female liberation.[80]

Technological and organisational change could radically affect the type of proto-industrial work which women did and its economic and social implications. In Shepshed in the eighteenth century men knitted and women spun, but with the mechanisation of spinning and its shift to factories women and youths began to get involved in framework knitting.[81] In northern Ireland machine-spun cotton drove out hand-spun flax so women in putting-out areas shifted into weaving alongside men.[82] Likewise in Auffay by 1851 there were three times as many female as male weavers and in the south of Scotland linen industry one-third of all weavers were women and children by the early nineteenth century.[83] A similar development occurred in south Lancashire after the mechanisation of spinning: women entered the coarser less-skilled branches of weaving which were the first to suffer from factory competition.[84]

Although the identification of weaving largely as men's work broke down following the removal of spinning from the household and with the extension of demand for cloths, this did not necessarily increase the status of women or their independence. Often by this time they were working in flooded labour markets, as in South Lancashire where wages were driven down by the influx of Irish and agricultural workers as well as former spinners.[85] In some areas a new sexual division of labour was established in weaving. In the Pays de Caux women were confined to lighter-weight fabrics and although these were amongst the most popular products of the region, women were paid only about two-thirds of male wages. It was recognised that there was a role for women in weaving but that role was socially defined from the outset as inferior, easier and 'less skilled'.[86] In cotton spinning in England the jenny and frame were mainly associated with female labour, but the more efficient mule rapidly became a male enclave. Women could and did work the early mules but they were gradually squeezed out by male workers and their union during the shift from short to long and 'doubled' hand mules. By the introduction of the self-actor the intergenerational transmission of female craft skills had been lost.[87] Similarly, new sorts of broad and jacquard looms introduced into silk and other weaving were reserved for men and defined as more highly skilled than the narrow and ribbon looms operated by women. The introduction of the dutch engine loom in Coventry, for example, separated ribbon weavers into a skilled male division using the new looms and an 'unskilled' female section using single handlooms.[88]

Technological change in most sectors produced a reworking of the sexual division of labour. Men usually retained their ability to define their superior social status through their work. Women, denied parity of status through work, were just as likely as in the past to seek their social definition through their domestic and mothering roles. Assumptions about women's weaker physical capacity and inferior intelligence were used to justify the male monopoly of most of the more lucrative and high-status processes of production. This was common in many regions and sectors experiencing the reworking of the sexual division of labour following technological changes. It has important general implications for the arguments about women's income levels, their self-esteem, the extent to which incomes were a route to economic and social independence, rather than supplemental to the family economy, and for the sexual division of housework.[89]

We have little evidence that women's involvement in commercial manufacturing released them from their traditional domestic priorities even in areas where the demand for female labour outstripped that for men. The labour-market was segmented so that excess demand for female labour did not translate itself into higher female wages. But it was not just a question of differential opportunity cost: proto-industrial tasks were usually added onto rather than substituted for women's normal work in the home or in agriculture. Hufton has shown the variety of tasks both domestic and waged, agricultural and industrial which women in France turned their hands to, of necessity, during the eighteenth century. The 'economy of makeshift' was particularly important in the lives of widows and *femmes soles*.[90] In areas like the Scottish Highlands spinning on the distaff continued well into the nineteenth century because it could absorb the cheap labour of older women, of children and particularly of women who were simultaneously engaged in other tasks. It added to the drudgery of female existence on the crofts and small farms.[91]

There were some exceptions to the general picture of intense effort, low wages and low status involved in many female branches of proto-industry. The metalware trades of the English Black Country had their share of degraded female employments: chain-making, saddlery, holloware, nail-making, lacquering and button-making. Most of these involved hier-archies of employment based on gender and age with women in the inferior sectors.[92] But the economic structure of Birmingham and its region, dominated by small family workshops also gave women access as widows to running a business themselves which they appear to have done in significant numbers and with considerable skill and knowledge. Wherever the small master family business structure predominated in proto-industry a route lay open for women as widows to use their skill and initiative in high-status work.[93] But it must be remembered that their access was via the family unit with its patriarchal attributes: in some regions where this structure predominated, for example in the Bas Meuse, the traditional household with its stress on resident training, late marriage (hence low fertility) and male skill resembled a peasant household economy more than a new departure in terms of gender relations.[94] In some countries, notably Russia, proto-industry could expand enormously without dis-rupting the traditional structure of extended households or peasant gender divisions.[95] On the whole, for the majority of women involved, proto-industry brought little change in their economic or social status relative to men.

Industrialisation

It is frequently argued that industrialisation created the separation of home and work: 'Facing a conflict between their family obligations and their ability to earn money, women ultimately altered their occupational choices, experienced a fundamental reformulation of their attitudes about work, and gradually developed a characteristically female work pattern.'[96] Industrial-ism diminished women's roles in economic production by drastically curtailing the role of the family as a market production unit.[97] Industrial-isation led to a spatial dislocation of child care and economic production and the gradual disappearance of the earlier unifying features of women's work, with its coherent link between domestic and non-domestic activ-ities.[98] This type of analysis was well established early this century and has received further support from feminist and Marxist writers of the last decade or so. They argue that it was specifically the rise of industrial capitalism which created the conditions for the increasing oppression of women. Industrial capitalism needed a cheap and flexible reserve supply of labour and the unpaid work of women in domestic reproduction, including housework, served to reduce the real costs of male labour in industry. Advancing capitalism thus fed upon the pre-existing subordination of women and this subordination then became a necessary element in the continued operation of the mode of production.[99]

But another very different interpretation of the influence of industrialisation on the economic and social status of women also exists which emphasises the effects of women being able to enter the labour-market as independent wage-earners outside the home. Shorter, for example, sees marked changes in power relationships between the sexes and the generations resulting from the economic changes of the nineteenth century in particular.[100] As women went out to work in greater numbers, marriage became a partnership, domestic work and child care were increasingly shared, affective individualism replaced family decisions about love and marriage, thus completing the transition (started with proto-industrialisation) to the symmetrical family. Both pessimist and optimist interpretations of the effects of industrialisation tend to be very influenced by a functionalist and economic determinist perspective which sees the family economy and intra-family relationships as passive and dependent variables in the process of change. They both assume that the family economy, women's work and female subordination differed markedly in the pre-industrial period from what was to follow. They also underplay regional and life-cycle diversity and the general problem of comparing relationships of power (inside the family and in the wider economy) within societies very different from one another.

Census data from a variety of European countries provides contradictory evidence about the impact of industrialisation on women's work. Although recorded female employment has increased and diversified, especially in recent decades, it remained relatively low in the nineteenth century and changes in occupational segregation have been modest. The British census of 1851 revealed a low rate of female labour-force participation, with approximately 2.8 million 'working' women (or just over 25 per cent of all British women of working age). By 1911 there were 5.4 million women in waged employment, although as a proportion of all British women there had been little change since the mid-nineteenth century. In the case of Germany there was evidence of an increased level of female employment between 1882 and 1907 in manufacturing and mining, but in absolute terms agriculture remained the largest source of registered employment for women.[101] The exodus of men from the land had led to an increased dependence on female labour. In France the number of women in full-time employment rose from 4.4 million (1856) to 7.7 million (1911) but the higher overall level of female labour-force participation has been attributed to the persistence of domestic production and the slow rate of population growth which necessitated a greater reliance on female labour than in other parts of Europe. Great care needs to be exercised in the utilisation of census data to determine general trends in female employment.

Persistent under-recording of women's work occurred because of the prejudices of enumerators, male household heads and of those who designed the schedules and reports. The British census of 1881, for example, excluded women's household manufacturing from the definition of those economically active and much seasonal and part-time work by women was not declared.[102]

Theoretically, late-eighteenth and nineteenth-century industrialisation should have tended to create additional opportunities for female employment. First, the advent of steam and then electrical power reduced the earlier reliance on physical strength which had promoted 'masculine monopolies' in certain trades.[103] Secondly, new technology in the long term led to a reduction in the earlier emphasis on skilled labour. Deskilling, the introduction of *Gewerbefreiheit*, and the final disappearance of male-dominated guilds represented important incentives for the maximisation of female employment. But official occupational statistics reveal little diversification in terms of women's sectoral employment. Industrial capitalism failed to transform the pre-existing sexual division of labour and adapted itself to pre-industrial social and organisational arrangements.[104] Women remained concentrated in a few occupations which frequently revealed affinities to housework or simply represented 'extended housework'. In Britain in 1911 a significant proportion of women were employed as domestic servants (35 per cent), as textile workers (19.5 per cent), or as garment workers (15.6 per cent). French data from 1896 reveal that 59 per cent of all women in employment were located in four occupations, with the garment industry (26 per cent) and textiles (14 per cent) particularly prominent. In Norway in 1900 women were only important in textiles (38.6 per cent) and food production (24.7 per cent).[105] There would appear to have been a sharp and persistent occupational segregation along the gender divide, with early industrialisation accompanied by a diffusion of a sex-specific division of tasks into the new workplaces, factories and occupations.[106]

Importantly from the perspective of the family economy, female employment during the century or so before 1945 saw greater emphasis on the role of single women and a diminished degree of participation in the formal economy by married women. In Britain in 1911, for example, 69 per cent of all single women worked, but only 9.6 per cent of married women. Similarly, in the case of France in 1896, 52 per cent of single women were recorded as being in full-time employment as against only 38 per cent of married women.[107] In the Lancashire cotton industry between 1841 and 1911, between 70 and 75 per cent of the female operatives were single and most 'mill girls' left the factory after marriage.

In attempting to explain the long-term determinants of the nature and extent of women's employment, life-cycle and age-related earning patterns were clearly important. Low levels of male wages especially in the less-skilled sectors during the nineteenth century along with large family size made it essential that women earned an income both before marriage and at least during the early years of marriage until children were old enough to replace the wife's income through their own wage-earning activities.[108] But, at the same time, women in cotton and other centralised sectors were likely to earn their maximum at around the age of 25 years. The fact that the greatest disparity between male and female wages occurred in the age range 31–36 would have been an incentive for married women with mounting domestic responsibilities to leave the regular workforce.[109]

Changes in the extent of married women's employment in the nineteenth and early twentieth centuries also reflected the growing dominance of a bourgeois family model, in which the breadwinner was the husband and the wife and children the dependants. Tensions between contemporary Christian moral values and those of emergent industrial capitalism were relieved by the middle-class cult of domesticity. The Victorian ideal of the 'angel in the house', reflecting the influence of evangelicalism and the over-riding view of women as domestic beings was clearly evident by the 1830s and 1840s, and this idealisation of femininity, with its implicit 'looking-glass function' limited adult women to a narrowly defined role as wives and mothers.[110] Diffusion of the bourgeois family model within nineteenth-century European society was underpinned and reinforced by a concept of the sexes which embodied great mental and emotional distinctions. The emergent medical profession, with its image of women as conspicuous consumptives also helped to maintain the view of women as invalid, weak, delicate and invariably prone to illness.[111]

Increased educational provision for women reinforced these views. Formal teaching of girls in schools was equivalent to 'professional mothering' and any higher education was pursued primarily in order to train women for their domestic role.[112] In this context education was a means to instil the women's belief in their destiny as wives, housekeepers and mothers, which would ensure the restabilisation of family life as an effective solution to the 'social question'. Increasing official concern with the potential deleterious effects on family welfare, particularly in relation to infant and child mortality, of full-time work by married women also tended to encourage the primacy placed upon domestic responsibilities. Similarly, in the late 1940s and 1950s the emphasis by psychologists on maternal adequacy as the key to 'normal' child development played a role in militating against the active participation of married women in the labour force.[113] The significant rise in home visiting from the 1860s onwards helped to inculcate in some working-class mothers the middle-class ideal of family behaviour.[114] But home visiting was often viewed as invasive and its effectiveness in transmitting social and class values must remain open to doubt. Similarly, although infant welfare centres sought to promote middle-class methods of child-raising in the pre-1914 period and later (with an emphasis on the domestic role of the mother), the overall impact of institutional initiatives of this sort must remain equivocal.[115] Notions of respectability were well entrenched within sections of the working class (for example, carding buttons at home was regarded as more respectable than making matchboxes).[116] Status consciousness and increasing social stratification within the working class may well have reinforced the cult of domesticity and contributed to the low profile of women's work and its contribution to family income.[117]

Organised labour and the family wage

A further important factor in accounting for the exclusion of married working-class women from the formal economy in England during the second half of the nineteenth century was increased pressure from the organised labour movement for a 'family wage'.[118] Individual cases, such as the Glasgow Scottish Spinners and the Dundee jute workers, reflect male–female disputes at the workplace. But it was increasingly accepted that 'A woman, become a worker, is no longer a woman', and the organised labour movement adopted the family wage concept as a main bargaining issue.[119] In Britain, the Trades Union Congress leader Henry Broadhurst in 1875 emphasised in clear patriarchal terms that a woman's proper sphere lay 'at home', and an Independent Labour Party pamphlet of 1900 proclaimed that true freedom for women could only be guaranteed if they did not have to earn 'any wage under any condition'.[120] The exclusionary tactics of male trade unions were a major element in the assertion of patriarchal attitudes in the world of work but recent research has also emphasised the key role of employers, male household heads and state policy in securing the exclusion of women from new industries of the twentieth century in particular. It may be that different types of patriarchal control worked to this end over time. In fact, in nineteenth-century British coal mining Mark-Lawson and Witz have suggested that before 1842 employers and male workers controlled female and child work through familial work systems but after the 1842 Mines Act the exclusion of women worked through employers' preference and the force of male trade unions. It is also the case that married women in full-time employment often faced the pity of their neighbours but this was largely a reflection of the immutability of gender-specific work roles at home, rather than evidence of a positive acceptance of the middle-class family model.[121]

Clearly, the attempted confinement of married women to the home, with its attendant domestic and family responsibilities derived from an ideology of gender that pre-dated industrial capitalism. But the emergence of the famly wage concept in the second half of the nineteenth century also reflected more immediate issues related to the contemporary processes of factory-based development, including the impact of technological change on demand patterns for gender-specific labour, long-run changes in real wages for male and female employees, and mounting international competition.[122] For example, the increasing emphasis on the family wage may have reflected changes in the productive process and the significance of skill in the construction of masculinity. The 'sexualisation' of skill was not new to the nineteenth century but it was promoted by industrial deskilling, particularly in sectors such as the printing industry. The development of supervisory authority as a function of the extended division of labour in many sectors was also important in the definition of skill. Women's increasing exclusion from technical education and knowledge prevented them from being able to substitute for men, made them dependent on male overlookers or supervisors and frequently made them objects of sexual harassment in the workplace. The replication of family-based gender relations not only strengthened patriarchal attitudes, but also contributed to the marginalisation of older, more experienced and married women in the productive process.[123]

Undoubtedly the concept of the 'family wage' furthered the adoption of gender-specific restrictive practices throughout Europe, and the increasing prevalence of the 'male-provider system' reinforced the continued sex-structuring of the workforce.[124] Trade-union support for the 'family wage' may well have reflected fear of competition from domestic workshops, but the concept was also a useful weapon against employers in the continuing struggle over wages.[125] The labour movement in Western Europe as a whole clearly took the path of least resistance in response to the threat of wage undercutting through the hiring of women workers from the 'reserve army' of labour. Male-dominated trade unions, despite the increasing involvement of women in the labour movement as a whole, prioritised employment rights of men, pressed for the curtailment or outright exclusion of female employees and continuously reiterated the aim of creating 'circumstances in which a woman can fulfil her duties as wife and mother'.[126] Although this campaign was never completely successful, it tended to drive married women out of industrial employment and increased their marginalisation within the labour force as a whole. As Clare Evans indicates, even at the time of the cotton famine, out-of-work women were projected not as unemployed labourers, but as individuals in need of 'proper and congenial employment'.[127]

To some extent, despite the apparent cost-cutting opportunities open to industrialists in employing poorly paid woman, the concept of the 'family wage' and the retention of a gender-specific wage differential were of direct utility to industrial paternalism and employer–labour strategies. Employers frequently attempted to re-organise production by securing a stable labour force through the reinforcement of traditional gender divisions and job segregation. In the Courtaulds silk mills in Essex, paternalistic structures were developed in which the work life of women was arranged to mimic the household, thereby attempting to reconcile domestic ideology with the employment of both single and married women, but emphasising their overall subservience.[128] The duplication of familial and workplace hierarchies (as in the case of the Lancashire cotton industry), pervasive gender discrimination in the workplace, and a heightened division of labour which necessitated increased male supervision of female labour functions, were important factors which reinforced the bargaining power of the employers. In the French cotton industry, for example, three distinct strategies were visible: direct support of Catholic workers' organisations (such as the *groupes du vingt*, which collected fines from female operatives who had 'sinned'); the use of nuns as spies; and the imposition of a variety of religious practices within the mills themselves.[129] Persistent wage differentials within most branches of industry could be justified as an attempt to sustain the concept of the 'family wage', but they also allowed employers to split strikers by sex. Low pay for women reinforced their continued dependence on the family economy, restricted their involvement in political activity and encouraged a self-definition and consciousness embedded in private rather than public life and in reproduction rather than production.

The role of the state

A further factor working towards an increased exclusion of married women from employment in the formal economy was state intervention in shaping the relations of capitalist production. From the English Factory Acts onwards there was a growing concern to secure the implementation of 'principles of protection for women' which embodied the assumption that married women were dependent and not free agents. Governments throughout Europe were increasingly forced to crystallise their position in respect to the employment of women in ways which were to be seen to be appropriate for developing industrial society.[130] English legislation in 1883 restricting the nature and extent of women's work, and protective measures in Germany (such as the *Gewerbeordnungsnovelle* of 1891) and other European states, sought to endorse society's sense of women's proper role.[131] But minimum wage and other protective legislation probably promoted the extension of women's work in unregulated sweatshops. There was mounting international pressure for more effective protection for married women employees. By 1919 the International Labor Organisation had recommended a minimum of twelve weeks' paid maternity leave, but all too frequently the net short-term effect of increased state intervention in this area, by increasing the costs of employing women, only tended to preserve traditional work forms and reinforced the latent belief that married women should really be fulfilling their family role.[132] Reforms were primarily concerned with the possible adverse effect of working conditions on women's behaviour and social role, and many legislators were still somewhat ambivalent about the rightful role of working-class wives when enacting protective legislation and national insurance regulations. These effectively controlled both the type of work available to women outside the home and limited the access of working-class wives to unemployment benefit.[133] Even at a time of acute labour needs, as during the Second World War, policy-makers in England still were unable to maximise the full use of women's labour because of persistent patriarchal attitudes about women's work and domestic role. In Germany, Nazi ideology concerning the rightful role of women continued to prioritise the withdrawal of married women from the labour force, despite the pressing labour requirements of the war economy.[134] The state throughout Western Europe also played an important role in re-establishing the sexual division of labour after both world wars, and the continued official ambivalence to women's work was reflected in unemployment and welfare legislation in the 1930s.[135]

Twentieth-century trends

Undoubtedly the scale of married women's involvement in the formal labour market has altered dramatically in the twentieth century. The post-1945 period in particular witnessed a rapid development in women's employment in advanced industrial economies despite the resurgence of a 'back to the kitchen ideology' in the 1970s fuelled by official concern about male unemployment. The abolition of the marriage bar in public-sector employment in Britain aided this trend.[136] There were significant changes in a variety of areas, with women increasingly dominating such occupations as clerical work, retail sales, elementary teaching and nursing. The increasing importance of 'new industries' in the 1920s and 1930s, including rayon manufacture, light engineering, food processing, and white goods provided a boost for female employment in the formal sector, although on a regionally selective basis and with an emphasis on 'semi-skilled' and 'unskilled' work.[137] Furthermore, the inter-war period generally was characterised by official restrictions on married women's employment as a reaction to male unemployment.

'New' female occupations in the service sector continued to expand after 1945, particularly in retailing, banking, public administration and other forms of clerical work. This trend was assisted by a variety of factors, including improved levels of female pay in certain sectors, shorter working hours, lower fertility, and the gradual provision of suitable, if still inadequate welfare support. As Ida Blom indicates, there was a strong correlation in Norway between married women's activity and the trend towards smaller families and, although the relationship between female labour-force participation and European fertility clearly requires further comparative analysis, the implications of a reduction in family commitments for working mothers was considerable.[138] Technological innovations in the production and conception of household consumer durables such as vacuum cleaners, cookers and electric irons were potentially a source of reduction of domestic burdens as they slowly percolated down the social scale, especially from the 1960s, but new higher standards of domestic cleanliness and decor put pressure on women to spend as much time as in the past on homemaking.

Despite growth in the employment of married women in the formal economy in the twentieth century, many of the factors which determined female labour force participation in the early stages of capitalist development continue to affect occupation choice, gender segregation and women's overall subordination in work. Married women frequently choose jobs which do not directly challenge the prevailing concept of a 'woman's proper place', and many people still 'view it unseemly and inappropriate for wives to work'.[139] Women's occupational choices are clearly influenced by a variety of factors, both work and non-work related. The nature of the labour-market is important but persistently negative facets of women's employment, such as sex-typed jobs, low-ranking position and low comparative earnings, reflect the continued operation of more long-term and deep-seated factors. Married women are still not expected to express any dissatisfaction with their domestic status, so that a return to formal employment frequently has to be legitimised in a socially acceptable fashion, with hours tailored to suit child care (for example, mothers' evening shifts in factories) and with earnings treated as 'pin money', or with work portrayed as an emergency measure.[140] As important is the assertion that women have a different relationship to money and wages from men, a notion which has helped to cement the social construction of gender dependency.

Just as women's wage labour in the early phases of capitalist development was frequently an extension of home-based skills, so the general expansion of the service sector, particularly in the twentieth century, has tended to replicate a similar bond between the domestic and work environments. There has been an unprecedented expansion in nursing services since the nineteenth century, accompanied by the formation of professional nursing associations, but these have been based on women's 'traditional' role as carer.[141] Moreover, gender segregation in the health sector as a whole has been associated with persistent low pay for nurses in comparison with other sections of the medical profession. Librarianship has also provided a fast-growing demand for low-paid, but educated, female recruits.

Women librarians have frequently been employed because of their sub-missive attitudes or, as in Tsarist Russia, because of their function as 'guardians of traditional culture'.[142] Even in the retail trades women have been employed not just because they were cheaper than men but because they had such positive virtues as 'politeness' and 'sobriety'. They could also function effectively in a 'world of women', linking women as workers with women as consumers.[143]

In the long term, therefore, despite an unprecedented expansion in the employment of married women in the formal economy, many of the earlier facets of women's work have been retained, particularly in relation to economic marginalisation, pay discrimination, occupational segregation and trade-union participation.[144] As Linda Grant notes, in Britain in the inter-war period women trade unionists had to struggle to establish their identity, both within mixed unions and in the TUC, and it is only recently that the question of the sexual division of labour has been put on the agenda of workers in Coventry car factories.[145]

Combined and uneven development

In order to understand long-term trends in the sexual division of labour, and the attendant ramifications for the structuring of gender relations and attitudes both within and outside the family, it is necessary for analysis to take in regional and sectoral, as well as temporal, variations and to consider the vital economic and social activities of women in informal productive activities, services and networks.

It is too simplistic to argue that industrialisation from the late eight-eenth century onwards produced a sharp division between women's domestic work and waged work away from the home. The process of capitalist development was uneven and subject to a significant degree of both temporal and spatial variation.[146] Separate processes within the same industry followed different paths of development and the impact of technological change, with its gender-specific implications, was often highly selective. Lace production, for example, was concentrated in steam-powered factories from the mid-nineteenth century, but finishing remained almost entirely domestically based until well into the twentieth century. Similarly, in the silk industry new machines were introduced in the 1830s and 1840s for removing the silk from the cocoons, for twisting thread and for weaving, a development which reinforced workshop and factory concentration. However, the nourishing of worms on mulberry leaves and the pulling of silk filaments from cocoons retained their traditional domestic context. The sectoral and regional distribution of factory-based production inevitably generated differentiated labour-markets with localised demand patterns for female labour.[147] As Franzoi has noted, the specific nature of industrial development in any given area in Western Europe determined the number of women working, as well as affecting relative sectoral wages for both men and women, and potentially influencing patterns of marital fertility.[148] Moreover, as we emphasised earlier, it is equally important to decompose the constituent elements of a particular labour process in order to analyse fully the sexual division of labour in its different and frequently distinct forms. Most production processes throughout the period covered by this book consisted of an extended variety of complicated tasks, each of which was allocated according to gender and/or age. It is on the basis of a far more selective and critical approach to the overall process of industrialisation and the labour process itself that the factors affecting the changing balance of gender-specific responsibilities in terms of production and family commitments can be understood. Attention must also be paid to historically derived localised and regional attitudes to female work. Across communities with similar occupational structures there were those where young female workers were in great demand and others where employers made little attempt to utilise this labour.[149]

Given sectoral lags in mechanisation and the application of new technology, the dynamic of capitalist development in the nineteenth century tended to generate an increased emphasis on cheap production methods in the form of domestic outwork. Regions which were characterised by a rapid development of consumer goods industries dependent on non-mechanisd, non-factory labour, as well as those where men's wages were low (as in the eastern counties of England) or irregular (as in the case of dock-related employment), witnessed a dramatic rise in female domestic production. The number of women employed in this area was substantial, and always much higher than the official records indicate. Whereas married women, including widows and separated women, constituted 21 per cent of the female industrial work force in Imperial Germany in 1907, they represented approximately 50 per cent of homeworkers. *Heimarbeit* for women was prevalent in linen-weaving, textiles, toy manufacture and cuckoo-clock production, but was most highly developed in the case of the German clothing industry.[150] In England, the 1901 census revealed that approximately one-third of women employed in the clothing trades were homeworkers. Moreover, many forms of domestic outwork, including such arduous tasks as fur-pulling and matchbox making, were performed almost exclusively by women. Many more women, especially married women, were employed on a part-time, casual or intermittent basis in homework which never entered historical record.

The growth in domestic production and the sweated trades generally was fuelled by a number of factors. Many firms in textiles, clothing, cleaning and food processing were confronted with an elastic market and significant seasonal fluctuations (particularly in the case of women's clothing), which necessitated or encouraged a heavy reliance on a flexible supply of cheap female labour. The fact that this form of employment was frequently treated as a marginal economic activity tended to force wage-rates further downwards and to make casual female homework more attractive to employers. Even after the tentative implementation of minimum wage legislation, as in the case of England in 1909, a significant proportion of homeworkers in those trades ostensibly covered by the Acts were still unable to earn the statutory minimum. Even when governments did attempt to regulate industry, as in the case of match manufacture, they frequently failed to allocate resources for the effective enforcement of legislation and its impact remained negligible.[151]

It has also been argued that the expansion of decentralised domestic production in the late nineteenth century was itself a reaction to regulatory legislation and increasing official constraints on worker exploitation.[152] *Hausarbeit* in Imperial Germany was only subject to legislative controls after 1911, and the predominance of sub-contracting on the basis of piece-rates reinforced the economic viability of this mode of production. In London in 1901 between 5.7 and 8.7 per cent of the total population (between 125,000 and 190,000 individuals) are estimated as having been involved as outworkers in the clothing trades, reflecting the continuing need for cheap female labour. Domestic production also mirrored the persistence of traditional work forms associated with proto-industrial structures. In many parts of Western Europe there was a persistence of a proto-industrial approach to manufacturing work, and in Saxony, for example, official encouragement for men to seek high-wage seasonal employment in railway construction led to married women assuming proto-industrial tasks, particularly in weaving.[153]

The informal economy

As long as male wages remained precariously low, or male employment was casual or seasonal, most married women were obliged to seek work in the non-formal economy. Wives were forced to supplement family income because of a persistent and serious economic need.[154] The increased importance of female recorded and unrecorded outwork towards the end of the nineteenth century may well have reflected the strength as well as the necessity of women's commitment to family support and survival.[155] Women were able to find supplementary income in childminding, casual cleaning and washing, and by taking in lodgers. Within the interstices of an expanding capitalist system, characterised by rapid urban development and increased labour mobility, there were numerous income-generating activities which married women could undertake. Laundry work, for example, was essentially homework as was petty production and trading in confectionary and consumables.[156] Much activity of this kind drew on women's neighbourhood and kinship networks and involved reciprocity and payment in kind as well as monetised transactions. So important were these sorts of informal sources of income that they made the difference in places like Barrow and Lancaster between working-class survival and starvation. This form of economic activity was attractive because of its flexibility in the face of changing domestic requirements and shifting life-cycle needs. It was also vital in the many regions and cities where the possibilities of formal paid work for women were limited. In Liverpool, for example, women's waged work was limited by the narrow manufacturing base whilst the predominance of casual and low-paid work for men made women's contributions to family earnings a necessity.[157]

It is sometimes suggested that women preferred non-formal activities or even domestic service, whether they were married or unmarried. They disliked factory work as 'it was too impersonal and likely to involve them with bad companions'.[158] Furthermore, it could be argued that women's work remained resistant to change, despite a significant narrowing of the gender-specific literacy gap and increased educational opportunities, because women continued by and large 'to select work options that were familiar to them'.[159] However, it should also be remembered that training opportunities remained limited, and girls' schools, as in mid-nineteenth-century Spain, still tended to restrict education to the rudiments of literacy and religion, and the 'labour of their sex', namely, embroidery, sewing and lacemaking.[160] Equally, the familial socialisation process anchored in the mother–daughter relationship may have been critical: working-class mothers, faced with the manipulation of limited physical and financial resources had no time to offer their daughters learning in other spheres. Employment choice was thus curtailed by the cumulative oppression of women.[161]

Women's work and family organisational models

The widespread extent of women's informal work together with marked regional variations of experience during industrialisation places in doubt the three models of family organisation originally suggested by Tilly and Scott. The absence of a life-cycle perspective also vitiates the general applicability of such models, and as Anne Meyering shows there are abundant examples of family organisation which did not conform to the three basic patterns.[162] The temporal sequence of organisational change from the traditional family economy to the family wage economy, and finally to the family consumer economy based on a 'symmetrical' marriage structure is of only limited usefulness. It is also problematic to view work at home for pay as constituting a 'transitional model', given both its

31

traditional and contemporary prevalence.[163] Even within the middle class, adherence to the Victorian cult of domesticity was not always translated into the reality of separate spheres of activity and maintaining the 'paraphernalia of gentility' was often financially impossible. With changing economic conditions participation by middle-class women in the public sphere became 'both respectable and necessary', and there is increasing evidence of their role in decision-making in relation to their husbands' careers and family businesses.[164] To this extent nineteenth-century middle-class practice was not too dissimilar from the joint responsibility for financial matters enshrined in the earlier German tradition of *Hausmutterliteratur*.[165] Furthermore, despite the apparent pervasiveness of patriarchy in the later nineteenth century, there were certain industries, such as pottery, where the male breadwinner ethos failed to take root, and where women retained a strong presence, even in trade-union organisations. A joint contribution to the family economy could also encourage mutuality in dealing with domestic responsibilities.[166]

Technological change was not uniformly a negative influence on women's employment opportunities, as earlier research on the impact of industrialisation on gender-specific work roles has implied.[167] Gender occupational segregation in bookbinding was essentially broken down by technological change, providing greater access for women. Over 70 per cent of all the employees in the early silk-weaving factories in Lyons were female *canutes* and in Germany, increasing mechanisation in metalworking industries in the second half of the nineteenth century also created employment opportunities for women.[168] Improved technology in office work (typewriters and telephones) was accompanied by the gradual dominance of this sector by women.[169] Equally, despite certain limitations, some of the new employment forms increasingly open to women from the mid-nineteenth century onwards, such as teaching and nursing, did allow the possibility of some economic independence, and in England an uncompromising education reform group rigorously opposed institutional segregation and the provision of special women's courses.[170] The retail trade, as in the case of the French department stores such as Bon Marché, may well have retained a strong element of paternalism, with their insistence on a uniform dress and supervised accommodation on the premises, but they offered wages at least four times higher than the average industrial wage for women.[171] New forms of 'fit work for women' which emerged with technological change and economic development were accorded some social and economic status, whereas the mainstay of the less respectable manufacturing and informal service activities went unrecorded, unrecognised and underpaid.

Conclusion

It is clear that some of the general assumptions concerning the impact of industrialisation on women's market and non-market employment, with their attendant implications for family organisational structures, are in need of modification and revision.[172] As we have consistently emphasised, the development of industrial capitalism was not a linear process and the gap between the prevailing ideology and the reality of women's economic roles was often very wide indeed. Aside from the importance of life-cycle variations, the local and regional structure of production was crucial in influencing gender-specific economic roles. Thus analysis of the impact of industrial capitalism on women's employment and gender roles within the family must be conducted first on a disaggregated level. Not only is it necessary to decompose the labour process itself, in order to establish the task-specific complexity of gender roles within particular industries, but the process of industrialisation needs to be examined as a highly diverse regional phenomenon, involving a variegated pattern of sectoral balance and attendant levels of technological development. This, in turn, generated regionally divergent gender-specific labour-markets and local configurations of female employment opportunities in both formal and non-formal activities. Only by neglecting some of the more generalised models of change in the family economy in favour of regional and local studies can one proceed to rebuild the general picture at a more sophisticated level. Richard Whipp's analysis of the pottery industry between 1890 and 1920 which witnessed a continuing role for married women in paid employment and a central function for family recruitment and work units, and Linda Grant's portrayal of the Coventry car industry in the inter-war period as a highly skilled male preserve emphasise this point in full.[173] The combined role of ideology, of law, and of technology in provoking change in the sexual division of labour and in the structure and nature of the family economy can best be pursued further in this way.

A disaggregated regional and sectoral approach is necessary also if we are to shed more light on the connection between social and personal life and gender-specific work roles. What effect did local female work experience play in the formation of occupational horizons and in job recruitment of girls and boys?[174] The relationship between women's work and the age and rate of marriage and the rate of illegitimacy as well as marital fertility is also important. These demographic measures exhibit marked spatial variations which bear a close connection with local economic structures.[175] It is clear, for example, that women's work experience before marriage provided a long-term as well as short-term alternative to traditional domestic roles. Evidence from the both the 1860s and the 1960s reveals that previous work experience was one of the major determinants affecting the decision of women to return

33

to the labour-market after marriage and childbirth and to restrict childbirth to the earlier years of marriage.[176]

It is also on the basis of a more localised analytical framework, drawing in particular on workforce ethnographies that the interrelationship between changing gender-specific employment patterns and power relations within the domestic sphere can be more precisely examined.[177] Power over resources and decision-making within the family unit remains in this context one of the most fundamental, yet little known, aspects of social interaction.[178] Even if women's experience of work in the formal economy was initially shaped by an assumption of dependency, the long-term expansion of job opportunities for women almost certainly impinged on traditional gender roles within the family but its effect was not straightforward. Women textile workers in Lancashire, for example, were assumed to have a 'roving and independent cast of mind' but they were not at the forefront of family limitation.[179] Even though pay for women workers was often derisory, and thwarted any desire for economic independence, it is important to explore the extent to which the increasing incorporation of married women within the formal economy since the Second World War was accompanied by any appreciable shift in family power relations or in the balance of concensus and conflict which forms these relations.[180] Although it is difficult to penetrate the dynamics of intra-family relations historically, it is clear that a mother's position within the family as an organiser of physical and financial resources was initially a strong one, at least in theory.[181] The Victorian ideal of separate spheres, with the daily absence of the husband from the home, could have strengthened female control over household management and consumption decisions. But female responsibility for the management of the household budget, as in the case of dockland Liverpool, may have been an onerous burden as much as a sign of female influence.[182] It is certainly the case that the economic, political and legal subordination of women (or indeed their emancipation) has not necessarily been replicated within the domestic environment.[183] The contributions to this volume highlight the fact that women's work, the family economy and family strategies are not merely reactive in the process of economic change but function in a pro-active manner which itself contributes to the material and ideological outcome of economic development.[184]

Research on women's work and role inside the household and in the wider economy has now reached a volume and importance which obliges full acknowledgement of its implications for economic and social history more generally. Old questions and debates like the standard of living during industrialisation, the formation of class and class fragmentation, the roots of demographic behaviour, the validity of formal national income measures, the assessment of labour productivity, structural shifts in employment over time and the relationship between unemployment, wage and benefit levels in advanced welfare economies all now need to be reassessed in the light of the vital role played by gender. As long as research about women's lives remains largely separate from wider issues such as these, the importance which society has attached to female activities and agency in the past (and in the present) will not change. Indeed the continuing separate treatment of women may serve to endorse their particularised and marginal status compared with men.[185] The chapters in this volume each endeavour to keep wider issues at centre-stage and to view the history of women as necessarily part of a much larger story of the interaction of gender, class, ethnicity, the construction of knowledge and the complex long-term interrelationship between the internal world of the family and the external functioning of local, national and international economies. With the current emphasis in Europe upon the need for more women in both the professional and manual workforce and a resurgence of homeworking in many countries, an understanding of the history of women's work, the family economy and its much wider economic, social and political implications is all the more urgent.

Notes

1 A classic example is E. Richards, 'Women in the British economy since about 1700: an interpretation', *History*, 59 (1974), pp. 337–57. E. Shorter's *The Making of the Modern Family*, New York, 1976, also derives most of its social analysis from official indicators of female economic participation whilst in a different tradition, attempts like that of L. A. Tilly and J. W. Scott in *Women, Work and the Family*, New York, 1978, to formulate different stage models of the family related to female economic activity flounder partly because of the restricted definition of such activity.

2 S. Shahar, *The Fourth Estate: A History of Women in the Middle Ages*, London, 1983; M. Segalen, *Love and Power in the Peasant Family*, Oxford, 1983, chapters 3 and 4; S. Alexander, 'Women's work in nineteenth century London: a study of the years 1820–50', in J. Mitchell and A. Oakley (eds.), *The Rights and Wrongs of Women*, London, 1976, pp. 59–111; E. Roberts, 'Working-class living standards in Barrow and Lancaster, 1890–1914', *Economic History Review*, 30, 2 (1977); P. Ayers, 'The hidden economy of dockland families: Liverpool in the 1930s', chapter 11 in this volume.

3 E. Power, *Medieval Women*, Cambridge, 1975, chapter 1; Shahar, *Fourth Estate* pp. 251–80; M. Wade Labarge, *Women in Medieval Life: A Small Sound of the Trumpet*, London, 1986, chapter 2.

4 Power, *Medieval Women*, chapter 3.

5 See for example B. Easlea's analysis of attitudes to women in this period in *Witchhunting, Magic and the New Philosophy: An Introduction to the Debates of the Scientific Revolution, 1450–1750*, Brighton, 1980. See also his *Science and Sexual Oppression: Patriarchy's Confrontation with Woman and Nature*, London, 1981.

6 P. Crawford, 'Attitudes to menstruation in seventeenth century England', *Past and Present*, 91 (1981), p. 72. For an interesting discussion of the points raised in this paragraph see Michael Roberts, 'Words they are women and deeds they are men: images of work and gender in early modern England', in L. Charles and L. Duffin (eds.), *Women and Work in Preindustrial England*, London, 1985, pp. 122–60.

7   Roberts, 'Words they are women', p. 144.

8   N. Z. Davis, 'Women in the *Arts Méchaniques* in sixteenth-century Lyon', in *Lyon et Europe, Hommes et Sociétés*, Université Lyon II-Centre Pierre Leon, 1980, p. 146, quoted in *ibid.*, p. 141.

9   E. Roberts, *Women's Work 1840–1940*, London, 1988; Sonya Rose, 'Gender at work: sex, class and industrial capitalism', *History Workshop*, 21 (1986), pp. 113–32; Wally Seccombe, 'Patriarchy stabilised: the construction of the male breadwinner wage norm in nineteenth century Britain', *Social History*, 11, 1 (1986).

10 C. Cockburn, *Brothers: Male Dominance and Technological Change*, London, 1983; and *Machinery of Dominance: Women, Men and Technical Know-how*, London, 1985.

11 Jane Lewis, 'Introduction: reconstructing women's experience of home and family', in idem (ed.), *Labour and Love: Women's Experience of Home and Family, 1850–1940s*, Oxford, 1986, p. 2.

12 K. E. Lacey, 'Women and work in fourteenth and fifteenth century London', in Charles and Duffin (eds.), *Women and Work*, pp. 24–82; Shahar, *Fourth Estate*, pp. 11–21, 90–3, 221–3.

13 Janet Thomas, 'Women and capitalism: oppression or emancipation? A review article', *Comparative Studies in Society and History*, 30, 3 (1988); Lee Holcombe, *Wives and Property*, Oxford, 1983.

14 Martha C. Howell, 'Women, the family economy and the structures of market production in cities of northern Europe during the later middle ages', paper presented at an International conference on custom and commerce in early industrial Europe, University of Warwick, 1986, pp. 25–8.

15 E. P. Thompson, 'The grid of inheritance: a comment', in J. Goody, J. Thirsk, E. P. Thompson (eds.), *Family and Inheritance*, Cambridge, 1979; Holcombe, *Wives and Property*.

16 Roberts, *Women's Work*, chapters 3 and 4.

17 See for example Power, *Medieval Women*, pp. 62–9; Shahar, *The Fourth Estate*, pp. 189–205, 239–44; Howell, 'Women, the family economy and the structures of market production'; Alexander, 'Women's work', *passim*; E. Roberts, 'Women's strategies 1890–1940', in Jane Lewis (ed.), *Labour and Love: Women's Experience of Home and Family, 1850–1940s*, Oxford, 1986, pp. 223–44.

18 C. Middleton, 'Women's labour and the transition to preindustrial capitalism', in Charles and Duffin (eds.), *Women and Work*, pp. 198–200; I. Pinchbeck, *Women Workers in the Industrial Revolution*, London, 1930, 3rd ed, 1981, *passim*; W. R. Lee, 'Women's work and the family: some demographic implications of gender-specific rural work patterns in nineteenth-century Germany', chapter 2 in this volume.

19 Shahar, *The Fourth Estate*, pp. 13–21, 81–93, 189–205, 220–30; Martha C. Howell, *Women, Production and Patriarchy in Late Medieval Cities*, Chicago and London, 1987; Howell, 'Women, the family economy and the structures of market production'; Sue Wright, 'Churmaids, Huswyfes and Hucksters': the employment of women in Tudor and Stuart Salisbury', in Charles and Duffin (eds.), *Women and Work*, pp. 100–121, especially p. 116; Pinchbeck, *Women Workers*, pp. 292–3, 203–5; J. Quataert, 'The shaping of women's work in manufacturing: guilds, households and the state in central Europe, 1648–1870', *American Historical Review*, 90 (1985); R. Braun, 'Early industrialisation and demographic change in the Canton of Zurich', in C. Tilly (ed.), *Historical Studies of Changing Fertility*, New York, 1978; H. Medick, 'The proto-industrial family economy: the structural function of household and family during the transition from peasant to industrial capitalism', *Social History*, 1 (1976); M. Berg, P. Hudson and M. Sonenscher (eds.), *Manufacture in Town and Country before the Factory*, Cambridge, 1983, especially chapters 3 and 5; M. P. Guttman and R. Leboutte, 'Rethinking proto-industrialisation and the family', *Journal of Interdisciplinary History*, 14, 3 (1983),

Maxine Berg, *The Age of Manufactures*, London, 1986, chapters 9–12; P. Deyon, 'L'enjeu des discussions autour du concept de proto-industrialisation' *Revue du Nord*, 240 (1979); G. L. Gullickson, 'Proto-industrialisation, proletarianisation and the sexual division of labour', *Proceedings of the Eighth International Economic History Conference, Budapest, 1982, Section A 2*, Lille, 1982.

20 Roberts, *Women's Work*; James A. Schmiechen, *Sweated Industries and Sweated Labour: The London Clothing Trades, 1860–1914*, Illinois, 1984; Alexander, 'Women's work'; Angela V. John (ed.), *Unequal Opportunities: Women's Employment in England, 1800–1918*, Oxford, 1986; S. Blackburn, 'Sweated labour and the minimum wage', unpublished Ph.D. thesis, University of London, 1983.

21 M. Berg, 'Women's work, mechanisation and the early phases of industrialisation in England', in P. Joyce (ed.), *The Historical Meanings of Work*, Cambridge, 1986, pp. 64–98; O. Saito, 'The other faces of the industrial revolution', *Institute of Economic Research, Hitotsubashi University*, 39, 2 (1988), pp. 180–184. On politics see M. Savage, *The Dynamics of Working-class Politics: The Labour Movement in Preston, 1850–1940*, Cambridge, 1987.

22 L. Davidoff and C. Hall, *Family Fortunes: Men and Women of the English Middle Class, 1780–1850*, London, 1987, pp. 114, 200–1, 209–13, 276–7, 313–15, 325; M. Anderson, 'The social position of spinsters in Mid Victorian Britain', *Journal of Family History*, 9, 4 (1984); K. D. M. Snell and J. Millar, 'Lone parent families and the welfare state: past and present', *Continuity and Change*, 2, 3 (1987).

23 G. L. Gullickson, 'Women and protoindustrialisation: a review of the literature and the case of the Caux', in M. Berg (ed.), *Markets and Manufacture in Early Industrial Europe*, London, 1990.

24 See for example, M. Freifeld, 'Technological change and the self-acting mule: a study of skill and the sexual division of labour', *Social History*, 10, 3 (1986).

25 C. Hakim, 'Occupational segregation; a comparative study of the degree and pattern of the differentiation between men's and women's work in Britain, the United States and other countries', Research Paper no. 7 Department of Employment, London, 1979.

26 See chapters 10 and 8 by Evans and Whipp in this volume, pp. 248–70 and 184–203. For the cotton industry in a later period see Savage, *The Dynamics of Working-class Politics*.

27 Power, *Medieval Women*, pp. 71–5; M. Roberts, 'Sickles and Scythes: Women's work and men's work at harvest time', *History Workshop*, 7, 1979, pp. 3–28; C. Middleton, 'The sexual division of labour in feudal England', *New Left Review*, 113, (1979), pp. 147–68, Segalen, *Love and Power in the Peasant Family*; Pinchbeck, *Women Workers*, Part One, especially pp. 53–65; Snell, *Annals*, pp. 15–66; Lee's contribution (chapter 2) to this volume.

28 C. Middleton, 'Women's labour under capitalism', in Charles and Duffin (eds.), *Women and Work*, p. 189.

29 Roberts, 'Sickles and Scythes', p. 15; Shahar, *Fourth Estate*, p. 239.

30 Shahar, *Fourth Estate*, pp. 240–2; Roberts, 'Sickles and Scythes', pp. 3–28.

31 Middleton, 'Women's labour under capitalism', p. 190; I. D. Whyte, 'Proto-industrial-isation in Scotland', in P. Hudson (ed.), *Regions and Industries: A Perspective on the Industrial Revolution in Britain*, Cambridge, 1989; J. Thirsk, 'Industries in the country-side', in F. J. Fisher (ed.), *Essays in the Economic and Social History of Tudor and Stuart England*, Cambridge, 1961; R. C. Richardson, 'Metropolitan counties: Bedfordshire, Hertfordshire and Middlesex', in J. Thirsk (ed.), *The Agrarian History of England and Wales*, vol. 5, 1, *1640–1750: Regional Farming Systems*, pp. 265–9; Pinchbeck, *Women Workers*, pp. 16–19; Snell, *Annals*, p. 64. Pinchbeck, *Women Workers*, pp. 65–6.

32 Roberts, 'Sickles and Scythes', p. 17.

33 Snell, *Annals*, chapter 1, especially pp. 61–2; For the situation in Scandinavia compare Bengt Ankerloo, 'Agriculture and Women's Work: Directions of Change in the West, 1700–1900, *Journal of Family History*, 4 (1979), pp. 111–20.

34 J.M. Neeson, 'Common right and enclosure in eighteenth century Northamptonshire', unpublished Ph.D. thesis, University of Warwick, 1977; J.M. Martin, 'Village traders and the emergence of a proletariat in south Warwickshire, 1750–1851', *Agricultural History Review*, 32, 2 (1984).

35 Snell, *Annals*, pp. 57–63.

36 See Lee in this volume, pp. 50–75.

37 *Ibid.*; Snell, *Annals*, pp. 46, 94–7; A. Kussmaul, *Servants in Husbandry in Early Modern England*, Cambridge, 1981, chapter 6.

38 Thirsk (ed.), *Regional Systems*, *passim*.

39 Pinchbeck, *Women Workers*, pp. 59–66; Lee in this volume, p. 59.

40 Pinchbeck, *Women Workers*, pp. 59–66; John (ed.), *Unequal Opportunities*, p. 4.

41 Lee in this volume, pp. 50–75.

42 H. Mendras, *La Fin des Paysans. Suivi d'une réflexion sur la Fin des Paysans vingt ans après*, Paris, 1984; N.G. Bermeo, *The Revolution within the Revolution: Workers' Control in Rural Portugal*, New Jersey, 1986.

43 A.P. Donajgrodski, 'Twentieth century rural England: a case for peasant studies?', *Journal of Peasant Studies*, 16, 3 (1989), pp. 425–42; W. Lem, 'Household production and reproduction in rural Languedoc: social relations of petty commodity production in Murviel-les-Bezier', *Journal of Peasant Studies*, 15, 4 (1988), pp. 500–30.

44 Shahar, *Fourth Estate*, pp. 196–8; Charles and Duffin (eds.), *Women and Work*, chapters 1–3.

45 Power, *Medieval Women*, p. 62; Shahar, *Fourth Estate*, p. 198; Roberts, 'Words they are women', p. 42.

46 Howell, 'Women, the family economy and the structures of market production', *passim*.

47 These varied from one city to another and men were usually involved in supervisory and controlling ways but more than one historian has claimed that there was no clear-cut sexual division of occupations in medieval towns: F. and J. Geis, *Women in the Middle Ages*, New York, 1978, pp. 174–7. Most would agree that, although there were powerful status differences within trades and crafts, women do appear to have been significantly represented in the majority. For examples of the range of female occupations in high-status crafts see Shahar, *Fourth Estate*, pp. 189–200.

48 Lacey, 'Women and work in London', p. 25.

49 Hutton, 'Women in fourteenth-century Shrewsbury', pp. 111–12; and Wright, 'Churmaids, Huswyfes and Hucksters', pp. 111–12; both in Charles and Duffin (eds.), *Women and Work*.

50 Lacey, 'Women and work in London', p. 47; Power, *Medieval Women*, p. 61, Howell, 'Women, the family economy and the structures of market production', p. 26; Shahar *Fourth Estate*, p. 193.

51 Shahar, *Fourth Estate*, pp. 191–2.

52 Power, *Medieval Women*, p. 60.

53 In Norwich women were banned from weaving with twine on the pretext that they lacked the necessary physical strength and in Paris women were prohibited from working on carpets known as *tapis sarrazinois* because the work was deemed too dangerous for pregnant women in particular. For these and other examples see Shahar, *Fourth Estate*, p. 198.

54 *Ibid.*, p. 199.

55 In London from about 1480 the numbers of female merchants seem to have declined and there were growing attempts by guild and livery companies to exclude single women: Lacey, 'Women and work in London', p. 25; Power, *Medieval Women*, p. 60; Wright, 'Churmaids, Huswyfes and Hucksters', p. 116; Shahar, *Fourth Estate*, pp. 201–2.

56 Howell, 'Women, the family economy and the structures of market production', *passim*; Shahar, *Fourth Estate*, p. 196.

57 The analysis in this paragraph leans heavily on Howell, 'Women, the family economy and the structures of market production'. See also A. Clark, *The Working Life of Women in the Seventeenth Century*, London, 1919, especially Introduction and Conclusion.

58 Davidoff and Hall, *Family Fortunes*, chapter 6.

59 Petty trading had always had dubious status implications, associated as it was with gossip and gadding and tainted with the popular distrust of dealing: Roberts, 'Images of work and gender', pp. 153–4, in Charles and Duffin (eds.), *Women and Work*.

60 Martin, 'Village traders'; Snell, *Annals*, chapter 1; W. Thwaites, 'Women in the market place: Oxfordshire 1690–1800', *Midland History*, 9 (1984); M. Prior, 'Women and the urban economy: Oxford, 1500–1800', in M. Prior (ed.), *Women in English Society 1500–1800*, London, 1985.

61 Shahar, *Fourth Estate*, pp. 201–2; A. L. Wyman, 'The surgeoness: the female practitioner of surgery, 1400–1800', *Medical History*, 28, 1 (1984); Clark, *Working Life*, chapter 6, pp. 236–89.

62 Hutton, 'Women in fourteenth century Shrewsbury', p. 97; Lewis, *Labour and Love*, pp. 1–20; Roberts, 'Working-class living standards' and 'Women's strategies'; P. Ayers, chapter 11 in this volume.

63 J. N. von Schwerz, *Beschreibung der Landwirtschaft in Westfalen und Rheinpreussen*, 2 vols., Stuttgart, 1816, vol. 1, p. 111, quoted by Medick 'The proto-industrial family economy', p. 312.

64 *Ibid.*, pp. 309–14, where Medick is relying heavily on E. Sax's 1888 study of Thuringia, J. N. von Schwerz's 1816 study of Rhineland and Westphalia, and on the work of R. Braun, see note 65.

65 R. Braun, 'The impact of cottage industry on an agricultural population', in D. S. Landes (ed.), *The Rise of Capitalism*, New York, 1966. See also Braun's 'Proto-industrialisation and demographic changes in the Canton of Zurich', in C. Tilly (ed.), *Historical Studies of Changing Fertility*, New York, 1978; and R. Braun, *Industrialisierung und Volksleben. Veränderung der Lebensform unter Einwirkung der verlagsindustriellen Heimarbeit in einen ländlichen Industriegebiet (Zürcher Oberland) vor 1800*, Erlenbach und Zürich, 1960. Braun relies heavily on the evidence of middle-class travellers and moralisers.

66 N. McKendrick, 'The consumer revolution in eighteenth century England', in N. McKendrick, J. Brewer and J. H. Plumb (eds.), *The Birth of a Consumer Society: The Commercialization of Eighteenth Century England*, London, 1982, pp. 9–33.

67 M. Berg, 'Women's work, mechanisation and the early phases of industrialisation in England', in P. Joyce (ed.), *The Historical Meanings of Work*, Cambridge, 1987, pp. 64–98; O. Saito, 'The other faces of the industrial revolution', *Institute of Economic Research; Hitotsubashi University*, 39, 2 (1988), pp. 180–4.

68 The activity rate for married women aged 20 to 39 in Cardington, Bedfordshire, in 1752 was 82 per cent. In Flanders the linen industry employed at least four times as many women as men and in the Canton of Auffay near Rouen in 1796, 75% of women were spinning for merchants and the cotton industry there employed almost eight times as many women as men. O. Saito, 'Who worked when: lifetime profiles of labour force participation in Cardington and Corfe Castle in the late eighteenth and mid nineteenth centuries', *Local Population Studies* (Spring 1979); F. F. Mendels, 'Agriculture and peasant industry in eighteenth century Flanders', in W. N. Parker and E. L. Jones (eds.), *European Peasants and their Markets: Essays in Agrarian Economic History*, New Jersey, 1975, pp. 183–4; G. L. Gullickson, 'Women and proto-industrialisation: a review of the literature and the case of the Caux', paper delivered at an international conference on custom and commerce in early industrial Europe, University of Warwick, 1987, pp. 3, 9. Published in revised form: see note 23.

69 For the best account of the role of women in a West European peasant society see M. Segalen, *Love and Power in the Peasant Family*, Oxford, 1983.

70 G. L. Gullickson, *Spinners and Weavers of Auffay*, Cambridge, 1986, chapters 2 and 10; Whyte, 'Proto-industrialisation in Scotland', Snell, *Annals*, chapter 1.

71 Berg, *Age of Manufactures*, p. 173.

72 Pinchbeck, *Women Workers*, p. 126.

73 Shorter, *Making of the Modern Family*, pp. 172–3.

74 Middleton, 'Women's labour and capitalism', pp. 199–200.

75 Pinchbeck, *Women Workers*, chapters 6–8; Gullickson, 'Women and proto-industrialisation', pp. 7–9; B. Collins, Proto-industrialisation and pre-famine emigration', *Social History*, 7 (1982), pp. 130–1.

76 P. Hudson, 'Proto-industrialisation: the case of the West Riding wool textile industry in the eighteenth and early nineteenth centuries', *History Workshop*, 12 (1981), pp. 34–61; J. Styles, 'Embezzlement, industry and the law in England, 1500–1800', in M. Berg, P. Hudson and M. Sonenscher (eds.), *Manufacture in Town and Country before the Factory*, Cambridge, 1983, pp. 173–210.

77 R. Wall, 'Age at leaving home', *Journal of Family History*, 3 (1978), pp. 182–201.

78 Gullickson, 'Women and proto-industrialisation', p. 9.

79 Berg, *Age of Manufactures*, pp. 154–5.

80 Hudson, 'From manor to mill', p. 130, in Berg, Hudson and Sonenscher (eds.), *Manufacture in Town and Country*.

81 D. Levine, *Family Formation in an Age of Nascent Capitalism*, London, 1977, pp. 28–33.

82 Collins, 'Proto-industrialisation and pre-famine emigration', pp. 130, 140.

83 Gullickson, 'Women and proto-industrialisation', p. 9; N. Murray, 'A social history of the Scottish handloom weavers, 1790–1850', unpublished D.Phil. thesis, University of Strathclyde, 1976, pp. 55–62; Whyte, 'Proto-industrialisation in Scotland', pp. 245–9; Berg, 'Women's work and mechanisation', p. 82.

84 A. P. Wadsworth and J. de L. Mann, *The Cotton Trade and Industrial Lancashire, 1600–1780*, Manchester, 1931, pp. 285, 323, 325, 336; M. Berg, 'The introduction and diffusion of the power loom', unpublished MA disssertation, University of Sussex, 1972.

85 *Ibid.*; Berg, 'Women and mechanisation', p. 82.

86 Gullickson, 'Women and proto-industrialisation', pp. 14–18.

87 Freifeld, 'Technological change and the self-acting mule'.

88 Berg, 'Women's work and mechanisation', p. 81.

89 For a general treatment of these issues see A. Phillips and B. Taylor, 'Sex and skill: notes towards a feminist economics', *Feminist Review*, 6 (1980).

90 O. Hufton, 'Women and the family economy in eighteenth century France', *French Historical Studies*, 9 (1975), and 'Women without men: widows and spinsters in Britain and France in the eighteenth century', *Journal of Family History*, 9 (1984).

91 Hugh Miller, 1823, cited by Richards 'Women and the British economy', p. 341, quoted in Berg, *Age of Manufactures*, p. 143.

92 Berg, 'Women's work and mechanisation', pp. 86–8.

93 *Ibid.*, pp. 97–8; Davidoff and Hall, *Family Fortunes*, pp. 250–1.

94 M. P. Guttman and R. Leboutte, 'Rethinking proto-industrialisation and the family', *Journal of Interdisciplinary History*, 14, 3 (1984).

95 R. L. Rudolf, 'Family structure and proto-industrialisation in Russia', *Journal of Economic History*, 40 (1980), pp. 111–22.

96 Theresa M. McBride, 'The long road home: women's work and industrialisation', in Renate Bridenthal and Claudia Koonz (eds.), *Becoming Visible: Women in European History*, Boston, 1977, p. 283.

97   For a discussion of this hypothesis, see Martha C. Howell, *Women, Production and Patriarchy in Late Medieval Cities*, Chicago and London, 1987, pp. 26–33.

98   Susan H. van Horn, *Women, Work and Fertility, 1900–1986*, New York, 1988, p. 4; Susan Yeandle, *Women's Working Lives: Patterns and Strategies*, London and New York, 1984, p. 2.

99   Alice Clark, *Working Life of Women in the Seventeenth Century*, 1919, new edn, London, 1968; Sheila Rowbotham, *Woman's Consciousness, Man's World*, Harmondsworth, 1973; M. Barrett, *Women's Oppression Today*, London, 1980; W. Seccombe, 'The housewife and her labour under capitalism', *New Left Review*, 94 (1975), pp. 47–58. For fuller discussion of this and alternative interpretations see Janet Thomas, 'Women and capitalism: oppression or emancipation? A review article', *Comparative Studies in Society and History*, 30, 3 (1988).

100   Shorter, *The Making of the Modern Family*. For other 'optimistic' interpretations see W. J. Goode, *World Revolution and Family Patterns*, New York, 1963; M. Young and P. Wilmott, *The Symmetrical Family*, London, 1973.

101   E. Higgs, 'Women, occupations and work in the nineteenth century censuses', *History Workshop*, 23 (1987); Robyn Dasey, 'Women's work and the family: women garment workers in Berlin and Hamburg before the First World War', in R. J. Evans and W. R. Lee (eds.), *The German Family: Essays on the Social History of the Family in Nineteenth- and Twentieth-Century Germany*, London, 1981, pp. 221–55.

102   Higgs, 'Women, occupations and work'; F. L. Jones, 'Occupational statistics revisited: the female labour force in early British and Australian censuses', *Australian Economic History Review*, 27, 2 (1987); Jane Lewis, 'Dealing with dependency: state practices and social realities, 1870–1945', in J. Lewis (ed.), *Women's Welfare, Women's Rights*, London, 1983, p. 17; C. Hakim, 'Census reports as documentary evidence: the Census Commentaries 1801–1851', *Sociological Review*, 28 (1980), pp. 556–8. The German census of 1907 presents a false picture of the extent of the female labour-force as it was carried out in a year of economic depression accompanied by an inflated relative level of female employment: see Barbara Franzoi, *At the Very Least She Pays the Rent: Women and German Industrialisation, 1871–1914*, Westport, Conn. and London, 1985, p. 17.

103   Mary Lynn McDougall, 'Working class women during the Industrial Revolution, 1780–1914', in Bridenthal and Koonz (eds.), *Becoming Visible*, pp. 257–79.

104   Yeandle, *Women's Working Lives*, p. 13.

105   Data for Norway and other Scandinivian countries, including Finland, in R. Hjerppe and P. Schybergson, 'Kvinnoarbetar i Industrins Genombrottsskede c. 1850–1913', in G. A. Blom (ed.), *Arbeits-lonns og rettsforhold for yrkesaktive Kvinner i de Nordiske land ca. 1810–1914*, Trondheim, 1978.

106   Tilly and Scott, *Women, Work and Family*.

107   C. Hakim, 'Occupational segregation'; van Horn, *Women, Work and Fertility*, p. 4. McDougall, 'Working class women', p. 268.

108   M. H. Fraundorf, 'The labor force participation of turn-of-the-century married women', *Journal of Economic History*, 39 (1979), pp. 401–17.

109   See Clare Evans' contribution to the present volume, chapter 10.

110   Deborah Gorham, *The Victorian Girl and the Feminine Ideal*, London and Canberra, 1982, pp. 4, 209; Catherine Hall, 'The early formation of Victorian domestic ideology', in Sandra Burman (ed.), *Fit Work for Women*, London, 1979, pp. 22–3.

111   Karin Hausen, 'Family and role-division: the polarisation of sexual stereotypes in the 19th century – an aspect of the dissociation of work and family life', in Evans and Lee, *The German Family*, pp. 51–85; Lorna Duffin, 'The conspicuous consumptive: woman as an invalid', in S. Delamont and L. Duffin (eds.), *The Nineteenth-Century Woman: Her Cultural and Physical World*, London, 1978, p. 26. Belief in psychological and

and biological gender differences remained remarkably persistent despite increasing scientific evidence to the contrary. G. T. W. Patrick of the University of Iowa, for example, continued to argue that women had smaller brains than men and were not as ambidextrous. See van Horn, *Women, Work and Fertility*, p. 10; J. L. Dubbert, *A Man's Place: Masculinity in Transition*, New Jersey, 1979, p. 91.

112 Julie A. Matthaei, *An Economic History of Women in America: Women's Work, the Sexual Division of Labour, and the Development of Capitalism*, New York, 1982, pp. 180–1.

113 Margaret Hewitt, *Wives and Mothers in Victorian Industry*, 1st edn, 1958 (Westport, Conn., 1975), chapter 8, pp. 99–122; Carol Dyehouse, 'Working-class mothers and infant mortality in England, 1895–1914', *Journal of Social History*, 12 (1978), pp. 248–67; Lewis, 'Introduction: reconstructing women's experience of home and family', p. 6; Denise Riley, *War in the Nursery: Theories of the Child and the Mother*, London, 1983.

114 Jane Lewis, 'The working class wife and mother and state intervention, 1850–1918', in Lewis (ed.), *Labour and Love*, p. 100; Anne Summers, 'A home-from-home – women's philanthropic work in the nineteenth century', in Sandra Burman (ed.), *Fit Work for Women*, London, 1979, pp. 33–4. See also Celia Davies, 'The health visitor as a mother's friend: a woman's place in public health, 1900–1914', *Social History of Medicine*, 1 (1988), pp. 39–60.

115 Lewis, 'Working class wife', p. 103.

116 Lewis, 'Introduction', p. 11.

117 See for example the bourgeois attitudes to women's wages in *La politique des femmes*, 18–24 January 1848, cited in Laura S. Strumingher, *Women and the Making of the Working Class: Lyon 1850–1870*, Vermont, 1979, p. 131. Such a view clearly reinforced the notion of women's earnings as 'pin money', see Sharlene J. Hesse, 'Women working: historical trends', in Karen W. Feinstein (ed.), *Working Women and Families*, London, 1979, p. 46.

118 Sonya O. Rose, 'Gender antagonism and class conflict: exclusionary strategies of male trade unionists in nineteenth century Britain', *Social History* 13, 2 (1988), Hilary Land, 'The family way', *Feminist Review*, 4 (1980), pp. 55–77, here p. 56; Malcolm I. Thomis and J. Grimmett, *Women in Protest, 1800–1850*, London, 1982, p. 16; Heidi I. Hartmann, 'The unhappy marriage of Marxism and Feminism: towards a more progressive union', in L. Sargent (ed.), *Women and Revolution: A Discussion of the Unhappy Marriage of Marxism and Feminism*, London, 1981, p. 21; Michelle Barrett and Mary Macintosh, 'The family way; some problems for socialists and feminists', *Capital and Class*, 1 (1980), pp. 53–4. See also Clare Evans' contribution to the present volume, chapter 10.

119 Norbert C. Soldon, *Women in British Trade Unions 1874–1976*, Dublin, 1978, p. 4; Eleanor Gordon, 'Women, work and collective action: Dundee jute workers, 1870–1906', *Journal of Social History*, 27–48 (1987), p. 31. See also Rose, 'Gender antagonism and class conflict', pp. 191–208.

120 McDougall, 'Working class women', p. 257, Lewis, *Women in England*, p. 49.

121 For a recent survey and restatement of the role of male trade unionists see Rose 'Gender antagonism and class conflict'. For a recent more complex view see Ellen Jordan, 'The exclusion of women from industry in nineteenth-century Britain', *Comparative Studies in Society and History*, 31, 2 (1989). For stress on the role of employers' preferences, male household heads, state policy, and the local housing market see M. Savage, 'Trade unionism, sex segregation and the state: women's employment in new industries in interwar Britain', *Social History*, 13, 2 (1988). For evidence from British coal mining see Jane Mark-Lawson and Anne Witz, 'From "family labour" to "family wage"? The case of women's labour in nineteenth century coal mining', *Social History*, 13, 2 (1988).

For neighbourhood attitudes see Elizabeth Roberts, *A Woman's Place: An Oral History of Working Class Women, 1890–1940*, Oxford, 1984.

122 Michelle Barrett, *Women's Oppression Today: Problems in Marxist Feminist Analysis*, London, 1980, p. 165. For a detailed argument about the relationship between ideology and material changes see Mackintosh, 'Gender and economics. The sexual division of labour and the subordination of women', in K. Young, C. Wolkowitz and R. McCullagh (eds.), *Of Marriage and the Market: women's subordination internationally and its lessons*, London, 1981, p. 10.

123 Rose, 'Gender at work', pp. 113–32; Cynthia Cockburn, *Brothers: Male Dominance and Technological Change*, London, 1985, *passim*; see also Sonja O. Rose, 'Gender segregation in the transition to factory: the English hosiery industry, 1850–1910', *Feminist Studies* (1987); Harriet Bradley, 'Technological change, management strategies, and the development of gender-based job segregation in the labour process', in D. Knight and H. Willmott (eds.), *Gender and the Labour Process*, Aldershot, 1986, p. 58; Strumingher, *Women and the Making of the Working Class*, p. 19ff.

124 See Ida Blom's contribution to the present volume, chapter 6; Yeandle, *Women's Working Lives*, p. 15.

125 Lewis, 'Working-class wives', p. 143. It was of course argued that a decent wage which met family needs would enable working-class wives to fulfil their familial and maternal responsibilties.

126 Soldon, *Women in British Trade Unions*, p. 6; Jill Liddington, 'Women cotton workers and the suffrage campaign: the radical suffragists in Lancashire, 1893–1914', in Burman (ed.), *Fit Work for Women*, pp. 104–6. W. Seccombe, 'Patriarchy stabilised: the construction of the male bread winner wage norm in nineteenth-century Britain', *Social History*, 21 (1986), pp. 53–76; *Hamburger Echo*, 19 November 1899, cited in R. J. Evans, 'Politics and the family: social democracy and the working class family in theory and practice before 1924', in Evans and Lee (eds.), *The German Family*, p. 272.

127 See chapter 10 below.

128 Judy Lown, 'Not so much a factory, more a form of patriarchy: gender and class during industrialisation', in E. Gormarnikov *et al.* (eds.), *Gender, Class and Work*, London, 1983, p. 36ff.

129 Patricia Hilden, 'Class and gender: conflicting components of women's behaviour in the textile mills of Lille, Roubaix and Tourcoing, 1880–1914', *Historical Journal*, 27 (1984), pp. 361–85. See also Lown, 'Not so much a factory', p. 39; J. C. Fout, 'Working-class women's work in Imperial Germany', *History of European Ideas*, 5 (1987), p. 625–32; Strumingher, *Women and the Making of the Working Class*, p. 34.

130 Yeandle, *Women's Working Lives*, p. 15; Quataert, 'The shaping of women's work in manufacturing', p. 1135.

131 Franzoi, *At the Very Least*, p. 69; Lewis, 'Dealing with dependency', p. 22. See also Dorothea Schmidt, 'Keine schutzende Hand. Die Bedeutung staatlicher Regelungen für die Frauenarbeit in Bremen in der Zeit des Kaiserreiches', *Beiträge zur Sozialgeschichte Bremens*, vol. 6, 1985, pp. 15–44.

132 Sheila B. Kamerman, Alfred J. Kahn and Paul Kingston, *Maternity Policies and Working Women*, New York, 1985, p. 15.

133 G. Braybon, *Women Workers in the First World War: The British Experience*, London, 1981, p. 20; Lewis, 'Dealing with dependency', p. 22; *idem*, 'The working class wife', p. 100.

134 Penny Summerfield, *Women Workers in the Second World War: Production and Patriarchy in Conflict*, London, 1984, *passim*; T. W. Mason, 'Women in Germany, 1925–40: family, welfare and work', *History Workshop*, 1 (1976), pp. 74–113, 2 (1976), pp. 5–32; Claudia Koonz, *Mothers in the Fatherland: Women, the Family and Nazi*

Politics, London, 1986; Barbara Rogers, *The Domestication of Women: Discrimination in Developing Societies*, London, 1980, *passim*; Gisela Bock, 'Frauen und ihre Arbeit im Nationalsozialismus', in Annette Kuhn and Gerhard Schneider (eds.), *Frauen in der Geschichte. Frauenrechte und die gesellschaftliche Arbeit der Frauen im Wandel*, Dusseldorf, 1981, pp. 113–49.

135 Savage, 'Trade unionism, sex segregation and the state', pp. 223–5; Yeandle, *Women's Working Lives*, p. 17; Helen Boak, 'The state as employer of women in the Weimar Republic', in W. R. Lee and Eve Rosenhaft (eds.), *The State and Social Change in Germany, 1880–1980*, Leamington Spa, Hamburg and New York, 1990; Lewis, 'Dealing with dependency', p. 22; see also Linda Grant's contribution to the present volume, chapter 9; Fiona McNally, *Women for Hire: A Study of the Female Office Worker*, London, 1975, p. 124.

136 Jane Lewis, *Women in England, 1870–1950: Sexual Divisions and Social Change*, Brighton, 1984, *passim*; H. G. Schaffer, *Women in the Two Germanies: A Comparative Study of a Socialist and a Non Socialist Society*, New York, 1985, pp. 55–109; Jerzy Piotrowski, 'Marriage and marriage dissolution and the changing status of women: the case of Poland', in M. Niphius-Nell (ed.), *Demographic Aspects of the Changing Status of Women in Europe*, Leiden, 1978, pp. 49–65.

137 Yeandle, *Women's Working Lives*, p. 7; McNally, *Women for Hire*, *passim*.

138 Kamerman, Kahn and Kingston, *Maternity Policies*, *passim*; van Horn, *Women, Work and Fertility*, *passim*; Ansley J. Coale and Susan Cotts Watkins, *The Decline of Fertility in Europe*, Princeton, 1974, p. 458. In the Princeton European Fertility Project the relationship between female labour-force participation and long-term trends in fertility was only analysed in the case of Ireland, Germany and Switzerland, although the findings clearly support the need for further research. In the case of Norway there was a strong correlation between smaller families and married women's economic activity, see Ida Blom's contribution to the present volume, chapter 6, p. 168. See also H. T. Groat, R. C. Workman and A. G. Neal, 'Labor force participation and family formation: a study of working mothers', *Demography*, 13 (1976), pp. 115–25.

139 van Horn, *Women, Work and Fertility*, p. 59; Kamerman, Kahn and Kingston, *Maternity Policies*, p. 33.

140 McNally, *Women for Hire*, p. 186; Hesse, 'Women working', p. 46.

141 See, for example, Brian Abel-Smith, *A History of the Nursing Profession*, London, 1960.

142 Dee Garrison, 'The tender technicians: the feminisation of public librarianship, 1876–1905', in M. Hartman and L. W. Banner (eds.), *Clio's Consciousness Raised: New Perspectives on the History of Women*, New York, 1974, pp. 159ff. McDermid also stresses the strength of the idea that women were the guardians of traditional culture in Tsarist Russia, see chapter 8 in this volume.

143 Theresa M. McBride, 'A woman's world: department stores and the evolution of women's employment, 1870–1920', *French Historical Studies*, 10 (1978), pp. 664–83; Michael B. Miller, *The Bon Marché: Bourgeois Culture and the Department Store, 1869–1920*, London, 1981, *passim*.

144 Hakim, 'Occupational segregation', *passim*, S. Dex and S. P. Perry, 'Women's employment changes in the 1970s', *Employment Gazette*, 92, 5 (1984). See also H. Hartmann, 'Capitalism, patriarchy and job segregation by sex', *Signs*, 3 (1976); and S. Dex and L. B. Shaw, *British and American Women at Work: Do Equal Opportunities Policies Matter?*, London, 1986; C. Craig, E. Garnsey and J. Rubery, *Pay in Small Firms: Women and Informal Payment Systems*, Department of Employment Research Paper, No. 40 (1985).

145 See chapter 9 below and Soldon, *Women in British Trade Unions*, p. 184.

146 Rose, 'Gender at work', p. 114; Pat Hudson (ed.), *Regions and Industries: A Perspective on the Industrial Revolution in Britain*, Cambridge, 1989, chapter 1; W. R. Lee,

'Economic development and the role of the state in nineteenth-century Germany', *Economic History Review*, 41 (1988), pp. 346–67.

147 Lown, 'Not so much a factory', *passim*; Strumingher, *Women and the Making of the Working-Class*, pp. 17–18; Sonya O. Rose, 'Proto-industry, women's work and the household economy in the transition to industrial capitalism', *Journal of Family History*, 13, 2 (1988), pp. 181–93.

148 Franzoi, *At the Very Least*, p. 13; Michael Haines, *Fertility and Occupation: Population Patterns in Industrialization*, New York, 1979.

149 Forms of the sexual division of labour are interestingly discussed by Middleton in 'Women's labour and the transition', pp. 186–200. For a specific empirical study which takes account of localised and life-cycle diversity in women's work see R. Pahl, *Divisions of Labour*, Oxford, 1984. See also Ellen Jordan, 'Female unemployment in England and Wales, 1851–1911: an examination of the Census figures for 15 to 19 year-olds', *Social History*, 13, 2 (1988).

150 Franzoi, *At the Very Least*, p. 129; H. Schafer, 'Die Heimarbeiterin und die Fabrikarbeiterin (1800–1945)', in H. Pohl and W. Treue (eds.), *Die Frau in der Deutschen Wirtschaft*, Stuttgart, 1981, p. 67; Dasey 'Women's work', pp. 221–5; Rosemarie Beier, *Frauenarbeit und Frauenalltag im Deutschen Kaiserreich. Heimarbeiterinnen in der Berliner Bekleidungsindustrie 1880–1914*, Frankfurt and New York, 1983.

151 See Lowell J. Satra, 'After the match girls' strike: Bryant and May in the 1880s', *Victorian Studies*, 26 (1982), pp. 13–14ff; James F. McMillan, *Housewife or Harlot: The Place of Women in French Society 1870–1940*, Brighton, 1981, *passim*.

152 J. Schmiechen, 'Sweated industries and sweated labour: a study of industrial disorganisation and workers' attitudes in the London clothing trades, 1867–1909', *Journal of Economic History*, 36 (1976), pp. 283–6; *idem*, *Sweated Industries and Sweated Labor*.

153 Quataert, 'The shaping of women's work', pp. 1122–48; *idem*, 'Teamwork in Saxon homeweaving families in the nineteenth century', in R.-E. B. Joeres and M. J. Maynes (eds.), *German Women in the Eighteenth and Nineteenth Centuries*, Bloomington, 1986, pp. 3–10; *idem*, 'Combining agrarian and industrial livelihood: rural households in the Saxon Oberlausitz in the nineteenth century', *Journal of Family History*, 10 (1985), pp. 11; Douglas R. Holmes and Jean H. Quataert, 'An approach to modern labor: worker peasantries in historic Saxony and the Friuli region over three centuries', *Comparative Studies in Society and History*, 18 (1986), p. 200.

154 Roberts, 'Working-class living standards'; Marlene Ellerkamp and Brigitte Jungmann, 'Unendliche Arbeit. Frauen in der "Jutespinnerei und -weberei Bremen" 1888–1914', in Karin Hausen (ed.), *Frauen suchen ihre Geschichte. Historische Studien zum 19. und 20. Jahrhundert*, Munich, 1983, pp. 128–45; Franzoi, *At the Very Least*, p. 125; Lewis, *Women in England*, *passim*; Lynn Jamieson, 'Limited resources and limiting conventions: working class mothers and daughters in urban Scotland, 1890–1925', in Lewis (ed.), *Labour and Love*, p. 50.

155 Winifred P. Wandersee, *Women's Work and Family Values, 1920–1940*, Harvard, 1981, p. 1: but the increasing importance of female 'outside' work also arguably reflected a commitment to family values. Oral evidence for urban Scotland fails to verify Scott and Tilly's view relating to the appearance of a modern individualistic attitude to work by married women: Jamieson, 'Limited resources', p. 65.

156 L. Davidoff, 'The separation of home and work? Landladies and lodgers in nineteenth- and twentieth-century England', in Burman, *Fit Work for women*, pp. 64–97. See also L. Davidoff and B. Westover (eds.), *Our Work, Our Lives, Our Words; Women's History and Women's Work*, London, 1986; Theresa M. McBride, *The Domestic Revolution: The Modernisation of Household Service in England and France, 1820–1920*, London, 1976, p. 145; Hilden, 'Class and gender', p. 361–85; Malcolmson, 'Laundresses and the

laundry trade', pp. 439–62. So common was prostitution that it was known commonly as 'the fifth quarter of the women's day'.

157 See Pat Ayers' contribution to the present volume, chapter 11. Roberts, 'Working-class living standards', *passim*; Ellen Ross 'Survival networks: women's neighbourhood sharing in London before World War One', *History Workshop*, 15 (1983).

158 Theresa McBride, 'Women's work: mistress and servant in the nineteenth century', *Proceedings of the Western Society for French History*, 3 (1975), pp. 390–7; *idem*, 'The long road home', p. 290.

159 Franzoi, *At the Very Least*, p. 30. See also McNally, *Women for Hire*, p. 4.

160 Richard L. Kagan, *Students and Society in Early-modern Spain*, Baltimore and London, 1974, p. 27.

161 John W. Shaffer, 'Family, class and young women: occupational expectations in nineteenth-century Paris', *Journal of Family History* (1978), pp. 62–77; Jamieson, 'Limited resources', p. 55; Sheila Rowbotham, *Women, Resistance and Revolution*, London, 1976, p. 127.

162 Tilly and Scott, *Women, Work and Family*, *passim*. See Anne Meyering's contribution to the present volume, chapter 5.

163 Matthaei, *An Economic History of Women*, p. 315–20; van Horn, *Women, Work and Fertility*, p. 21.

164 Lewis, 'Introduction', p. 7; Gorham, *The Victorian Girl*, p. 415; M. Jeanne Petersen, 'No angels in the house: the Victorian myth and the Paget women', *American Historical Review*, 89 (1984), pp. 677–708; see also Catherine Hall's contribution to the present volume, chapter 4; and Davidoff and Hall, *Family Fortunes*, *passim*.

165 Marion W. Gray, 'Prescriptions for productive female domesticity in a transitional era: Germany's *Hausmutterliteratur*, 1780–1840', *History of European Ideas*, 8 (1987), pp. 413–26.

166 Holmes and Quataert, 'An approach to modern labor', p. 187; Gullickson, *Spinners and Weavers*, p. 151.

167 Bradley, 'Technological change', pp. 54–73; Rose L. Glickman, 'The Russian factory woman, 1880–1914', in D. Atkinson, A. Dallin and G. W. Lapidus (eds.), *Women in Russia*, Stanford, 1977, p. 66. Sonia Cliff, 'Technical change and occupational sex-typing', in David Knight and Hugh Wilmott (eds.), *Gender and the Labour Process*, Aldershot, 1986, pp. 74–93. Technological change in agriculture, as in the development of the centrifuge, however, has frequently been accompanied by an erosion of women's role in production: see Bodil K. Hansen, 'Rural women in late nineteenth-century Denmark', *Journal of Peasant Studies*, 9 (1981), pp. 225–39; Maureen M. Mackintosh, 'Domestic labour and the household', in Burman (ed.), *Fit Work for Women*, p. 179.

168 Lewis, *Women in England*, p. 179; Richard T. Vann, 'Toward a new lifestyle: women in pre-industrial capitalism', in Bridenthal and Koonz (eds.), *Becoming Visible*, pp. 192–216; Strumingher, *Women and the Making of the Working Class*, p. 17; Franzoi, *At the Very Least*, p. 31.

169 McNally, *Women for Hire*, p. 27; Graham S. Lowe, *Women in the Administrative Revolution*, Oxford, 1977, *passim*. See also Meta Zimmeck, 'Strategies and stratagems for the employment of women in the British civil service, 1919–1939', *Historical Journal*, 27, 4 (1984).

170 Anne Summers, *Angels and Citizens: British Women as Military Nurses*, London, 1988, *passim*; Matthaei, *An Economic History of Women*, p. 182; Sara Delamont, 'The contradiction in ladies' education', in Sara Delamont and Lorna Duffin (eds.), *The Nineteenth-Century Women: Her Cultural and Physical World*, London, 1978, p. 154.

171 Miller, *The Bon Marché*, *passim*.

172 See the contributions by Robert Lee (chapter 2), Sheilagh Ogilvie (chapter 3), Anne Meyering (chapter 5) and Ida Blom (chapter 6) to the present volume.

173 See Richard Whipp, chapter 7 and Linda Grant, chapter 9 in this volume.

174 Tamara Hareven, *Family Time and Industrial Time*, Cambridge, 1982, *passim*; Michael Anderson, *Family Structure in Nineteenth Century Lancashire* Cambridge, 1971; R. Whipp and M. Grieco, 'Family and workplace: the social organisation of work', *Warwick Economic Papers*, 239, 1983; R. Whipp 'Labour markets and communities: an historical view', *The Sociological Review*, 33 (1985), pp. 768–91.

175 D. Levine and K. Wrightson, *Poverty and Piety in an English Village: Terling, 1525–1700*, New York, 1979; P. Laslett and K. Oosterveen (eds.), *Bastardy and its Comparative History*, London, 1980, *passim*; Eilidh M. Garrett, 'The trials of labour – motherhood versus employment in a nineteenth century textile centre', unpublished paper presented to the Annual Conference of the British Sociological Association, University of Edinburgh 1988; Haines, *Fertility and Occupation*, *passim*.

176 Garret, 'The trials of labour'; van Horn, *Women, Work and Fertility*, p. 71. For contemporary and Third World work on the fertility implications of female employment see Mercedes B. Concepcion, 'Female labor force participation and fertility', *International Labor Review*, 108 (1974), pp. 503–17; Juan C. Elizaga, 'The participation of women in the labour force of Latin America: fertility and other factors', *International Labor Review*, 109 (1974), pp. 519–38; Eva Mueller, 'The allocation of women's time and its relation to fertility', in R. Anker, M. Buvinic and N. H. Youssef (eds.), *Women's Roles and Population Trends in the Third World*, London, 1982, pp. 59ff.

177 See, for example, the ongoing research in Liverpool University being undertaken with the support of the Leverhulme Trust, the National Museums and Galleries of Merseyside and Liverpool University by the Docklands History Project: Alan Johnson and Kevin Moore, *The Tapestry Makers: Life and Work at Lee's Tapestry Works, Birkenhead*, Liverpool, 1987; Pat Ayers, *The Liverpool Docklands: Life and Work in Athol Street*, Liverpool, 1988; Alan Johnson, *Working the Tides: Gatemen and Masters on the River Mersey*, Liverpool, 1988. See also Lydia Morris, 'Local social networks and domestic organisations: a study of redundant steel workers and their wives', *The Sociological Review*, 33 (1985), pp. 327–42; and Martin Bulmer, 'The rejuvenation of community studies? Neighbours, networks and policy', *The Sociological Review*, 33 (1985), pp. 430–48.

178 R. E. Cromwell and D. H. Olson, 'Power in families', in R. E. Cromwell and D. H. Olson (eds.), *Power in Families*, New York, 1955. In this context power over family resources and decision-making was one of the most fundamental aspects of social interaction.

179 Hewitt, *Wives and Mothers*, *passim*; Roberts, *A Woman's Place*, p. 101.

180 Hilden, 'Class and gender', pp. 361–85.

181 Jamieson, 'Limited resources', p. 65.

182 See Richard Whipp, chapter 7 and Pat Ayers, chapter 11 in this volume.

183 Segalen, *Love and Power*, *passim*; also contributions by Sheilagh Ogilvie, Ida Blom, Jane McDermid and Robert Lee in the present volume, chapters 3, 6, 8, and 2 respectively; and Glickman, *The Russian Factory Woman*, p. 64.

184 For a thought-provoking exposition of this view see D. Levine, *Reproducing Families: The Political Economy of English Population History*, Cambridge, 1987.

185 For an interesting statement of the need to move from a separate treatment of women's history and to create a more radical feminist history incorporating aspects of post-structuralist epistemology see J. W. Scott, *Gender and the Politics of History*, London, 1988, pp. 1–11 and chapter 1.

PART ONE

Agriculture and proto-industry

Chapter Two

Women's work and the family: some demographic implications of gender-specific rural work patterns in nineteenth-century Germany

W.R. LEE

Introduction

This chapter examines the work role of women within German rural society in the eighteenth and nineteenth centuries and, in particular, the familial context of female work. An attempt is made to delineate between the biological, cultural and economic factors influencing changes in the pattern of female work, and to explore the domestic repercussions of these changes within rural families. The demographic implications of the shifting balance between women's domestic and outside responsibilities will be examined in terms of contemporary trends in various indicators – including infant mortality, fertility, maternal mortality and gender-specific death-rates.

It is generally assumed that women played a subordinate role in pre-industrial rural society.[1] There is no tangible evidence of a reduction in the production function of the family economy, and in various regions of Germany traditional family structures and the implicit value system of peasant society, persisted well into the twentieth century.[2] Within this world, where family relationships were primarily determined by work needs and marriage contracts continued to reflect purely material considerations, the overall position of women could frequently appear to have been unfavourable. Indeed, evidence of direct discrimination against women can be found in a number of areas. In terms of inheritance practices, women were clearly disadvantaged. Whether in Württemberg, the Eiffel, or in the rural hinterland of Lübeck, male offspring, and in particular eldest sons, were accorded preferential treatment over female siblings.[3] In those areas where impartible inheritance was customary, this, in turn, emphasised even further the central importance of the *Hof* (farm).[4] Equally, as a function of a relatively high average age at first marriage which was a feature of the general European marriage pattern,[5] the expected social and economic role

50

of women would have been inculcated during an extended period of service, either within a domestic environment or more commonly as a maid on a large peasant holding.[6] However, among the *Dienstboten* (domestic servants) the individual spheres of work were closely defined on a gender-specific basis, and an internal hierarchy was rigidly maintained, both at work, at meal times and during periods of rest and recuperation. Even if female servants were integrated into the *Hof*, they were seldom accorded equal rights with other family members, inter-marriage was precluded, and their level of remuneration was often very low.[7] The general retention of the traditional *Tischgemeinschaft* (table community) until the second half of the nineteenth century provided tangible evidence of women's subordinate role, which state legislation during the post-Napoleonic period attempted to reinforce.

The assignment of specific female spheres of responsibility and influence was also reaffirmed by sex-specific group endogamy, particularly in relation to the choice of marriage partner.[8] Although rural mobility may well have been substantial, the majority of marriage partners still tended to come from within a limited radius of individual villages. Discrimination against women was also evident in the context of re-marriage. The customary year of mourning was seldom applied to men and ecclesiastical dispensation was readily available to widowers on their choice of a new wife. In South Germany, for example, over 50 per cent of widowers had remarried within the space of three months, but it was generally assumed that widows required no such dispensation from customary practice.[9] Moreover, the chances of re-marriage for a widow declined markedly after the age of 50, whereas the age barrier for widowers appears to have been far less rigid.[10]

Gender work roles

The role of women in German rural society in terms of their economic contribution to the family economy has seldom been examined in detail, and no attempt has been made to assess the extent to which gender-specific work roles conformed to traditional norms or affected the actual position of women within peasant households. Indeed, ethnographers have generally neglected such topics as work and economic activity, and too often processes of change in gender-specific work orientation are not explicitly confronted. The available evidence would seem to support the general view that there was no natural division of labour between the sexes. Although the sex-specific division of labour may reflect the operation of a number of different factors, the scale of work segregation by gender, both in a contemporary and historical context, is most pronounced.[11] The variety of tasks required from a rural family was itself very extensive, ranging from hard labour, daily management, to intensive watchfulness, and the allocation of these variegated responsibilities on a sex-specific basis is likely to have fluctuated considerably over the family life cycle.[12]

The historical evidence for Germany fails to reveal any rigid or inflexible pattern in gender work roles. Although under certain conditions, women tended to be excluded from specific agricultural tasks, such as ploughing, and agricultural work was often assigned according to its relative importance, a great deal of work appears to have been substitutable on a sex-specific basis.[13] If unmarried sons from peasant holdings were employed outside the immediate locality, their sisters are known to have assumed the traditional tasks of a *Knecht* (farm labourer).[14] An interplay of demand and supply factors was also visible in the direct use of unmarried daughters for agricultural work, when this was necessary. The earlier work of Weber-Kellerman and Wiegelmann has emphasised not only the persistence of regional work customs in terms of the sex-specific division of labour on the land, but also an extensive variation in the allocation of individual tasks within the peasant household.[15]

Although the claim that agricultural work in earlier centuries was largely done by women is undoubtedly an exaggeration,[16] a number of factors encouraged women to assume a broad spectrum of agricultural tasks. In the eighteenth century, the specific nature of seigneurial labour services in certain regions of Germany could occasionally deprive the peasant family of male labour at critical times in the harvest year. The magistrate of Oldenburg and Friezland, for example, had the power to order out all peasant landowners for 20 days each year in order to mend and maintain existing roads, and 'the poor man must leave his own work and go'.[17] In these circumstances, responsibility for the fulfilment of outstanding agricultural tasks on the peasant holding would devolve on the remaining female household members. Similarly in north-west Germany *Heuerlinge*, or smallholders, who leased additional land, were frequently obliged to pay a partial labour rent which obliged their wives to provide annually between 20 and 25 days of agricultural work.[18] Indeed peasant women were often required to take on a full range of agricultural tasks, if only on a short-term basis, when their husbands were involved in seasonal labour migration (such as to Holland (*Hollandgängerei*) and Saxony (*Sachsengängerei*).[19] This practice remained extensive in the eighteenth and nineteenth centuries (figure 2.1). Increasing male mobility in the course of this period, whether as a function of military conscription, or the geographical expansion of markets, probably reinforced the involvement of women in agricultural tasks.[20] In the absence of the *Knecht*, on larger peasant holdings, the wife was often obliged to take over many of his duties.[21]

Thus despite an ostensible gender-specific division of labour, women were probably prepared and frequently obliged to do anything in agriculture.[22] There was clearly a general intermeshing of tasks, with any

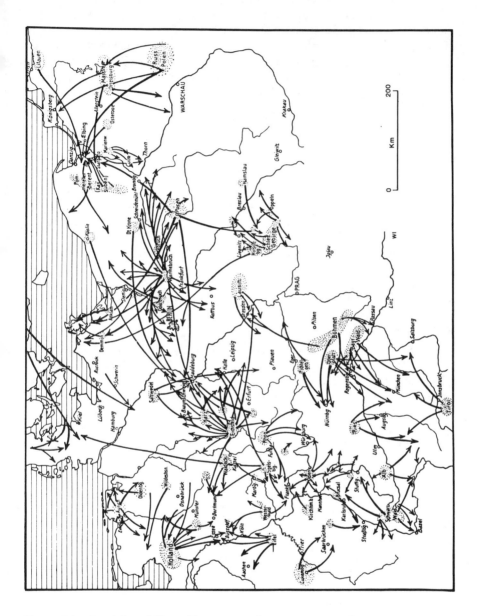

Figure 2.1 *Spatial mobility of harvest workers in nineteenth-century Germany*

Source: I. Weber-Kellermann, *Erntebrauch in der ländlichen Arbeitswelt des 19.Jahrhunderts*, Marburg, 1965. (For the earlier ethnographical material upon which this is based, see references in note 19.)

division of family labour structured in a way which would maximise complementarity and allow a high degree of short-term substitutability.[23] Indeed, given the premature dissolution of marriages through the early death of the husband, many widows were obliged to manage the family economy for a considerable length of time.[24] The range of tasks which women were required to do, in addition to domestic and non-domestic activities which were traditionally assigned to them, could be considerable. On the basis of more modern data, peasant wives were probably expected under normal circumstances to perform a higher work quota than the husband, and if male work was relatively well defined and bound by routine, the wife was frequently expected to modify her work in step with changing economic conditions and the overall labour requirements of the family economy.[25] To this extent, the economic functioning of the family holding was largely dependent on the active role of the wife, whose work was seldom limited to household duties, often encompassed the domestic production of clothing, responsibility for the family's garden plot, as well as a broad range of agricultural tasks, particularly at certain times of the year. According to a proverb from the Bremen region, 'Wo die Frau arbeitet nicht, da gibt kein brodt im Hause.'[26]

Given that the gender-specific division of agricultural work seldom reflected bio-social demands, and women were often to be found carrying out heavy physical work on the land, the precise allocation of agricultural tasks evinced a high degree of variance, both over time and space.[27] The distribution of agricultural work within the family economy was itself affected by a number of important variables. According to Wiegelmann, 'work custom', which was itself highly mutable, often determined the choice of agricultural implements, and therefore the gender-specific allocation of labour tasks.[28] Equally, the maximisation of a woman's potential labour input on the land was often a function of holding size and relative pauperisation. The family dependants of smallholders, including wives and children, were of necessity condemned to extra work, and the wives of day-labourers in Germany, as in many other regions of Europe, almost certainly worked the greater part of the agricultural year.[29] Although the *Bauersfrau* (farmer's wife, of an integral holding) undoubtedly worked as well, in order to generate a net surplus, the pressures on women within the rural household were consistently more severe and continuous lower down the socio-economic hierarchy.[30] This would have been particularly the case during periods of depressed agricultural wages for male day-labourers, and at times of extended economic hardship in the primary sector as a whole.

The interrelationship between dominant handtool technology, holding size and the gender-specific division of labour has been emphasised by a number of authors.[31] The type of harvesting tools and agricultural implements employed by the peasantry varied considerably, even within what were assumed to have been fairly homogeneous districts.[32] Whereas the sickle continued in use as the primary harvesting tool in southern Germany for rye and wheat, it was increasingly displaced in northern Germany for harvesting winter grains by the scythe.[33] Also, whereas women continued to use the sickle, particularly for cutting rye, the scythe increasingly became a male preserve.[34] However, the choice of a suitable handtool technology was, in part, a function of the local pattern of cultivation and the state of the crop at harvesting time. 'Strong' grains in Pomeramia continued to be harvested with the sickle, and in Saxony the final choice of harvesting implement was dependent on whether the grain was dry or wet.[35] The size of the peasant holding also affected local handtool technology, with small-holdings tending to retain the more traditional sickle.[36] Equally, in terms of plough types, a similar division was apparent according to holding size. Only the larger peasant holdings could invest in more modern or specialist ploughs (such as the *Beetpflug*), but these again often required a modification in earlier gender-specific roles on the land. Whereas the more traditional plough had been worked by the peasant and his wife, the *Beetpflug* (edging plough) was managed by the peasant himself, at best with the assistance of a *Kleinknecht*.[37]

The range of female work tasks on the land was wide. Women were generally employed in hand operations, and the relatively limited extent of farm mechanisation, even towards the end of the nineteenth century, meant that they remained indispensable for many agricultural jobs.[38] Although the actual pattern of women's work was subject to considerable local, regional and class-specific differentiation, women everywhere carried out a wide variety of agricultural tasks. In North Germany women participated in ploughing, and on steep arable fields they were frequently involved in the transportation of soil, if any slippage had occurred. They were also employed in hoeing and harrowing. Women played an even greater role in terms of harvesting agricultural crops, in mowing hay, cutting grain with the sickle, with their work effort concentrated particularly in the harvesting of hay and rye. In addition, women were regularly employed in processing crops after the harvest period, for example, in binding winter barley and threshing grain. The cartage and carrying of agricultural produce was also frequently carried out by women, and female assistance in the loading and spreading of dung was also recorded.[39]

Moreover, certain spheres of activity were often directly associated with women, including the planting and care of fruit and vegetables (frequently in a small garden area attached to the peasant cottage); dairy and livestock activities, including the milking of cows and the making of butter; the care of pigs and poultry.[40] Equally, the different tasks associated with root-crop cultivation, including the preparation of the soil, hand-hoeing, weeding and *Verkrehlen*, were almost uniformly undertaken by women.

The extensive range of ancillary tasks which could be undertaken by women is fully reflected in individual estate accounts:

Female agricultural tasks, Hofmark Thalhausen

Sowing vegetables
Making fences
Cutting grass
Cutting wood
Cutting corn
Mowing of oats
Mowing of hay
Weeding
Hop-picking
Cutting hop sticks
Cleaning picked flax
Threshing
Washing clothes

Source: Staatsarchiv für Oberbayern, Hofmark Thalhausen, Rechnungen, 1812–13.

In addition to these tasks, many authors have naturally argued that domestic responsibilities remained the *main* sphere for female work.[41] Although it has been suggested that the impoverished conditions of rural life tended to reduce the extent of domestic tasks, including the washing of clothes, cooking and cleaning,[42] pauperisation may well have reinforced the importance of household management and an optimal utilisation of existing family resources, necessitating in many cases additional female work. Apart from the direct and indirect reproduction of the family's labour power, women were also heavily involved in domestic craft production, specifically in the making of textiles, either for family use, or for sale within the framework of existing putting-out systems. Although the regional development of proto-industrial production in the textile sector could often lead to women being displaced from some of these tasks,[43] they continued to undertake many of the processes involved in textile production. In relation to linen production, for example, they were employed in the intermediate preparation of flax, cleaning flax once it was picked, and in beating it in order to separate the fibres. In this as in other areas the yearly work cycle for women often involved a fluctuating and complementary combination of both indoor and essentially outside work.[44]

Although there tended to be some structuring of distinct fields of responsibility within the family economy on a gender-specific basis, it is patently incorrect to assume that the maternal function was the prime determinant of women's economic activities on the land in the pre-capitalist era.[45] What emerges on the basis of recent research is a picture of overlapping gender-specific boundaries, diverse and changing 'work customs' and a division of agricultural roles frequently affected by local and regional factors, including the dominant cultivation pattern and the overall structure of landholding. If social value systems in any sense constrained the nature of female work on the land, this was less likely to have been the case in relation to smallholders and the rural proletariat, and in general there was a high degree of substitutability in terms of the roles of men and women, with women frequently doing men's work particularly during the hay harvest.

The nature and impact of agricultural change

The high degree of complementarity and substitutability and the shifting balance within the peasant household in the gender-specific allocation of work are of central importance in any analysis of the broader social implications of women's economic function in the nineteenth century. The central concern of this chapter is to elucidate the dualism of women's work in production and reproduction by focussing on the impact of primary-sector development on the gender-specific division of labour, and hence on infant mortality and child care, maternal and female mortality, and fertility. The growing commercialisation of German agriculture during the nineteenth century inevitably affected the labour role of peasant women, and this, in turn, may well have been the central factor determining contemporary trends in sensitive demographic indicators. Moreover, if work orientation, as Weber-Kellermann suggests, was an important determinant of family relationships,[46] it will be interesting to explore the intra-familial implications of changing gender-specific work patterns as a result of increasing agrarian specialisation and the diffusion of new technology on the land during this period.

It is important in the first instance to examine the impact of patterns of change in agrarian production on the relative demand for female labour on the land and the specific tasks open to women.[47] Within this context, three factors were of substantial importance. First, agrarian reform in the early nineteenth century arguably provided the organisational basis for the further expansion of agricultural production. Although official legislation did not initiate such an expansion, it undoubtedly modified farm organisation and production, and affected the regional pattern of labour demand.[48] For the purpose of the present analysis, it is sufficient to emphasise the differential extent of land transfers and the relative severity of the enclosure movement. In the case of Prussia, for example, following the legislation of 1807, 1811 and 1821, peasant land losses, as a result of regulation cases involving land compensation, were noticeably greater in the eastern provinces than in the west, and the enclosure movement was also severer in uprooting peasants along a similar east–west axis.[49] The immediate post-reform period also witnessed a further increase in the number of smallholdings, and a significant change in the average size of peasant holdings.[50] However, if the early subdivision of common land in Westphalia hastened the emergence of a rural 'sub-class', the main beneficiaries of the sale of seigneurial demesne and secularisation in Bavaria after 1803 were often small-holders and day-labourers. Given that the work role of women on the land was closely correlated with holding size and family income constraints, the differential impact of structural change in German agriculture in the post-reform era would inevitably have affected the regional pattern of gender-specific work allocation.

Secondly, the nineteenth century was marked by a reinforced trend towards regional specialisation in the primary sector. Given the problems surrounding the available estimates of trends in agricultural output, particularly for the early decades of the nineteenth century, it is difficult to construct a reliable index of regional specialisation. However, it is important within the framework of analysing changes in the gender-specific division of labour to elucidate some of the major characteristics in the pattern of increasing regional specialisation. The eastern provinces of Prussia were increasingly characterised by extensive cereal production, primarily for export, and the growing emphasis on grain mono-culutre was accompanied by a continuing reliance on traditional cultivation methods, with agricultural labourers largely dependent on potato cultivation to meet their subsistence requirements.[51] In the western regions of Germany, however, there was a perceptible shift towards intensive cultivation, with an emphasis on commercial crops and the dairy–livestock sector. In those regions of Germany where the domestic production of textiles, particularly linen, had developed to meet growing export opportunities, flax cultivation had become widespread.[52] Equally, given official tax incentives, the cultivation of sugar-beet was expanded extensively in the post-1815 period, with a particular concentration on the Magdeburger Börde and, to a lesser extent, in a number of Rhineland districts.[53] Regional specialisation was also increasingly evident in relation to viticulture and livestock–dairy production, although it would be false to overstate the extent of such trends, or the degree to which a rational division of labour on a regional or local basis had effectively been achieved during the period under consideration.

Thirdly, there had been a general tendency towards a more labour-intensive system of cultivation, whether in relation to specific crops, such as sugar-beet, or in terms of rotation systems. The introduction of root crops into existing cultivation patterns, the increasing application of *Koppel-wirtschaft* (alternate husbandry), and the extension of stall-feeding, all implied a significant rise in the relative demand for agricultural labour. If certain Prussian provinces, such as Pomerania, Posen, East and West

Prussia, raised output through an expansion in the total cultivable area, other regions, such as Mecklenburg, Schleswig-Holstein and Saxony, by adopting new crops or through applying more modern means of production, benefited from improved yields from existing land. In both cases, however, the pattern of agricultural development required a substantial infusion of additional labour. Certainly in many regions of Germany land expansion was a very 'high-powered' absorber of labour. The registered growth in primary-sector output was essentially dependent on increased labour input at an almost constant, or slowly rising, level of output per head.[54]

The pattern of agrarian change in the nineteenth century undoubtedly produced a re-structuring of the sex-specific division of labour. Given the different labour requirements of individual crops and cultivation systems, the process of regional specialisation, the labour-intensive expansion of the cultivable area, and the adoption of new commercial crops would have had a perceptible influence on the local nature of gender-specific labour requirements. The overall importance of women within the primary sector was reinforced by the limited extent of farm mechanisation, with the exception of the introduction of threshing machines.[55] Although areas of increasing commercial production were more receptive to mechanisation, and sugar-beet cultivation was associated with technological development and the growth of the artificial fertilizer industry, many regions of Germany remained dependent on manual labour to meet their production needs. Also, as Boserup has noted, 'a half-mechanized agriculture' often raises the demand for female labour, whereas increased technical innovation is commonly associated with a higher degree of male participation in the production process.[56]

There can be little doubt that the nature of agricultural change in the nineteenth century required a greater involvement of women in outside work in the German primary sector.[57] Inevitably the proportion of rural women actively employed in agricultural work varied both regionally and seasonally, dependent on a woman's health and strength, family life-cycle considerations, including her age and number of children, as well as the availability of alternative occupations. However, most of the new crops introduced during this period, in particular commercial crops, such as sugar-beet, and root crops, including potatoes, as well as the expansion in the cultivable area, led to a direct increase in the demand for female outdoor labour. Potato digging was generally recognised as hard work for women, and around All Saints' Day all root crops were pulled out and cut, normally by women, which required a triple work shift.[58] Amongst the most arduous tasks for women were turnip-pulling and potato digging, although the hay harvest was the most fatiguing of all, requiring all available female and child labour and the use of every minute on good days for a period that lasted for over a month. Evidence also points to the increasing demand for female labour in viticulture, with women constrained to work hard both at home and in the fields, and suffering from premature ageing as a result.[59] The regional expansion of livestock and dairy farming, at least before the introduction of the centrifuge, undoubtedly imposed a more severe burden on women, involving long hours of work throughout the year.[60] Stall-feeding, in itself, required a significantly increased labour input, and according to Bavarian evidence, women simply could not do more than they did. They were obliged to rise at 4 o'clock in the morning, clean out the stable, then work with the sickle in the fields until 9 o'clock in the evening.[61]

On the other hand, it has frequently been argued that one of the most salient forms of technical change in the nineteenth century – the substitution of the sickle by the scythe – tended to displace women from certain agricultural tasks. Although it is still unclear as to whether the introduction and disseminationn of the scythe was primarily a response to a feared diminution in the supply of agricultural labour, or a reflection of changing climatic and farming conditions, this important shift in rural handtool technology in certain areas of north-western Europe pushed women into less well-paid jobs, as followers or rakers, or affected the seasonal pattern of their agricultural employment, by reducing female participation in the annual harvest.[62] Although there was a similar trend in nineteenth-century Germany towards the use of labour-saving tools, as previously indicated, there was no uniform transition. The specific choice of harvesting tools continued to vary according to the type of land, the condition of individual crops and the size of the peasant holding. The sickle continued to be used for cutting both rye and wheat in southern Germany, and the scythe was only used extensively in the North German plain for cutting these crops. However, the scythe was used for harvesting oats and barley, both in North and South Germany, as well as in the Mittelgebirge.[63] If any displacement of female labour tasks did take place, this would have occurred on a regionally selective basis. Moreover, women were reported using certain types of scythe themselves. Although the seasonal pattern of women's work may well have been affected by this shift in handtool technology, its overall impact on the role of women in the primary sector was more than compensated by the rising demand for female labour in many other facets of contemporary agricultural work.

The demographic implications of changing patterns of women's work

Given the inherent substitutability of agricultural tasks in rural society, the labour-intensive emphasis of primary-sector production in the nineteenth century, and the unavoidable reality of economic necessity, it is clear that women on the land arguably played an increasingly critical role within the peasant family economy. The precise nature of changing crop and cultivation patterns, and shifts in handtool technology during this period inevitably impinged on the economic role of all family members. But by altering the focus of female work, macro-economic change had both a direct and indirect effect on a number of sensitive demographic indicators, particularly through its impact on the work regimes of married women of child-rearing years.

Throughout most of the nineteenth century differential mortality rates in the age group 0–1 continued to determine the overall mortality profile of most European states, as well as specific regional mortality trends. In the case of Germany, infant mortality tended to increase during the course of the early nineteenth century and family reconstitution data has confirmed the existence of pronounced regional differences at the village level (figure 2.2). Although a final explanation of the causative factors behind this variegated pattern must await a more rigorous analysis of the economic and environmental background to each of the village studies,[64] a number of factors point to the central explanatory relevance of changes in women's work roles and domestic responsibilities.

There is increasing evidence from studies of so-called Third World economies that infant care and nurture during the late pre-natal and early post-natal period, although affected by cultural norms, is primarily a function of the mother's economic activities and non-household roles.[65] Various economic roles, including field-work away from the village, are often incompatible with adequate child care, confirming Nerlove's cross-cultural analysis that female subsistence activity is generally associated with an earlier start to harmful supplementary feeding, a termination of breast feeding and higher infant mortality and morbidity.[66] In absolute terms infant and child care is the activity that suffers most, if a mother is constrained to maximise outside work.[67] It is therefore appropriate to examine the impact of agrarian change on the employment of women in Germany within an ecological paradigm, focussing on the consequences of a shifting allocation in gender-specific non-household functions for trends in infant mortality. Undoubtedly infant mortality rates were determined by a broad spectrum of cultural, economic and environmental factors, but the work role of married women may well have been an important variable. Although the precise extent of increased female participation in the labour-market varied both regionally and locally, depending on the specific context of agrarian development, there were three areas in which the pattern of change in the primary sector affected infant mortality trends.

First, there may have been a direct connection between the increased involvement of women in agricultural production and infant feeding patterns. Data from the early twentieth century reveal a high degree of regional variation in the practice and extent of breast feeding, and a negative

61

correlation with both illegitimacy and female labour-force participation.[68] Evidence for Bavaria confirms the negative effect of women's work, particularly during the summer period, on breast-feeding patterns. The increased dependency on female labour in the course of the nineteenth century frequently meant that women were obliged to resume full-time agricultural work almost immediately after delivery, with a concomitant decline in the extent of breast feeding and the overall amount of care shown to newborn infants.[69] In other parts of Europe a similar process appears to have been underway. Hard work outside the home was a critical reason why infants were not breast fed, or were breast fed for too short or too irregular a period of time: it was also inconsistent with regular lactation.[70] Given the frequently lethal nature of supplementary feeding for infants and generally unhygienic conditions, any diminution in the extent of breast feeding would have had negative repercussions on infant mortality trends.[71] To this extent the markedly regional and local nature of infant feeding practices may well reflect the differentiated effect of agrarian change on the relative exploitation of female labour in the German primary sector.

Secondly, the nature of agricultural development also affected the seasonal distribution of work. Individual crops had their own pattern of seasonal labour requirements and different labour input rates. If rye cultivation, which became increasingly important in the eastern provinces of Prussia, necessitated a higher level of labour input in the autumn, root-crop cultivation had an inordinately large demand for labour per unit of land and a pronounced seasonality in overall labour requirements.[72] Family reconstitution data reveal a significant shift in the seasonality of infant mortality, allowing for changes in relative risks, particularly during the second half of the nineteenth century.[73] The cessation of breast feeding in communities where at least some level of breastfeeding was normally maintained, particularly if this occurred during the summer months, would have had immediate and adverse effects on local infant mortality levels. Given that most family members had to participate in work-related activities during peak agricultural periods, mothers were less likely to spend sufficient time with newborn infants than in other noticeably slacker seasons of the agricultural year.[74] Infant mortality was frequently most excessive during the summer months, precisely because the enforced involvement of married women in harvest work either precluded the adoption of breast feeding, or necessitated the premature introduction of supplementary feeding.[75] To this extent changes in the seasonal pattern of weaning evident in nineteenth-century data may also reflect the differential effect of contemporary shifts in cultivation patterns on female labour requirements.

Thirdly, evidence also indicates that the type of infant feeding was often determined by the work needs of the mother, which, in turn, was a

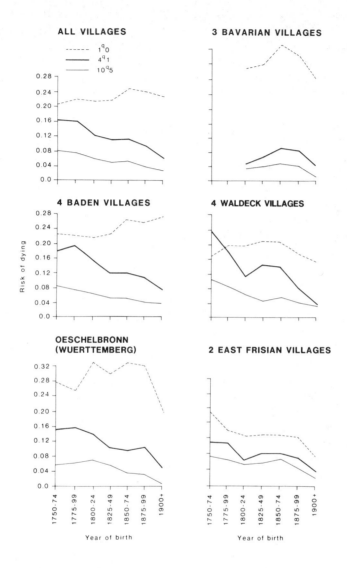

Figure 2.2 *Trends in infant and child mortality in selected nineteenth-century German village populations*

Note: Calculations of 1q0 include stillbirths

Sources: J. Knodel, 'Two centuries of infant, child and maternal mortality in German village populations', unpublished paper, 1986; *idem, Demographic Behaviour in the Past: A Study of Fourteen German Village Populations in the Eighteenth and Nineteenth Centuries*, Cambridge, 1988, figure 3.1, pp. 41–3.

function of holding size.[76] Time is of central importance in determining the absolute quality of infant care, and simultaneously represents the dominant household resource of poor families. If the practice of breast feeding was itself a function of the level of parental attention, the negative impact of agricultural development in the nineteenth century on infant mortality trends would have been most pronounced in those regions and localities which witnessed a further proliferation in smallholdings, the creation of a landless rural proletariat or severe pauperisation.[77] If a heavy workload for women was broadly synonymous with a decline in breast feeding and inflated infant mortality levels, then the nature of agrarian change, in terms of land distribution patterns, would once again have produced a highly differentiated regional effect. Extensive female work was frequently a function of relative impoverishment and regional studies have highlighted the extent to which both agrarian reform legislation and the increasing commercialisation of the German primary sector affected land distribution patterns and holding size.[78] Sugar-beet cultivation in the Magdeburger Börde, for example, was associated with the emergence of a rural proletariat, and the expansion of grain mono-culture in the eastern provinces of Prussia resulted in a disproportional increase in the number of day-labourers.[79] In these, as in other cases, the specific process of agrarian change, by affecting the socio-economic structure of rural society, may have also contributed to the higher levels of infant mortality evident within these individual regions.

Similarly in relation to trends in maternal mortality, it has been argued that increasingly adverse work conditions for women, associated primarily with the intensification of agricultural production, led to a higher level of maternal deaths. The 'discovery of childhood', and a higher self-defined sickness threshold for women were undoubtedly ancillary factors, but the major cause ws to be found in the extended workload for peasant women. Under these conditions, women increasingly had to ignore the difficulties of pregnancy in order to carry out continuous outside work. Significantly a number of studies indicate a noticeable rise in maternal mortality, which peaked in one case in the 1840s, and in a further sample of villages in the period 1825–74.[80] However, despite the fact that the risk of maternal mortality was many times higher than in the recent past, English and Swedish data confirm the fact that childbirth was only a significant, although a still minor cause of death, among women in their mid twenties to mid thirties.[81] Despite the fact that there was an approximately 1 per cent chance of death associated with each confinement, this did not normally constitute a significant proportion of background deaths.[82] However, the marginal increase in maternal mortality risks during the central decades of the nineteenth century provides additional evidence of the potential negative consequences of agrarian change on married women.

More significantly gender-specific mortality data confirm the persistence of excess female mortality, particularly for women in their thirties throughout most of the nineteenth century. In the Duchy of Oldenburg, for example, women had a 25 per cent higher probability of dying than men in their thirties (Table 2.1), and Prussian data for 1880/81 reveals a similar excess female mortality (at least in rural areas) in the age groups between 25 and 40.[83] Indeed, there appears to have been a widening over time in the gender-specific mortality gap in individual areas of Germany.[84]

Table 2.1   *Age-specific mortality rates (0/00) in Prussia, 1880–81*

Age	1		2		3		4	
	M	F	M	F	M	F	M	F
2–3	40.49	40.78	38.70	38.58	35.12	34.46	32.72	32.31
3–4	28.00	29.25	26.90	26.39	23.34	23.17	22.48	21.93
4–5	21.26	21.50	18.46	19.24	16.14	16.79	15.62	16.53
5–10	11.21	10.50	6.88	6.96	8.96	9.24	9.01	9.75
10–15	3.61	4.03	2.53	2.64	3.76	4.11	3.98	4.45
15–20	5.53	4.30	5.41	4.60	4.93	4.95	4.98	4.63
20–25	7.17	6.20	7.30	6.52	7.93	6.80	7.42	5.91
25–30	9.66	7.87	10.30	9.68	8.81	8.93	7.31	7.63
30–35	12.61	9.98	13.87	9.99	11.93	10.35	8.01	8.81
35–40	16.41	11.11	16.61	12.42	14.56	11.63	10.11	10.44
40–45	20.40	11.89	20.77	13.04	18.17	12.22	12.80	11.22
45–50	25.15	13.65	25.71	14.48	22.24	13.77	16.26	12.85
50–55	11.11	16.43	32.73	18.34	27.80	18.04	21.78	17.14
55–60	39.50	22.75	40.52	24.95	36.47	26.05	30.14	26.20
60–65	53.00	32.16	52.70	35.15	48.00	36.22	42.20	39.13
65–70	69.23	47.51	71.36	53.40	66.72	50.5	63.03	60.52
70–75	100.4	75.91	104.3	80.68	98.92	86.5	96.70	95.15
75–80	147.5	88.70	142.6	123.1	143.0	128.5	142.7	138.56
80–85	248.7	176.35	213.8	183.1	213.9	196.35	216.3	210.7
85–90	315.5	288.1	273.5	271.3	293.9	265.7	300.8	286.2
90–95	500.0	268.4	363.1	341.3	355.0	327.2	384.8	340.7

Notes: Col. 1 8 large cities (>100,000)
2 medium cities (20,000–100,000)
3 small towns
4 rural communities

Source: C. Ballod, *Die mittlere Lebensdauer in Stadt und Land* (Staats- und socialwissenschaftliche Forschungen, Bd 16, Heft 5), Leipzig, 1899, pp. 112–13.

Women were particularly disadvantaged in rural areas primarily as a result of increasing work burdens and their low nutritional status. Nutritional status is often dependent on the type and timing of labour inputs, and aggravated by a maldistribution of resources and labour requirements. Not only do the very poor do more physical work and receive less food, but the intra-household distribution of resources is frequently unequal.[85] This is relevant in terms of the present analysis in two particular ways. First, poor nutritional status is associated with a low birth weight and infant vulnerability to disease. An inadequate maternal diet will also tend to curtail the output of breast milk. Secondly, poor nutritional status will have an adverse effect on female life expectancy in general.

There is considerable evidence to support the existence of a low nutritional status for women in the nineteenth century. Working-class diets remained relatively poor, even in the last decades of this period and meat consumption per capita in Prussia in the period 1801–49 may well have declined marginally.[86] The family distribution of nutrition mirrored the unequal distribution of social power, above all between men and women, and the gradual diffusion of a male provider ideology arguably encouraged mothers even more to sacrifice their own share and that of their children to keep their husbands working.[87] The evidence of birth-weight data, despite its urban provenance, provides a further indication of the adverse effects of a cumulative sub-standard diet, compounded by gender inequality in the distribution of family nutritional resources.[88] The general process of agrarian change in the nineteenth century, by affecting the gender-specific distribution of work tasks within the family would have aggravated this situation, forcing many married women into a more insidious system of constant overwork, undernutrition, and weakened resistance to tuberculosis and infectious disease.

Finally, change in female nutritional status may also help to account, at least in part, for registered shifts over time in both fecundity and fertility. Knodel's analysis of a sample group of village populations testified to the existence of important regional differences in these two indices.[89] Moreover, the application of the Coale–Trussell index of underlying fertility levels, M, as well as evidence from other family reconstitution studies (table 2.2) indicate a perceptible increase in fertility in the early decades of the nineteenth century. The process of agrarian change may well have affected fertility trends in a number of ways. However, in the context of the present discussion, it is important to focus on the potential implications of changes in female work patterns on marital fertility. On the one hand, increased work pressure, whether in connection with the introduction of stall-feeding, or labour-intensive sugar-beet cultivation, may have reduced fecundity, or restricted the ability of women to carry to term. More significantly, reduced female nutritional status together with an extension in labour requirements outside the home, arguably produced a reduction in the length of breast feeding, and in post-partum amenorrhea, and a concomitant rise in fertility. In terms of the length of the non-susceptible period (NSP), which provides some indication of the relative extent of breast feeding, South German evidence reveals a marginal decline in breast feeding in the first half of the nineteenth century (table 2.3). It may well be the case,

Table 2.2 *Age-specific fertility rates in Heuchelheim, Massenhausen and Leezen (by five-year age group)*

	15–19	20–24	25–29	30–34	35–39	40–44	45–49	20–49[a]
Heuchelheim								
1691–1720	0.400	0.431	0.357	0.335	0.234	0.104	0.013	7.37
1721–1750	0.154	0.379	0.346	0.273	0.169	0.089	0.013	6.34
1811–1840	0.714	0.464	0.427	0.285	0.232	0.125	0.018	7.75
Massenhausen								
1750–1799		0.555	0.589	0.457	0.330	0.245	0.016	10.96[b]
1800–1849		0.688	0.647	0.538	0.429	0.257	0.035	12.97[b]
Leezen								
1720–1769	0.346	0.480	0.407	0.321	0.243	0.114	0.016	7.91
1770–1819	0.442	0.482	0.409	0.352	0.272	0.123	0.013	8.26
1820–1869	0.526	0.550	0.423	0.322	0.223	0.091	0.004	8.07

Notes: [a] TMFR (Total Marital Fertility Rate) equals the sum of the fertility rates for each five-year age group above age 20 multiplied by 5.
  [b] The high TMFR for Massenhausen, which is also evident in the three Bavarian villages studies by Knodel, almost certainly reflects the impact of the total absence of breast feeding, which would have reduced the average interval between births by reducing the period of post-partum amenorrhoea.
Sources: Heuchelheim: A. E. Imhof (ed.), *Historische Demographie als Sozialgeschichte: Giessen und Umgebung vom 17. zum 19.Jahrhundert*, Darmstatt and Marburg, 1975, *passim.*
Massenhausen: W. R. Lee, *Population Growth, Economic Development and Social Change in Bavaria, 1750–1850*, New York, 1977.
Leezen: R. Gehrmann, *Leezen 1720–1870. Ein historisch-demographischer Beitrag zur Sozialgeschichte des ländlichen Schleswig-Holsteins* (Studien zur Wirtschafts- und Sozialgeschichte Schleswig-Holsteins, Bd 7), Neumünster, 1984, pp. 224–5.

Table 2.3 *Non-susceptible period in months, by holding size in settlements in the Hofmark Massenhausen, 1750–99/1800–49*

Holding size	1750–99	1800–49
1	7.50	6.96
1/16	8.04	6.90

Source: Author's calculations.

therefore, that the variegated local fertility trends in Germany will only be finally understood by a closer analysis of the specific effects of agrarian change on local cultivation patterns, with their attendant gender-specific labour demands.

Conclusion

Economic change is invariably associated with changes in peasant family structure and household organisation, and in their demographic profile.[90]

The evidence of significant variations in population parameters continues to pose substantial research problems, both in a German and a wider European context. Aggregate studies, such as the Princeton Fertility Project, cannot provide an adequate insight into the operation of causal mechanisms behind patterns of demographic change. On the other hand, available micro-level studies frequently fail to distinguish between the causal role of biological, behavioural and environmental factors. The analysis of demographic change in any specific society must itself be based on the specification of the relations of production in which individuals participate, with an emphasis on the means of consumption and the means of work. Within this context it is particularly important to focus both on the eco-logical parameters affecting individual activity and to examine the potential and actual interactions between processes of economic change, cultural systems and demographic regimes.

In the case of nineteenth-century rural Germany registered changes in a number of demographic indicators, specifically infant and female mortality and fertility, can be usefully analysed within the context of the processes of change in the primary sector. By focussing specifically on the centrality of women's work, and the changing balance between domestic and non-domestic labour responsibilities, it has been argued that the nature of agrarian change impinged directly on the labour role of women in rural society, and thereby affected demographic trends. Non-domestic work by married women had always been important to the peasant family economy. However, in the context of the increased demand for labour, particularly female labour, in German agriculture in the nineteenth century, the extent of their incorporation into non-domestic work processes grew substantially. The precise consequences of such a change fluctuated on a local and regional basis, dependent on the specific form of localised agricultural development and the absolute and seasonal demand for female labour. But the overall effect, in terms of various demographic indicators, was generally negative, especially as the increased involvement of married women in arduous out-side work was not accompanied by any realignment of domestic respon-sibilities. The present analysis has hopefully indicated the potential benefits of focussing on the changing pattern of women's work for understanding long-term demographic changes, and the behavioural and adaptive processes underlying different stages of the demographic transition.

Notes

1   E. Shorter, *The Making of the Modern Family*, New York, 1976, *passim*; German edn, *Die Geburt der modernen Familie*, 1977, pp. 76–7.
2   P. Fried, 'Die Situation auf dem Lande', in R. H. Müller and M. Henken (eds.), *Aufbruch ins Industriezeitalter. Aufsätze zur Wirtschafts- und Sozialgeschichte*

Bayerns, 1750–1850, Band 2, Munich, 1981, pp. 412–42; M. Mitterauer and R. Sieder, *Vom Patriarchat zur Partnerschaft. Zum Strukturwandel der Familie*, Munich, 1977, p. 74.

3   F. Elsass, *Zur Frage des Anerbenrechtes in Württemberg*, Stuttgart, 1913, *passim*; J. Hartwig, 'Vom Anerbenrecht im früheren lübeckischen Landgebiet', *Archiv für Bevölkerungswissenschaft und Bevölkerungspolitik*, 1941, p. 383.

4   D. Sauermann, 'Hofidee und bäuerliche Familienverträge in Westfalen', *Rheinische-Westfälische Zeitschrift für Volkskunde*, 17 (1970), pp. 58–78; R. Schulte, 'Life and work in peasant households in nineteenth century Bavaria', unpublished MS, 1988.

5   J. Hajnal, 'Two kinds of pre-industrial household formation systems', *Population and Development Review*, 8 (1982), pp. 449–94.

6   R. Schulte, 'Dienstmädchen im Herrschaftlichen Haushalt. Zur Genese ihrer Sozial-psychologie,' *Zeitschrift für Bayerische Landesgeschichte*, 42 (1979), pp. 879–920.

7   Sauermann, 'Hofidee'.

8   I. Kothe, *Das Mecklenburgische Landvolk in seiner bevölkerungsbiologischen Entwicklung, dargestellt am Beispiel der Dörfer Göhlen, Lohmen und Grüssow*, Leipzig, 1941, pp. 44–5; W. R. Lee, 'Family and ''modernisation'': the peasant family and social change in nineteenth century Bavaria', in R. J. Evans and W. R. Lee (eds.), *The German Family: Essays on the Social History of the Family in Nineteenth and Twentieth-Century Germany*, London, 1981, p. 100.

9   W. R. Lee, *Population Growth, Economic Development and Social Change in Bavaria, 1750–1850*, New York, 1977, p. 281.

10   W. Norden, *Eine Bevölkerung in der Krise. Historisch–demographische Untersuchungen zur Biographie einer norddeutschen Küstenregion (Butjadingen, 1600–1850)*, HIldesheim, 1984, pp. 179–80; S. B. Ortner and H. Whitehead, *Sexual Meaning: The Cultural Construction of Gender and Sexuality*, Cambridge, 1981, p. 1; S. H. Coontz, *Population Theories and Economic Integration*, London, 1957, *passim*; F. Edholm, O. Harris and K. Young, 'Conceptualising women', *Critique of Anthropology*, 11 (1978), pp. 101–30.

11   P. R. Sanday, *Female Power and Male Dominance. On the Origins of Sexual Inequality*, Cambridge, 1981, pp. 77ff.

12   See, for example, the interesting work of B. D. Miller, 'Farming families and sex roles in rural India: a classic pattern and new questions,' *Peasant Studies*, 11 (1983), pp. 19ff.

13   Women were also traditionally excluded from cutting wood, and from the long-distance transportation of agricultural commodities, see M. Mitterauer, 'Geschlechtsspezifische Arbeitsteilung in vorindustrieller Zeit', *Beiträge zur Historischen Sozialkunde*, 1981, pp. 77–87. In parts of Britain, on the other hand, women were excluded from mowing, see J. A. Perkins, 'Harvest technology and labour supply in Lincolnshire and the East Riding of Yorkshire, 1750–1850', *Tools and Tillage*, 3 (1976), p. 128.

14   [ ] Wagner, 'Bevölkerungsstatistisches aus der Gemeinde Bernloch und Meidelstetten, OA Münsingen', *Württembergisches Jahrbuch für Statistik und Landeskunde*, 1916, pp. 30–64.

15   I. Weber-Kellermann, *Erntebrauch in der ländlichen Arbeitswelt des 19. Jahrhunderts*, Marburg, 1965, *passim*; G. Wiegelmann, 'Erste Ergebnisse der ADV-Umfragen zur alten bäuerlichen Arbeit', *Rheinische-Vierteljahrsblätter*, 33 (1969), pp. 208–62; *idem*, 'Bäuerliche Arbeitsteilung in Mittel- und Nordeuropa – Konstanz oder Wandel?', *Ethnologia Scandinavica* (1975), pp. 5–22. Wiegelmann's analysis, for example, concentrated on the diffusion of different work practices, including the hand tools utilised for pulling potatoes from garden plots and for cutting winter grain, together with their gender-specific work implications.

16   A. Wolf-Graaf, *Frauenarbeit im Abseits. Frauenbewegung und weibliches Arbeits-vermögen*, Munich, 1981, p. 303.

17 T. Hodgskin, *Travels in the North of Germany*, 2 vols., London, 1820, reprinted New York, 1969, p. 277.

18 F. Wunderlich, *Farm Labor in Germany*, Princeton and New York, 1961, p. 17. Similarly, hired male labourers in Northumberland also had to supply the labour of their wives as part of their contractual obligations, see E. Hostetler, 'Women farm workers in 18th and 19th century Northumberland', *North East Labour History Bulletin*, 16 (1982), p. 40. For a discussion of the Swedish *statare* system, which also involved contractual labour obligations on the part of the wife, see J. Rogers and I. Eriksson, *Rural Labor and Population Change: Social and Demographic Development in East-central Sweden during the Nineteenth Century*, Studia Historica Upsaliensia, 100, Uppsala, 1978, *passim*.

19 Weber-Kellermann, *Erntebrauch*, Karte 3 (see figure 2.1). This important work was largely based on the earlier ethnographical material collected and published by Th. von der Goltz, *Die Lage der ländlichen Arbeiter im Deutschen Reich*, Berlin, 1875, tables pp. 246–425, and by W. Mannhardt, *Wald- und Feldkulte aus nord-europäischer Ueberlieferung*, Berlin, 1877, *passim*. This pattern of female labour substitution was also very common where men supplemented their agricultural livelihood by other forms of employment, such as fishing, which necessitated extended periods of absence: see R. Pedersen, 'Die Arbeitsteilung zwischen Frauen und Männern in einem marginalen Ackerbaugebiet – Das Beispiel Norwegen', *Ethnologia Scandinavica*, (1975), p. 43. See also the evidence from Upper Bavaria, where the absence of the husband invariably entailed an increase in the labour input of the wife and older children: Museum für Deutsche Volkskunde, Berlin, *Das Bild von Bauern. Vorstellungen und Wirklichkeit vom 16. Jahrhundert bis zur Gegenwart*, 1978, p. 125.

20 Mitterauer, 'Geschlechtsspezifische Arbeitsteilung', p. 84.

21 A. Hauser, 'Der Familienbetrieb in der schweizerischen Landwirtschaft. Eine historische und sozio-ökonomische Analyse', *Zeitschrift für Agrargeschichte und Agrarsoziologie*, 26 (1978), p. 209.

22 S. Lewenhak, *Women and Work*, London, 1980, p. 170.

23 M. Segalen, *Love and Power in the Peasant Family: Rural France in the Nineteenth Century*, Oxford, 1983, p. 81.

24 Norden, *Bevölkerung*, p. 177; J. Dupaquier, E. Helin, P. Laslett, M. Livi-Bacci, S. Sogner (eds.), *Marriage and Remarriage in Populations of the Past*, London, 1981, *passim*. See also P. N. Stearns, 'Old women: some historical observations', *Journal of Family History*, 5 (1980), p. 44, who claims that there was virtually no re-marriage for widows after 50 years of age. This issue is also discussed within a proto-industrial context in G. L. Gullickson, *Spinners and Weavers of Auffay: Rural Industry and the Sexual Division of Labor in a French Village, 1750–1850*, Cambridge, 1986, pp. 167ff. For various means of survival open to widows, see O. Hufton, 'Women without men: widows and spinsters in Britain and France in the eighteenth century', *Journal of Family History*, 9 (1984), pp. 355–76.

25 See, for example, the evidence on gender work roles in K. v. Dietze, M. Rolfes and G. Weippert, *Lebensverhältnisse in kleinbäuerlicher Dörfern*, Hamburg, 1952, pp. 130ff.; H. Scharnagl, 'Straussdorf, eine sozialökonomische und soziologische Untersuchung einer oberbayerischen Landgemeinde mit starkem Flüchtlingsanteil', unpublished Ph.D. dissertation, University of Erlangen, *passim*; Lee, *Population Growth*, pp. 284–5.

26 Hodgskin, *Travels*, p. 266.

27 Mitterauer, 'Geschlechtsspezifische Arbeitsteilung', pp. 77ff.

28 Wiegelmann, 'Erste Ergebnisse', p. 256; Pedersen, 'Arbeitsteilung', p. 42.

29 H. J. Rach, 'Zur Lebensweise und Kultur der Bauern unter den Bedingungen des Kapitalismus der freien Konkurrenz (etwa 1830–1900)', in H. J. Rach and B. Weissel (eds.), *Bauer und Landarbeiter im Kapitalismus in der Magdeburger Börde. Zur*

Geschichte des dörflichen Alltags vom Ausgang des 18.Jahrhunderts bis zum Beginn des 20.Jahrhunderts, Berlin, 1982, Teil II, p.52; D.H. Morgan, *Harvesters and Harvesting 1840–1900: A Study of the Rural Proletariat*, London, 1982, p.46.

30 K. Müller, *Die Frauenarbeit in der Landwirtschaft*, München-Gladbach, 1913, p.29. Within a contemporary context the range of permissible activities undertaken by women also tends to vary according to class, see E.I. Holmstrom, 'Changing sex roles in a developing country', *Journal of Marriage and the Family*, 35 (1973), pp.546–53.

31 See, in particular, Wiegelmann, 'Bäuerliche Arbeitsteilung', p.17.

32 U. Bentzien, 'Der Mecklenburgische Haken im 19. Jahrhundert', in I. Balassa (ed.), *Getreidebau in Ost- und Mitteleuropa*, Budapest, 1972, p.488.

33 U. Bentzien, 'Der agrartechnische Standard in Deutschland am Vorabend der bürgerlichen Agrarreformen', *Probleme der Agrargeschichte des Feudalismus und des Kapitalismus*, 9 (1977), pp.62ff.

34 O. Højrup; 'Die Arbeitsteilung zwischen Männern und Frauen in der bäuerlichen Kultur Dänemarks', *Ethnologia Scandinavica* (1975), pp.28ff. Significantly, the exclusion of women from using the scythe could not have been due to physical constraints – women did in fact use the *Heidekrautsense* which was an even heavier instrument. The harvesting of rye remained dependent on female labour.

35 Weber-Kellermann, *Erntebrauch*, pp.316, 339ff.

36 *Ibid.*, p.323.

37 U. Bentzien and R. Quietsch, 'Pfluggeräte 1850–1870. Erläuterungen zum Kartenausschnitt DDR', *Jahrbuch für Volkskunde und Kulturgeschichte*, 19 (1976), pp.179–87.

38 E. Boserup, *Women's Role in Economic Development*, New York, 1970, *passim*.

39 B. Huppertz, *Räume und Schichten bäuerlicher Kulturformen in Deutschland*, Bonn, 1939, pp.304ff.; H. Caesar-Weigel, *Frauenarbeit in der Feldwirtschaft*, Berlin, 1941, pp.235ff.; Wiegelmann, 'Erste Ergebnisse'; *idem*, 'Bäuerliche Arbeitsteilung', *passim*; Staatsarchiv Oberbayern, Hofmark Thalhausen, Amts-Rechnungen, 1808–09, 1818–19, 1824–25.

40 Müller, *Frauenarbeit*, p.26 (on the basis of the 1907 census); Wiegelmann, 'Erste Ergebnisse', p.6.

41 Wolf-Graaf, *Frauenarbeit*, *passim*.

42 O. Hufton, 'Women and the family economy in eighteenth-century France', *French Historical Studies*, 9 (1975/76), pp.7–22.

43 Mitterauer, 'Geschlechtsspezifische Arbeitsteilung', p.82.

44 B. Bergreen, 'The female peasant and the male peasant', *Ethnologia Scandinavica* (1986), pp 72ff.

45 K. Müller, 'Demographische Aspekte der Einbeziehung der Frau in den Berufsprozess', *Jahrbuch für Wirtschaftsgeschichte* (1974), Teil 1, p.173.

46 I. Weber-Kellermann, 'Die Familie auf dem Lande in der Zeit zwischen Bauernbefreiung und Industrialisierung', *Zeitschrift für Agrargeschichte und Agrarsoziologie*, 26 (1978), p.70.

47 For a general introduction to the development of German agriculture during the period under consideration see R. Berthold, *Agrargeschichte. Von der bürgerlichen Reformen zur sozialistischen Landwirtschaft in der DDR*, Berlin, 1978.

48 For a general survey of reform legislation see C. Dipper, *Die Bauernbefreiung in Deutschland 1750–1850*, Stuttgart, 1980. For more detailed regional studies see E. Schremmer, *Die Bauernbefreiung in Hohenlohe*, Stuttgart, 1963; W. von Hippel, *Die Bauernbefreiung im Königreich Württemberg*, 2 vols., Boppard, 1977; H. Harnisch, *Kapitalistische Agrarreform und Industrielle Revolution. Agrarhistorische Untersuchungen über das ostelbische Preussen zwischen Spätfeudalismus und bürgerlich-demokratischer*

Revolution, Weimar, 1984; H. Schissler, *Preussische Agrargesellschaft im Wandel*, Göttingen, 1978.

49   H. Harnisch, 'Statistische Untersuchungen zum Verlauf der kapitalistischen Agrarreformen in den Preussischen Ostprovinzen (1811 bis 1865)', *Jahrbuch für Wirtschaftsgeschichte* (1974), pp. 157, 169; D. Saalfeld, 'Zur Frage des bäuerlichen Landverlustes im Zusammenhang mit den preussischen Agrarreformen', *Zeitschrift für Agrargeschichte und Agrarsoziologie*, 2 (1962), pp. 163–71; W. R. Lee, 'Mortality levels and agrarian reform in early 19th century Prussia: some regional evidence', in T. Bengtsson, G. Fridlizius and R. Ohlsson (eds.), *Pre-industrial Population Change: The Mortality Decline and Short-term Population Movements*, Stockholm, 1984, pp. 162–3.

50   R. Berthold, 'Die Durchsetzung der kapitalistischen Produktionsweise in der deutschen Landwirtschaft und die Veränderungen in der Sozialstruktur des Dorfes', *Probleme der Agrargeschichte des Feudalismus und des Kapitalismus*, 8 (1977), pp. 7–24. For an insight into the extent of socio-economic differences at a regional level, see Weber-Kellermann, *Erntebrauch*, pp. 65ff.

51   In Mecklenburg, for example, there was a pronounced expansion in potato cultivation from the 1770s onwards, reflecting an increasing shortage of traditional grains, see F. Mager, *Geschichte des Bauerntums und der Bodenkultur im Lande Mecklenburg*, Berlin, 1955, p. 271.

52   For examples of the extensive literature on proto-industrial production in Germany, see P. Kriedte, H. Medick and J. Schlumbohm, *Industrialization before Industrialization: Rural Industry in the Genesis of Capitalism*, Cambridge, 1981, *passim*; W. Mager, 'Haushalt und Familie in protoindustrieller Gesellschaft: Spenge (Ravensberg) während der ersten Hälfte des 19.Jahrhunderts', in N. Bulst, J. Goy and J. Hoock (eds.), *Familie zwischen Tradition und Moderne. Studien zur Geschichte der Familie in Deutschland und Frankreich vom 16. bis zum 20.Jahrhundert*, Göttingen, 1981, pp. 141–81; H. Schultz, *Landhandwerk im Uebergang vom Feudalismus zum Kapitalismus. Vergleichender Ueberblick und Fallstudie Mecklenburg-Schwerin*, Berlin, 1984. See also Sheilagh Ogilvie's contribution to the present volume, chapter 3.

53   H.-H. Müller, 'Zur Geschichte und Bedeutung der Rübenzuckerindustrie in der Provinz Sachsen im 19.Jahrhundert unter besonderer Berücksichtigung der Magdeburger Börde', in H. J. Rach and B. Weissel (eds.), *Landwirtschaft und Kapitalismus. Zur Entwicklung der ökonomischen und sozialen Verhältnisse in der Magdeburger Börde vom Ausgang des 18.Jahrhunderts bis zum Ende des ersten Weltkrieges*, vol. 2, Veröffentlichung zur Volkskunde und Kulturgeschichte, vol. 66, no. 2, Berlin, 1979, pp. 9–61; J. A. Perkins, 'The agricultural revolution in Germany, 1850–1914, *Journal of European Economic History*, 10 (1981), pp. 87ff.; *idem*, 'Fiscal policy and economic development in XIXth century Germany', *Journal of European Economic History*, 13 (1984), pp. 311–44; W. R. Lee, 'Die Deutsche Zuckerrübenindustrie und Wirtschaftswachstum – eine kritische Bilanz', in T. Pierenkemper (ed.), *Landwirtschaft und industrielle Entwicklung. Zur ökonomischen Bedeutung von Bauernbefreiung, Agrarreform und Agrarrevolution*, Stuttgart, 1989, pp. 58–62.

54   Schissler, *Preussische Agrargesellschaft*, p. 156; R. A. Dickler, 'Labor market pressure: aspects of agricultural growth in the eastern region of Prussia, 1840–1914: a case study of economic–demographic interrelations during the demographic transition', unpublished Ph.D. thesis, University of Pennsylvania, 1970, p. 84. The *Mecklenburgische Koppelwirtschaft*, for example, involved an intensification of production to meet the needs of new crops, and required a deeper and more thorough preparation of the soil: see L. Werner, 'Die Entwicklung des Thünenschen Mustergutes Tellow (Mecklenburg) in den Jahren 1810 bis 1850. Ein herausragendes Beispiel

der kapitalistischen Intensivierung der deutschen Landwirtschaft in der ersten Hälfte des 19.Jahrhunderts', *Jahrbuch für Wirtschaftsgeschichte*, 1983, pp. 71–98.

55 Perkins, 'Agricultural revolution' p. 114. The overall situation in England was not too dissimilar, in terms of the introduction of mechanised production, see D. H. Morgan, *Harvesters and Harvesting 1840–1900: A Study of the Rural Proletariat*, London, 1982, pp. 34–46.
56 Boserup, *Women's Role*, p. 80.
57 A. E. Imhof, 'Women, family and death: excess mortality of women in childbearing age in four communities in nineteenth-century Germany', in R. J. Evans and W. R. Lee (eds.), *The German Family. Essays on the Social History of the Family in Nineteenth- and Twentieth-Century Germany*, London, 1981, pp. 148–74; G. Heller and A. E. Imhof, 'Körperliche Ueberlastung von Frauen im 19.Jahrhundert', in A. E. Imhof (ed.), *Der Mensch und sein Körper von der Antike bis Heute*, Munich, 1983, pp. 137–56. The broader implications of agricultural change for the nature of women's work are highlighted in G. P. Murdock and C. Provost, 'Factors in the division of labor by sex: a cross-cultural analysis', *Ethnology*, 12 (1973), pp. 203–27.
58 J. Griessmair, 'Die Entwicklung der Wirtschaft und der Bevölkerung von Baden und Württemberg im 19. und 20. Jahrhundert', *Jahrbücher für Baden-Württemberg*, Band 1, 1954, p. 51. A similar point was made in relation to England by Ivy Pinchbeck, *Women Workers and the Industrial Revolution, 1750–1850*, London, 1930, p. 95.
59 Dr. Kuby, 'Zur geburtshilflichen Statistik auf dem Lande', in *Aerztliches Intelligenz-Blatt*, 13, Munich, 1866, pp. 453–4.
60 B. Wachowiak, 'Die Entwicklung der Landwirtschaft Hinterpommerns in den Reiseberichten des Regierungsrates Haese aus den Jahren 1835 und 1837', *Jahrbuch für Wirtschaftsgeschichte*, 1977, p. 132; Snell, 'Agricultural seasonal unemployment', pp. 422ff.; B. K. Hansen, 'Rural women in late nineteenth-century Denmark', *Journal of Peasant Studies*, 9 (1981), pp. 225–40.
61 Museum für Deutsche Volkskunde, *Bild von Bauern*, p. 125 – evidence from Habach, Oberbayern, 1916.
62 For the debate on the substitution of the sickle by the scythe, see J. A. Perkins, 'Harvest technology and labour supply in Lincolnshire and the East Riding of Yorkshire, 1750–1850', *Tools and Tillage*, 3 (1976), pp. 54–125; E. J. T. Collins, 'Harvest-technology and labour supply in Britain, 1790–1870', *Economic History Review*, 22 (1969), pp. 453–73; idem, 'Labour supply and demand in European agriculture, 1800–1880', in E. L. Jones and S. J. Woolf (eds.), *Agrarian Change and Economic Development*, London, 1969, pp. 61–94; K. D. M. Snell, 'Agricultural seasonal unemployment, the standard of living and women's work in the South-East, 1690–1860', *Economic History Review*, 34, 3 (1981), pp. 407–37. M. Roberts, 'Sickles and scythes: women's work and men's work at harvest time', *History Workshop*, 7 (1979), pp. 3–28; A. Lühning, 'Die Schneidenen Erntegeräte', unpublished dissertation, University of Göttingen, 1951.
63 Wiegelmann, 'Bäuerliche Arbeitsteilung', *passim*.
64 W. R. Lee, 'Infant, child and maternal mortality in Western Europe: a comparative critique', in A. Brändström and L. G. Tedebrand (eds.), *Society, Health and Population during the Demographic Transition*, Umeå, 1988, pp. 9–22.
65 R. Anker, 'Demographic change and the role of women: a research programme in developing countries', in R. Anker, M. Buvinic and N. Youssef (eds.), *Women's Roles and Population Trends in the Third World*, London, 1982, p. 38.
66 E. Mueller, 'The allocation of women's time and its relation to fertility', in R. Anker, M. Buvinic and N. Youssef (eds.), *Women's Roles and Population Trends in the Third World*, London, 1982, p. 76; S. B. Nerlove, 'Women's workload and infant feeding practices', *Ethnology*, 13 (1974), p. 212.

67 E. King and R. E. Evenson, 'Time allocation and home production in Philippines rural households', in M. Buvinic, M. A. Lycett and W. P. McGreevey (eds.), *Women and Poverty in the Third World*, Baltimore, 1983, p. 51; J. de Vanzo and D. L. P. Lee, 'The compatability of child care with market and non-market activities: preliminary evidence from Malaysia', in *ibid.*, p. 88.

68 H. J. Kintner, 'Trends and regional differences in breastfeeding in Germany from 1871 to 1937', *Journal of Family History* (1985), pp. 163–82.

69 Dr. Henkel, 'Die ländlichen Säuglingsverhältnisse im Regierungsbezirk Oberbayern', *Blätter für Säuglingsfürsorge*, 1913, p. 21; W. R. Lee, 'The impact of agrarian change on women's work and child care in early nineteenth-century Prussia', in J. C. Fout (ed.), *German Women in the Nineteenth Century: A Social History*, New York, 1984, pp. 234–55.

70 U. B. Lithell, 'Infant mortality rate and standard of living in the past', *Scandinavian Journal of History* (1981), p. 315; idem, 'Childcare – a mirror of women's living conditions: a community study representing 18th and 19th centuries Ostrobothnia in Finland', in A. Brändström and L. G. Tedebrand (eds.), *Society, Health and Population during the Demographic Transition*, Umeå, 1988, pp. 91–108.

71 H. Bernheim, 'Die Intensitäts-Schwankungen der Sterblichkeit in Bayern und Sachsen und dessen Factoren', *Zeitschrift für Hygiene*, (1988), p. 577; W. R. Lee, 'Germany', in W. R. Lee (ed.), *European Demography and Economic Growth*, London, 1979, p. 155.

72 W. Müller-Wille, *Der Feldbau in Westfalen im 19. Jahrhundert*, Band 1, 1938, pp. 305ff.; Perkins, 'Agricultural revolution', pp. 100–1.

73 J. Knodel, 'Seasonal variation in infant mortality: an approach with applications', *Annales de Démographie Historique* (1983), p. 213.

74 Anker, 'Demographic change', p. 46.

75 [ ] Behrens, 'Der Verlauf der Säuglingssterblichkeit im Grossherzogtum Baden von 1852–1895', *Beiträge zur Statistik der inneren Verwaltung des Grossherzogtums Badens*, 46 (1901), pp. 3–23; Dr. Geigel, 'Kindersterblichkeit in Würzburg', *Vierteljahrschrift für öffentliche Gesundheitspflege*, 3 (1871), pp. 521–35; K. Kisskalt, 'Epidemiologisch–statistische Untersuchungen über die Sterblichkeit von 1600–1800', *Archiv für Hygiene und Bakteriologie*, 137 (1951), pp. 26–42.

76 B. Duden and U. Ottmüller, 'Der süsse Bronnen', *Berliner Frauenzeitung Courage*, 2 (1978), pp. 15–21.

77 E. King and E. Roberts, 'Time allocation and home production in Philippines rural households', in M. Buvinic, M. A. Lycett and W. P. McGreevey (eds.), *Women and Poverty in the Third World*, Baltimore, 1983, p. 51.

78 See, for example, R. Berthold, 'Der sozialökonomische Differenzierungsprozess der Bauernwirtschaft in der Provinz Brandenburg während der industriellen Revolution (1816 bis 1872/82)', *Jahrbuch für Wirtschaftsgeschichte* (1974), pp. 13–50; idem, 'Zur Herausbildung der kapitalistischen Klassenschichtung des Dorfes in Preussen', *Zeitschrift für Geschichte*, 25 (1977), pp. 565–74. See also R. Sandgruber, 'Innerfamiliale Einkommens- und Konsumaufteilung. Rollenverteilung und Rollenverständnis in Bauern-, Heimarbeiter- und Arbeiterfamilien Oesterreichs im 18., 19. und frühen 20. Jahrhundert', in P. Borscheid and H. J. Teuteberg (eds.), *Ehe, Liebe, Tod*, Münster, 1983, pp. 135–49; Harnisch, 'Statistische Untersuchungen', pp. 157ff.

79 H. Plaul, *Landarbeiterleben im 19. Jahrhundert. Eine volkskundliche Untersuchung über Veränderungen in der Lebensweise der einheimischen Landarbeiterschaft in den Dörfern der Magdeburger Börde unter den Bedingungen der Herausbildung und Konsolidierung des Kapitalismus in der Landwirtschaft*, Veröffentlichungen zur Volkskunde und Kulturgeschichte, Band 65, Berlin, 1979, *passim*.

80 Imhof, 'Women, family and death', pp. 148–74; Heller and Imhof, 'Körperliche Ueberlastung', pp. 137–56; J. Knodel, 'Two centuries of infant, child and maternal mortality in German village populations', in A. Brändström and L. G. Tedebrand (eds.), *Society, Health and Population during the Demographic Transition*, Stockholm, 1988.

81 R. Schofield, 'Did the mothers really die? Three centuries of maternal mortality in "The world we have lost"', in L. Bonfield, R. M. Smith and K. Wrightson (eds.), *The World We Have Gained: Histories of Population and Social Structure*, Oxford and New York, 1986, pp. 231–60; *idem*, 'Dimensions of danger: the causes and consequences of maternal mortality in pre-industrial England re-examined', paper presented to the International Symposium on Infant, Child and Maternal Mortality, Liverpool University, 1988.

82 Knodel, 'Two centuries', *passim*.

83 *Statistische Nachrichten über das Grossherzogtum Oldenburg*, Band 11, 1870, p. 224, cited in E. Shorter, *A History of Women's Bodies*, London, 1982, p. 229; C. Ballod, *Die mittlere Lebensdauer in Stadt und Land*, Staats- und sozialwissenschaftliche Forschungen, Band 16, Leipzig, 1899, *passim*.

84 A. Bek, 'Die Bevölkerungsbewegung im ländlichen Raum in den letzten 250 Jahren', unpublished dissertation, University of Hohenheim, n.d, p. 120.

85 S. Schofield, 'Seasonal factors affecting nutrition in different age groups and especially preschool children', *The Journal of Development Studies*, 12 (1974), pp. 22–40. The adverse effects of hard physical work for women are discussed extensively in M. Mayer, 'Zur Frauenarbeit in der Landwirtschaft', *Zentralblatt für Gewerbehygiene*, 2 (1914), pp. 281–4.

86 E. S. Riemer and J. C. Fout (eds.), *European Women: A Documentary History, 1789–1945*, Brighton, 1980, p. 183; Dickler, 'Labor market pressure', p. 126.

87 W. Seccombe, 'Patriarchy stabilised: the construction of the male breadwinner wage norm in nineteenth-century Britain', *Social History*, 11 (1986), pp. 53–76; V. Maher, 'Possession and dispossession: maternity and mortality in Morocco', in H. Medick and D. W. Sabean (eds.), *Interest and Emotion: Essays on the Study of Family and Kinship*, Cambridge, 1984, pp. 103–28.

88 W. P. Ward and P. C. Ward, 'Infant birth weight and nutrition in industrializing Montreal', *American Historical Review* (1984), pp. 324–45; M. Rosenberg, 'Birth-weight, breastfeeding, post-partum amenorrhea and infant mortality in three Norwegian cities during the late nineteenth and early twentieth century', in A. Brändström and L. J. Tedebrand (eds.), *Society, Health and Population during the Demographic Transition*, Umeå, 1988.

89 J. Knodel, 'Natural fertility in pre-industrial Germany', *Population Studies*, 32 (1978), p. 483; *idem*, 'Child mortality and reproductive behavior in German village populations in the past: a micro-level analysis of the replacement effect', University of Michigan, Research Report, 1981, p. 59.

90 C. D. Deeve and A. de Janvey, 'A conceptual framework for the empirical analysis of peasants', *American Journal of Agricultural Econmics*, 61, 4 (1979), pp. 601–11.

Chapter Three

Women and proto-industrialisation in a corporate society: Württemberg woollen weaving, 1590–1760

SHEILAGH C. OGILVIE

Introduction

Women's work is distinguished from that of men by the superior household productivity of females, a consequence of both biology and socialisation. Because women take into account their productivity in the household as well as in alternative market occupations in deciding how much time to allocate to the market,[1] and because women are often located close to the boundary between market work and household work, female employment reacts very sensitively to demographic and institutional changes altering the rewards of different uses of time. This mobile, flexible reserve of female labour plays a special role in greasing the wheels of the most petrified labour-market. How, then, does it change with economic opportunities? In particular, how did it change with the expansion of domestic manufacture in Europe in the early modern period?

Two theories give diametrically opposed answers to this question. One, the theory of proto-industrialisation, sees the expansion of domestic manufacture and the consequent 'transition to capitalism' as having greatly widened women's market role. The other, which one might call the English empirical historiography, sees the transition to 'capitalist organisation' as having decreased women's work in the market. Testing these theories using data from a particular European society – that of the former Duchy of Württemberg in south-west Germany – exposes lacunae in both, which can only be filled by taking into account the social and legal institutions which constrained the value of women's time in the market. The theory of proto-industrialisation rightly sees the expansion of rural industry as initially increasing women's market opportunities, but ignores subsequent institutional tightening which often restricted women to a narrow range of work in the new industry. The English empirical historiography rightly recognises that women were excluded from many occupations as cottage industry expanded, but wrongly assigns responsibility to 'capitalism' rather than to the restrictive institutions which developed in some societies around an expansion of economic opportunities.

Proto-industrialisation is a name invented in the last decade for the rapid expansion of dense, export-oriented cottage industry in many parts of Europe between the sixteenth and the nineteenth centuries.[2] It is supposed to have paved the way for factory industrialisation and a 'transition to capitalism' by loosening communal and corporate institutions, opening up the countryside to capitalist markets, and breaking down the old homeostatic demographic regime by leading peasant households to 'exploit themselves', to expand their workforce and output (through earlier marriage and higher fertility) at below market wage-rates.

According to the theory, the new organisation of the proto-industrial family under the new form of production, and especially the new working role of women, was crucial in the development of capitalism. Proto-industrialisation is supposed to have broken down the traditional peasant sexual division of labour, as both men and women began to work at the same market-oriented tasks.[3] As female market labour increased in importance, the economic and social freedom of women increased.[4] Because women's market work was now more significant to rural households, and because of the 'pauperisation' the theory associates with the process of proto-industrialisation, the expansion of rural industry brought about a more individualised selection of marriage partners, on the basis of work skills, instead of property and parental planning.[5] In the wake of these changes came, it is said, a loosening of political and patriarchal controls on female sexuality[6] and greater freedom and mobility for women.[7]

These are wide and interesting claims. They are especially interesting in that they run counter to earlier English studies which view the transition to capitalism as having narrowed the range and extent of women's work in the market. Pinchbeck, who can be viewed retrospectively as a representative of this English empirical school, remarks on the decline in female employment during the eighteenth century, especially in crafts,[8] and concludes that rural industry weakened women's earlier economic position, by establishing a tradition of low wages and causing the decline of female apprenticeship.[9] In the rural woollen industries, she finds that 'women's work was most varied where the influence of capital in the trade was negligible ... As the industry became more highly organised their employment was attacked as competing wtih that of men, and on these grounds they were excluded from certain branches of the trade.'[10]

In the same vein, Clark portrays the transition to capitalism as having disenfranchised women of their medieval and early modern equality: 'many trades which in later times have become entirely closed to women were then so dependent on their labour that sisters are mentioned specifically in rules concerning the conditions of manufacture'.[11] She sees women gradually being forced into household labour and dependence on their husbands: 'As capitalistic organisation developed, many avenues of industry were ... gradually closed to married women.'[12]

Berg, in a more recent echo of this school of thought, argues that the 'availability of more household employment in cottage manufactures in the eighteenth century' may have contributed to the decline not only in female apprenticeship, but also in adolescent service for girls, making them more subject to 'patriarchal authority at home'.[13] She suggests that the flexibility of women workers in domestic industry, allocating time between 'household chores and casual industrial employment', resulted in 'a very irregular training for women', which tended to exclude them from lucrative or powerful positions in the trade. She concludes that 'the control of these industries went to men'.[14] Using local settlement and apprenticeship records for the south of England, Snell likewise finds 'relatively more equal and sexually shared labour before the nineteenth century ... The late eighteenth and early nineteenth centuries saw a narrowing of the possibilities for female artisan activity.'[15]

These English studies record outcomes – the narrowing of women's work in the market – but often assign causation unspecifically to the development of capitalist organisation. What specific dynamics or institutions of capitalist organisation were responsible for restricting women's work roles? Were they 'capitalist' institutions, strictly speaking?

The theory of proto-industrialisation ignores the variations in demography, and in industrial opportunities for women, resulting from the very great local and regional differences in industrial organisation and legal and corporate institutions in early modern Europe. Because female labour functioned as a 'reserve' of market labour, close to the boundary of choice between market work and household work, it adapted itself flexibly to the local organisation of specific rural industries, and resists classification by theories that try to view it in isolation from industrial and demographic structures.

The shortcomings of both general theories can be made empirically relevant by investigating women's labour-force participation in a rural industry quite unlike any in England. In the 1580s a new form of weaving, of the finer New Draperies, arose in the Nagold Valley of the Duchy of Württemberg, situated in the Swabian Black Forest south-west of Stuttgart. It drew in large numbers of peasants, rural artisans from other trades, old-style 'coarse woollens' weavers, unemployed journeymen, and women.[16] For the next two hundred years, cloths from the valley were exported as far afield as northern Germany, France, Austria, and Italy. By the beginning of the eighteenth century, as many as 40 per cent of households in the most densely proto-industrial communities were at least partly dependent on weaving for a livelihood. The Nagold Valley therefore experienced classic proto-industrialisation: dense and initially very rapidly expanding rural industry for export markets.

However, the social results of the expansion of rural industry in this region diverge from the predictions of the theory in two important respects. First, the demographic changes predicted by the theory are largely absent. Some densely industrial communities did experience faster population growth than agrarian communities; others did not. Weavers married at much the same age as other men, and they married older, rather than younger, women. By the early eighteenth century, weavers' fertility was lower than average, and in small towns and villages alike, they had smaller than average households. The demographic expansion irrespective of economic opportunities which the theory predicts does not seem to have taken place.[17]

Secondly, the expansion of rural industry in this region did not loosen social and communal institutions or pave the way for capitalist market society in the countryside. As soon as the new form of weaving began to expand, a new corporate group, the New Draperies weavers' guild, was formed around it, by a process of grass-roots lobbying.[18] The guild exercised jurisdiction over village and small-town weavers alike. Quantitative and qualitative analysis of the annual guild accounts and local court records demonstrates that from its establishment in 1598 at least until 1760 the guild intensified its control over entry,[19] output, technological change, industrial lobbying and labour practices.[20] It elicited impressive financial and moral support from its members, and its regulations were actively enforced by village and small-town councils and by the dense network of Ducal bureaucrats and local officials.[21] Weavers were heavily represented on village and town councils,[22] and the exclusionary powers of the corporate communities relating, for example, to citizenship requirements, continued to be actively enforced throughout the period of proto-industrialisation.[23] In 1650, the distribution end of the industry was also granted a corporate monopoly by the Ducal government: for the next 150 years all weavers were legally obliged to sell their cloths to a single company of merchant-dyers, which also developed impressive local and national political clout and regulatory powers.[24]

Thus with the advent of capitalism to the Württemberg countryside came an intensification of the economic power of the state, and a strengthening rather than a weakening of corporate groups. This result is by no means unique to Württemberg. Cross-cultural comparison reveals the existence of proto-industries – in Bologna, Castile, Languedoc and northern Germany – where corporate and regulatory institutions remained strong throughout the expansion of rural industry, where new guilds and merchant companies were set up in response to the industrial expansion, and where capitalism came hand-in-hand with a strong regulatory state.[25] On the other hand, it shows agrarian countrysides – in England and The Netherlands – where corporate and regulatory institutions were already weak before proto-industrialisation.[26]

It is no coincidenece that cross-cultural comparisons show a similar variety in the demographic response to expanding rural manufacture. In some areas of rural industry – Shepshed in England, the Flemish communities studied by Mendels – there was population expansion, early marriage, high fertility, and large and complex households. In others – southern Flanders, Ireland, Bavaria in southern Germany, the Ravensberg area in northern Germany, Thimerais in southern France, and Bethnal Green and Sudbury in southern England – there was population stability, late marraige, low fertility, and small and simple households.[27] The demographic and productive choices of rural artisans did not exhibit a spontaneous reaction to the introduction of dense, export-oriented cottage industry, but rather adapted to it flexibly, according to the specific institutional context in each case.

In Württemberg, as in England, there was a strong popular tradition prior to and independent of proto-industry, in which women's rights to be economically active were recognised and informally tolerated. When new economic activities arose (such as proto-industry), women did initially move into them and take up a share of the new opportunities. Female labour was adaptable, but it was corporately and regulatively powerless. As corporate and bureaucratic regulation of the rural economy became more intense, women were often forced out of the unregulated niches they had previously occupied. In Württemberg, it was not the market-oriented or 'capitalist' organisation of expanding rural industry which narrowed women's opportunites, but rather the activities of interest-groups, which came in the wake of the expansion, concerned to regulate its allocation among social groups.

Forms of female work

Throughout the seventeenth and eighteenth centuries women from peasant, proto-industrial, and traditional artisan households remained active in agriculture. Farming continued to be an important livelihood in both small towns and villages, as rural manufacture expanded. In 1736, after 150 years of proto-industrialisation, more than one-third of all family earning units in the most densely proto-industrial community in the Nagold Valley, the small town of Wildberg with 1,400 inhabitants, depended for a living partly on their own land.[28] In the town one-fifth of New Draperies weaving households and two-fifths of other households owned some land; in the villages more than three-quarters of both New Draperies weaving and non-weaving households owned land.[29] Agriculture thus played a major role in the livelihood of households even under advanced proto-industrialisation.

Church court prosecutions for Sabbath-breaking record women carrying on the habitual daily toil of farmyard and field: 'mucking out the cowstall' on a Sunday,[30] or 'carrying hay out to the stall during the sermon'.[31] Conflicts arose among females over the borrowing of farmyard implements and alleged agricultural trespasses. In 1632 one butcher's maid 'asked to borrow a dung cart in the plainant's house, whereupon his daughter is supposed to have said, they thought so much of themselves, why didn't they buy one? The maid went home and carried to her mistress's ear that his daughter had said that she should take the money from the stolen beasts and buy a cart with it'.[32] There was a heavy seasonal demand for females in summer and autumn for haymaking and harvest. In the small towns, young women worked in gangs as grass-cutters. In 1616 a village forest warden sued a gang of eight female grass-cutters and New Draperies journeymen for jeering and throwing stones at him as he was leaving the town of Wildberg.[33]

Among villagers engaged in agriculture, a woman's strength was a quality particularly valued in her by men. One woman, the young wife of a village shepherd, reported to the church court in 1658 that as she was walking home from penning the sheep, a village farmer had walked with her and 'on the way he said to her, he would like to sleep with her, she was so pretty and strong'.[34]

Women could conduct whole agricultural businesses on their own. In 1619, the widow of the Wildberg *Kleemeister*, the 'untouchable' who doctored and buried animals and suicides, and did a multitude of other odd and dirty work in the pastoral sector, submitted a petition to the duke, asking for the right of free fodder in winter, 'since other masters receive hay and straw to feed those beasts which are put on ... in the wintertime because of the wolves ... so she petitions that she also should receive her share'.[35] She regarded it as no more than her right to be treated on the same footing as 'other masters'. In a petition of 1642, one village widow described how she was gradually bringing the family farm back under cultivation after the Imperial invasion. Although she had three sons, she was the chief mover in the business, and in the petition she entered into technical agricultural details concerning proper manuring, the state of the farm buildings, the quality of various fields, and the grain yields and tax obligations of different parts of the estate.[36]

It might be argued that although women were active in agriculture, proto-industrialisation decreased the extent of non-market-oriented labour on family land. But proto-industrialisation does not seem to have decreased dependence on family farm land in the villages, but rather sustained it.

In the Nagold Valley, dense New Draperies weaving was associated with a less than average polarisation of village society into landed and landless groups: as late as 1736, 39 per cent of households in the six least proto-industrial villages were landless, compared to only 28 per cent in the three densely proto-industrial villages.[37] Of course, there were more purely agricultural households in the non-weaving villages (28 per cent compared to 19 per cent in the dense weaving villages), but it is essential to note that weaving did not bring about the disappearance of agricultural work on the household's own land in those villages in which weaving was most densely practised. There is no evidence that the less polarised, more by-employed pattern of livelihoods in the weaving villages involved either less or more participation by women in an economy in which they were already very active.

So active were women in selling agricultural products that they could get commercial reputations in the community. In a defamation case in 1622 a man insulted a neighbour's wife by telling her that 'people in town were talking about the way she sells her lard ... if [she] only sold a quarter of lard, it would be found to be lacking half a quarter'.[38]

Women were also active in the food and drink trade. In 1602, when proto-industry had hardly begun, among the six tavern-keepers presenting their guarantors to the district court was a married woman running a drinking-house as her own business, responsible for naming her own guarantor.[39] Her husband did not appear in the matter.

Even heavy crafts such as milling, fulling and building were practised by women. In 1603 a woman appeared before the administrative court in Wildberg, who had bought a mill some years previously, had paid the considerable licence fee to the community, had invested her dowry in improvements, and had been supporting herself and her children from milling ever since.[40] A petition of 1657 for tax relief shows that one widow had been operating one of the three town mills herself and supporting herself on the proceeds; the petition stated that 'apart from the mill, [she] has no means'.[41] In 1706, a miller's widow was fined by the church court for milling during the sermon.[42] A 1736 population register lists a widow in the town supporting a household of four on a fulling mill and some land, and a widow in a village supporting a household of six on an ordinary grain mill and some land.[43] The female village grain miller can hardly be seen as a result of proto-industrial emancipation of women and it would surely be more appropriate to see both female millers as part of a long-standing economic tradition, independent of proto-industrialisation.

It was the wife who was often a craftsman's main assistant, even in such a heavy craft as building. One defamation case in 1656 arose between a mason's customer, and the mason and his wife who had been rebuilding a wall together. Although it is evident that the mason's wife was expected to do the auxiliary tasks, she was present throughout the job, assisting in the whole course of the work, acting as journeyman or partner to her husband.[44] An artisan's natural partner even in heavy work was his wife, unless he was prosperous enough to keep a journeyman: in 1709 a fifty-year-old cooper and his wife were summoned before the church court, because 'on a day of repentence before the sermon, he made barrel wood and carried it in with his wife after the sermon'.[45] A serious dispute between a miller's and a fuller's wife arose in 1711 around the construction by a labouring gang of the waterway in the mill-ditch, a job which the miller and the fuller left to their wives to oversee.[46]

Not only proto-industrial, but also other crafts were seen as being the business of both husband and wife. Serious marital conflict could arise from disputes about work. A Wildberg tailor and his wife were brought before the church court in 1715 for a dispute which arose, according to the wife, 'concerning the making of a [coat] breast'. The husband's defence was that 'his wife always wants to have the last word, and made him so angry that he gave her a couple of boxes on the ear, and when she wouldn't be quiet he beat her some more; if only she would give way to him such things would not happen'.[47]

It was taken for granted that in the absence of her husband, a woman would carry on his craft. A furrier petitioned for release from military service in 1633 on the grounds that 'no woman can fulfil his craft'.[48] A woman evidently *would* be able to fulfil almost any other craft. A baker, petitioning in the 1640s to be let out of the first military muster in the town, claimed that 'because his wife is ill, if he had to go out again he would miserably lose everything he has'.[49] In 1668 a citizen complained to the governor's court that 'the fountains by the upper gate and in the market are running very poorly, the well- and fountain-master sees to it very carelessly, sends only his wife; better provision should be made'.[50] Even official tasks were exercised by the officeholder's wife in his absence. One of the town constables complained to the governor's court in 1670 that 'the butchers, also to some extent the other citizens, refuse to obey when in his absence something is commanded by order of the authorities through his wife; and instead resist, on the grounds that it is not she who is the town constable'. The authorities saw it as perfectly proper that the constable's wife should exercise his office in his absence, and issued an order to that effect.[51]

Whether the family gained its living from proto-industry, traditional crafts, or agriculture, a wife was seen as absolutely essential to the maintenance of a household, as is shown by the very low proportion of widowers in the population. In 1736, only 5 per cent of earning units in the town and villages of the district of Wildberg were headed by single or widowed males, and in the censuses of 1717 and 1722, only 1 per cent of households (residential units) were headed by such males.[52]

The central importance of a wife is also shown by the petitions made by men of all occupations to be permitted to marry during Lent or Advent, or to remarry before the legal six months has elapsed since the death of the previous wife. In 1636 a farmer from the town of Nagold petitioned to be permitted to marry during Lent 'so that he can attend that much more properly to his lands'.[53] That year in a single month four villagers from the district of Wildberg petitioned to be allowed to remarry less than five months after the deaths of their wives, so essential was the wife's labour contribution to the household. One villager petitioned in 1657 to be permitted to remarry before the six-month time-limit, and to marry a woman to whom he was too closely related, on the grounds that '[he] has children and a heavy load of lands, for which reason he can no longer get along without a wife ... If he had to wait out the time, the field work would come in the middle, and he would thereby suffer noticeable impediment to the field work.'[54] A villager petitioned for tax relief on his land in 1664 on the grounds that 'he has been a widower for three years now ... can no longer maintain these lands and keep them under cultivation'.[55]

But it was not merely in farming that the labour of a wife was essential. One Wildberg New Draperies weaver petitioned in 1620 to be divorced from his wife who had been officially consigned to the leper-house, on the grounds that 'without a wife he could not conduct a household, [but] must work for a master'. He had, in fact, already been obliged to leave Wildberg and work as a servant in Tübingen.[56] In 1627 a Wildberg butcher and tavern-keeper petitioned to remarry twelve weeks after his wife's death, on the grounds that he 'keeps a tavern, cannot without injury keep house with strangers'.[57] In 1636 a Wildberg shoemaker petitioned for dispensation to remarry only nineteen weeks after his wife's death 'on account of his craft, grievous military quartering and great disturbance in the household';[58] another man on the grounds that 'he has four small children, great poverty, and can keep no servants';[59] and a third because he held a town office.[60] A wife's assistance, therefore, was essential in every walk of life.

Certainly women were active in woollen weaving, as they were in other crafts. A case brought before the Wildberg court in 1623 reveals an underground network of women dealing in low-quality wool which did not meet guild standards. The women's husbands claimed that their wives had dealt without their knowledge while they were away on business.[61] It is evident that considerable latitude was given to a wife to deal in the husband's absence. The weavers in this case were not, however, proto-industrial weavers, but rather old-style coarse woollens weavers selling to local markets. Proto-industrialisation was clearly not necessary for the active involvement of women in rural textile production.

The old-style weavers sold a large volume of cloths collectively to the Ducal court each year and in return had the right to buy a shipment of wool from the Ducal flocks, known as the *Herrenwollen*. When this shipment arrived, it was shared out among the masters' wives, and the women went up to collect it. It was an event for the women of the district, a matter for envy and conflict among weavers' wives, an occasion for female street culture. This is shown in a defamation case of 1624, in which an old-style weaver's wife sent her sister up to fetch 'her' *Herrenwollen*, and a female neighbour challenged the woman's right to the wool on the grounds that it was rumoured among the women in the town that the woman's husband was weaving New Draperies instead of old-style woollens.[62] Proto-industry and old-style weaving co-existed in the same community, often in the same household, and old-style weaving already involved the weaver's wife as co-owner of the rights and practice of the craft: a woman would employ her female relative to go and fetch 'her' wool 'in her name', gossip about industrial practice was spread 'about her', and it was an affair of public female sociability for women to envy and insult one another about economic privileges. Proto-industrialisation was not required for women to be economically active: it was happening already in the non-proto-industrial sector.

Not only the wool and yarn supply was female work. Many weaving tasks, such as the job of stretching out a newly made weft, were two-person jobs. Censuses show that by the early eighteenth century most New Draperies weaving households were small, with a mean size of 3.95 (compared to the non-weavers' 4.49), and almost one-fifth of weavers' households consisted only of the weaver and his wife (compared to one-tenth among the non-weavers). The obvious pair to stretch wefts together was the married couple. Many weaving couples appeared before the church courts in the seventeenth and eighteenth centuries for 'stretching a weft during the sermon'.[63] But women outside the proto-industrial sector also appeared in such presentments: in just the fifteen years from 1705 to 1720, the wives of smiths, carpenters, coopers, innkeepers, and rope-makers, all were fined with their husbands for working on the Sabbath.[64]

In the financial and investment sector of the textile industry women had been active long before the growth of New Draperies weaving. Women would lend money *auf Tücher* ('on [old-style] woollens') to male weavers from their inheritances or dowries. Sometimes women investing in this way would charge a somewhat higher rate of interest than the 5 per cent legal maximum, and cases appeared before the civil court, where weavers would plead 'not to have to pay more than the lawful interest'.[65] Of course the court would enforce the law, deciding that 'the plaintiff shall be satisfied with the money that has already been received, plus the lawful interest';[66] and the woman would be done out of her little profit. One New Draperies weaver reported to the civil court in Wildberg how 'he had to pay his sister for the second time, and not with cloths but rather a usurious interest;

to which he objected, saying he would no longer pay interest like this on the 60 Gulden; in the end his sister agreed that he might pay the lawful interest on the money, which he then continued to do for three years'.[67] Although the new weaving with its new capital needs offered new hopes of independence for women, the regulation of finance prevented women deriving from it an enduring increase in security.

Dense, export-oriented cottage industry did not bring about great changes in the scale or the nature of women's work in the small agrarian towns and villages of the Nagold Valley. Women were active in agriculture, in retailing, in heavy trades both in their own rights and as assistants to their husbands, and in the traditional textile crafts. When men were absent, it was taken for granted that women did their work. Little difference can be discerned in the work women did in the households of New Draperies weavers, compared to those of traditional textile and non-textile artisans.

Single women

This popular tradition of female involvement in all sectors of the economy, and the tendency for flexible female labour to fill the gaps created by shortages in male labour supply, should not be interpreted as showing that the early modern period was a golden age of female economic independence.[68] Married women or widows working under a husband's licence or on the family's land were a matter of course. Daughters and maidservants were similarly permitted in crafts and agriculture, although in crafts their work could be circumscribed by regulation. Women filling a labour shortage or operating in peripheral sectors of the economy were tolerated. Single women earning their own bread, operating their own businesses independently of any economic right derived from husband or father, were given a special pejorative name, *Eigenbrötlerinnen* (literally, '[females] earning their own bread'), and were subject to perpetual harassment by the community and the authorities to whom respectable citizens constantly reported them.[69]

Court records from the sixteenth to the late eighteenth century bear witness to a long tradition of attempts by officials, communities, and male craft groups to control independent women. There was general disapproval of single women earning a living without being formally contracted to a master. At the yearly governor's court in 1646, at which each citizen was asked in the presence of the whole citizenry if he had anything to report, one man complained that 'several single girls are lodging with several citizens here, who in his view should be instructed to engage themselves to masters'.[70] He named four citizens with whom such single women were lodging. The response of the authorities was immediate and severe: 'the whole citizenry is enjoined on pain of a *Frevel* fine [three Gulden] to engage such girls to masters within three weeks, for if afterwards any are discovered [still unengaged], the said fine will without fail be inflicted'.[71]

Similar complaints in following years reveal some of the grounds for communal anxiety about these women. For one thing, they were too mobile. In 1647 a man complained that 'there are two *Eigenbrötlerinnen* in the town who dwell here on and off, and will serve no honourable master, which is counter to the Ducal ordinances'.[72] The following year a citizen complained that 'there were unmarried girls here on their own, who do not bind themselves, or work for a master, which is not to be endured, namely one from Rotfelden in Mike The Board's house, one from Jesingen in Jeremiah's Hans's house, and from time to time one in Veit's house, who wanders in and out'.[73] Such women did not stay in one household like proper servants, but moved in and out of the town, threatening the settlement controls imposed by the corporate community as a means of licensing access to collective rights and privileges. In 1650 after further popular complaints the authorities decreed that such women should be expelled from their lodgings within fourteen days.[74]

Service by single women was tolerated; independence was not. In 1660, a Wildberg linen-weaver reported that 'the girl who had been at the carpenter's place, and was recently ordered away by the authorities, is dwelling here again in the middle mill'; the response of the authorities was that 'so long as she day-labours she shall be endured; but should she try to be independent again, she shall be thrown out'.[75] So long as such women provided part of the pool of cheap labour for town citizens, they were permitted to stay; as soon as they started competing with citizens for employment, they were moved on.

They were also accused of competing with citizens for other resources. In 1660, for instance, one male citizen complained that 'there are some *Eigenbrötlerinnen* here, should be gotten rid of; in the market everything is grabbed away by them, no citizen can get anything any more'.[76] The community took this accusation seriously, and ordered that 'in the next few days there shall be a house-to-house visitation to see what *Eigenbrötlerinnen* there are here, whereupon the court shall consider the matter'.[77]

Single women were supposed to go into service, married women to stay with their husbands. In 1623 the regulatory court ordered a Wildberg citizen to get rid of 'young Meg The Bucket' who was lodging in his house, 'but who has a husband in Effringen named N. Sper; is not to be put up with'.[78] In 1641 a neighbour reported to the court that 'the Öschelbronn pastor's wife, who has separated herself from her husband, is not to be put up with in the town'.[79]

The expansion of New Draperies weaving does not seem to have relaxed the pressures forcing would-be independent women back under family authority. Neither the corporate community nor the authorities cared for the idea of women achieving independence from family and masters alike by spinning. In 1626, when it might be expected that proto-industrialisation would have begun to emancipate women, two different citizens complained that 'Michel Fronmiller is lodging a lass who has been in at least three different services in one year, and spins perpetually at the wheel.'[80]

Even in conditions of considerable male labour shortage, such as prevailed in the worst years of the Thirty Years War, a girl could be brought up before the regulatory court on the charge that she was 'said to go to no sermon or prayer session, to swear wantonly, and to spin every Sunday between the sermons';[81] the authorities put her in the stocks.

Provisions in successive weaving ordinances limited the kinds of work which might be done by 'single girls and other persons' who, in addition to spinning yarn for the weavers (which they were entitled to do), made and sold wefts.[82] The ordinances alleged that they thereby 'caused great damage to the wefts and the yarn'.[83] This unfitting work was also keeping single women from their proper places in the economy, and must be abolished so that 'such daughters may be caused to apply themselves to other and necessary house work and business, or enter into honourable service'.[84] Poorer masters saw the making and selling of wefts to richer masters as an important part of their prerogatives, and women caught infringing on it were fined heavily. Yet according to the theory, proto-industrialisation should have caused a *decrease* in the sexual division of labour.[85]

Women were allowed to spin – indeed there was always a shortage of spun yarn – but the rural guild colluded with even its usual opponent, the merchant company, to prevent the army of female spinners from charging the high prices which scarcity would otherwise have commanded. Petitions and guild accounts are replete with the sufferings of weavers, caused by the price ceilings on cloths imposed by the state under pressure from the merchant lobby; but the weavers in turn imposed grievous price ceilings on the spinners. Maximum piece-rates for spinners, and penalties for weavers who paid higher rates, were laid down in the first and every subsequent New Draperies weaving ordinance.[86] The 1654 ordinance turned over completely the periodic revision of spinners' rates to the merchant company and the weavers' guilds, which allied in order to minimise their own production costs against the unincorporated spinners.

The ordinances were actually enforced. Even in the first, comparatively unregulated, phase of the industry's expansion, town and village weavers successfully acted together to protect their cheap source of spun yarn. In July 1618 two guild foremen froze the assets of rival weavers competing with the Wildberg corporation for cheap female labour in a comparatively distant village.[87] Similar initiatives against the 'current disorders' among the spinners were undertaken even in the darkest years of the Thirty Years War.[88]

As the century passed, the control of spinners increased. In 1670, when 'foreign' putters-out tried to have spinning done in some remote hamlets of the Nagold Valley, the guild instantly sent an official up to the hamlets, who informed the local authorities and confiscated the wefts and yarn.[89] The problem of regulating the spinners' attempts to evade the price ceiling was then taken under the control of the Ducal government. In 1671 the Ducal authorities issued prohibitions to two villages against spinning for 'foreigners', and ordered 'a list of all those in the villages who spin wool, with the addition of where to and whom for, with names, 13 pages', which was paid for by the rural weavers' guild.[90] Not long after, prohibitions were sent out to ten villages in the district of Wildenberg forbidding all wool-spinning 'out of the country', again paid for by the weavers.[91]

Both guild and local courts enforced the absolute prohibition against single females weaving or combing wool. In 1669, for instance, one citizen reported to a local court that 'a year ago Hannß Schrotten was forbidden to set his servant girl behind the loom and have her weave, on pain of a *Kleine Frevel* [3 Gulden] fine; however he does not comply with this, but rather has been having this girl weave from time to time all year'. The authorities' response was immediate and severe: 'Because he ignored the previous prohibition, he is fined a *Kleine Frevel* to the Duchy, and is commanded once again, absolutely not to have this girl do weaving; if he does not comply with this, he will be fined a *Kleine Frevel* again.'[92]

As late as the second half of the eighteenth century, several masters were being fined each year for such offences as 'allowing his maid to comb, as though she were a journeyman, counter to the ordinance',[93] 'keeping single [female] combers, counter to prohibition',[94] or 'because he had a female work for him'.[95] Females were unable to escape regulation of their work even in the villages, for village masters were fined no less frequently for this offence than masters from the small town. Nor does it appear that this was only a pro forma enforcement of a much more widespread and uncontrollable delict, for on one occasion six masters were fined for keeping single female wool-combers 'as a first offence and just as a warning'.[96] The guild behaved as if by and large it was keeping the phenomenon under control.

One way in which the New Draperies industry did open new chances to women, at least in its more prosperous phase, before the Thirty Years War, was if they bound themselves to masters as servants. A list of servants and their wages in each community in the district of Wildberg in 1631 shows that communities which had a high proportion of weavers also had an excess of female over male servants (see table 3.1). In the three

Table 3.1   *Sex of servants in the district of Wildberg, July 1631*

Community	Male		Female		Total	
	No.	%	No.	%	No.	%
Weaving						
Wildberg	34	47	38	53	72	100
Sulz	14	40	21	60	35	100
Ebhausen	9	53	8	47	17	100
Total weaving	57	46	67	54	124	100
Non-weaving						
Oberjettingen	12	55	10	45	22	100
Gültlingen	11	48	12	52	23	100
Schönbronn	4	100	0	0	4	100
Total non-weaving	27	55	22	45	49	100
Grand total	84	49	89	51	173	100

Note: Servants of unknown sex are omitted.
Source: WHSA A573 Bü 5597, list of servants and their wages, July 1631.

most dense centres of New Draperies weaving in the district 54 per cent of servants were female, compared to only 45 per cent females among servants in non-weaving villages. The highest mean wages for female servants were in the town and one of the weaving villages (see table 3.2); but the lowest mean wage for female servants was in another weaving village, suggesting that the employment opportunities of women in this society depended less on proto-industrialisation, than on other, more local, characteristics of the labour-market.

According to the theory, proto-industry is supposed to have made women more mobile. In the weaving village of Sulz, for which the 1631 list records servants' communities of origin, female servants were much less mobile than males: four-fifths of male servants, but only one-half of the female servants were from outside the village in which they were serving (see table 3.2). Here one can see the operation of the corporate community on individuals' economic opportunities, for on average the highest wage rates in Sulz were being paid to servants native to the village. 'Foreign' servants earned 10 per cent less on average than servants native to the village.

But servants were not the primary source of labour in the New Draperies weaving industry. By 1736, in the dense weaving communities of Wildberg and Ebhausen, only one-fifth of New Draperies weaving households, but almost one-third of non-weaving households, had servants. It was in family roles within the household, or as unmarried spinners operating on the margin of subsistence, that women had to find their principal place in New Draperies weaving.

Table 3.2 *Wages of servants in the district of Wildberg, July 1631*

Community	Male		Female		Total	
	Mean wage	No.	Mean wage	No.	Mean wage	No.
Weaving						
Wildberg	10.0	33	4.0	36	6.8	69
Ebhausen	6.6	9	3.2	8	5.0	17
Sulz:						
total	7.6	16	4.4	20	5.6	36
native	9.7	3	4.6	10	6.0	13
outsider	5.6	13	4.2	10	5.2	23
Total weaving	8.8	58	4.0	64	6.2	122
Non-weaving						
Oberjettingen	6.3	12	3.7	10	5.1	22
Gültlingen	9.3	11	3.8	12	6.4	23
Schönbronn	12.0	4	–	–	12.0	4
Total non-weaving	8.4	27	3.8	22	6.3	49
Grand total	8.7	85	3.9	86	6.2	171

Note: Wages are given in Gulden.
Servants whose wages were not recorded are omitted.
Source: WHSA A573 Bü 5597, July 1631.

Why was this so? There are two reasons: one is that corporate communities, rural guilds and merchant companies formed a powerful coalition of pressure groups which, in seeking state enforcement of their own economic interests, obtained the desired profits at the expense of groups with little lobbying power. Women operating within the household under the licence of a male member of one of these pressure groups did considerably better than unorganised independent women. It was not that the weaving industry did not provide opportunities for women, but that its organisation into corporate pressure groups led to the exclusion and exploitation of unorganised (especially female) labour.

The other reason for this restriction of the economic opportunities of women is that the system of risk-sharing and collective insurance provided by the Württemberg system of corporate communities was threatened by the mobility, poverty, disorder, and unlicensed sexuality represented by the phenomenon of independent women.

The theory argues that proto-industrialisation saw a loosening of political and patriarchal controls on women and on female sexuality. In particular, illegitimacy and pre-marital pregnancy are supposed to have become more common. Nothing can have been further from the case in the Nagold Valley. As the seventeenth century progressed, Pietist pastors in town and villages increased the controls and penalties on pre-marital sexual activity. In 1645, Pietist church 'convents' or church 'censures' were established, which met every few weeks and called before them all suspected moral delicts, previously covered less systematically by administrative courts. The baptism of a child born less than 36 weeks after the marriage of the parents was recorded as such in the register, and the phrase 'conceived in concubinage' written in the margin. Couples marrying when the woman was known to be pregnant were wedded in a special penitential prayer-session rather than the usual church service, and this too was recorded in the marriage register. In household listings, *Unehelich* (illegitimate) was included as part of an individual's census identity. By the late seventeenth century, all illegitimate births were being entered upside-down in the parish registers. In the early eighteenth century, after almost a century and a half of proto-industrialisation, illegitimacy rates, despite such conscientious registration, were extremely low, compared with densely industiral communities of comparable size in England.[97] Illegitimate births were about 4 per cent of the total for the population as a whole, but only 2 per cent among births to mothers with any connection with New Draperies weaving. The regulation of female sexuality does not seem to have become less strict as proto-industrialisation progressed.

This, too, can be associated with the corporate structure of local society. Illegitimate children could not inherit, they could not become a citizen of a town or village, save by special dispensation, and they could not be apprenticed to a craft. There was thus no room for them in New Draperies weaving, or any other sector of the economy, and they would merely become a burden on their mothers, and on the village or town poor-rate. In sheer self-protection, it was logical for the risk-sharing corporate community to place restrictions on the work and residence of unmarried women. The evidence suggests that it was largely successful in doing so.

Married women and widows

Women were permitted to be involved in proto-industry in their own right through inheriting the right to weave from a husband when he died. Although in this way large numbers of widows were permitted to earn a living, and thus participated in proto-industrialisation, it is not at all clear that it opened up new opportunities for them. A glance at household size shows that proto-industry enabled women to support fewer dependants than did other occupations. The households of New Draperies weaving widows in 1717 had a mean size of 2.56, whereas the non-weaving female-headed households had a mean size of 3.17. A female New Draperies weaver could feed and support 0.61 fewer people than her non-proto-industrial counterpart.

Nor did proto-industry open new working opportunities to women by enabling them to marry earlier in life. In the Nagold Valley, contrary to the predictions of the theory of proto-industrialisation, New Draperies weaving was associated with later than average marriage for women. Among some three hundred reconstituted marriages in Wildberg at the beginning of the eighteenth century, the brides of New Draperies weavers were on average and on median almost a year older (at 26.5 years) than the brides of men of other occupations (at 25.6 years).[98] Parental consent was apparently still required for the marriages of village weavers' offspring, seventy years after the onset of proto-industrialisation. In 1655, a village weaver's son refused to consider himself betrothed to a girl, on the grounds that 'besides, [his] father will not consent that he take Schüz's daughter'.[99] The girl justified her insistence on the betrothal on the grounds that 'her stepfather Schüz is also of that opinion [that the betrothal should be kept] and this betrothal is not unacceptable to him'.[100]

Just as the expansion of rural industry did not open up new opportunities for women through earlier or freer marriage, so also married women's work options continued to be circumscribed. Both the rural guild and the local courts excluded from New Draperies weaving widows and wives who had not inherited from their husbands the right to practise. At the quarterly regulatory court in 1629, for instance, a neighbour reported that 'Michell Henni's widow buys up yarn from time to time among the New Draperies weavers, although her late husband was no New Draperies weaver'.[101] Only a year after the invasion of 1634, the guild, still in control of the industry in the countryside, exacted the maximum guild fine from a village widow of an old-style coarse woollens weaver for practising the New Draperies craft on the grounds that her husband had never been apprenticed to it.[102]

Although women could inherit the right to weave, the corporation prevented them from transmitting it to their children. The coming of proto-industry had not made economic life more open for one woman, whose father had been a Nagold Valley New Draperies weaver, but who had married a non-Württemberger, and who petitioned in 1657 to be permitted to apprentice her son to the craft; the guild would not accept the boy 'on the grounds that he is foreign'.[103]

The theory of proto-industrialisation argues that the expansion of cottage industry brought women out of 'private' household production, in which they took a subordinate, domestic role, and where their relationships with the outside world were mediated through the market labour of the husband, into 'public' market production, in which they took an active role in the outside world.[104] The English empirical historiography argues, on the contrary, that as cottage industry expanded women were gradually being forced into household labour and dependence on their husbands.[105] For Württemberg, this is a false dichotomy: both market and household work by women was a matter of public knowledge in corporate communities. This is one of the factors which made it easier to regulate, as church court presentations for Sabbath-breaking show. In 1707 three women were fined by the church court for doing laundry on the monthly Day of Prayer and Repentance.[106] In 1711, a woman reported by a female neighbour for spinning for her New Draperies weaver son charged in turn that the neighbour 'also sews on Sunday, which the [neighbour] did not deny, saying that ecclesiastical and temporal [persons] had done the same'.[107] Both women were punished.

Distinctions between public market work and private household production were blurred by the corporate nature of this society, and it would be wrong to draw a firm line between the two, or to assign very different roles to women on either side of the line. Women moved in and out of the market flexibly according to changes in productivity and regulatory constraints; even in household work they were publicly engaged in the economic and social life of the community. For instance, communities required that hot-water laundry be done in the public wash-house, as a fire-protection measure; court minutes bear witness to the careful enforcement of this regulation. Whereas men might be able to preserve social distinctions, all women, regardless of social status, had to work publicly together at the communal washhouse.

This apparently held good for the very highest echelons of rural society. As late as 1657, the highest-ranking Ducal official in the district, the *Keller*, reported to the Wildberg church court that 'his wife had complained to him woefully that when she went into the washhouse today, Hanß Georg Haug's wife and daughter came up to her and accosted her with bitter words, saying that Haug's son had been unjustly put in the stocks, and unjustly driven out of town'.[108] Far from refusing to have anything to do with these women, who came from a far poorer section of the community, the *Keller*'s wife was stung into defending her husband's actions, saying that the woman's son 'was not treated unjustly; they don't sit up there to do injustice to people, the *Herren* [members of the communal court] had a hard job to do, they take their oaths to do as little injustice as possible to anyone'.[109] The *Keller*'s daughter became involved in the quarrel, saying 'her father does injustice to no-one, her father did not do it alone, the church-censors did it'.[110] The dispute ended in physical violence (the *Keller*'s wife threw a washing-slab at Haug's wife) and general recrimination, with the two Haug women using the female privacy of the wash-house to criticise the behaviour of the community officials as a group.

A complex picture emerges of a vigorous female working life surrounding the washhouse and its well, in which women accused and defended their menfolk and expressed forthright opinions about the public life of the community. The case ended not with a hardening of the social gap between the official's female relations and those of the petty offender, but with a public apology between the two women, and a personal plea on the part of the *Keller* and his wife to the court to be lenient with Haug's wife – a reaffirmation of corporate female sociability. Was this public or private production?

Nor did it require proto-industry to endow women with economic and moral authority within marriage. Marriage was a partnership, in which the law gave dominance to the man, but in which the logic of the situation could easily redress the balance. For instance, women continued to view the land which they brought into marriage as their own, and went to considerable lengths to defend it. In the early seventeenth century one woman whose husband was facing foreclosure for debt, argued in the court that 'she ... had not acquiesced in this contract and debt; they should go after the husband, for her husband brought nothing to her; what she has is hers'.[111] One Wildberg woman petitioned for divorce in 1640 on the grounds that her husband 'did not farm her land equally with his own'.[112] A villager's wife justified leaving her husband in 1651 on the grounds that her husband 'had dissipated her property'.[113] In 1652 the elderly wife of a Wildberg man asked the church court to see that her and her husband's property was inventoried because he 'dissipates what she earns'; the court ordered that inventories be made.[114] Another villager's wife complained to the church court that 'he alienated and sold what she brought [to the marriage], for which reason she could not keep house with him ... but if he gave back what he had sold, then she would keep house with him as is right; ... she brought with her some 50 Gulden, which he spent on a piece of land, and sold the piece of land without her prior knowledge and consent'.[115] The conflict was resolved by the man 'promis[ing] to provide her with other security on it [the 50 Gulden] within a month'.[116]

A woman could also exert enough economic authority within the marriage to force her husband to go back on an agreed sale. In 1613, one husband reported to the court that 'when he told his wife of the sale she refused to acquiesce in it, saying it was her inheritance, her third share was not for sale'.[117] Pressed by the other party and by the court, the man stuck by his guns throughout six pages of court minutes, repeating that he could not go ahead with the sale 'since it simply did not please his wife', and finally naming eight witnesses to give evidence of her resistance.[118] In one household where the house was owned by the woman from a previous marriage, the woman's new husband was evidently merely living on sufferance. The sixty-year old couple came before the church court in 1712, six months after their marriage, 'charged with living evilly with one another ... he complains that he gets no bread to eat; [the wife answers] that it occurred on account of eating, that it was impossible for them, in these expensive times, to keep the man with as much bread as he eats; she would allow him what he earns'.[119]

The theory also argues that proto-industrialisation gave rise to a 'more individualised selection' of marriage partners, a weakening of patriarchal controls within the family, and the rise of the affectionate, egalitarian, companionate marriage.[120] However, the evidence indicates that notwithstanding their legal subordination, women traditionally had a great deal of economic and moral authority within marriage. As Wrightson put it for seventeenth-century English marriages, 'it would seem unwise to make too sharp a dichotomy between the "patriarchal" and the "companionate" marriage, and to erect these qualities into a typology of successive stages of family development'.[121] It is improbable that the allocation of economic and other decision-making powers within marriage was a simple function of the occupation of the family. It may be that the optimal allocation of these powers did not change so much as we imagine, but rather merely the external structure of prices, technology and institutions within which these powers were expressed. So long as rural society was corporative and the rural economy subject to regulation and corporate lobbying, even the external expression of women's powers within marriage may have changed very little.

Conclusion

In the Nagold Valley we have observed a society in which women were economically very active, but where their activity was strictly channelled. Neither of the two general theories of women's work under expanding cottage industry can explain this. The theory of proto-industrialisation focusses on the expansion of flexible female labour into market gaps, but because it ignores institutions cannot explain either the previous economic power of women or the subsequent process of exclusion of women from the new opportunities. The English empirical historiography takes the traditional economic powers of women, and their subsequent restriction, as its starting-point, but assigns responsibility unspecifically to capitalism, rather than identifying specific social constraints. A theory of women's work which takes into account both its flexibility in allocating time between the market and the household, and its sensitive response to institutional changes altering the rewards of different uses of time, can explain both the enduring economic powers of women, and the expansions and contractions in women's market work under rural industry.

Demographic shifts (including the effects of war) and technological changes (such as the expansion of New Draperies weaving) could open up niches in labour-markets which male labour could not for the moment fill. Women, with their greater flexibility and more limited existing opportunities, could readily shift out of the household and into the market. But the system of legal and corporate institutions in the society was such that women were pushed out of these niches when the male labour supply adjusted to fill them. Without corporate groups of their own to represent them, in the longer term women tended to occupy only those interstices of the local economy where the earnings were not worth lobbying for – or they adopted a position in the household of a male, who did have the right to industrial practice.

Repeatedly we have seen how the flexibility of women's labour was an essential element in all parts of the early modern economy. Women were active in farming, distribution, retailing, heavy trades and textiles; and were sexually valued for their strength. A craftsman or farmer's wife was his main assistant, exercising the craft in his absence, and rendering householding untenable when she died. For similar reasons, we may guess, communities which harassed women in independent business tolerated them when they entered service or provided day-labour. New Draperies weaving edged single women out of weaving, combing and weft-making, which competed with men, but set them to work to fill the scarcity of spun yarn. Married women, on the other hand, moved flexibly in and out of public and private production, between which there was no sharp dichotomy. In so far as women greased the wheels of the labour-market, they were permitted an enormous range of economic activity; their flexibility was a valued attribute to the whole economy.

The obverse of the flexibility women's labour was its exploitability, which was due to its lack of corporate organisation in an economy dominated by corporate pressure groups. What enabled women to be squeezed out of certain forms of economic independence was their very flexibility: the fact that women were not organised into pressure groups and were thus at the mercy of government regulation in response to those who were so organised. When put under pressure by corporate groups, it was more worthwhile for female labour to return to household production, to exercise market production from within a male-headed household, or to adapt by moving to a less constrained (but consequently less lucrative) part of the market.

Why did women not in turn set up pressure groups? Partly, their flexibility and fragmentation made the relative costs of adapting far lower than the costs of organising to lobby, which were very high. Almost all the women with resources to spend on such a project were already yoked into the system of male corporations, by the close working partnership of marriage, with the additional incentive of inheriting the husband's rights on his death. Those women with an interest in economic independence, specifically in organising in opposition to existing pressure groups, exercised far less economic power; they were scattered, poorly informed, and completely lacking in support from the authorities. The grass-roots organising campaign of the New Draperies weavers to obtain their guilds in the 1590s, or that of the merchant-dyers to obtain their company monopoly in the 1640s, show the absolute necessity of state support for corporate organisation. Existing corporations were certain to oppose the establishment of organised female labour (for example, a spinners' guild) since independent women were already seen as competing for resources and livelihood niches against men with families to support. Situated, as they were, close to the boundary of subsistence, early modern communities and individuals were rationally averse to risking innovations in economic and social organisation which posed even a potential threat to livelihoods.

This institutional inertia raised the costs of organising female labour to an unrealistic level, and the flexibility of female labour reduced the costs of adapting to institutional constraints. Thus women tended, as we have seen, to drift to the (powerless) periphery of the economy, except where there was a shortage of male labour, or a powerful male pressure group which was able to exploit female labour to reduce its own costs. In explaining ebbs and flows in women's work in the market, it is not necessary to invoke a spontaneous reaction of households to the spread of a new occupation, nor a widespread change in social mores concerning women's independence accompanying 'the spread of the capitalistic organisation of industry'.[122] Changes in relative productivities of working in the household and the market are sufficient to explain women's allocation of time to different forms of work. The findings of this chapter indicate that a knowledge of the specific functioning of institutional constraints on these relative productivities is indispensible for an understanding of the great shifts in the European economic and demographic system between the early modern period and the present.

Notes

1 This is a commonplace of labour economics; see, for example, R. G. Ehrenberg and R. S. Smith, *Modern Labour Economics: Theory and Public Policy*, 2nd edn, 1985, Glenview, Ill., pp. 193–218.
2 The term first appeared in F. F. Mendels, 'Proto-industrialization: the first phase of the industrialization process', *Journal of Economic History*, 32 (1972). The most exhaustive development of the theory is in P. Kriedte, H. Medick and J. Schlumbohm, *Industrialization before Industrialization: Rural Industry in the Genesis of Capitalism*, Cambridge, 1981, first published as *Industrialisierung vor der Industrialisierung*, Göttingen, 1977.
3 Kriedte, Medick and Schlumbohm, *Industrialization before Industrialization*, pp. 61–2.
4 *Ibid.*, p. 51.
5 *Ibid.*, p. 56.
6 *Ibid.*, pp. 63, 70.
7 *Ibid.*, p. 70.
8 I. Pinchbeck, *Women Workers and the Industrial Revolution, 1750–1850*, London, 1930, p. 293.

9 *Ibid.*, p. 126.
10 *Ibid.*, p. 121.
11 A. Clark, *Working Life of Women in the Seventeenth Century*, London, 1982 (originally published 1919), p. 183.
12 *Ibid.*, p. 196.
13 M. Berg, *The Age of Manufactures 1700–1820*, London, 1985, p. 156.
14 *Ibid.*, p. 158.
15 K. Snell, *Annals of the Labouring Poor 1660–1900*, Cambridge, 1985, p. 309.
16 W. Troeltsch, *Die Calwer Zeughandlungskompagnie und ihre Arbeiter: Studien zur Gewerbe- und Sozialgeschichte Altwürttembergs*, Jena, 1897.
17 S. C. Ogilvie, 'Corporatism and regulation in rural industry: Württemberg woollen weaving 1590–1740', unpublished Ph.D. dissertation, University of Cambridge, 1985, chapter 6.
18 *Ibid.*, chapter 2.
19 *Ibid.*, chapter 4.
20 *Ibid.*, chapter 5.
21 *Ibid.*, chapter 2 and *passim*.
22 *Ibid.*, chapter 5.
23 *Ibid.*, chapter 2.
24 *Ibid.*, chapter 2.
25 C. Poni, 'A proto-industrial city: Bologna: XVI–XVIII century', in *Eighth International Economic History Congress 'A' Themes*, Budapest, 1982; A. G. Enciso, 'Economic structure of Cameros' dispersed industry: a case study in eighteenth century Castilian textile industry', in *ibid.*; J. K. J. Thomson, *Clermont-de-Lodève 1633–1789: Fluctuations in the Prosperity of a Lanquedocian Cloth-making Town*, Cambridge, 1982; and H. Kisch, 'From monopoly to laissez-faire: the early growth of the Wupper Valley textile trades', *The Journal of European Economic History*, vol. 1 (1972).
26 On England, see K. Wrightson, *English society 1580–1680*, London, 1982; on The Netherlands, J. de Vries, *The Dutch Rural Economy in the Golden Age, 1500–1700*, Berkeley, 1974.
27 On Shepshed, see D. Levine, *Family Formation in an Age of Nascent Capitalism*, London, 1977; on Flanders, Mendels, 'Proto-industrialization'; on southern Germany, J. Knodel, 'Demographic transitions in German villages', Population Studies Centre Research Report, University of Michigan, no. 82, 1982; on the Ravensberg villages, W. Mager, 'Haushalt und Familie in protoindustrieller Gesellschaft: Spenge (Ravensberg) während der ersten Hälfte des 19. Jahrhunderts: Eine Fallstudie', in N. Bulst, J. Goy, and J. Hoock (eds.), *Familie zwischen Tradition und Moderne: Studien zur Geschichte der Familie in Deutschland und Frankreich vom 16. bis zum 20. Jahrhundert*, Göttingen, 1981; on Thimerais, see B. Derouet, 'Une démographie sociale différentielle', *Annales ESC*, vol. 35 (1980); on southern Flanders, C. Vandenbroeke, *Handlingen van de Geschieden Oudheidkundige Kring*, Oudenaarde, 1976; on Ireland, L. Clarkson and B. Collins, 'Proto-industrialization in an Irish town, 1820–21', in *Eighth International Economic History Congress 'A' Themes*, Budapest, 1982; on Bethnal Green and Sudbury, see M. Clarke, 'Household and family in Bethnal Green 1851–1871', unpublished Ph.D. dissertation, University of Cambridge, 1986.
28 Württembergische Hauptstaatsarchiv (Württemberg State Archive, henceforth WHSA) A573 Bü 6967, *Seelentabelle*, 1736. Even including the mostly single-person female-headed fragments of families, lodging with other households, but deriving a separate livelihood from spinning or charity, more than one-quarter of earning units owned land.
29 *Ibid.*

30 Pfarrarchiv Wildberg (Wildberg Parish Archive, henceforth PAW) Kirchenkonvents-protokolle (henceforth KKP) I, 26 August 1646, fol. 3v–4v: 'dem Küehstall gemüstet'.

31 PAW KKP I, 26 August 1646, fol. 5r: 'vnd. der Predig hew, in stall getrag'.

32 WHSA A573 Bü 86 Jahresvogtgericht (yearly governor's court, henceforth JVG), 19 November 1632, fol. 169r: 'habe, Friderich bub. Magt, ein Mistbehren, in anbringers hauß entlehnen wollen, darüb. sein dochter gesagt haben solle, Sie haben sonnsten all hoffart, warumben Sie das nicht auch Kauffen, die Magdt were heimb zogen, Unnd Ihrer Frawen zu ohren getragen, ob hette sein dochter vermelt, solls gelt, von dem gestohlenen Vich nemmen, Unnd ein beeren darumb Kauffen.'

33 WHSA A573 Bü 15 fol. 298v 25 January 1616.

34 PAW KKP I, 7 May 1658, fol. 190r: 'habe Er vnderweegs Zue Ihren gesagt Sie seye so hipsch vnd starckh Er möchte bey Ihren schlaffen'.

35 WHSA A573 Bü 122 fol. 61r, 15 December 1619: 'Nachdem man Andere Maister hew unnd Straw zuerhalltung des Jenig vüchs so man zue wintters Zeitten uff das Luder, wegen der wölff thuett, besolldung haben, ... Alls Pittett Sie, man wolle Auch derselben Thaylhafftig mach.'

36 WHSA A573 Bü 128 fol. 69r, 22 June 1642.

37 WHSA A573 Bü 6967, *Seelentabelle*, 1736.

38 WHSA A573 Bü 15 fol. 568v, 16 January 1622: 'die leütt redeten In d. Statt, Wie sie Ihr schmalz Verkauffe ... Wann sein fraw nuhr ein Vierling schmalz Verkaufft, so fehle es ein halber vlg.'

39 WHSA A573 Verhörstag (administrative court, henceforth VHT) Bü 25 fol. 22v, 23 December 1602.

40 WHSA A573 VHT Bü 24 fol. 25r, 23 February 1603.

41 WHSA A573 Bü 129b fol. 19r, 5 January 1657: 'habe auß. d. Mühlin sonst Keine mittel'.

42 PAW KKP IV, 26 February 1706, fol. 254r.

43 WHSA A573 Bü 6967, *Seelentabelle*, 1736.

44 PAW KKP I, 5 September 1656, fol. 141r.

45 PAW KKP IV, 31 May 1709, fol. 268v.

46 PAW KKP IV, 17 July 1711, fol. 280v–281v.

47 PAW KKP IV, 4 January 1715, fol. 315r–315v.

48 WHSA A573 Bü 127 fol. 83v, 28 October 1633.

49 WHSA A573 Bü 127 fol. 95v: 'müeste allso, weil er ein Kranckhe Fraw wann er widerumben fort müesste ehlendtlich Umb dz seinige kommen'.

50 WHSA A573 Bü 90 Vogt- und Rüggericht (governor's and regulatory court, henceforth VRG), 1 December 1668.

51 WHSA A573 Bü 90 JVG, 24 October 1670.

52 WHSA A573 Bü 6967, *Seelentabelle*, 1736; WHSA A573 Bü 6965, *Seelenregister*, 1717; WHSA A573 Bü 6966, *Seelenregister*, 1722.

53 WHSA A573 Bü 128 fol. 3v, 16 February 1636: 'damit er desto füeglicher seinen güettern abwartten'.

54 WHSA A573 Bü 129b fol. 19v, 9 January 1657: 'habe Kinder Und ein schwehr Gueht, dahero Er sich ohne einer weib nicht mahr außbringen khönde ... Sintemahlen wan Er der Zeith erwarten müeste die Veldt geschäfften ins mittel kämen, Und Er dardurch an Veldt geschäfften merckhlich impediert werde.'

55 WHSA A573 Bü 129c fol. 21v, 6 February 1664: 'Motiven: Seye ein Witwer bey 3 jahren her ... khönne die güether nimmer manuteniren und im baw erhalten.'

56 WHSA A573 Bü 122 fol. 79v, 23 April 1620: 'khende ohne weib nit heußlich. whonen, mießte einem Maister schaffen'.

57 WHSA A573 Bü 125 fol. 28v, 9 April 1627: 'Treibt würthschafft, Kann mit frembd. leüth. ohne schad. nit haußen.'

58 WHSA A573 Bü 128 fol. 2r, 27 January 1636: 'wegen seiner handthierung, beschwehrlicher quartierung und grosßer haußunruhr'.

59 WHSA A573 Bü 128 fol. 2r, 27 January 1636: 'hatt 4 Kleine Kinder grosße Armutey, kan kein gesindt zue erhalten [sic]'.

60 WHSA A573 Bü 128 fol. 3v, 21 February 1636: 'er der Statt diener'.

61 WHSA A573 Bü 16 fol. 15r ff 9 December 1623.

62 WHSA A573 Bü 16 fol. 79v, 19 August 1624.

63 For instance, PAW KKP I, 26 February 1647, fol. 15r: 'haben u.schinen Sonntag vnder der Predig ein Zettel angespannt'.

64 PAW KKP IV, 1705–20.

65 WHSA A573 Bü 15 fol. 379r, 15 December 1618: 'verhof weit.s nitt dan den landleüfigen Zins Zegeben schuldig'.

66 *Ibid.*, fol. 379v: 'der Clager mitt [inserted: den] empfangnen geltt samptt dem landleüfigen Zins, verniget sein soll'.

67 WHSA A573 Bü 16 fol. 3r, 20 August 1623: 'hette er ermellter seiner schwester, die thuech nicht, Aber dargegen einen Wucherlichen zinß Zum Andern Mahl raichen muessen, da er sich nuhn beschwehrt, dz er solche 60f nicht mehr Also Verzinsen Wolle, Were sie, die schwester mit Ihme eins Word., das gellt, landtleüffig zu Verpensioniren, Welches er Also 3 Jahrlang Continuirt'.

68 As Alice Clark portrays the situation of women in seventeenth-century England, in *Working Life of Women*.

69 The term *Eigenbrötlerinnen* referred to single women who 'earned their own bread', without either supporting a family of their own, or being a servant or dependent in the family of an adult male or a widow with land or an inherited right to practice a craft. They were generally disapproved of in Swabian society, and ultimately the term became one of opprobrium, referring to an eccentric or a recluse.

70 WHSA A573 Bü 86 fol. 265r, 24 November 1646: 'bei etlichen burgern alhie, hielten sich etliche ledige magden auff, welche seines erachtens dahin anzuehallten weren, daß Sie sich verding. thetten'.

71 *Ibid.*: 'Einer gantzen burgerschafft Verbotten bei einer frevel straff, dergestallten, daß sich solche möchten in 3 Wochen Verdingen [crossed out: sollen] dann wo sich eine oder die ander hernach erfinden solle würdt obbemellte straff Unnachläßig eingezogen werd.' Three Gulden was more than half a year's wages for a servant-girl, and a considerable sum for most households in the community.

72 WHSA A573 Bü 86 fol. 384r, 2 November 1647: '2 Aigen bröthlerin hats in der Statt, die hin unnd wider sich aufhalten, Unnd Keinem Ehrlichen maister dienen wöllen, So wider die Fürstl: ordnungen.'

73 WHSA A573 Bü 86 fol. 211r, 17 November 1648: 'weren ledige Madtlen für sich selbsten alhie, die sich nit verdingen: oder einem Maister schaffen thetten, so nit zuegeduld, Namblich Ins Bretten Michelins hauß eine von rothfelden, Ind des Jeremiaßen hanßen hauß eine von Jesingen, so Jeweilen ins Veiten hauß, auß Und ein wandern thette'.

74 WHSA A573 Bü 86 fol. 300r, 29 October 1650.

75 WHSA A573 Bü 90, 16 July 1660.

76 WHSA A573 Bü 90, 29 October 1660.

77 *Ibid.*

78 WHSA A573 Rüggericht (regulatory court, henceforth RG) Bü 86 fol. 95r, 23 May 1628: 'die Jung Kübelgretha ... die doch ein Mann von Effringen Namens N: Sper, habe, were nit zugedulden'.

79 WHSA A573 JVG Bü 86 fol. 225, 1 November 1641: 'des Pfarrers weib von Eschelbronn, so sich selbsten von Ihrem man schaidet, in der Statt nicht zue gedulden'.

80 WHSA A573 JVG Bü 86 fol. 58r, 30 October 1626: 'Michel Fronmiller haltte ein dürnen uff, die in einem Jahr wohl drey dienst gehabt, spinne Immertz am radt.'

81 WHSA A573 RG, Bü 86 fol. 206r, 4 June 1640: 'Margretha Michel Geckhlins see: dochter solle in kein Predigt Undt bettstundt gehen, Leichtfertig schwören, Undt alle Sontag zwisch. d. Predigt. spinnen.'

82 Troeltsch, *Die Calwer Zeughandlungskompagnie*, p. 445: 'Ledige döchtern und Andere Persohnen'.

83 *Ibid.*: 'grossen ufschlag In den zug und das Garn verursacht'.

84 *Ibid.*, p. 446: 'dergleichen Töchtern zu andern und nohtwendigen hauss Arbaiten und geschäfften Auzuehallten, oder sich in Ehrliche Dienst einzuelassen verursacht werden'.

85 Kriedte, Medick, and Schlumbohm, *Industrialization before Industrialization*, pp. 44, 51–2, 60–2, 91, 95.

86 Troeltsch, *Die Calwer Zeughandlungskompagnie*, pp. 446ff.

87 WHSA A573 Bü 791 fol. 19r.

88 WHSA A573 Bü 816 no folio, 6 March 1641: 'vorlauffend Vhnordnungen'.

89 WHSA A573 Bü fol. 38–9, 8 January 1671.

90 WHSA A573 Bü 826 Zettel 15: 'ein Designation aller der Jenigen in Dorffschafften, welche wolle spinnen, mit dem Anhang wahin? vnd wem mit Namen, 13 Blatt'.

91 *Ibid.* 'vßer Landts'. Similar initiatives were undertaken in following years, e.g., WHSA A573 Bü 827 fol. 46 and Zettel 1, 10 February 1672.

92 WHSA A573 Bü 90, 1 November 1669.

93 WHSA A573 Bü 896 (1744–45): 'um willen Er seine Magd der Ordnung zuwider gesellenweiß kammen laßen'.

94 WHSA A573 Bü 897 (1745–46): 'haben wider das verbott ledige Wollen Kämmerin gehalten'.

95 WHSA A573 Bü 908 (1756–57): 'weil sich durch 1 weibs bild schafen lassen'.

96 WHSA A573 Bü 897 (1745–46): 'zum erstenmal nur Zur Warnung'.

97 For further discussion of illegitimacy see S. C. Ogilvie, 'Coming of age in a corporate society: capitalism, pietism and family authority in rural Württemberg, 1590–1740', *Continuity and Change*, vol. 1 (1986).

98 Ogilvie, 'Corporatism and regulation in rural industry', chapter 6.

99 PAW KKP I, 31 August 1655, fol. 127v: 'vnd will der vatter Balthas Pfeiff. auch nicht Zuegeben, daß Er deß Schüz. Tochter nemme'.

100 PAW KKP I, 31 August 1655, fol. 127v: 'der Stieffvatter Schüz ist auch der mainung vnd solcher Ehe v.spruch Ihme nicht zue wid'.

101 WHSA A573 Bü 86 fol. 132v, 27 October 1629: 'Michell hennis Wittib, Kauffe hin Unnd Wid. bey der Knappenschafft garn auff, da doch Ihr mann seeliger Kein Knapp gewees.'

102 WHSA A573 Bü 810 no folio.

103 WHSA A573 Bü 129b fol. 28f, 5 January 1657: 'Ess wolle aber dz handwerckh daß Knäblin nicht recipiren vß ursach. daß es frembd sey.'

104 Kriedte, Medick, and Schlumbohm, *Industrialization before Industrialization*, pp. 61–3.

105 Clark, *Working Life of Women*, p. 126.

106 PAW KKP IV, 28 January 1707, fol. 261r.

107 PAW KKP IV, 21 August 1711, fol. 283v.

108 PAW KKP I, 11 June 1657, fol. 160v: 'daß Ihme von seiner haußfrawen were wehemuethig clagendt Angebracht worden, daß alß sie heutigs tags in daß wäsch hauß gangen, seye hanß Georg haug. fraw vnd dochter Zue ihren in dz wäschhauß kommen, sie mit rawen wortten angefahren Zue ihren vermeldt man [inserted: habe] ihren deß haug. bueben ohnschuldiger weiß in dz narrenhäußlen gelegt und ohnschuldiger weiß außer der Statt vertriben'.

109 *Ibid.*, 'mann werde Ihne nicht ohnrecht gethon haben man sitze nicht droben dz

man d. leüth ohnrecht thüe die herrn haben ein schwehres auff ihnen sie thuen ihren aiden darauff dz sie souihl müglich niemandt ohnrecht thuen wollen'.

110 *Ibid.*, fol. 165r: 'ihr vatter thüe Niemandt ohnrecht, Ihr vatter habs nicht allein gethon die Kirchen censores habens gethon'.

111 WHSA A573 Bü 15 fol. 157r: 'Sie hab ... nitt In diß Contract vnd schuldtt bewilligt, soll dem Mann Angreiffen, dann er Ir Mann nichts Zue Ihr gebrachtt, waß sie hab, sey Ihr.'

112 WHSA A573 Bü 128 fol. 50v, 20 August 1640: 'bawte Ihre güetlin nit gleicher die seinen'.

113 PAW KKP I, 3 September 1651, fol. 66v: 'habe er Ihro daß Ihrige verthan'.

114 PAW KKP I, 15 October 1652, fol. 82r: 'verthue, was Sie auffbringen'.

115 PAW KKP I, 10 December 1652, fol. 87r: 'Er Ihr das Zugebrachtt abalieniert vnd verkhaufft, desswegen Sie nicht mit Ihm haussen khönde ... so Er aber das verkhauffte wider erstatten werde, als dan wölle Sie mit Ihm hausen, wie recht ist. ... Sie Ihn in die 50f Zugebracht, so Er auff ein giltlein gewendet, vnd das gütlein ohn Ihr vorwissen vnd willen verkhauffet.'

116 *Ibid.*: 'verspricht, innerhalb monats frisst, Sie vmb solches anderwerts Zuversichern'.

117 WHSA A573 Bü 15 fol. 141r, 28 January 1613: 'da nun er c: solchen Kauf seiner hausf: Angezaigt, Hab sie In solchen Kauff nitt bewilligen wöllen, sey Ir Erbguett, Sey Ir drittertheyl nitt fayhl'.

118 *Ibid.*: 'dann seinem weib Ain mahl der Kauf nitt Lieb'.

119 PAW KKP IV, 21 October 1712, fol. 292v.

120 Kriedte, Medick, and Schlumbohm, *Industrialization before Industrialization*, pp. 61–3.

121 Wrightson, *English Society*, p. 104.

122 Clark, *Working Life of Women*, p. 41; see pp. 306–8 for a succinct statement of the argument that the advent of capitalism changed beliefs concerning women's independence.

PART TWO

Women's work and the family economy

Chapter Four

Strains in the 'firm of Wife, Children and Friends'? Middle-class women and employment in early nineteenth-century England

CATHERINE HALL

If the stock of our bliss is in strangers' hands rested
The fund ill secured oft in bankruptcy ends,
But the heart is given bills which are never protested
When drawn on the firm of *Wife Children and Friends*.

Wolverhampton travelling salesman, 1811

In 1776 a baby girl was born to Captain Weeton and his wife in Lancaster. Her father regretted that she was a girl; 'unless a father can provide independent fortunes for his daughters', he argued, 'they must either be made mop squeezers, or mantua makers, whereas sons can easily make their way in the world'.[1] Miss Weeton never became either a mop squeezer or a mantua maker, but her struggles to survive economically and socially, powerfully recorded in her journals and letters, vividly demonstrate the difficulties for middle-class women in living as independent persons in late-eighteenth- and early-nineteenth-century England. Her father was a sea captain, the son of a farmer. Her mother had been a lady's maid before her marriage and was the daughter of a butcher. She would take in lodgers during the Lancaster Assizes to provide a little extra money. In 1782 Captain Weeton died at sea and his widow was left with the little girl and her younger brother and only a small property on which to live.

In 1784 the three of them moved to the village of Up-Holland and there Mrs Weeton established a school with the help of her daughter who cooked, cleaned and sewed for the household, allowing them to manage without a servant. The son and heir, the focus of all the hopes and prayers of his mother and sister, was meanwhile sent to a clergyman's school as a dayboy and was articled at the age of fourteen in Preston. The two women suffered many deprivations and hardships for the sake of the boy, expecting that they would benefit in later life. As his sister acidly commented, however, 'it was a vain expectation, for like all his sex, when he was grown up, he considered what had been done for him was right; that he owed no gratitude to us, for we were but *female* relatives, and had only done our duty'.[2]

In 1797 Mrs Weeton died but Miss Weeton kept up the school to maintain her brother during his clerkship. Once finished he made a successful marriage with the daughter of a factory owner and was launched into the professional classes. Neither he nor his in-laws liked the idea of his sister running a village school for it was too public a display of her need for money. Nor did they want her to go governessing. They would have preferred her to take a few acres, keep a cow and a servant, and manage on her income.

In 1809 Miss Weeton gave up the school, left the village having let her cottage and bought the one next door as an investment, and for some time lived in lodgings on Merseyside. She invested some money in property in Liverpool without consulting her brother, and further asserting her independence she took a job in December 1809 as a companion and governess in the Lake District. Her brief was to act as improver and educator to the younger woman, previously a servant, who had married the gentleman son of a Preston banking family, and who needed training in the ways of gentility. 'My dear Tom', Miss Weeton explained to her brother,

> It is not mere education in language, manners, books, and work I have to attend to, but to persist in the proper direction and management of the servants and the household ... if any rules of etiquette with which it is probable I may be unacquainted, should occur to you or Mrs. Weeton, I should really be obliged to you to write them down for me, particularly at the dinner or supper table.[3]

Miss Weeton's initially favourable impressions of the Pedder household, Dove's Nest, did not last. She was shocked by the effects of marrying across ranks and commented on the innumerable humiliations Mrs Pedder suffered at the hands of her husband who 'seems to think that by lording it over two or three women he increased his own consequence'.[4] In her opinion Mr Pedder treated his wife worse than the servants, knowing that she could not leave him. It was perhaps her many discussions with Mrs Pedder as to her husband's autocratic ways that inspired her to write a short essay on women in which she argued that women are equal to men and 'ought to be treated as such in every respect'.[5]

In 1811 she left the Pedder household and after staying with friends for some months and holidaying on her own in the Isle of Man where she took long walks by herself (an unusual practice for a woman, as she knew), she went as a governess to a mill-owning family in Yorkshire. Here she experienced the social marginality which Charlotte Bronte was to evoke so powerfully with the image of Jane Eyre sitting on the edge of the 'company', there but not there. Two years in Yorkshire with the 'plodding, money-getting' manufacturers and farmers were enough for Miss Weeton and soon after leaving she married Aaron Stock, a cotton-spinner in Wigan.[6] Ten months later, when she was thirty-nine, a daughter, Mary, was born.

The marriage was a disaster. In retrospect she was convinced that Stock only married her for her small fortune, over which he gained complete control. In earlier years she had thought of marriage, tired of the contempt associated with being an old maid, of the strange looks and comments that were passed on her independence, and the restrictions that went with being a woman on her own, yet fearful of 'the conviction that one is merely addressed for the sake of the money one is worth'.[7] The reality of marriage she found unbearable, for she was cruelly treated both mentally and physically by her husband. In 1822 the couple separated. As a married woman Mrs Stock was at the mercy of her husband with no rights either to her child or her property. The rest of her life she lived in lodgings, excluded from society as a separated woman with no money. She constantly struggled with her husband both to extract an allowance equal to the interest on her property and to be permitted to see her daughter. She found her main sustenance in reading, from Mme de Stael to Shakespeare and from Lady Mary Wortley Montague to the newspaper. She wrote bitterly:

> When man injures woman how can she defend herself? Her frame is weaker, her spirit timid; and if she be a wife, there is scarce a man anywhere to be found who will use the slightest exertion in her defence; and her own sex cannot, having no powers. She has no hope from law, for man, woman's enemy, exercises, as well as makes those laws. She cannot have a jury of her peers or equals, for men, every where prejudiced against the sex, are her jurors; man is her judge.[8]

Miss Weeton's life, spanning the years 1776–1844, gives us fascinating if disturbing glimpses into the working lives of middle-class ladies. Schoolmistress, lady companion, governess, wife, independent lady living in genteel penury, these were familiar routes for a middle-class woman in this period. In this chapter I attempt to explore the working world of middle-class women, to look at the kinds of work they did in the late eighteenth and early nineteenth centuries and the ways in which their work contracted and was re-defined, while that of their husbands, fathers and brothers opened up. It is these changes which provide the context for the feminist demand in the 1850s for more training and employment for middle-class women, together with a change in the laws on married women's property. Miss Weeton's private cry of despair, that 'every female should know how to earn a living' was to become a rallying cry for England's first organised feminist movement.[9]

Brewer argues that 1 million out of a population of 7 million in eighteenth-century England can be described as of the 'middling sort' and claims that their numbers were expanding by the closing decades of that century.[10] This tallies with the estimates of historians of the early nineteenth century who are roughly agreed in their estimate of 20–25 per cent of the total population being middle class.[11] That middle-class world was peopled with farmers, merchants, manufacturers, tradesmen and professionals. Their fortunes rested on either the manufacture and sale of an immense variety of material goods – from Derbyshire stockings to Birmingham candlesticks, from Gloucestershire cheeses to Suffolk lawnmowers, from Yorkshire woollens to Kidderminster carpets; or the production and sale of material and cultural services – the clergyman tending the spiritual welfare of his flock, the dentist caring for their teeth, the physician and surgeon their health, the lawyer their property, the architect their buildings, the novelist and poet their imaginative fare, the essayist their moral and political diet. Within the sector levels of income varied widely and a broad line of distinction can be drawn between the upper and the lower middle class with different styles of economic enterprise, different patterns of housing, different ways of organising their inheritance and varieties of religious and political affiliation. A strong case, however, can be made for the creation of a cultural identity across these boundaries which drew together in some ways the disparate elements of the class.[12]

Estimates as to how many of the women within this class worked in the sense of 'gainful employment' are extremely hard to make. The fundamental difficulty lies in the ways in which the sources mask the work of married women since family enterprises are listed under the male head of household. Women appear in the trade directories, for example, as widows and single women running their own businesses, but the team of husband and wife almost never achieved formal recognition. Similarly, up to 1851 the census gives little help with women's work. Those of 1811 and 1821 focussed on asking about the occupations of families, 'which question had entirely failed, from the impossibility of deciding whether females of the family, children, and servants were to be classed as if of no occupation, or of the occupation of the adult males of the family'.[13] This difficulty was resolved in 1831 by deciding to focus on adult males, a focus which gives us little help in establishing women's occupations. In 1841 both men and women were questioned and some evidence exists as to the work of single women and widows but the Registrar-General in his comments on the figures felt bound to explain the numbers of women without any occupation returned as consisting 'generally of unmarried women living with their parents, and of the wives of professional men or shopkeepers, living upon the earnings, but not considered as carrying on the occupations of their husbands'.[14] Such generalised assumptions tell us more about the values and expectations of the Registrar-General than the everyday lives of these women. The major occupations listed in 1841 which were most likely to be taken up by middle-class women included those in the retail trades, hotel and innkeepers, dressmakers and schoolmistresses.[15]

By 1851 there was some recognition of the partiality of the previous figures and it was acknowledged that, 'Women ... in certain branches of business at home render important services; such as the wives of farmers, of small shopkeepers, innkeepers, shoemakers, butchers' and should be listed as such.[16] At the same time a major new category was introduced in the census, that of 'wife, mother and mistress of an English family', a category that gave formal status to the ideological construction of women as dependants of men.[17] This census, which revealed to the horror-struck nation that one in four wives and two in three widows were 'engaged in some extraneous occupation' also gave official status to the English wife and mother and argued that the 'proper duties' of women 'cannot be neglected without imminent peril to their children – to the nation of the next generation'.[18]

The economic activities of middle-class women were underpinned by a set of legal and property relations which crucially affected both expectations and possibilities. Widows and single women had independent legal status but married women had no separate legal identity, could not enter a partnership, could not make contracts, could not sue or be sued. Legally they were 'covered' by their husbands and could only operate in the market on behalf of their men.[19] Customary practice assumed that it was men who would be active in the world of commerce, women would be provided for. A study of inheritance patterns, for example, amongst the Birmingham, Essex and Suffolk middle class in the period from 1780 to 1850, has shown that though sons and daughters tended to inherit equally the sons were given forms of property which they were expected to work with and would provide a basis for expansion and accumulation. The daughters inherited forms of property which would provide an income and allow them to be dependent – a life assurance, an annuity, money in trust. The development of life assurance and the annuity are significant in that they allowed middle-class men who did not have land to provide in a secure way for their widows and daughters. The trust, a device heavily utilised by the upper middle class in the late eighteenth and early nineteenth centuries, allowed men to ensure an income for dependants while the capital in trust could be utilised by the overwhelmingly male trustees.[20] The law, together with such testamentary practices, ensured that women did not operate freely in the market. Their actual wealth, in urban properties, in bonds, in shares, was extensive – their potential to use that wealth in order to expand it was extremely limited. It is hardly surprising that amongst the first concerns of the feminists of the 1850s were the demands to change the law on married women's property and to educate middle-class women in the ways of business.

Miss Weeton's mother, the daughter of a tradesman, thought nothing of taking in lodgers or establishing a small village school in the 1770s and 1780s. In this she was simply following the pattern of the majority of middle-class women who would expect to contribute to the family income, or as widows to provide, in whatever ways possible. Considerable evidence has now been accumulated of the economic activity of middle-class women in the early modern period. This evidence suggests an extremely varied range of economic activities carried on in a world dominated legally, socially and financially by men.[21] Patterns of occupational segregation, so familiar in the twentieth century, are already apparent with the clustering of working-class as well as middle-class women in certain trades and sectors. In London there was a high concentration of women in spinning, laundering and nursing by the early eighteenth century.[22] In Oxford the businesses most often run by women were the food and drink trades, leather working (specifically glove- and shoemaking) and clothing – sectors which clearly connected with women's domestic activities.[23] In the Midlands women's activities as market traders were limited and were to become more so.[24] A study of the Birmingham Directories in this period, however, makes it clear that within the metal trades occupational segregation as we now know it was not yet clearly established. The late eighteenth-century Directories, for example, reveal women agents, awl-blademakers, bell founders, bellow-makers, edge-toolmakers, iron founders, lock-makers, hinge-makers and platers. By the 1850s no women active in these sectors are recorded. Indeed the pattern of occupational segregation was by then far more fixed and the main women's trades listed by the 1830s and 1840s were the familiar ones of milliner, stawbonnet-maker, stay-maker, hosier and dressmaker, shopkeeper, innkeeper, lodging-housekeeper and schoolmistress.[25]

In the trades where women were active with men their opportunities and powers were restricted. In Oxford, as Prior's work has shown, those widows running businesses were tacitly exluded from office in the guilds and there is no evidence that they attended regular meetings of the guilds and companies. The common law allowed single women and widows to trade but borough custom made it difficult. Some guilds, as for example the tailors, did not encourage widows to maintain their husbands' businesses and actively discouraged them by only allowing them to take one apprentice. Furthermore, the form of apprenticeship undertaken under the supervision of a woman inevitably neglected some aspects of training which only a man could do.[26] Women seem to have taken small numbers of apprentices generally and usually the apprenticeship deeds appear in the name of the couple.[27] In the southern and eastern counties, as Snell has shown, there was a high level of apprenticeship for girls in as wide a variety of trades as boys.[28] But the differential meaning of apprenticeship for the two sexes may well have been considerable. Lantz's research on eighteenth-century Essex and Staffordshire suggests high levels of apprenticeship for girls but with strictly limited thresholds both in skill and training.[29] Their training in most trades included the learning of feminine values and behaviour just as young men learnt the symbols and meanings of masculinity through the rituals and games of apprenticeship and its rites of passage.[30]

A major field of women's economic activity in the eighteenth century was as wives, daughters, mothers and sisters active in family enterprises. In farming as Pinchbeck argues, 'it was still customary for the wife of a large farmer to take an active share in the management of the household'.[31] This could involve the production of food, in the large kitchens beloved of Cobbett, a good deal of the clothing would also be provided for the household by the mistress in the intervals between the care of the dairy, the calves, pigs and poultry, the garden and orchard. It was the dairy which was the most productive aspect of the work of farmers' wives and 'on all but the largest farms, the mistress superintended every stage of the business and performed all the more difficult operations herself'.[32] She would also be responsible for the business side of the dairy, taking her butters and cheeses to market herself or dealing with the relevant tradesmen, and training and managing the young women who helped her. It was perfectly acceptable for a widow or daughter to carry on a farm if a farmer died without a male heir, as Young's frequent mentions of women farmers make clear.[33]

The same pattern can be found both in traditional trades and in new areas of manufacture. Family enterprises were informal partnerships between husband and wife in which the labour of both was essential. The wives of retailers were responsible for running the large households with their children, apprentices, paid workers and servants, as well as minding the shop when necessary and looking after business affairs when their husbands were away.[34] Their services could include anything from doing the books to mending the apprentices' socks, from checking the credit-worthiness of customers on the gossip networks to entertaining regular customers with 'open house' on market days.[35] Daughters would be expected to help in whatever ways were most useful. Sarah Robinson, for example, the younger daughter of a Birmingham cooper and his wife, born in their town-centre home and shop in 1767, helped in the retail side of the business.[36]

The essential contributions made by wives were extremely varied. Jedediah Strutt, the son of a farmer and maltster in Derbyshire, was apprenticed at the age of fourteen to a wheelwright and fell in love with the daughter of the house, Elizabeth.[37] She went into service with the master of the dissenting academy in the town, and then to London as the servant of a Nonconformist divine, a Dr Benson, who became very attached to her and was so horrified at the idea of her getting married that he offered to make her financially independent at his death. The courtship between Jedediah and Elizabeth lasted for seven years and they finally married in 1755. Jedediah started in business as a wheelwright but turned to farming having been left some stock. He then invented a process of making ribbed stockings by machine. Elizabeth, contributing in whatever ways she could, investigated the possibility of her late employer, the doctor, lending them some capital but she was unsuccessful in this. She visited London and canvassed among relatives and Nonconformist friends for orders for her husband and her brother who was working with him. She also checked out possible sources of supply. She was always active and well informed as to the business and her letters reveal details of the ins and outs of ribbed stockings as well as the relative values of different kinds of thread. She was a 'partner in herself' as the family biographers describe her, but without the legal appurtenances of partnership since these were denied to married women.[38] As the business grew, turning from hosiery production to the establishment of a silk mill before moving into cotton in partnership with Richard Arkwright, it provided sustenance for Jedediah's younger brother as well as Elizabeth's brother and their children. Elizabeth's eldest daughter helped in the warehouse while the three sons all entered the business. By the time the younger daughter was growing up the family was wealthy and well established and Martha perhaps was more in favour of trips with the Arkwrights (as in 1775 when she went with them to Birmingham, dressed like Miss Arkwright in a 'genteel riding dress' and provided with 'pen and ink and Memorandum Books that they may see which writes the best journal'), than with checking stock or managing the household.[39]

The contribution of middle-class women to family enterprise remained extremely significant throughout the early nineteenth century for family enterprise was at the heart of economic organisation.[40] It was only late in the century that companies with limited liability (which had been introduced in mid century) came to dominate over single-person enterprises and partnership. Partnership was the major way for businesses to expand in the early nineteenth century for a partner could provide much needed capital, skills and labour. The informal partner, as we have seen, was often the wife. Wives may have had no legal rights but the informal partnership between husband and wife was the starting point for many enterprises, for a marriage meant two sources of capital, two sets of hands, two lots of skills, two sets of relatives and friends.

Many women brought capital into their marriage, as did Rebecca Smith whose father provided five hundred pounds for her on her marriage and another five hundred pounds a year later when she was twenty-one. This capital was crucial to her husband Archibald Kenrick, who had been a bucklemaker in Birmingham, suffered from the decline of that trade, and was able to set up as an iron founder in 1791. Subsequent Kenrick men benefited in similar ways from their marriages which opened up possibilities of loans and sources of credit as well as the lump sums which might be given as a wedding settlement.[41] Among the lower middle class, women's resources were constantly used to start off small businesses and provide credit. The death of a wife's father was often a time at which further capital could be invested in the business and provide for expansion, or simply help out at a time which might otherwise have been disastrous, for bankruptcy always lurked round the corner for middle-class households in this period of acute economic instability. Indeed a wife's inheritance could provide sustenance in face of bankruptcy, but such settlements were the exception rather than the rule and great care had to be taken over the legal arrangements. A Birmingham Methodist bucklemaker in the 1780s recorded the unfortunate case of the Gardner family, who were members of his chapel. Mr Gardner was declared bankrupt and the carelessness of Mrs Gardner's trustees meant that her property was not safeguarded. A Mr Guest had been 'the principal manager in all the business', conducting the Commission of Bankruptcy:

> It was he who found a flaw in a lease of some premises recently erected by order of some trustees to a sum left for the use and at the disposal of Mrs. Gardner; this money had been lent by her consent to her husband. She at length agreed to it being laid out in some building; and as the original trustees lived at a distance in Cheshire, they desired Mr. Charles Nevill and Mr. Gardner's eldest son, Richard Gardner, not only to overlook the management thereof, but likewise to have the lease of the land made out in their name. All this was done: but for want of a legal transfer of authority from the former trustees to those deputed to act in their stead, Mr. Guest was of the opinion (as did the other Commissioners appear to be) that the interest if any in the lease in question belonged to the private creditors of Mr. Gardner. Mr. Barker, the attorney, made the lease, whose fault it was in making this capital error, whereby Mrs. Gardner and her family are likely to be great sufferers.[42]

Women brought their own contacts and skills into an enterprise as well as their capital. In addition their relatives and friends might provide useful connections, lines of supply or further sources of expertise. Their brothers and husbands might go into partnership, their nephews might be educated and trained by them in the family business. Mrs Strutt used her contacts in London, as we have seen, to build up their hosiery business in its early days. George Dawson, the well-known preacher and protagonist of the 'civic gospel' in Birmingham in mid century, married into the established merchant family of Crompton. One Crompton son had gone into the ministry, another was a doctor; Susan (Dawson's wife) and her sister Sarah were intellectual women, writers and teachers, friends of Harriet Martineau in whose house in the Lake District the Dawsons enjoyed their honeymoon. Susan edited her husband's sermons and prayers for publication while Sarah was the superintendent of the Sunday school at her brother-in-law's Church of the Saviour, and wrote numerous children's books, seeing it, as so many middle-class women did, appropriate to their sphere to write for younger readers. Together they pioneered the 'Evening Schools for the Education of Women' in Birmingham in the 1850s, schools for working-class wives which aimed to train their pupils in 'the womanly habits of civilised life', including reading, writing and domestic economy, which were written up by Martineau in *Household Words* and achieved considerable attention. George, Susan and Sarah shared a belief in their educational responsibilities as middle-class people, they brought their different skills to bear on the problems of ignorance, inactivity and misunderstanding between classes. In the name of improvement they were ready to 'sacrifice themselves and their pleasures to the claims of the times'. Together they made a formidable team, an extended family enterprise.[43]

The contribution of wives to the enterprise did not stop at capital, contacts and skills. Their labour was also vital. Sometimes they were directly involved, as was Annie Gillott, whose brothers were in the steel-pen trade. She married Joseph Gillott and together they worked in the manufacture of steel pens in Birmingham, an enterprise which became extremely lucrative.[44] Similarly, the wives of shopkeepers continued to serve in the shop, the wives of farmers to organise the dairy, the wives of innkeepers to supply food and drink. Other women provided indirect support for an enterprise, the doctor's wife who took messages, the bank manager's wife who cleaned the bankhouse, the town missionary's wife who was available to work with women and girls when delicacy required it. Meanwhile all wives were engaged in the work of managing the household for the provision of food, the supply and maintenance of clothes, the upkeep of standards of cleanliness and tidiness, the education and training of small children, the management of servants, the care of apprentices, pupils or trainees; all this had traditionally been part of women's work and continued to be so. When workplace and home were the same as was so frequently the case in the late eighteenth and early nineteenth centuries, this could be a very substantial responsibility. The schoolmaster with living-in pupils, the surgical-instrument maker with his apprentices, the land agent with his living-in clerk all relied on the mistress of the house to feed them, clothe them, darn their socks and iron their neckerchiefs, order the fires laid and the water heated.

Furthermore, women had the vital task of bearing children, a labour riven with significance in a predominantly Christian middle-class culture. That culture regarded children as a blessing and sorrowed for those who did not have them. Until the 1860s and the beginning of the decline in family size, middle-class women, who like their husbands married relatively late, could expect to spend a large portion of their married lives pregnant, childbearing or breast feeding.[45] Take Martha Gibbins, the wife of a Birmingham button manufacturer and banker, who married young in 1778 when she was twenty and her husband twenty-two and had 17 children between 1779 and 1806, 13 of whom survived. Or, Sarah Lea Hill, the wife of the schoolmaster and founder of the well-known Benthamite school Hazelwood, who married in 1791 when she was twenty-six and her husband twenty-eight and had 8 children between 1792 and 1807. When her last daughter was born in 1807 Sarah had 5 children under nine and 3 in their teens while Martha in 1800, when baby Sarah was born, had an infant of one, a toddler of two, a little boy of four, one of seven, one of eight and one of nine in addition to the 5 boys and girls in their teens and the 3 who were still to come. The responsibilities involved were unending.[46]

Wives indeed were indispensable. It was difficult for a man to operate alone in many fields of business as Julius Hardy, the Birmingham button manufacturer, found to his cost in the late 1780s. His house was next to his business in the centre of the town and he employed between thirty and forty men, women and boys. One of his workmen and his wife lived with him rent-free in exchange for the wife's cooking and domestic help. She was assisted by a servant girl. The workman, however, was sacked and Hardy seriously considered marriage at this point, but felt the need of 'much deep and long consideration' on 'so momentous an affair'. His worries on the subject were brought to a head when he discovered that the servant girl was pregnant and he feared that he would be blamed. He summarily dismissed her and decided it was his 'duty' and 'interest' to marry. It was not possible to run a decent and trouble-free household without a wife.[47]

In a different sector of the middle-class world clergymen found it difficult to do their parochial work properly without a wife, and indeed part of a Protestant minister's duty was to marry, for celibacy was dangerously associated with Catholicism. For the serious Christians of the early nineteenth century, inspired with religious passion by evangelicalism, that wife must have the love of Christ as her 'spring of action'. Only a properly Christian woman could make a good clerical wife. Husband and wife together would make 'the welfare of his [sic] flock an object of *primary* solicitude'. This would inevitably involve the loss of much domestic enjoyment but that loss would be as nothing compared with the pleasure in doing one's Christian duty. The Rev. John George Breay, Anglican Evangelical and minister of the new Christ Church, especially built for the working classes in Birmingham's town centre in the early nineteenth century, found in Miss Phillis Peyton 'the chosen partner of his future life'. John and Phillis shared a commitment to serious Christianity and a certainty of their mutual duty to create a new moral world. On their wedding day in

1827 the money usually spent on wedding cake was instead given to poor widows in the vicinity of Haddenham, the Rev. Breay's first living. Before her marriage Phillis had devoted much time to philanthropic and religious causes together with the two women friends with whom she had lived. As a clergyman's wife she immediately helped to set up a Sunday school and train the necessary teachers, while running the household which consisted of herself and her husband, four pupils whose fees made a substantial contribution to the household economy, and her old friend Miss Lamb, whom she had lived with before her marriage. One of the special responsibilities of 'the ladies' was to organise the clothing club which provided respectable clothing for the poor and they helped to found the various schools for both adults and children which Breay, in his untiring evangelical enthusiasm, had inspired. In 1832 the family, now with three young children, moved to Birmingham and again Phillis launched into Sunday schools, clothing clubs and schools of industry, as well as being personally involved with the new Birmingham Magdalen Asylum. In 1837 a new school room was built, able to cater for one thousand children, a monument to the joint endeavours of the Breay family enterprise. Phillis' efforts, however, were never directly remunerated. Just as the married woman was 'covered' by her husband in law, so she was 'covered' by his stipend or salary. In 1839 the Rev. Breay caught scarlet fever from one of his sons and died, leaving his widow with five young children. His congregation, recognising their plight raised £3,000 to be invested for them and Phillis stayed in Birmingham for the rest of her life, bringing up her children and working for varied philanthropic causes.[48]

Marriage was a partnership, a partnership without legal guarantees but nevertheless the basis of most successful family enterprises. It was wife, children and friends who made the venture of life worthwhile, who could be relied on for support in a shifting and dangerous world. A Wolverhampton salesman writing to his loved one during their courtship, captured this spirit in a poem he quoted to her,

> If the stock of our bliss is in strangers' hands rested
> The fund ill secured oft in bankruptcy ends,
> But the heart is given bills which are never protested
> When drawn on the firm of *Wife Children and Friends*[49]

Assumptions as to the nature of women's involvement with the 'firm of Wife Children and Friends' were, however, changing, changing in ways which were to lead to a crisis over the question of middle-class women's employment by the 1850s. The increased specialisation and more advanced division of labour characteristic of agrarian and industrial capitalism affected the middle classes as well as their employees. The varied tasks of the eighteenth-century attorney became the specialised professions of solicitor, surveyor, estate agent, auctioneer or stockbroker; the iron founder who had lent some money on the side became a fully fledged banker; the producer and retailer turned either to manufacture or his shop. Such specialisation meant the need for more training and of different kinds; the 'sound commercial education' so sought after by the English middle classes for their sons, which would enable them to operate in the elaborating world of business. A young stockbroker, for example, needed not only numeracy and literacy, a grasp of the financial market and its dealings (which middle-class women were extremely unlikely to have), but also the social skills and contacts to operate within the market. In the early nineteenth century those contacts were informal but middle-class men worked hard to develop the infrastructure of their commercial world. They organised committees of manufacturers and chambers of commerce to articulate and represent their interests. They built market halls and exchanges to centralise their dealings and codify their practices. Their clubs were for men only, their purpose-built buildings designed for the male commercial world. Women were increasingly marginalised and excluded from this world, both formally and informally.

Let us take farming, where the traditional responsibilities of the farmer's wife, or daughter were under attack. In the dairy more scientific methods of cheese-making combined with more specialised and large-scale organisation to marginalise women. They had relied on traditional skills, handed down from mother to daughter, skills which could not compete with the increasingly approved methods of empirical observation and experiment. 'By 1843', as Leonore Davidoff points out, '*the Royal Commission on Women and Children in Agriculture* announced that the patience, skill and strength needed to produce cheese made this work unsuitable for women.'[50] Those women who tried to go on farming independently found themselves operating in an increasingly specialised market. More capital investment was needed to survive but this presented difficulties since women were seen as less creditworthy than men both by their kin and by the country banks which helped to sustain middle-class lines of credit.

Women who were actively engaged in family business when home and workplace were the same found their patterns of daily life significantly different when and if the two were separated. By the 1830s and 1840s such separation was becoming more common amongst both the upper middle and sections of the lower middle classes as suburban housing was more extensively developed.[51] Often it was a relief, particularly for the mothers of young children, to be away from the 'business house', with its noise, its dirt, its associations with the dangers of a town centre. As the daughter of a Birmingham retail chemist wrote about her mother,

When our dear mother was first married, she went to the business house in Bull St ... there were several young men resident in the house, and many callers and visitors to be provided for, and my mother has sometimes told us that the two or three years before the removal to Camp Hill were years of considerable trial. At Bull St. it was a noisy thoroughfare in the centre of the town, our mother went to her brother's house in Gt. Charles St. when the two elder of her children, Anna Mary and Ellen were born.[52]

Later the family moved to a small house about 2 miles from the business and a few years afterwards into Edgbaston, Birmingham's premier suburb. Similarly, the Best family, manufacturers of lamps in Birmingham in the early nineteenth century, lived close to the town centre for many years in a Georgian house with a small factory built in the yard next door. In 1858 they also moved into Edgbaston, concerned that their neighbourhood had been 'going down' and no doubt enjoyed their view of the Botanical Gardens rather more than the factory outlook they had lived with so long.[53]

The separation between workplace and home was undoubtedly connected in part with the increased desire amongst sections of the middle class to demonstrate their gentility by ensuring that their womenfolk had nothing directly to do with productive enterprise. While economic activity gave men dignity and worth it threatened women's femininity which was primarily assured by being a wife and mother. Such ideas, articulated most powerfully in the writing of women such as the Evangelical Hannah More in the 1780s and 1790s and the ubiquitous Mrs Sarah Stickney Ellis in the 1830s and 1840s depended on the notion of 'separate spheres' for the two sexes and assumed that men's and women's natures and interests were fundamentally different.[54] By mid century it was deemed unladylike and ungenteel for a middle-class woman to be seen to be economically active. One indication of this is in the slightly embarrassed way daughters and granddaughters, in memoirs and letters, explained to themselves and their friends that their mothers and grandmothers had been involved in business. Ann Bassett, who had taken over from her brother as a saddler, collar and whip-maker in central Birmingham in the 1780s, relied on her two nieces and a foreman to help her with the shop and workshop. One of the nieces 'often remarked that saddlery was a very unsuitable trade for ladies'.[55] When her aunt died in 1811 the business was sold and eventually the two sisters moved to Edgbaston.

It was necessity that drove middle-class women to make money and necessity was likely to hit widows and single women hardest, though a husband's lack of success or illness could mean that wives too had to become the main source of support within a family. It was necessity that drove Mrs Weeton to start a school and necessity that drove a Yorkshire woman, the youngest daughter of a minister, to take over her brother-in-law's haberdasher's shop in Halifax. She had gone to live with him and look after his motherless children when her sister had died. Two years later he died and she had to take responsibility for the shop as well as the children. When she herself married 15 years later three of her nieces continued to run the shop for another 16 years until their retirement.[56]

The demands of necessity could on occasion provide a welcome escape from the monotony of a genteel life. Harriet Martineau recognised that her father's death and the failure of the family business were a blessing in disguise as far as her writing was concerned. Her family came to accept the idea of her earning money and even offered her some grudging recognition.[57] Sometimes it was some kind of breakdown that offered an escape route as in the well-known cases of Florence Nightingale or Isabella Bird, the veteran lady travel writer. Isabella came from the heartlands of Evangelical Anglicanism. Her father, a Birmingham clergyman in the 1840s, was related to the Wilberforce family and was himself a prominent fighter for the evangelical cause. Her mother was active in the parish while her Aunt Mary and Cousin May both became well-known missionaries. Isabella taught Sunday school, trained the choir, and engaged in philanthropic work. From her early adulthood, however, she suffered from aches and pains, from lethargy, insomnia and backache and her doctor in desperation eventually prescribed a long sea voyage. Her first trip was to America and in later years she travelled to Hawaii, the Rockies and Japan. Her *A Lady's Life in the Rocky Mountains* was immensely successful. Abroad she was able to climb mountains and volcanoes, ride, sleep out, live rough and generally be 'privileged to do the most improper things with perfect propriety'.[58] Harriet Martineau, Florence Nightingale and Isabella Bird, however, were the success stories, and all came from families where confidence and ambition were part of their stock-in-trade. Behind them clustered the shadowy forms of seamstresses and governesses whose plight was to become public and who were to inspire the first organised feminist attempts to improve economic opportunities for middle-class women.

As early as 1792 Mary Wollstonecraft in her *Vindication of the Rights of Woman* commented on the lowly status of the middle-class milliners, mantua makers and governesses who were scarcely fitted for the humiliating situations into which they were forced by necessity. Like Mary Wollstonecraft, Miss Weeton had also longed for the day when 'honest, independent women' would be able to fill 'respectable stations' as physicians, farmers and shopkeepers, able to stand erect, 'supported by their own industry' rather than reduced to dependence.[59] By the 1840s the possibilities of women filling those 'respectable stations' looked ever more remote and the first wave of publicity over the pathetic conditions of elderly governesses was to be reinforced with the evidence from the 1851 census of the numbers of women who were employed, in official terms, and the revelations as to those half million 'redundant women' who were not married and therefore had no proper place. It was in this context that the subject of middle-class women's employment became a matter of public debate and concern.[60]

For commentators such as W.R. Greg the 'redundant woman', as Vicinus has argued, provided a potent symbol of the wider social disorders associated with industrialisation and urbanisation.[61] Unattached women could have no rhyme or reason in their lives since Greg's concept of true womanhood (one which was widely publicly shared) was being supported by and ministering to men. But a growing number of middle-class women, especially those who were single, were becoming more vocal in their search for economic opportunities both because they needed them and because they wanted them. The injunctions on middle-class fathers to provide for their dependants could often not be met and many unmarried daughters were left without resources in a world where working for money meant loss of gentility. Widows could find themselves desperately in need of employment and wives could discover that their husbands were less than adequate providers. At the same time, some women confined to a life of gentility longed for the independence and interest which could be associated with employment and the status and power which went with certain kinds of labour. Florence Nightingale's passionate demand for some greater meaning in her life, some sphere where her intellect and moral sense could be exercised, was echoed by many others, not just in the privacy of their diaries and journals but also on an increasingly public stage.[62] In beginning to articulate the limitations of their 'separate sphere' women had to reflect on and make sense of the new conditions which confronted their class and their sex in mid century England.

Take Barbara Leigh Smith, one of the first group of students at the Ladies' College in Bedford Square, who in 1854 wrote the pamphlet on women and the law which was to act as a focus for the agitation on married women's property and the subsequent founding of the *English Woman's Journal*.[63] Barbara Leigh Smith came from a wealthy Radical and Unitarian mercantile and landed family. Her grandfather had been the leading parliamentary spokesperson for the Dissenters in the early nineteenth century, a strong protagonist of the repeal of the Test and Corporation Acts and heavily involved in the anti-slavery movement with his childhood friends, but political antagonists the Wilberforces and the Thorntons. He was a close friend of the well-known Unitarian Thomas Belsham and a strong believer in the importance of reason and the necessarian doctrine, propounded by Joseph Priestley, that the moral and natural universe worked according to laws set in motion by God, that these laws were inevitable but that man, by using reason, could understand the laws and conform to them. It was man's positive duty to do this and to advance the divine plan. Each man was the maker of his own fortune.[64] Barbara's father, Benjamin, who restored the family fortunes in time of trouble with his successful distillery, also became a Member of Parliament and a well-known philanthropist. In 1823 he met Anne Longden, a milliner's apprentice, with whom he lived and who had five children before she died. Barbara, therefore, was illegitimate, undoubtedly a considerable social stigma at the time and one which placed the Leigh Smiths beyond the pale for some of their relatives. Indeed, Mrs Gaskell attributed Barbara's unconventional feminist opinions, to which she was not sympathetic, to the taint on her birth.[65]

Barbara's own thinking was shaped by this radical, Unitarian, slightly unconventional world to which she belonged.[66] She was used to a stress on improvement and progress, she had learnt an optimism about the human capacity to grow and change, she trusted in the power of reason. Unitarians, with their commitment to rationality and intellectual inquiry, were usually serious in their consideration of girls' education – though the female pursuit of knowledge took place within narrower boundaries than that of the male. Unitarians were used to criticism and disapproval, to being rebels (though after the 1830s they were substantially represented in local government), to being linked with dangerous ideas such as deism and Owenism, to the assumed link between their theological doctrines and reforming politics.[67] Indeed, the *Monthly Repository* under the editorship of W. J. Fox, advocated the emancipation of women and the liberalising of divorce laws, a stance which many Unitarians could not stomach and which provoked heartfelt complaints that the journal could no longer be left on respectable sideboards. Fox's sexual politics, including his separation from his wife and living openly with another woman, led to his expulsion from the association of Unitarian ministers, for Unitarian radicalism in politics and religion was rarely matched by a radicalism on familial relations.[68] However, their faith, in its encouragement of the rational pursuit of knowledge and its belief in individual responsibility, provided a space within which women could challenge assumptions of male superiority.

Mary Wollstonecraft, Harriet Martineau and Barbara Leigh Smith all had connections with Unitarianism. But they did not stand alone. In Unitarian congregations across the country women had claimed the right to organise activities for their sex, whether girls' Sunday schools or female Schools of Industry. They had long been accustomed to involvement in mixed discussion groups for young adults, sometimes they were even privileged to cast a vote in chapel meetings when a new minister was to be appointed.[69] But such rights could not be assumed. They were constantly fought over and contested, with the heavy weight of not only conventional conservative thinking about sexual difference but also the new doctrines of separate spheres ever present.

It is in this context that Barbara Leigh Smith published her book

Women and Work in 1857. On the title-page she quoted St Paul's Epistle to the Galatians,

> There is neither Jew nor Greek, there is neither
> bond nor free, there is neither male nor female:
> for ye are all one in Christ Jesus.

This text had long been a critical text for Christian women since it asserted women's spiritual equality with men. Drawing on the debates as to women's place within the church or chapel which had been a prominent feature of the previous decades, as women claimed the right to be active as philanthropists, Leigh Smith extended this claim and insisted on women's social equality. Women were God's children equally with men, she argued, a theory which was proclaimed in Christian society but not lived in practice. As the necessarian doctrine had taught, all are God's tools, sent into the world to forward progress. No human being, whether male or female had the right to be idle. Women *wanted* work.[70]

Leigh Smith's claim for social equality and the right to work reflected the middle-class insistence on the dignity of labour. For middle-class men, faced with the aristocratic and gentry code which maintained that true gentility depended on the capacity to live on the labour of others, a central issue was their demand that there was no disrespect associated with the counting-house, the stock-room or the office.[71] Indeed, progress and improvement depended on the reason and action of men like them who would steer the great engine of expansion with their quills, their theodolites and their bibles. It was they who stood at the prow of the good ship British Enterprise. It was not uncommon for middle-class people to explain mechanisation and industrialisation in terms of the rise of their class, as did Harriet Martineau in her powerful intervention 'On female industry' in the *Edinburgh Review*. For her it was the rise of the middle class which brought with it the need for and supply of female industry, an indication of the sense of power and agency which entrepreneurship bestowed.[72] Women like Barbara Leigh Smith and Harriet Martineau wanted to share that potential – not to work meant serfdom, as Elizabeth Barrett Browning had so eloquently written in the lines that Leigh Smith quoted next to St Paul,

> The honest earnest man must stand and work;
> The woman also; otherwise she drops
> At once below the dignity of man,
> Accepting serfdom.[73]

That same year John Duguid Milne, an eloquent friend of feminism, in his discussion of the *Industrial and Social Position of Women in the Middle and Lower Ranks* echoed these sentiments. He argued that it was a waste for middle-class women to live such purposeless lives and that, although it was exhausting to work, such work carried the satisfaction of being useful and interesting, quite apart from that of making money. Despite the difficulties of operating ethically in the market, industry could have good moral influence since it demanded honesty and honour. 'The moral culture of an upright man of business', he suggested, 'cannot but exceed far what is possible in a sedentary life or in affluent leisure':[74] an astonishing belief in a society which was used to the argument that women, by nature, and by virtue of their seclusion in the home, were more moral than men.

Women like Barbara Leigh Smith and her great friend Bessie Rayner Parkes had the *class* confidence which allowed them to speak in a society in which the bastions of inherited power had been successively broken down by their fathers, their grandfathers and their great-grandfathers. Their sense of themselves as ladies who should be publicly silent was broken by the tensions between the aspirations of their class and their sex. Middle-class men, in claiming rights for themselves, had claimed the right to support, protect and represent their womenfolk. But some of those womenfolk, surrounded by the discourses of power yet condemned by their sex to social and political marginality, broke the boundaries of genteel femininity and transformed the languages with which they were familiar, the languages of Christian duty and individual fulfilment, into weapons for themselves.

The language of liberal individualism was clearly present in the writing of Bessie Rayner Parkes. Her great-grandfather was the famed Radical, Unitarian theologian and chemist Joseph Priestley, whose necessarian doctrines influenced successive generations of Unitarians and the example of whose exile at the hands of a 'Church and king' mob was a potent reminder of the dangers associated with radical politics. Her father, the Radical Utilitarian lawyer Joseph Parkes, had been active, in the Benthamite initiatives in Birmingham since the early 1820s, was heavily involved in the struggle for the Reform Act in 1832, and soon after moved to London to work on the Municipal Corporations Commission. Both the Reform Act and the local government acts enfranchised and empowered middle-class men while for the first time formally excluding women. When the Parkes family moved to London they lived above the offices of the Municipal Corporations Commission, 'a great convenience' for Parkes and an arrangement which must have familiarised young Bessie with the ways of the political world.[75] By the time she was writing her articles on women's work for the review she co-edited, the *English Woman's Journal*, she had lost her father's faith in the hidden hand of the market. The market could not be left entirely to itself, she argued, to sort out the problem of middle-class women's work. Active intervention was needed if women were to claim their rightful place as workers. As long as families educated daughters only to be wives and mothers the opportunities associated with an ever expanding economy could not be taken up. Prejudices would have to be tackled and attitudes changed, unrestricted production could not be seen as the only good. Even such modest criticisms of the orthodoxies of political economy as those offered by Parkes were greeted with severe disfavour, by her father as well as other commentators.[76]

For those feminists such as Harriet Martineau and Bessie Rayner Parkes who had been heavily influenced by Utilitarianism with its belief in the potential benovolence of the market, there was a deep confidence in the economy's capacity to expand. Men's 'monopolising spirit', their fear of the threat to their jobs and conditions of work if women were allowed in, their jealous protection of their exclusive crafts and skills, were castigated on the grounds that there could be openings for all and that the exclusion of women from large sectors of the economy meant that their 'powers' and 'industry' were wasted. Harriet Martineau quoted the ironic case of the British watchmakers who refused to allow women into the trade with the result that Swiss watches were being imported which had been made by men and women. Her central argument was that there must be a proper recognition of the reality and extent of women's work. This reality had been demonstrated in the census of 1851 with its revelation that 'three millions out of six adult English women work for subsistence; and two out of the three in independence'.[77] Changes in the law were not necessary – it was changes in attitude that were required. The assumption that all women were supported by men was patently not true. A recognition of the reality of women's work in agriculture, in fishing, in domestic service, in the retail industries, in manufacturing or as landladies was a necessary first step in exploding masculine fantasies that the market was not big enough for both the sexes and the popular myth that all women were dependent. The liberal feminist case for the right of all individuals to fulfil their full potential had to be built, in the time-honoured Utilitarian tradition, on empirical investigation and a proper statistical base. Women already were in employment, in large numbers. The world should stop pretending they were not, recognise the value of that work and provide more openings, especially for middle-class women.

For the ladies of the *English Woman's Journal* the issue of the restricted employment possibilities available to middle-class women occupied them greatly. They wrote about it, organised around it, set up practical initiatives to try and change it. They were mainly born in the decades of the 1820s and 1830s so their mothers were the generation whose engagement with the family enterprise was likely to have been reduced as the business world became more organised around men. They had moved into the suburbs or modernised their farms with parlours and front doors; they learned to be professional wives and mothers. Their daughters demanded the re-entry of women into family enterprises and the education of women in the ways of the business world. They did not challenge the importance of the profession of wife and mother but argued forcefully that 'the middle class is at the mercy of a thousand accidents of commercial or professional life, and thousands and thousands of destitute educated women have to earn their daily bread'. Most *Journal* readers, they thought, would have a female relative or intimate friend who had been affected by trade failures, by death or by the 'exigencies of a large household'.[78] Some of these women could be absorbed into family businesses but others had no conveniently placed relatives.[79] Such women needed either salaried positions, or to be able to set up in business themselves.

Bessie Rayner Parkes bemoaned the lack of available capital for women. 'Girls never have any capital, they hardly know what it means', she wrote and, reflecting on the commonplace assumption that the financial world was not a world that women needed to know anything about, she argued that girls needed to be taught, just as boys were, 'how to make capital reproductive, instead of merely how to live upon its interest'.[80] It was the property laws in part which had encouraged such assumptions and it is hardly surprising that the demand for economic opportunities for women went hand-in-hand with the demand for a change in the laws on married women's property.

The importance of an active engagement with the world of business was recognised in the financial organisation of the *English Woman's Journal* itself. Middle-class women had long been used to the organisation of philanthropic committees, of church and chapel auxiliary societies. Barbara Leigh Smith had herself been actively involved in the establishment of a school and had set up a women's discussion group, where members showed each other their artistic productions. She and her friends took these established skills along different routes. They set up a committee to agitate on married women's property, they even established a joint-stock company themselves. The *Journal* was set up on joint-stock principles though Leigh Smith actually bought most of the initial shares with the independent income her father had settled on her.[81] Joint-stock was seen as a way forward for women, for if they would co-operate they could establish a business even with very limited capital. 'If twenty ladies in any town', wrote Bessie Rayner Parkes, 'would club together £5 a piece, they might open a stationery shop in which, if they gave all their own custom and tried to get that of their friends, they might secure a profit after employing a lady as manager, and if the business increased female clerks also'.[82] If joint-stock represented the financial organisation of the future, women must not be afraid of it and must learn to make use of it.

Jessie Boucherett, an early enthusiast for the *Journal* who became actively involved in setting up the Society for Promoting the Employment of Women, was so shocked by the recognition that the possibilities for women to work in shops were partly limited by the fact that they could not add up properly that she set up a school to train them.[83] Her enthusiasm for the genius and benevolence of a capitalist economy spread to life assurance, that instrument designed specifically to deal with the problem of financial dependants, usually women. Rather than criticising such a form she saw it as 'one of the positive duties of women to foster and disseminate an elastic principle which if carried out to its fullest extent would nearly banish poverty from our land'. It was a part of woman's mission to talk to people about this 'beautiful system' and life assurance needed the powerful aid of female influence. She set out to explain the benevolent principles of life assurance in simple terms without using the technical jargon which made it so particularly inaccessible to women. She proposed the establishment of a woman's life assurance mutual society, enrolled under the Act or Friendly Societies or registered under the Joint Stock Act, in which women could be trained to serve as clerks. Initially it would have to have male directors and a male secretary but she looked forward to the time when 'vital economics', mathematics and statistics would not be 'deemed improper subjects for female instruction'.[84] Indeed, even the agents to the company could be women, conveniently combining such work with their domestic duties. In this utopian dream women would raise the capital, they would act as clerks and agents, they would secure incomes for themselves and benefit the whole society. The new Jerusalem of the middle-class feminists of the 1850s was peopled with female insurance agents, female accountants, female doctors, female lawyers, female photographers, female designers and female artists as well as the more traditional female teachers and dressmakers. Their Jerusalem would recognise women as active subjects, treat them as independent persons legally, encourage and develop their skills and capacities, give them the opportunity to thrive in the world as businesswomen or as wives and mothers.

Such a dream provoked a deep sexual antagonism. The feminists, like most of their class and their generation, believed in the immense potential of the British economy. But they also knew and experienced men's fears, jealousies and 'monopolising spirits'. A group of Birmingham women in the 1850s established a 'Maidens' Club' that would have warmed the heart of Miss Weeton. The society consisted of young unmarried women who were committed to remaining single and to restricting their relationships with the male sex to their relatives. They held weekly discussion meetings at a clubroom in the town centre where they discussed such issues as whether men should be allowed to enjoy their men-only clubs. One week the question for debate was 'Are men the competent subjects they assume to be?'[85] Whatever their conclusions, both the society and its subject matter were another indication of a new willingness amongst some middle-class women to voice their grievances, make new claims as independent persons and speak for their sex.

Notes

Thanks to Rosalind Delmar and Keith McClelland for comments on this chapter.

1 N. Stock, *Miss Weeton's Journal of a Governess*, 2 vols., Newton Abbot, 1969, vol. 1, p. 6. Miss Weeton's story is all drawn from this source. Subsequently only direct quotes are noted.

2 *Ibid.*, vol. 1, p. 23.

3 *Ibid.*, vol. 1, p. 211.

4 *Ibid.*, vol. 1, p. 259.

5 *Ibid.*, vol. 1, p. 312.

6 *Ibid.*, vol. 2, p. 72.

7 *Ibid.*, vol. 1, p. 78.

8 *Ibid.*, vol. 2, p. 376–7.

9 *Ibid.*, vol. 2, p. 396.

10 J. Brewer, 'Commercialization and politics', in N. McKendrick, J. Brewer and J. H. Plumb (eds.), *The Birth of a Consumer Society: The Commercialization of Eighteenth Century England*, London, 1982, p. 24.

11 For estimates of the size of the middle class see, for example, J. Foster, *Class Struggle and the Industrial Revolution*, London, 1974, p. 74; J. Burnett, *A History of the Cost of Living*, Harmondsworth, 1979, p. 77. For a more detailed discussion of the size of the middle class see L. Davidoff and C. Hall, *Family Fortunes: Men and Women of the English Middle Class 1780–1850*, London, 1987. Much of this chapter draws on the joint research done with Leonore Davidoff and the extensive discussions we have had over the years. Much of that research is written up in *Family Fortunes*.

12 The lines of division were, of course, always fluid and flexible. For this argument see Davidoff and Hall, *Family Fortunes*; see also the work of R. J. Morris, particularly 'Voluntary societies and British urban elites, 1780–1850: an analysis', *The Historical Journal*, 26, 1 (1983).

13 Parliamentary Papers, *The Population Returns of 1831*, London, 1832, p. 2.

14 Parliamentary Papers, *Occupation Abstract of the Census Returns, 1841*, London, 1844, p. 9.

15 See the useful appendix on women's occupations in 1841 in I. Pinchbeck *Women Workers and the Industrial Revolution 1750–1850*, new edn, London, 1969.

16 Parliamentary Papers, *Census of Great Britain 1851*, Population Tables, Report and Summary Tabls, part 2, vol. 1, London, 1854, LXXXXVIII.

17 *Ibid.*

18 *Ibid.*

19 E. Reiss, *Rights and Duties of Englishwomen*, Manchester, 1934; L. Holcombe, *Wives and Property: Reform of the Married Women's Property Law in Nineteenth Century England*, Oxford, 1983.

20 Davidoff and Hall, *Family Fortunes*. Chapter 4 is a discussion of gender and property and this paragraph draws heavily on it. For the standard history of insurance see H. Rayne, *A History of British Insurance*, London, 1948.

21 For a discussion of this literature see M. Berg, 'Women's work, mechanisation and the early phases of industrialisation', in P. Joyce (ed.), *The Historical Meanings of Work*, Cambridge, 1987; see also M. Berg, *The Age of Manufactures 1700–1820*,

London, 1985. For a helpful discussion of feminist approaches to women's employment see V. Beechey's introduction to her *Unequal Work*, London, 1987.

22 K. Lacey, 'Women and work in fourteenth and fifteenth century London', in L. Charles and L. Duffin (eds.), *Women and Work in Pre-industrial England*, London, 1985.

23 M. Prior, 'Women and the urban economy: Oxford 1500–1800', in M. Prior (ed.), *Women in English Society 1500–1800*, London, 1985.

24 W. Thwaites, 'Women in the market place: Oxfordshire 1690–1800', *Midland History*, 9.

25 A sample of Birmingham Directories was taken from 1767 to 1852.

26 M. Prior, 'Women and the urban economy'.

27 M. Roberts, 'Images of work and gender', in Charles and Duffin (eds.), *Women and Work in Pre-industrial England*.

28 K. Snell, *Annals of the Labouring Poor*, Cambridge, 1985.

29 D. Lantz, 'The role of apprenticeship in the education of eighteenth century women', unpublished paper in *Warwick Working Papers in Social Hisotry – Workshops on Proto-Industrial Communities*, 1986. I owe this reference to Maxine Berg.

30 For some discussion of the ways masculinity was learnt in the workshop see K. McClelland, 'Time to work, time to live: some aspects of work and the reformation of class in Britain, 1850–1880', in P. Joyce (ed.), *The Historical Meanings of Work*, Cambridge, 1987.

31 Pinchbeck, *Women Workers*, p. 8.

32 *Ibid.*, p. 11.

33 See *Annals of Agriculture, and other Useful Arts*, collected and published by Arthur Young, 1784–1815, 46 vols.: vol. 6, p. 123, vol. 8, p. 82. Quoted in Pinchbeck, *Women Workers*, p. 10.

34 For an account of one such family business see C. Hall, 'The butcher, the baker, and candlestickmaker: the shop and the family in the Industrial Revolution', in L. Whitelegg et al. (eds.), *The Changing Experience of Women*, Oxford, 1982.

35 See the fictional account of the Furzes, ironmongers, in M. Rutherford, *Catherine Furze*, new edn, London, 1985.

36 I. Southall, W. Ransom, M. Evans (eds.), *Memorials of the families of Shorthouse and Robinson and others connected with them*, Birmingham, 1902.

37 This account is drawn from R. S. Fitton and A. P. Wadsworth, *The Strutts and the Arkwrights 1758–1830*, Manchester, 1958.

38 *Ibid.*, p. 111.

39 *Ibid.*, p. 77.

40 For a much longer discussion of the family enterprise and the character of men's and women's work see Davidoff and Hall, *Family Fortunes*, especially part 2.

41 A. Kenrick, unpublished manuscript diary 1787–89, Birmingham Reference Library 110/24; Mrs W. Kenrick (ed.), *Chronicles of a Nonconformist Family: The Kenricks of Wynne Hall, Exeter and Birmingham*, Birmingham, 1932; R. Church, *Kenricks in Hardware: A Family Business 1791–1966*, Newton Abbot, 1969.

42 Unpublished diary of Julius Hardy, Buttonmaker of Birmingham, 1788–93, transcribed and annotated by A. M. Banks, 1973, Birmingham Reference Library 669002, p. 8.

43 W. Wilson, *The Life of George Dawson 1821–76*, Birmingham, 1905; E. P. Hennock, *Fit and Proper Persons: Ideal and Reality in Nineteenth Century Urban Government*, London, 1973; S. Crompton, *Evening Schools for the Education of Women*, Birmingham, 1852; H. Martineau, 'The new school for wives', *Household Words*, 107 (1852); G. Dawson, *A Letter to the Middle Classes on the Present Crisis*, Birmingham, 1848, p. 4.

44 E. Edwards, 'Joseph Gillott', in *Personal Recollections of Birmingham and Birmingham Men*, reprinted from the *Birmingham Daily Mail*, Birmingham, 1877.

45 For a longer discussion of this see Davidoff and Hall, *Family Fortunes*, especially part 3.

46 E. Gibbins, *Records of the Gibbins Family, also Reminiscences of Emma J. Gibbins and Letters and Papers relating to the Bevington Family*, Birmingham, 1911; T. W. Hill, *Remains of the Late Thomas Wright Hill*, London, 1859; F. Hill, *An Autobiography of Fifty Years in Time of Reform*, edited with additions by his daughter Constance Hill, London, 1893; R. and F. Davenport-Hill, *The Recorder of Birmingham: A Memoir of Matthew Davenport Hill*, London, 1878; R. and G. E. Hill, *The Life of Sir Rowland Hill and the History of Penny Postage*, 2 vols., London, 1880.

47 Unpublished diary of Julius Hardy, pp. 36, 55.

48 Rev. J. G. Breay, *Memoir of the Rev. John George Breay Minister of Christ Church, Birmingham*, 5th edn, Birmingham, 1844, p. 124. References to Mrs Breay's activities in later life have been found in charitable records.

49 Shaw Letters, Birmingham University Library, no. 4.

50 L. Davidoff, 'The role of gender in the "First Industrial Nation": agriculture in England 1780–1850', in R. Crompton and M. Mann (eds.), *Gender and Stratification*, Cambridge, 1986, p. 204. This paragraph is heavily dependent on this article.

51 L. Davidoff and C. Hall, 'The architecture of public and private life: English middle class society in a provincial town 1780–1850', in D. Fraser and A. Sutcliffe (eds.), *The Pursuit of Urban History*, London, 1983.

52 Southall *et al.* (eds.), *Memorials of the Families of Shorthouse*, p. 68.

53 R. D. Best, *Brass Chandelier: A Biography of R. H. Best of Birmingham by his son R. D. Best*, London, 1940.

54 See, for example, Hannah More's best selling novel, *Coelebs in Search of a Wife Comprehending of Domestic Habits and Manners, Religion and Morals*, 2 vols., 9th edn, London, 1809; Mrs S. Ellis's series *The Women of England, The Wives of England, The Daughters of England, The Mothers of England* were immensely popular in the 1830s and 1840s.

55 A. W. Matthews, *A Biography of William Matthews, Expositor of Gas and Water Engineering*, London, 1899, p. 5.

56 J. Wilson, 'Mrs. William Rawson and her diary', *Transactions of the Halifax Antiquarian Society*, 1958. Thanks to Dorothy Thompson for this reference.

57 H. Martineau, *Autobiography with Memorials by Maria Weston Chapman*, 3 vols., London, 1877.

58 P. Barr, *A Curious Life for a Lady: The Story of Isabella Bird, Traveller Extraordinary*, Harmondsworth, 1958, p. 185.

59 M. Wollstonecraft, *A Vindication of the Rights of Woman*, new edn, Harmondsworth, 1975, p. 262; Stock, *Miss Weeton's Journal of A Governess*, vol. 2, p. 396.

60 For an account of the emergence of the debate see R. Strachey, *The Cause: A Short History of the Women's Movement in Great Britain*, new edn, London, 1978; L. Holcombe, *Victorian Ladies at Work: Middle Class Working Women in England and Wales 1850–1914*, Newton Abbot, 1973; for the most famous 'naming' of the redundant women see W. R. Greg, 'Why are women redundant?', in *Literary and Social Judgements*, Boston, 1873; for an interesting discussion of Greg see J. Worsnop, 'A re-evaluation of "the problem of suplus women" in nineteenth century England, in the context of the history of gender', unpublished MA dissertation, University of Essex, 1983.

61 M. Vicinus, *Independent Women: Work and Community for Single Women 1850–1920*, London, 1985, p. 3. See chapter 1 for Vicinus' account of 'The revolt against redundancy'.

62 F. Nightingale, 'Cassandra', reprinted in Strachey, *The Cause*.

63 On Barbara Leigh Smith who became Barbara Bodichon see H. Burton, in *Barbara Bodichon 1827–91*, London, 1949; S. R. Herstein, *A Mid Victorian Feminist, Barbara Leigh Smith Bodichon*, New Haven, 1985; J. Rendall, 'A "moral engine"? Feminism,

liberalism and the English Woman's Journal', in J. Rendall (ed.), *Equal or Different: Women's Politics in the Nineteenth Century 1800–1914*, Oxford, 1987.

64 On necessarian doctrines seee R. K. Webb, *Harriet Martineau: A Radical Victorian*, New York, 1960.

65 Herstein, *A Mid Victorian Feminist*, pp. 15–16.

66 Barbara Leigh Smith was taught for some time by an Owenite, see Burton, *Barbara Bodichon* and B. Taylor, *Eve and the New Jerusalem: Socialism and Feminism in the Nineteenth Century*, London, 1983, chapter 9.

67 On Unitarianism and middle-class culture see J. Seed, 'Unitarianism, political economy and the antinomies of liberal culture in Manchester 1830–50', *Social History* 7, 1 (1982); J. Seed, 'Theologies of power: Unitarianism and the social relations of religious discourse 1800–1850', in R. J. Morris (ed.), *Class, Power and Social Structure in British Nineteenth Century Towns*, Leicester, 1986.

68 F. E. Mineka, *The Dissidence of Dissent: The Monthly Repository 1806–36*, Chapel Hill, NC, 1944.

69 For a longer discussion of church and chapel government and the relative places of men and women see Davidoff and Hall, *Family Fortunes*, chapter 2.

70 Leigh Smith, *Women and Work*, London, 1857.

71 On the dignity of work see, for example, T. Carlyle, *Selected Writings*, Harmondsworth, 1971.

72 H. Martineau, 'Female industry', *Edinburgh Review*, 109, 222 (1859).

73 Quoted in the title-page of Leigh Smith, *Women and Work*; E. Barrett Browning, *Aurora Leigh*, new edn, London, 1978; see the introduction by Cora Kaplan.

74 J. Duguid Milne, *Industrial and Social Position of Women in the Middle and Lower Ranks*, London, 1857.

75 J. K. Buckley, *Joseph Parkes of Birmingham*, London, 1926, p. 118.

76 Rendall, 'A "moral engine"?', documents Joseph Parkes' criticism of his daughter for her ignorance of political economy, fn. 66.

77 The phrases are those of Harriet Martineau, 'Female industry', pp. 333, 335.

78 B. R. Parkes, *Essays on Women's Work*, London, 1865, p. 76. Most of the material in this book was reprinted from the *English Woman's Journal*. On the question of attitudes to married women and work see M. Maconachie, 'Women's work and domesticity in the *English Woman's Journal* 1858–64', in S. Alexander (ed.), *Studies in the History of Feminism 1850s–1930s*, University of London, Dept of Extra-Mural Studies, Work in Progress, 1984.

79 J. D. Milne took up this point particularly, *Industrial and Social Position*.

80 Parkes, *Essays on Women's Work*, pp. 143, 146.

81 On the business arrangements behind the *EWJ* see Burton, *Barbara Bodichon*; Herstein, *A Mid Victorian Feminist*; Rendall, 'A "moral engine"?'.

82 Parkes, *Essays on Woman's Work*, p. 182.

83 On the varied enterprises associated with the *EWJ* see Holcombe, *Victorian Ladies at Work*; Alexander (ed.), 'Studies in the History of Feminism.'

84 'J.B.', 'Life assurance', *English Woman's Journal*, 2, 11 (1859), pp. 310–11, 316–17.

85 'Newspaper Cuttings Relating to Old and New Birmingham 1864–1905', collected by J. Macmillan. Thanks to Doug Reid for this reference.

Chapter Five

La Petite Ouvrière surmenée: family structure, family income and women's work in nineteenth-century France

ANNE MEYERING

Introduction

Louise Tilly and Joan Scott offer one way of understanding the relationships between family structure, family income and women's work for working-class families in France during the last two centuries.[1] In their book, *Women, Work and Family*, the lives of women are explained in terms of three models of family organisation: the family economy, the family wage economy, and the family consumer economy. All three models imply a developmental cycle of the family and a life cycle of women.[2] Both families and the women in each model have a dynamic existence. They change over time in predictable but important ways.

The historical evidence Tilly and Scott use to illustrate the models is drawn from a wide variety and vast number of sources. However, little of this evidence shows the same families moving through the developmental cycle associated with each of the model families. Nor do many of the examples show the same women moving through the different life cycles prescribed by each of the three models of family organisation. Nevertheless, there is good reason for Tilly and Scott to employ this method. Few histories of working-class families or biographies of working-class women were written.[3] The evidence for their depiction of women's lives is like a film in which each frame pictures different women at a different stage in their life or different families at different stages in their developmental cycles, rather than a continuous reel of the life of one woman or of one family. This collage provides a less satisfactory gallery of portraits of families of women than would a picture based on evidence for the same families and the same women as they move through time.

This chapter uses family monographs compiled by Pierre-Frédéric-Guillaume Le Play and his school to examine the three models of family organisation formulated by Tilly and Scott. These monographs were published in *Les Ouvriers européens* and *Les Ouvriers des Deux Mondes* between 1857 and 1913.[4] Le Play was an early French sociologist who developed a method for systematically studying working-class families in relation to the locality in which they lived and their work environment. The monographs offer detailed evidence on family income, family structure and women's work.

The purpose here is twofold: first, to see whether any of the French families fit the models used by Tilly and Scott and, secondly, to see what the most obvious differences are between the models developed by Tilly and Scott and the families described by Le Play. This analysis will describe concrete examples of the developmental cycle of families and of the life cycle of women under the family economy, the family wage economy and the family consumer economy; it will also suggest ways in which the models may need to be refined or elaborated in order to account for a wider variety of experiences than the three models alone imply.

Three models of family organisation

To a large extent, the three family models developed by Tilly and Scott correspond to different historical periods: the family economy to the pre-industrial period, the family wage economy to the period of 'high' industrialisation in the nineteenth and early twentieth centuries, and the family consumer economy to the period of 'late' industrialisation or mature industrial capitalism in the late nineteenth century and the twentieth century. Nevertheless, examples of each type of family organisation can be found in all three periods.

The 'family economy' characteristic of the pre-industrial economy designates a domestic or household mode of production. Households organised according to the family economy were generally small units of production, most frequently small peasant farms, but sometimes artisanal workshops. If it was a peasant farm, the family that ran it either owned or rented the land they farmed. If it was an artisan's workshop, the artisan was self-employed. While he might rent the premises, he owned the tools and the raw materials and dealt directly with his customers. Most workers were family members, usually only parents and children, but sometimes other kin, apprentices or domestic servants might be found in the household, especially when the household head's children were too young to work in the family enterprise. Home and work were often the same place. Most work consisted of labour co-ordinated with other family members to produce the basic necessities which would assure the subsistence of the household members. On the farm this was the food the family ate and the fibres they spun to make their clothing and the household linens, as well as produce and livestock they sold in the local markets to obtain cash to purchase the things they could not produce on the farm. In the shop this was the income the artisan and his wife and children needed to pay their rent, to purchase food and to cover the cost of heat, light, tools, raw materials and equipment they needed to practise the trade. There was a division of labour based on age and sex, but every able-bodied person living in the household who was old enough to assist in some way worked. These small productive units rarely produced a surplus over the long term. Any temporary surplus would soon be wiped out by bad weather conditions or by a drop in the market for the goods they produced.

With industrialisation, the family economy gave way to the 'family wage economy'. The concentration of production in capitalist enterprises meant that factories and large commercial farms replaced the small artisanal workshops and peasant family farms as typical units of production. Work and home no longer coincided. Factories and mines, iron works and engine houses became the workplaces of dozens and even hundreds and thousands of men, women and children. More workers left home to go to work and they no longer produced goods consumed by themselves and other household members. Rather, they went out to earn wages which they used to purchase food, to pay rent, to buy fuel and light, clothing and other necessities which many families had previously produced themselves. Where wage labour predominated, men more often than women left home to work. Because it was increasingly difficult, with the concentration of production into large, capitalist units, for women to combine housekeeping and child-rearing with paid labour, more women became dependent upon their husband's earnings for support. The women spent less time on productive or wage-earning activities, not because they were slothful, but because these types of labour could less often be performed in their own homes. As a result, women contributed less to the family income and became more dependent upon their husbands for economic support. Of course, some people worked as proletarian wage-earners before the factory, both in agriculture and in manufacturing. But the implication of Tilly and Scott's heuristic use of the new family wage economy as characteristic of the nineteenth-century industrial working class is that it was more prevalent than in the pre-industrial period.

The third form of family economic organisation that Tilly and Scott describe explains women's work in the twentieth century. They call this form the 'family consumer economy', where the wages of the husband and father increasingly provided the primary means of supporting the entire family. Men's earnings rose to the point where the husband and father alone could support his wife and children for two reasons. First, labour organisation led to the successful negotiation of labour contracts that raised working men's wages. Secondly, economic growth and the expansion of capitalist production created many more jobs, especially low-level, white-collar positions, that paid workers at higher rates than manual labour did. Children now went more often to school than to work. Women were spending less time on productive or wage-earning activities and more time on child-rearing and home-making.[5] Some women still worked, but most often they were single, or, if they were married, they worked only sporadically in order to raise the family's standard of living rather than to provide basic necessities. Ironically, just when most couples were limiting the number of children they had to two or three, just when the physical and biological demands of motherhood were declining sharply, changes in the economic structure, particularly in the composition of the labour force and in men's earnings, converged to make women's role as mother and homemaker important.

An example of the family economy: the family of a peasant in the Laonnais region of the Aisne, May 1861

The first example from the Le Play collection of family monographs is a peasant family living in the Laonnais region of the department of the Aisne in 1861,[6] which fits the model of the family economy quite well. It illustrates that in nineteenth-century France there really were families organised according to the characteristics of the family economy described by Tilly and Scott.

In May 1861, when the schoolteacher who carried out this investigation visited the family, Jean-Baptiste and Rosalie's farm included 4.14 hectares (10.35 acres) of land. Their holdings placed them in the middle ranks of the peasantry in the local commune among those who owned between 1 and 5 hectares of land.[7] Jean-Baptiste and Rosalie's family raised hemp, Jean-Baptiste hauled black ashes to farmers in the Ardennes, and their sons worked in the peat bogs to supplement the living they so laboriously made from the land. Although the family was not as poor as some others, they were able to achieve this position and maintain it only with the greatest toil. Jean-Baptiste and Rosalie's modest farm was divided into a garden (0.07 hectares) and the fields (4.07 hectares). The family kept 2 horses, 1 cow and 1 heifer, 2 pigs which they fattened for sale, 18 chickens and 6 rabbits. On their land they produced rye, butter, milk, cheese, eggs, pork, rabbits, vegetables, potatoes, beans and cabbage, or most of the food they needed.[8] Assisted by his teenage sons, Jean-Baptiste spread manure, ploughed and sowed the land, cut, gathered and threshed the grain. All the family members helped in this work, the husband, his wife, their two sons who lived at home and their two daughters before they married.

In the winter months the family prepared hemp for sale in the local markets. Jean-Baptiste rose at four o'clock in the morning to begin combing hemp on his hackle, Rosalie rolled the skeins and put them in bundles of 5 kilograms and the children assisted in this work. Because the dust from the hemp bothered Rosalie so much, Jean-Baptiste preferred to sell the bundles in the neighbouring markets than to have Rosalie spin it. In March when the work in the fields still left Jean-Baptiste a little spare time, he bought black ashes and hauled them to sell in the Ardennes.[9] He spent about 32 days a year transporting black ashes and earned about 1 franc a day.

Rosalie's principal occupations were to prepare the family's food, to wash and mend the family's clothes and linens and to take care of the barnyard animals. It was her special task to take care of the vegetable garden and the crops that needed hoeing. When her sons became strong enough to replace her, she no longer helped with cutting the grain or with drawing the harrow when the fields were sown. But she still occasionally helped with the threshing and was no stranger to any of the work on the farm. When she accompanied her husband and sons to the fields she left to go home a little earlier than the others to prepare the meals and to feed the animals. Since she was almost always in the fields when the weather was good, she had little time to make the family's clothing which was made by someone outside the family. Her daughters helped her with the laundry, even though they were married and no longer lived at home, and she did the same for them. Rosalie was also in charge of selling farm produce at local markets.

In 1861 Jean-Baptiste and Rosalie had been married for 31 years. He was 54 and she was 52, old enough so that two of their children had already married. Thus, the monograph contains information on the transition from one generation to the next. Jean-Baptiste and Rosalie had been married in 1830, when he was 24 and she was 22. He was exempt from military service. Their union was more the result of their parents' satisfaction with the prospective spouse's dowry, than of the spouses' mutual attraction. They purchased a house using the cash portion of their dowries to make a down-payment, and the remainder of the purchase price was covered by a debt of 1,200 francs. By hard work and strict frugality they had paid off this sum in less than five years. Thus, Jean-Baptiste and Rosalie began their married life together in a house subsidised by gifts from their parents. With additional parental bequests and with savings they succeeded in increasing the size of their landholding to 4.14 hectares. In the 15 years between 1832 and 1847 Rosalie had seven children. Three died at very young ages; the four who survived were born in 1833, 1842, 1846 and 1848 respectively, when Rosalie was 25, 34, 38 and 40 years old. Most likely the children who did not survive were born between 1833 and 1842.

This monograph is particularly helpful as an illustration of the family economy because it indicates how the mother handled the competing demands of child care and housework, on the one hand, and income-generating activities, on the other, when her children were young. Rosalie's mother took care of the children so that Rosalie could help Jean-Baptiste in the fields. This was unusual: according to the investigator, most women in this region, while they worked in the fields alongside their husbands, left their children in dark, damp, cold cabinets, out of harm's way. Many of these children became ill and their parents would then usually spend money on novenas, prayers and pilgrimages, rather than call in a physician.[10]

Children really only began to be useful to the parents when they reached the age of nine. Their first jobs consisted of taking the cows to graze along the sides of the road and taking care of the barnyard chores in their mother's absence. They also gathered grass to feed the barnyard animals and worked at easy tasks associated with hoeing, cutting, retting, and scutching the hemp. As soon as they grew strong enough the sons were given a harrow, a plough and a cart; then they cut the grain, threshed it and worked the land just like their father. In the winter, like him, they worked hemp. In March when their father went to sell black ashes in the Ardennes, the boys worked in the peat bogs. This job consisted of transporting hunks of peat in a wheelbarrow and laying them out on the grass to dry. The boys were paid 0.50 francs per 1,000 bales and could manage about 1,000 per day.[11]

In 1852, after 22 years of marriage, when the surviving children were nineteen, ten, six and four years old, Jean-Baptiste replaced the thatched roofs on all the outbuildings with new tiles and completely remodelled the inside of the house. These improvements put the family back in debt, which was not entirely acquitted when his oldest daughter, Rosalie Victoire, married in 1853 at the age of twenty. Nevertheless, her parents gave her a dowry of 500 francs. Four years later, when her younger sister, Eugenie-Rose, got married, she, too, was given a similar dowry.[12] In 1861 the family worked to put together dowries for their two sons, Jean-Baptiste-Victor, aged fifteen years and Prosper-Eugène, aged thirteen. The investigator speculated that in a few years, when these sons married, the couple would sharply reduce their agricultural work. Jean-Baptiste would sell his agricultural equipment and divide the land among his children on the condition that they paid him and his wife a life annuity to cover their basic expenses.

The wife Rosalie performed many tasks that were also undertaken by the men in the family, in addition to chores which were exclusively her own 'women's work': cooking, mending, laundering, tending the vegetable garden and the barnyard animals. Her labour was needed for the primary tasks associated with cultivation and for the preparation of hemp in the winter months. The one job usually performed by women that Rosalie did not do was making the family's clothing.

According to the investigator, Rosalie worked harder than her husband Jean-Baptiste. His labour was estimated at 357 ten-hour days per year,[13] and accounted for about 51 per cent of the family's income. Rosalie's was estimated at 405 ten-hour days a year, involving a little over eleven hours a day, 365 days a year. Her labour accounted for about 20 per cent of the family's total income, not including time spent on housework; if this is added in, her share rises to 22 per cent of the family's income. The labour of each of the sons equalled about 15 per cent of the family income. Even in this family which owned enough land to grow most of its own food, family members worked to earn cash. The preparation and sale of hemp, as well as Jean-Baptiste's involvement in the black ash trade and his sons' work in the peat bog, were undertaken as small business enterprises, where they were self-employed, rather than working for wages.

This peasant family fits closely the model of the family economy outlined by Tilly and Scott. The work of the wife and mother changed somewhat as the structure of the family changed. Before the children were old enough to assist with work in the fields or with the preparation of hemp, it was their mother who worked alongside her husband, cultivating fields in the spring, summer and autumn and retting, scutching and spinning hemp in the winter. In addition, Rosalie was responsible for cooking and cleaning, the laundry, the barnyard animals and the vegetable garden. Even when her sons were old enough to take over some of the field work and she had given up spinning hemp, Rosalie still worked longer hours and more days than anyone else in the family.

Apparently the kind of work Rosalie did remained much the same throughout her life. As the daughter of a couple of small peasant cultivators living in the same commune, Rosalie very likely worked in the fields as a girl and a young single woman, helping her parents, much as her daughters did before they married. Apparently she did not go out to work as a domestic servant, and neither did her daughters. The only relief Rosalie got from this life of constant drudgery and toil was when her sons were old enough to work like adults in the fields. Even so, she still helped with field work and carried on her work in the house, barnyard and garden.

An example of the family wage economy: the family of a weaver in the Vosges, May 1862

When this family was visited in the spring of 1862, it consisted of seven members: Constant, 45, born in Sainte-Marie-des-Mines in the department of the Upper-Rhine, his wife Madeline, aged 48, born in the Lower-Rhine and five children, Josephine, 20, Constant, 19, Adolphe, 17, Adèle, 10 and Emma, 6. All the children were born in Sainte-Marie-des-Mines.[14]

The oldest, Josephine, worked as her mother had before her marriage, as a domestic servant for a local family. She used her wages for clothing and for recreation, and the remainder of her earnings were placed in a savings account under her father's supervision. Unlike her mother, Josephine did not contribute to the support of her parents or her siblings. Nevertheless, by going out to work as a domestic, she no longer drew on her parents' resources for food, clothing and shelter. Also, since her savings were under her father's supervision, her parents could draw on them if necessity demanded.

The two boys, Constant and Adolphe, on the other hand, worked in the same atelier as their father and under the same conditions, weaving fashionable cotton fabrics on a Jacquard loom. They all worked by the piece from five o'clock in the morning to noon and from one o'clock in the afternoon until seven o'clock in the evening. Each boy worked about 302 days a year, and earned about 1.50 francs a day or about 453 francs a year. They were given about 15 francs for pocket money, and the rest went into the family pot to help defray general expenses. Each boy's earnings accounted for between 15 and 20 per cent of the family's total income. In addition, Constant, the father, earned about 2.50 francs a day, or 755 francs a year working at the mill. In his spare moments he also gathered and cut wood for the family's fuel; this work was evaluated at 8 francs. Constant's earnings accounted for between 36 and 42 per cent of the family's income.

At age 48 Madeline's principal occupation was housework; she purchased and prepared the family's food, took care of the children, cleaned the house and furniture, made and mended clothes for the family, and washed the family linens. The time spent sewing and washing for the family was estimated at 132 days, each worth 1 franc, or 132 francs a year. This figure represented 7 per cent of the family's earnings, but it did not include time spent on housework. Madeline spent an additional 168 days purchasing and preparing food for the family's meals, caring for the children and cleaning the house. Her total contribution to the family income can, therefore, be evaluated at 300 days or 300 francs a year. In terms of the time she spent, she contributed just about as much as each of her sons or her husband. It is only because the wages paid to women were so low that the monetary value of Madeline's labour appears to be so much less than that of her husband or her sons. Moreover, her housework was indispensable to her husband and sons who would not have had time to provide for themselves the services Madeline performed. Having to be at work at 5.00 a.m. and staying until 7.00 p.m. made a fourteen-hour day; her labour contribution was, therefore, essential for the family's well-being. It was just as important as men's wages, even if the investigators carrying out the family surveys which appeared in the Le Play monographs assigned it no monetary value.[15]

The two youngest daughters, Adèle and Emma, attended school. When their studies permitted, they sewed and knitted, but this small contribution to the family's welfare was not accorded any monetary value. The girls attended the local communal school free of charge which represented a subsidy to the family equal to about 13 francs a year for each girl.

In addition to the work Constant and his sons did in the cotton mill and the housework done by Madeline, the family took in a few more francs by sub-letting a room in their home to an old weaver, who was not a relative but had worked in the same shop as Constant for 25 years. The old man paid them 33.80 francs a year in rent and bought his own food. Unlike some other households organised according to the model of the family wage economy, Constant and Madeline's family did not cultivate a vegetable garden.

Constant and Madeline were married in Sainte-Maire-des-Mines in 1840, when they were 24 and 28 years old respectively. Both had been orphaned at an early age. Constant's father, who worked as a mason, died when Constant was one year old. Constant's mother had remarried and his stepfather, a weaver, made him an apprentice at the age of 15. Chance had exempted him from military service. Madeline's father had been a cultivator, who died when she was very young. As soon as she was old enough, she found work as a domestic servant and she gave the 200 francs that she had inherited from her father's estate and anything she could save from her wages to her elderly mother who had no income. Unlike Jean-Baptiste and Rosalie, Constant and Madeline do not seem to have had dowries to help them set up and support their new household. They had to earn wages to support themselves and their children. In 1862 Constant and Madeline had been married for 21 years. Madeline bore seven children: two had died, one a girl at age 10 or 11, and a boy who lived only 8 months.

Madeline had not spent her entire married life only doing housework and taking care of the children. Until 1858, when her sons were old enough to work in the textile mill, she and the children wound bobbins. All the spare time Madeline had after housework and the children had after school was devoted to winding bobbins, which brought in about 2 francs a week. While Madeline was not currently engaged in wage-earning activities, her life fitted the one predicted for women living in a family wage economy in several ways. First, she had worked as a domestic servant as soon as she was old enough and had used her earnings to help support her family of origin, in this case, her widowed mother. Secondly, she was actively engaged in wage-earning at home, winding bobbins for the mill where her husband worked as a weaver, when her children were too young to earn wages to help cover the family's basic needs. Thirdly, she gave up this activity when her two sons were old enough to work alongside their father in the mill and contribute to the family income.

Life offered slightly more opportunity to Madeline's children. If the two youngest daughters were typical, they went to school until they were old enough to work as domestic servants or in the cotton mill. As long as the children lived at home, they were expected to contribute to the family's expenses, when they worked. However, since both their parents were still alive, they could provide a large part of the family's needs. This allowed the children to save some of their wages for future needs, such as a dowry, as seems to have been the case with the oldest daughter, Josephine. However, at no stage in this family's history had they been able to manage only on Constant's wages. In addition to his earnings, the family's needs required income from at least one other source, either the wife and mother or one of the children, in order to make ends meet. This case is typical of the family wage economy described by Tilly Scott.

An example of the family consumer economy: the family of a corporal in the Republican Guard in Paris, 1881

Only a very few of the families in *Les Ouvriers européens* and in *Les Ouvriers des Deux Mondes* matched the criteria of the model of the family consumer economy. In addition to the case discussed here,[16] one other family probably fitted this model, the family of a primary schoolteacher living in a rural commune in Normandy in 1860.[17] But this family was scarcely distinguishable from the families of the poor peasants whose children attended classes in the school. In the investigator's opinion this was mainly because the schoolteacher's wife was illiterate and worked for day-wages in the fields of local farmers.

Eugène-Jacques lived and took his meals at the Napoleon barracks on the rue de Rivoli, where he had daily guard duty. Because of the time-consuming demands of his service in the Republican Guard, Eugène-Jacques performed no manual labour for the family. However, he did give his wife a hand from time to time. His wife Eugénie, and two children lived 2 kilometres away on the rue Saint-Jacques near the Val de Grâce hospital. They chose to live there, rather than closer to the barracks, because the rent was lower, they enjoyed the fresh air of the Luxembourg Gardens and Eugénie's parents lived in the quartier. Also, many of her clients lived in adjoining streets.

Eugène-Jacques and Eugénie had two children, a daughter, Germaine, 5 years old, who was born in 1876, and a son, Armand, aged 3½, born in 1877. Eugénie directed the household and the family budget in co-operation with her husband. She was a very frugal housewife and raised her children with the greatest care and attention, keeping them very clean and giving them baths at home. For a time the little boy attended a nursery school, but his parents withdrew him due to his poor health. His father was teaching him the alphabet and planned to send him to a school run by the Brothers of the Christian Doctrine when he was 6 years old.

The little girl, Germaine, was raised without charge by the Sisters of Charity, who had a house in the quartier, and by the same sister who had raised Eugénie. Germaine attended school for ten months of the year and went every day, except Thursdays and Sundays, from 9.00 a.m. until

4.00 p.m. in the winter and from 8.00 a.m. to 4.00 p.m. in the summer. She came home between 11.30 a.m. and 1.00 p.m. for the midday meal.

Eugénie's housework kept her very busy. She got up at 6.00 a.m. every morning, and first tended to her household chores. Towards 6.30 in the summer and 7.00 a.m. in the winter she woke up the children, dressed them, fed them and took the little girl to school. The rest of the morning she used to take care of the house, her son, the family's clothes and linens, and to prepare the midday meal. Her productive work began at 1.00 p.m. With the help of her sewing machine she made clothes for herself, her children and her clients. At 4.00 p.m. Eugénie went to pick up her daughter and returned home to prepare supper. After supper she put the children to bed and then went back to sewing until 11.00 p.m. or midnight. She even stayed up all night when work was pressing. The income she earned from sewing varied from season to season. She set aside one day a week for repairs and alterations, and never worked on Sundays or holidays. One task Eugénie did not do was the family laundry, since she used so much of her time to sew for customers. It would have been very costly to send it out to a professional laundress. Instead, Eugénie's mother did much of the family's washing and her parents also gave her gifts of cloth and clothing. Eugénie did do the family ironing. While she made most of her own clothes and her children's, her husband's clothes were purchased.

Even though Eugénie worked as a seamstress most afternoons and evenings, her work was not indispensable to the family's well-being. Her husband's salary, 1,734 francs a year, was more than enough to cover the family's basic needs. Eugène-Jacque's position as an *officier* in the Republican Guard brought in twice as much as Jean-Baptiste earned farming in the Aisne and Constant earned as a weaver working in a cotton mill in Sainte-Marie-des-Mines. Eugénie's labour was worth about 461 francs a year, of which 300.09 francs came from the sewing she did for clients. This figure did not include the value of the time she spent shopping, cooking, cleaning and taking care of her children. Including the 182.09 days a year she spent on housework and child care, she worked 336.5 days every year.

As the investigator Monsieur Joseph Paviez pointed out, Eugénie could have made an even greater contribution to family income if she had used the time spent making clothes for herself and her children sewing instead for clients and purchasing clothes for the family ready-made. But as Eugénie herself told him, she preferred to dress herself and her children in clothes she had made with her own hands. In her view, the time she spent sewing for clients was only spare time left over 'after she had fulfilled all her duties as a mother'.[18] To Eugénie doing housework, caring for her children and sewing their clothes were all part of performing her duty as a mother. The economic rationale for the choices she made about how she spent her time was secondary.

The *brigadier*, Eugène-Jacques Michel, and his wife, Eugénie, were married in 1874. He was from the village of Olet in the Pyrénées-Orientales, and came from a large family. He still had three brothers and four sisters. Of his brothers, one was a captain in the cavalry, another was a department head in the Orleans railway company and the third was a priest at Prades. His four sisters all joined the order of the Sisters of the Holy Sacrament, whose mother house in Perpignan was directed by Eugène-Jacque's oldest sister. Like himself, all of Eugène-Jacque's siblings had the equivalent of white-collar or lower-middle class occupations.

Both his father and his grandfather on his father's side had also been born in Olet, and both had been soldiers. Eugène-Jacque's was born in Olet in 1838. In 1850 when his mother died he was twelve and he lived with his father in several garrisons until joining the army himself at the age of seventeen.[19] As a soldier he served in campaigns in Italy, Morocco, Syria, Mexico and the Franco-Prussian War, when he was made a prisoner-of-war. After his return to France, he joined the Republican Guard, rapidly becoming a corporal. He was 36 when he married Eugénie in 1874.

When his mother died in 1850, her children agreed to give the land and the house she left in Olet to the eldest child, the son who worked for the Orleans railway company, on condition that he would indemnify each of the other sons with the sum of 4,000 francs. When he married in 1874 Eugène-Jacques took 2,200 francs of his inheritance to set up a household for his wife in Paris. He used the remaining 1,800 francs to buy a small house which belonged to one of his uncles and managed by one of his aunts. Eugène-Jacques planned to take his wife and children and his wife's parents there to live when he retired from the Republican Guard, which was not too far in the future. When he retired he would get about 1,200 francs and would be able to live on his property in the Pyrénées-Orientales and easily obtain a tobacco licence at Olet. During the summer he could work at the mineral springs at Garous, 4 kilometres away, which were served by public transport.[20]

Eugénie was 24 when she married Eugène-Jacques and had lived in Paris all her life. Her mother's parents had come to Paris to make enough money to buy land back in their native Auvergne; her father was from Burgundy. The monograph does not state what Eugénie's father's occupation was, but since his son was a locksmith and one of his sons-in-law was a copper-turner, he was probably an artisan or small tradesman, perhaps in one of the metal trades. However, he had enjoyed the respect of everyone in the quartier, where he served as director of the Society of Saint Vincent de Paul for many years. This also suggests that he was a respectable lower-middle-class artisan or tradesman. Eugénie's parents succeeded in acquiring a modest position and observed many of the old customs of their native provinces.

Besides Eugénie, her parents had two other children, a married son who was a locksmith, and a daughter who married a copper-turner. The children all lived in Paris and visited each other and the parents regularly. Eugénie herself was a serious, hard-working woman who enjoyed work and family life. She was energetic and able at sewing and at housekeeping. Eugénie's daughter arrived within a year of her marriage and her son was born two years later. Her deliveries were easy and each time she was assisted by a midwife. She breast fed both the children. She looked forward to leaving Paris, where she believed she and her children seemed to grow weaker with each passing day, when her husband retired from the Republican Guard.

This family fits the model of the family consumer economy, even though Eugénie worked. The work she did, she did at home and only if it did not interfere with fulfilling her duties as a wife and mother. Clearly her paid labour was not crucial to the family's survival as Eugénie and Eugène-Jacques could have made ends meet on his salary alone. Also, like her children, Eugénie attended school when she was a girl. In addition, there is no evidence that Eugénie did anything other than help her mother with housework and sewing when she lived at home before her marriage, unlike both Rosalie and Madeline.

Examples of families that do not fit the models

Each of the three model families is based on the assumption that the household contains a working adult male, a wife who may or may not contribute to family income depending upon her husband's and her children's employment opportunities, and children who also may or may not work, depending upon their father's incomes, their ages, and the number of children in the family. However, other types of households existed. From the point of view of family structure, family income and women's work, some of the most interesting examples of households that do not fit one or another of the three models are households without adult males.

The Le Play monographs contain several families that are interesting for this reason. One describes the life of a seamstress living in Lille who was a 39-year-old single mother with a 7-year-old son.[21] Another family consisted of a widow and her three daughters who were employed in the porcelain works in Limoges.[22] A second widow's family living in a Paris suburb in 1904 consisted of the widow and her two daughters, Berthe, 28, and Hélène, 17, who supported themselves as corset-makers.[23] To these three female-headed households one could add the household of a toy-maker in Paris who had divorced her husband and who alone was supporting her two sons.[24]

Besides these female-headed households, the monographs contain examples of still another type of family organisation. These are very large, usually farming households which the Le Play school called *communautés* (in English, communities, communes or, perhaps more accurately but most awkwardly, family compounds). These include more than one married couple, usually parents and one or more married children and their children. Le Play referred to these large, complex households as patriarchal families, because the 'patriarch' kept his married sons and sometimes married daughters together and the family patrimony was passed on intact from one generation to the next. Examples in the monographs are a family of peasants living in Lavedan in the Hautes-Pyrénées,[25] a family of sharecroppers living in the Confolentais,[26] and another family of sharecroppers living in the Nivernais.[27]

In addition to these large peasant family compounds the monographs include an example of another type of family organisation, dear to Le Play and his followers, known as the stem family. This was also a type of extended family household, which usually includes, besides the parents, only one married child, his or her spouse, their children, and sometimes single siblings of the married child. The married child living with his or her parents is the child designated to inherit the family farm. It is usually the eldest son, but when there are no sons, it is the eldest daughter. An example of a stem family household is that of a sharecropper living in the Pays d'Horte in the department of the Landes in 1879.[28]

Although Le Play expressed some fondness for patriarchal families, he preferred the stem family. He believed these family structures were intrinsically more desirable than nuclear family households, which were created when the parents' estate was divided among the children. The extended family forms preserved patriarchal authority and perpetuated the family on the land. The stem family offered a means of establishing, however meagerly, those children who did not inherit, because the child who inherited the farm was usually obliged to indemnify other siblings by paying them in cash their share of the family estate, not unlike the arrangement Eugène-Jacques, the corporal in the Republican Guard, and his brothers made when dividing up their mother's property.

Subsequent research has shown that the majority of French households at any given moment in the eighteenth and nineteenth century consisted of what Le Play referred to as 'disorganized, unstable' nuclear family households.[29] The notion that large, multi-generational, extended family households were the most common family structure has gone the way of the unicorn. Although it was a nice idea, it never did exist.

However, following Berkner's argument, it is important to point out that the demographic regime of relatively late marriage and high mortality meant that in the nineteenth century, as in earlier periods, few parents lived to see their children marry or their grandchildren born.[30] Even if an extended family household was the ideal, or the model, which French couples tried to emulate, households like these were fairly difficult to create. In other words, more extended famils households might have existed in nineteenth-century France if demographic conditions had been different. Admittedly conditions were now changing in ways that made it more possible to establish extended family households than it had been in earlier centuries. Life expectancy was increasing and age at first marriage was declining. Nevertheless, this type of family structure still remained relatively rare.

In addition to the demographic constraints on household composition and structure, it should also be pointed out that by the second third of the nineteenth century, when Le Play and his disciples began collecting data for the family monographs, land was already fairly finely fragmented into very small plots and the average size of farms was small. This meant that even if land were passed down intact from one generation to the next, most farms were too small to support more than one couple and their children. Furthermore, industrialisation and the expansion of trade and commerce were accompanied by increased urbanisation. Towns and cities were attracting people born in rural villages to work and eventually to settle permanently. Consequently jobs were increasingly available to those siblings who would not inherit the family plot, if they were willing to move. The ideal family organisation may well have been some kind of extended family structure, in which some of the married children lived with their parents until they died or turned over the management of the family farm to the next generation and where other siblings were given two choices. Either they could stay, if they remained single, in the parental house under the tutelage of their married brother or sister and his or her spouse, or, if they wished to marry, they could seek their fortunes elsewhere. Small plots and more attractive job opportunities in expanding urban centres clearly mitigated against the formation of many extended family households. Nevertheless, the presence of several of these large, complex households among the nineteenth-century French families in the Le Play monographs is further proof that not all working-class households conformed to the three models outlined by Tilly and Scott.

What follows then are examples of households which do not conform to the three basic models of working-class family households. By comparing these examples to the models sketched by Tilly and Scott, we are able to see the possible ways in which the three models of the family economy over-simplify the history of family structure, family income and women's work in nineteenth-century France. This comparison may alert us to events and incidents that were perhaps not all that uncommon in the lives of women and their families and that made their lives distinctively different from those who lived in families that resembled the family economy, the family wage economy and the family consumer economy.

An example of a female-headed household: a seamstress in Lille, July 1858

Sophie Victoire, aged 39, lived with her son Alphonse, aged 7, on rue de Fives in Lille.[31] They lived in a room on the second floor of a two-storey house in which the family of one of Sophie's brothers was the principal occupant. Sophie worked as a seamstress, either making men's shirts or working as a thread-puller, pulling out one thread every centimetre from a piece of fabric which was cut as a shirt front. The seamstress then brought together two of the channels from which the threads had been pulled, sewing them together to make a tube of fabric which was then pressed with a hot iron. A series of these produced a row of vertical tucks across the front of the shirt. Such work was given only to the best seamstresses and was paid in 1858 at a piece-rate of 3.50 francs for every 100 pleats. It took twenty hours to do 100 pleats. Most seamstresses could not work more than ten hours a day at this task, so in the best times, when there was work, they earned 1.75 francs a day. This is what Sophie earned. She worked at home, rather than in workshops under employer supervision six days a week. Sophie devoted Sundays to cleaning her room, to doing the laundry and to making and mending clothes for herself and her son. Taking into account days lost due to sickness and other unforeseeable interruptions, and periods when no work was available, Sophie worked about 222 days a year. Her total annual earnings were estimated at 450 francs, slighly less than Eugénie, the wife of the corporal in the Republican Guard, earned from her sewing.

Sophie's earnings were so low that her brother paid her rent of 6 francs a month. Her earnings barely covered the cost of food, heat, light, clothing and washing for herself and her son. She used fabric salvaged from cast-off shirts and other second-hand articles of clothing to make her own clothes. Her son attended without charge a school run by the Brothers of the Christian Doctrine.

Sophie's story is that of the struggle of a single working woman for dignity who bore the added stigma of being a single mother. When Sophie was interviewed in 1858, her parents had been dead for quite a while. Her father, who was born in a faubourg in Lille and worked as a yarn twister, died suddenly in 1827 of complications from an illness he suffered after lowering himself into a lavatory to pull out Sophie, who had accidentally fallen in. At the time she was eight years old. When her father died, her mother was left a widow with eight children; a ninth had died. At first Sophie's mother did not do badly, supporting herself and her children as a lacemaker, but in 1842 she was completely ruined when her employer, to whom she entrusted all her savings, left the country. Soon after, Sophie was left an orphan when her mother died of a tumour. She immediately looked for work and found it as a seamstress. Sophie and all her brothers and sisters were born in Lille. Three of her brothers worked as yarn twisters; the fourth and the youngest, who was doing his military service, had been trained as a diamond cutter. Of her three sisters, one married a locksmith, one was a chambermaid, and the third entered a convent.

Sophie got pregnant when she was seduced by a locksmith who promised to marry her. He had already got another young woman pregnant, who died of shame. At the time Sophie met him she was 31 or 32 years old. When her brothers and sisters learned what had happened, they were scandalised but the seducer was persuaded to fulfil his promise to marry Sophie. Whether Sophie's seducer was a migrant to Lille or a native like Sophie herself is not known. However, Sophie's brothers did try to persuade him to make good on his promise of marriage. Their efforts were thwarted when the culprit absconded by train to Paris.

This story confirms much of what Tilly, Scott and Miriam Cohen have said about illegitimacy in the nineteeth century.[32] They argue that increased illegitmacy was the result of people adhering to old values under new circumstances. In pre-industrial times, back in rural villages, if a young man and a young woman consorted together and she got pregnant, pressure from her family and from the other villagers often forced the man to make an honest woman of her through marriage.[33] Pre-marital intercourse was like an engagement, which signalled the intention to marry. Rapid urban growth in the nineteenth century provided greater anonymity. Girls still got pregnant when men seduced them, promising to marry them, but it was easier for young men to abandon their mistresses, because it was more difficult to bring family and community pressure to bear on the responsible party. In large cities people living and working in one quartier might not know people living in another part of town. Many townspeople were recent migrants who had few obligations to their neighbours, co-workers or acquaintances. They had less to lose by not complying with social pressure which might be exerted on behalf of a young pregnant woman. In addition, skilled workers could probably find work fairly easily in another town. Both anonymity and mobility were greater in nineteenth-century France than they had been earlier.

In the investigator's judgement Sophie's status as an unwed mother placed her on the botton rung of the social ladder and she received little pity or sympathy from those around her. Living as she did in a poor neighbourhood and having little possibility of obtaining a better job or better accommodation, she seemed reconciled to her impoverished existence. In fact her prospects were not good. Her brothers were all workers whose jobs scarcely provided for their own needs, her sisters were in precarious circumstances, and her aunt, as a lacemaker, earned barely enough for her own subsistence. Sophie had had proposals of marriage, but she rejected all of them because she believed they were not in her son's interest. Her greatest hope was that

Alphonse's success in school would enable him to become an office clerk, because she believed that he was not physically strong enough to practise a manual trade.

Sophie's case illustrates that it was practically impossible for a woman alone to support herself and her child or children. Sophie and her son lived miserably, even though Sophie earned high wages and worked regularly. She and her son depended upon her brother to pay the rent, and they relied on other forms of charity for clothing and schooling.

The patriarchal nature of social organisation in nineteenth-century France is underscored by this example. Women needed the partial support a man's income provided, even if they worked long hard hours themselves. A single woman might live with a brother or a sister, but if he or she were married, and the likelihood was that they were, the single sister would be relegated to a lower status than her sister-in-law or her married sister. A second possible alternative for a single adult woman was to work as a live-in domestic servant. However, this solution posed serious problems. One was old age, when a maid was no longer useful to the family, and the family had no more reason to keep her on. Where could she go in her 'retirement' but to the poorhouse? She could not go to live with her children, now grown, because as a young woman it would have been almost impossible to have obtained a position as a live-in domestic with a young child in tow, who would have been viewed as a useless distraction and an added expense. All the other households in the Le Play monographs with no adult men living in them consisted of combinations of several adult women, except the household of the toy-maker. Together adult females could earn enough to make ends meet, but how these households managed to achieve this stage merits further study. The monographs fail to examine the lives of women living alone, and cast no light on the expediencies single women resorted to in order to keep body and soul together.

An example of an extended family household: a family of sharecroppers in the Confolentais, 1888

To illustrate the relationships between family structure, family income and women's work in large, extended family households or family compounds, the example of the family of sharecroppers living in the Confolentais region of the department of Charente is used.[34] This household contained four generations and four married couples. In 1881, when Pierre du Maroussem visited the family, the household's oldest member was the 81-year-old patriarch, Martial: next came his 50-year-old daughter Anne and her husband Pierre, aged 55. After Anne and Pierre came two of their four married daughters, Jeanne, 28, and Anne, 24. Jeanne's husband, Martial, aged 35, was also her cousin. The younger Anne's husband, Pierre was

28 years old. Each of the married daughters living with their parents had a child of her own. Jeanne had an 11-year-old son named Pierre, and Anne had a 21-month-old daughter named Marie. The other two married daughters had left the household. Anne and Pierre senior's other surviving daughter, also named Anne, was 17 years old and single. In addition to their five living daughters, Anne and Pierre senior had had two other daughters, one who died when she was only 1 month old and another who died when she was 10. The family was still in mourning over the loss of this child when the investigator visited them in 1888. In all the household contained ten persons.

This monograph provides no information on the pregnancies or the early child-rearing practices of women living in family compounds in the Charente. The women in this family all married at fairly young ages, Anne senior at 20, and the resident daughters at 18 and 21 respectively. The monograph does not state at what ages the two non-resident daughters married but in 1888 they were 26 and 21 respectively. When six of Anne's seven daughters were born, she was 23, 25, 27, 30, 34 and 41 years respectively and the seventh daughter, who died in her first month of life, was probably born when Anne was between 34 and 41 years old.

Anne probably grew up on the farm her father worked as a sharecropper and her childhood was spent much like that of her daughters. The division of labour among the household's members and the responsibilities of the youngest will furnish some clues to the earlier stages of Anne's life. The household worked a holding that measured just over 40 hectares (or 100 acres),[35] about 9.6 hectares were meadows, 4.1 pastures, 25.0 grain fields, 0.4 vineyards and just under 1.0 planted with chestnut trees. The family maintained 8 cows, with 5 or 6 calves, and a flock of 70 sheep.

Work on the farm was divided according to age and sex. Both the oldest, Grandfather Martial, and the youngest, baby Marie, did not work, but the rest shared all the work on the farm. Pierre senior was the 'governor', which meant that he was in charge of the livestock. He drove them in the fields and took them to the fairs, and also shared in all the work that his sons-in-law performed. Anne senior, the mistress of the household, reigned over the barnyard and this job gave her a great deal of importance in the household, because the profits that came from fattening pigs were often considerable. It also absorbed a great deal of her time, because most of the pigs' feed was cooked first. In addition, Anne was responsible for the housework, for spinning, knitting, and taking care of the garden. She also sold the animals she fattened or raised. The division of labour between Pierre and Anne was the common way in which agricultural tasks were divided between men and women in this part of France.

The two sons-in-law, while they helped Pierre senior with the livestock, were primarily responsible for cultivating the soil using a biennial crop rotation. By 1888, the cultivation of rye was receding in importance, while wheat cultivation was still expanding. The most fertile land was sown every year, with alternating crops. If potatoes, corn, beans or buckwheat were sown one year, then wheat, rye, barley, or oats were sown the next season. In addition Jerusalem artichokes and beets were planted among the cultivated crops and turnips, peas and vetch were also planted.

All the farming methods were traditional and taught by the older generation. Tasks that were reserved to the men only included pruning the trees and bushes and preparing fuel; cutting hay, cleaning the drainage ditches and repairing the hedges; pruning the vines and making and repairing agricultural tools. The two daughters, Jeanne and Anne, participated in the harvest just like the men. Women in this part of France worked the flail and sometimes ploughed, but not in this particular household. These women helped their mother wash the clothing and the household linens, prepare and spin skeins of hemp and wool, make clothes and linens, and take care of all the other household chores.

Pierre and Anne Senior's 17-year-old daughter, Anne, was the family's shepherdess. Sometimes she was given the proceeds from the sale of one of the cows and calves. When she was not tending a herd, she did the same work as her sisters. Pierre III, the son of Jeanne and Martial junior, went to school, tended the livestock, and helped with small agricultural chores. The work undertaken by the family was for their own benefit. It produced goods they consumed themselves or that they had to forfeit to the land-owner, from whom they leased the farm they operated.

The lives of the women in this extended family household of sharecroppers differed somewhat from that of their counterparts in the Laonnais peasant family in 1861 which was used to illustrate the family economy. The women in the sharecropper's family were exempt from most of the hard physical labour associated with cultivating the land. One reason may have been that the sharecropper's family was more heavily involved in raising livestock, than in intensively cultivating small fields, as Jean-Baptiste and Rosalie's family did. Another reason may have been that Anne and Pierre's household contained three adult males to do the field work, while the family economy example included only two adolescent sons, in addition to the husband and father, Jean-Baptiste. Rosalie worked in the fields helping her husband and her sons, while Anne and her daughters, Jeanne and the two Annes, left this work for Anne's husband, Pierre, and his two sons-in-law, Pierre and Martial.

This monograph is silent on a subject that would give us a better idea of the family's developmental cycle. It says nothing about how many brothers and sisters Pierre and Anne had. While much of the property owned by Pierre and Anne, by the younger Martial and Jeanne and by the younger Pierre and Anne came from the succession of the husband's parents, it is not clear how much the husbands of the two daughters who left the household were worth.[36] It is impossible, therefore, to determine whether marrying and staying in a family compound or moving out was more advantageous. However, in describing the inheritance system in the Confolentais, Du Maroussem states that it was divided equally and that any departure from a strictly equal division was vigorously disputed.[37]

What emerges, then, is a family compound that was a form of labour organisation for the exploitation of rather large, 40 hectare *métairies*, into which the large estates in the Confolentais were divided and which were leased to sharecroppers. At the same time these sharecroppers, in turn, owned and often rented out to other peasants and agricultural labourers cottages and small fields. Because much of the land was either in *métairies* or in holdings too small to support a family, access to a *métairie* lease was very desirable.

In terms of inter-generational changes, this monograph offers some very striking evidence. Although Anne senior married in 1857 at the age of 20 and had seven children before she reached 42, her eldest daughter Jeanne married in 1878 at the age of 18. By 1888, when the investigator visited the family, Jeanne, then 28, had only one child, an 11-year-old son, Pierre.[38] The third daughter, Anne, married when she was 21, in 1885, and had one 21-month-old daughter. The two other married daughters were 26 and 21, but the monograph does not state how long they had been married or whether or not they had any children. The fifth surviving daughter was 17, still living at home and single. It appears, therefore, that family limitation had begun to take hold in this part of France as it had in many other regions by this time.[39]

Conclusion

In general the lives of the women living in the extended family household differed little from the lives of women living in nuclear households. For all of these women, even Eugénie, the wife of the corporal in the Republican Guard, work began at an early age, first helping at home with small tasks and then working alongside their mothers and fathers doing their share of the work that had to be done in order to provide the family's necessities. Only Madeline and her daughter Josephine went out to work as domestic servants before they married. The other women lived at home until they married. Rosalie, Anne and Anne's daughters, Jeanne and the two Annes, worked on their parents' farms. Sophie began to work as a seamstress as soon as she was able. Eugénie learned to be an expert seamstress before she married. When these women married, they all continued to work long hours most days of the week and most weeks of the year.

Not only did these women all work very hard and from a very early age, but the composition of the household they lived in seems to have had very little effect on how much they worked or on the value of their labour. Except for Rosalie, all the wives were reported to have worked less than their husbands. However these estimates do not include housework. If shopping, cooking and cleaning are added into the hours that these women spent on tasks to which Le Play's investigators assigned a monetary value, the figures change substantially. Rosalie worked eleven hours a day, 365 days a year; Madeline worked 300 days a year, only 4 less than her husband and 2 less than her adolescent sons. Eugénie worked 300 days a year, even though she and her two young children could have managed without her work as a seamstress. Sophie worked 325 days a year, and the four women in the sharecropper's household 319.5 days a year, only 2.5 less than the men. Nevertheless, in every case, including that of Rosalie who worked longer hours than her husband, the value of these women's work was estimated to be less than that of their husband's.

There were two reasons why women's earnings were so much lower than the men's. A large portion of their time was discounted by Le Play's method which gave women no credit for shopping, cooking or cleaning. Each woman spent a significant amount of time keeping house for the other members of the family, from 47 days a year for each of the four women in the sharecropper's household, to 183 days a year for Eugénie. But, even giving the women credit for the time they spent on housekeeping fails to bring their contribution to the family income close to that of their husbands.

The reason, of course, is that wage rates for 'women's work' were invariably less than those of the men in their households. Wage rates for farm women such as Rosalie and the women of the sharecropper's household were less than 1 franc a day. Wages were higher for women living in towns and cities. The work Madeline did in Sainte-Marie-des-Mines in the Upper Rhine was worth 1 franc a day. Sophie earned about 1.75 francs a day in Lille and Eugénie earned an enormous 3.00 francs a day in Paris. These last two women were considered skilled seamstresses, and their wages reflect their proficiency. Men's wages, in contrast, only rarely fell below 1 franc a day and were generally 1.50 francs or more.

Even counting the time they spent on housekeeping at the rate they were paid for other work, the labour of every woman was estimated to account for a smaller percentage of the family's total income than the husband's labour. The women contributed between 14 and 36 per cent of the family's total earnings. Their husband's earnings varied from 21 per cent for each of the married men in the extended sharecropper's household in the Confolentais to 64 per cent for Eugène-Jacques, the corporal in the Republican Guard. Only in Sophie's case did a woman's labour account for most, indeed all, of household income, if we disregard the various subsidies she received. The devaluation of women's work accounted for a large part of the disparity between male and female contributions to family income in nineteenth-century France.

Within the framework of the present analysis, the use of the detailed information contained in the Le Play monographs has provided a means of testing the overall applicability of the basic models of family organisation originally propounded by Tilly and Scott. Drawing on the detailed observations recorded by individual investigators it has been possible to portray a series of household types which did not conform to the basic models of working-class family households. Despite the explicit downgrading of women's domestic responsibilities, in terms of their equivalent monetary value, the Le Play monographs also provide an important means of analysing the changing interaction between family structure, family income and the nature and extent of women's work. They effectively provide a vital insight into the shifting pattern of women's work within the context of the individual and familial life cycle. To this extent the material presented in this chapter highlights a number of important directions for future research in this field.

Notes

I would like to thank Sharon Comwell, Lisa Fine and Leslie Page Moch for reading and commenting on an earlier version of this paper.

1 It would be interesting to examine the family in nineteenth-century France as a kinship network linking parents, children, grandparents, aunts and uncles, nieces and nephews and to determine what the obligations owed to and benefits derived from these kin ties were. We know that kinship varies from one culture to another. The configuration of obligations and benefits of kinship are very different among most of the peoples of Africa from what they are among the peoples of Western Europe, to cite one example of marked contrast. Kinship ties also vary from class to class, from region to region and from one time period to another within France. See Emmanuel Le Roy Ladurie, 'Family structures and inheritance customs in sixteenth-century France', in Jack Goody, Joan Thirsk and E. P. Thompson (eds.), *Family and Inheritance in Rural Society in Western Europe, 1200–1800*, Cambridge, 1976, pp. 37–70; and Hervé Le Bras and Emmanuel Todd, *L'Invention de la France: Atlas anthropologique et politique*, Paris, 1981. Kinship often concerns questions of inheritance, but it is difficult to find systematic information on inheritance and kinship for nineteenth-century France.

   As interesting as questions about inheritance and kinship are, we know that the dominant residential pattern in Western Europe including France in modern times has been the nuclear family household: see Peter Laslett, 'Introduction', in Peter Laslett (ed.), *Household and Family in Past Time*, Cambridge, 1972, pp. 1–90.

   In this chapter the family refers to the nuclear family of a married couple and their children residing together as a single unit. When other relatives or unrelated persons are included in the analysis, the unit will be called the household. If kin ties beyond the nuclear family are implied, the unit will be referred to as an extended family.

2 Louise Tilly and Joan Scott, *Women, Work and Family*, New York, 1978, 2nd edn, New York, 1987: all references in this essay are to the first edition.

3 Tilly and Scott, *Women*, pp. 113, 118–19 for references to the life of Jeanne Bouvier

and pp. 107, 108 and 123 for references to the life of Juliette Sauget. Louise Tilly has also translated and edited the autobiography of another working-class French woman who lived between the Franco-Prussian War and the 1960s: see Mémé Santerre, *Mémé Santerre*, New York, 1985.

4 *Les Ouvriers européens*, 1st edn, Paris, 1855; *Les Ouvriers des Deux Mondes*, series 1, 1–5, Paris, 1857–85; series 2, 1–5, Paris 1887–99; series 3, 1–2, Paris, 1904–08. The second edition of *Les Ouvriers européens* contains those in the first edition and some published in the five volumes of the first series of *Les Ouvriers des Deux Mondes*. *Les Ouvriers des Deux Mondes* includes none of the monographs which appeared in the first edition of *Les Ouvriers européens*, but together the first edition of *Les Ouvriers européens* and the 12 or 13 volumes of *Les Ouvriers des Deux Mondes* provide a complete set of the monographs.

5 Tilly and Scott, *Women*, pp. 176–7.

6 'No. 29, Paysan d'un village à banlieue morcelée du Laonnais (Aisne-France)', *Les Ouvriers des Deux Mondes*, series 1, 4, Paris, 1862, pp. 37–82.

7 Of the 776 landowners in the commune, 612 owned less than 5 hectares, or 12.5 acres: see *ibid.*, p. 40.

8 *Ibid.*, pp. 70–1.

9 Black ashes were a produce of lignitic pyrite deposits found in the hills of the Laonnais and the Soissonnais. These deposits were formed of vegetable waste and iron sulphate. They were mined, then left exposed to the air. The substance caught fire and burned after it was dry. When it had cooled, it was pulverised, then delivered to farmers who spread it on fields like lime.

10 *Les Ouvriers des Deux Mondes*, series 1, 4, Paris, 1862, p. 43.

11 *Ibid.*, p. 47. In the description of the boys' work in the peat bog, the school teacher writes that they were paid at the rate of 0.50 francs per 1,000 bales of peat bog. In the budget section of the monograph, however, the wage rate given for their work in the peat bog is only 0.40 francs per day, which works out at only 20.80 instead of 26.00 francs a year: see *ibid.*, p. 57.

12 On p. 52 the monograph states that the second daughter married four years after the first one who married in 1853. This would put her marriage in 1857. However, it also states that this second daughter, Eugénie-Rose was 17 years old when she married, which would place her birth in 1840. However, in 1861, when the investigator visited the family, he reported that Eugénie-Rose was 19 years old. If this age is correct, it would place her birth in 1842, not 1840, and her age in 1857 at 15 years. Perhaps these discrepancies can all be explained by the inaccuracies that crop up in writing about age and lapsed time in whole years, when fractions of a year would be more accurate in calculating the age at which a specific event occurred.

13 In the monographs the standard workday consisted of ten hours.

14 'No. 26, Tisserand des Vosges (Haut-Rhin-France)', *Les Ouvriers des Deux Mondes*, series 1, 4, Paris, 1862, pp. 363–404.

15 See Olwen Hufton, 'Women and the family economy in eighteenth-century France', *French Historical Studies*, 9 (1975), pp. 1–22, which argues that women's work was essential to the family's survival, not 'pin money' used for little extras that made life less unpleasant than it otherwise would have been.

16 'No. 43, Brigadier de la Garde republicaine de Paris', *Les Ouvriers des Deux Mondes*, sereis 1, 4, Paris, 1885, pp. 261–314.

17 'No. 26, Instituteur primaire d'une Commune rurale de la Normandie', *Les Ouvriers des Deux Mondes*, series 1, 3, Paris, 1861, pp. 326–71.

18 *Ibid.*, p. 268.

19 The text of the monograph states that Eugène-Jacques became an 'army brat' when his

father died in 1858. But Eugène-Jacques would have been 20 years old at that date. It also states that Eugène-Jacques enlisted in the line infantry at the age of 17, which would have been in 1855, and that he became a grenadier in the Imperial Guard when he was 18, which would have been 1856. It is possible that the investigator meant to say that Eugène-Jacques became an 'army brat' when his mother died in 1850 when he would have been 12 years old and clearly this makes more sense.

20   *Ibid.*, p. 277.
21   'No. 24, Lingère de Lille', *Les Ouvriers des Deux Mondes*, series 1, 3, Paris, 1861, pp. 247–84.
22   'No. 98, Decoreuse de Porcelaine de Limoges', *Les Ouvriers des Deux Mondes*, series 3, 1, Paris, 1908, pp. 391–434.
23   'No. 106, Corsetière du Raincy, Banlieue de Paris', *Les Ouvriers des Deux Modes*, series 3, 2, Paris, 1908, pp. 377–431.
24   'No. 76, Ouvrière mouleuse de jouets parisiens', *Les Ouvriers des Deux Mondes*, series 2, 4, Paris, 1885, pp. 173–224.
25   'No. 3, Paysans en communauté de Lavedan', *Les Ouvriers des Deux Mondes*, series 1, 1, Paris, 1857, pp. 107–60.
26   'No. 65, Métayers en communauté du Confolentais', *Les Ouvriers des Deux Mondes*, series 2, 3, Paris, 1890, pp. 1–60.
27   'No. 38, Fermier à communauté taisible du Nivernais', *Les Ouvriers des Deux Mondes*, series 1, 5, Paris, 1885, pp. 1–50.
28   'No. 53, Métayer du pays d'Horte', *Les Ouvriers des Deux Mondes*, series 2, 1, Paris, 1887. For another example of stem family organisation, see Pierre Bourdieu, 'Marriage strategies as strategies of social reproduction', in Robert Forster and Orest Ranum (eds.), *Family and Society: Selections from the Annales: Societies, Economies, Civilisations*, Baltimore, 1976, pp. 117–44.
29   See also Peter Laslett, 'Introduction', in Peter Laslett (ed.), *Household and Family in Past Times*, Cambridge, 1972, pp. 1–90.
30   See Lutz Berkner, 'The stem family and the developmental cycle of the peasant household: an eighteenth-century Austrian example', *American Historical Review*, 77 (1972), pp. 398–418.
31   'No. 24, Lingère de Lille'.
32   See Louise Tilly, Joan Scott and Miriam Cohen, 'Women's work and European fertility patterns', *Journal of Interdisciplinary History*, 6 (1976), pp. 447–76.
33   On courtship, see Jean Louis Flandrin, *Les Amours paysannes: Amour et sexualité dans les campagnes de l'ancienne France (XVIe–XIXe siècles)*, Paris, 1975; on illegitimacy under the Old Regime, see also Cissie Fairchild, 'Female sexual attitudes and the rise of illegitimacy: a case study', *Journal of Interdisciplinary History*, 8, (1978), pp. 627–67; Jean-Louis Flandrin, 'A case of naiveté in the use of statistics', *Journal of Interdisciplinary History*, 9 (1978), pp. 309–15; Cissie Fairchild, 'A reply', *ibid.*, pp. 316–22; by far the most absorbing of any of these studies of seduction leading to illegitimate births is Richard Cobb, 'A view on the street', in his *Second Identity*, London and New York, 1969.
34   'No. 65, Métayers en communauté du Confolentais'.
35   References to bequests can be found on pp. 18–19; see pp. 6–7 for data on the size of the farm.
36   *Ibid.*, pp. 18–19.
37   *Ibid.*, p. 30.
38   *Ibid.*, pp. 11, 28.
39   Etienne van de Walle, *The Female Population of France in the Nineteenth Century*, Princeton, 1974.

Chapter Six

'Hun er den Raadende over Husets økonomiske Angliggender'? Changes in women's work and family responsibilities in Norway since the 1860s

IDA BLOM

Introduction

In 1864 three district councils in western Norway decided to investigate the work done by women in the region to keep their families clean and well groomed. The reason was the idea that leprosy thrived particularly well because of unsatisfactory cleanliness in the farmhouses. A prize was set up for the best investigation, which was also expected to indicate the means of improving what was supposed to be the lack of cleanliness of the women.[1] The father of Norwegian sociology, Eilert Sundt, took part in the competition, describing and explaining how women managed to keep their homes reasonably clean, given the precarious circumstances of their daily lives. His work was not awarded the prize by the initiators, who did not share his views. Among other participants was a teacher, K. L. Huus, who found women failing in cleanliness because the men did not and could not control female labour. According to Huus, the powerful and independent wife of a farmer did anything but scrub floors:

> She decides the economic affairs of the household according to old customs giving her this right. She manages the goods of the family, assuring – by a wise government – the welfare and happiness of everybody. Everything, not only in the house and kitchen, but also in the cellar, the barn and the cowshed is subject to her will, as no one in the family has the authority to give her advice or in any way control her government.

He thought farmers exceedingly stupid when they explained that excellent health and good bodily strength for working in the fields at harvest time, being able to compare to most other women in pulling and carrying heavy loads, etc., were the qualities they valued most in their wives.[2]

The remedy to this situation in the opinion of Huus was to admonish farmers to control their wives and teach them that cleanliness and diligence in domestic duties were what was expected of a proper housewife.

These conflicting views of the priority given to different parts of women's work are indicative of a conflict between two systems of family survival. The system used by the farmers was what has been termed the *family economy system*, i.e., a system where all members of the family, regardless of sex and age-group, took part in the work necessary to cover the basic needs of the family unit. This was the strategy for family survival used not only by agrarian families, where remuneration for work was given in kind, but also by urban families, where all members might work for money.[3] The teachers, doctors, and local politicians represented the bourgeois family, dependent on the salary of the husband, combined with work performed by the wife in the house and kitchen. Within this system, *the male provider system*, children old enough to work were usually attending school. Boys were socialised to provide for a family, while girls were taught to give priority to work done in the home. Around the 1960s a third system of family survival may also be discerned, *the two-wage system*. This brought women, including mothers of small children, into the workforce, giving families a female as well as a male provider. The main difference between the systems was thus not changes in male, but in female responsibilities to the family.

The purpose of this chapter is to trace the typical characteristics of the division of labour in the family within the three systems, to discuss explanations for the transition from one system to the other, and the implications of the different systems for power relations between wife and husband. In this process, the concepts and theories applied may to some degree overshadow the multi-faceted historical realities. However, to obtain a clear analysis of changes over a long span of time, typical characteristics must be accorded greater attention than individual variations.

The characteristics of women's work within the three systems

Compared to the bigger European nations, Norway industrialised late. In 1875 still well over half the economically active population was found in the primary sector. In 1900 this was down to 40 per cent, in 1950 to 25 per cent. The breakthrough came just after the turn of the century, as industrial production soared between 1905 and 1916 with 83 per cent growth.[4] The last decades of the nineteenth century nevertheless witnessed major changes in demographic, economic and social structures. The first of the bigger waves of emigrants to the USA occurred in the 1860s, the second in the 1880s and the third from the middle of the 1890s until the First World War. The three biggest cities, Cristiania, Bergen and Trondheim, grew considerably and their combined share of the total population in Norway rose from

18 per cent in 1870 to 28 per cent around 1900.[5] But a great deal of industrial production continued to be located in the countryside along the coast,
where electric power generated from waterfalls along the fiords constituted
the main source of energy. This situation prolonged the period of a mixed
agrarian–industrial economy, so that the family economy system and the
male provider system co-existed until after the Second World War. This was
due, among other factors, to the fact that mechanisation was only slowly
introduced into agrarian production, partly owing to the small average size
of farms and the combination of farming and fishing, and partly due to the
mountainous character of farm land (table 6.1). The family economy system
survived in most agrarian areas until after the Second World War; a situation markedly different from large-scale farming in England, but similar
to family-run farms in France.[7] The growing urban middle classes, as we
shall see, adopted the male provider system from the middle of the nineteenth century onwards.[8]

Table 6.1   *Norwegian farms according to size of cultivated area (dekar), 1907–49*

Size	1907	1949
Less than 5	34	43
5.1–10.0	15	9
10.1–20.0	17	15
20.1–50.0	18	20
50.1–100.0	9	8
100.1–200.0	5	3
200.1–1000.0	2	1
Over 1000.1	1	1
Total	100	100
No.	246, 634	345,125

Source: Norges Offisielle Statistikk, *Census of Agriculture*, 1949.

   In the agrarian family economy, women's first priority was work
designed to secure food and clothing for the family and household members.
If the family lived off their own farm, the wife would take part in production,
especially through her work in the cowshed and with dairy production, but
also through an extensive list of other outdoor activities, ranging from haymaking, potato-planting and harvesting, to the gathering of leaves for animal
food and seaweed for dung. She was also responsible for the smaller animals
on the farm, including poultry, pigs and sheep. Only the horse was a male
responsibility, but then many small farmers and crofters, especially in the
mountainous western parts of the country, did not use horse-driven agricultural machinery until after 1870. Before that, the tilling of the soil was
done by spades, using women's as well as men's labour.[9]

Where farmers combined fishing and farming, as was the case along the coast and in the fiord areas of the western and northern part of the country, wives were responsible for the work on the farm for a greater part of the year. In addition they would assist in many areas in the laborious rinsing and hanging of stockfish – split and air-dried cod – exported especially to southern Europe. This combination of activities and the absence of husbands over long periods of time made women in these areas responsible for the farmwork to such a degree that they have been characterised as female farmers, not as farmers' wives.[10]

Crofters comprised about 60 per cent of all farmers around 1850, but urban migration and emigration reduced their numbers by more than half at the end of the century. In spite of wide regional variations, generally all members of crofter families, would also work for the farmer – in addition to taking care of their own land and livestock. The crofter's wife helped in washing, cooking, baking, slaughtering, etc., on the farm and children guarded cows and sheep, picked potatoes and so on.[11] Children were also a guarantee of support during old age. Indeed, during the nineteenth century the system of pensioning off the old couple by securing them certain rights and services on the farm, at least in some regions, seems to have grown in importance.[12]

As long as towns were mainly centres of administration and trade, even middle-class and upper-class women, to a great extent, took part in the production of food and clothing required for family consumption.[13] Families in the capital – Cristiania, later Oslo – kept cows for the home consumption of dairy products, well after the middle of the nineteenth century.[14] Artisans' wives, as well as the wives of small traders, took part in producing and selling goods. Only gradually, and mainly after the Second World War, when residential areas were separated from the production and trading areas of towns, did the families of artisans and small traders shift more fully towards the male provider system.

Working-class women added to family resources by working in factories or by cleaning, cooking and sewing in other people's homes. Taking in lodgers and minimising expenditure by the artful management of household budgets were also important.[15] As has been shown for nineteenth-century America, scavenging and, in extreme cases, theft may also have been a way out for the most unfortunate Norwegian working-class wives.[16]

Within the system of the family economy, the care of small children, sick and old people was also the responsibility of the wife. When resources were limited, such caring activities would be given low priority. Small children would be left in charge of bigger children, or on their own; the sick and the old would go without help. In more extreme cases, the local community would have to take over, and in the agrarian districts this would be done by sending the needy from one farm to the other, the so-called *legd*. In towns, the poorhouses and a few hospitals would provide assistance for individuals with no family care.[17]

It must be pointed out, however, that this did not necessarily mean a family life without emotional ties between family members. Sentiments were shown, not by physical caresses and sweet words, but as Eilert Sundt put it:

> They show their feelings in this way: he works his farm diligently and she is a careful housewife. There is no lack of happiness, cordiality and joy, but there is more seriousness and thoughtfulness. The beautiful means little compared to the useful.[18]

As far as the children were concerned, sources indicate much love and endearments, and very little punishment among farmers' families all through the nineteenth century.[19]

The transition to the male provider system started within upper- and middle-class urban families. A number of factors may explain the transition. Family production of food and clothes became rarer among such families in the last half of the nineteenth century. The number of servants declined, as alternative jobs were found in developing industries and emigration drained the country of especially male, but also some female labour.[20] Children's work declined in importance and was gradually seen as demeaning. Married women's work outside the family, especially if paid in cash, was condemned. Discussions around the turn of the century in periodicals edited by and read by bourgeois women, especially in the three main cities, amply document the expectations of the wife as the manager of the home, and strongly opposed the idea of a married woman taking part in providing for the family. Even in a situation with impending social degradation, because of a reduction in the wage gap between workers and civil servants (table 6.2), the idea of married women being economically active outside the home was wholeheartedly condemned.[21] The ideal of the husband as the sole provider can also be traced in sources discussing family survival strategies.[22] Husbands were sometimes given the credit even for producing and educating the children, obliterating wives' responsibilities in these fields.[23]

The ideal of the husband as sole provider spread to working-class families around the turn of the century, and was clearly reflected even in the socialist women's organisation.[24] Legal restrictions on women's and children's work in factories were meant to safeguard them against exploitation, but seem to have taken for granted the existence of a male provider. When this was not the case, such restrictions could result in illegal work or dire hunger for some of the families involved.[25] A law of 1892 prohibited women from working in factories for six weeks after giving birth, without

Table 6.2   *Trends in Norwegian occupational wage differentials, 1900–20 (in kroner)*

Occupation	Annual salary (kroner)		
	1900	1910	1920
Industrial worker	100	100	100
Civil Servant	396	336	186
Clerk in municipal services	194	168	110

Source: NOS *Samfunnsøkonomiske Studier*, no. 3, p. 181, table 91.

making provision in any way for their economic subsistence. The law therefore placed in direct contrast the female responsibility of providing for the family and caring for the newborn. In 1909 some support via the system of health insurance was given to women provided they were themselves members of the insurance scheme. As membership depended on a personal wage relationship, this mainly related to unmarried women. Only in 1915 were wives of insured husbands included.

However, the way these and similar laws were implemented in local communities indicates, at least until 1940, that the responsibility of providing for the family was considered above all that of the father of the child. If he could not or would not shoulder this responsibility, the pressure on unmarried mothers to give priority to earning their own living instead of looking after infants was considerable.[26] During the 1920s, however, the idea that daily contact between a mother and a newborn child would improve the mother's moral standards, helped to make municipal authorities a little more inclined to apply the new laws in a way that allowed unmarried mothers the possibility of taking care of their infants with public support.

Such public regulations, however, only applied to a minority of women. Nevertheless, they provide evidence of the growing acceptance of the principle of the husband as sole provider, the wife as dependent housewife, taking care of the children. Even for unmarried mothers, between the wars the moral consequences of mothering paved the way for increased public support.

Other changes bear witness to the same idea. Studies of changes in the labour force within specific branches of industry show that around the turn of the century the number of married women employed in telecommunication, as seamstresses and in the textile industry was already in decline.[27] According to official statistics in 1920 and 1930 married women were to a lesser degree than ever before engaged in full-time economic activities (table 6.3):

Table 6.3   *Employment of married women in Norway, 1875–1970 (per 100)*

1875	3.4
1900	4.6
1919	4.0
1920	2.1
1930	3.1
1940	5.4
1960	9.5
1970	19.6

Source: O. Ljones, *Female Labour in Norway*, Oslo, 1979, table 2.3, p. 27.

It should be explained that the economic depression of the post-war years and its accompanying unemployment did not hit Norway until 1921 and that the crisis years of the inter-war period were between 1931 and 1934.[28] Between the wars the antagonism against married women employed in public services became so strong that the hiring of married women was banned in the local administration of the two biggest towns, Oslo and Bergen. Even with a high court decision to support them, married female teachers also found it difficult to retain their jobs.[29]

The male provider, however, was not opposed to female labour as such. From the 1860s legislation opened up education and jobs to women and gave *unmarried* women better opportunities to earn their living outside the family, thus easing the economic burden for fathers and also possibly for brothers, who, until then, were normally expected to provide for unmarried female relatives.

A final important point underlining male responsibility as sole provider can be found in tax regulations. When in 1863 a law codified the right to deduct a certain amount from taxable income, according to the number of persons to be provided for, wives were *not* classified in this category. This finally did become the case in 1882, however, when urban communities were given the right to allow a reduction in the taxable income of married men, if they considered the wife economically dependent. This principle was only adopted in agrarian communities in 1911. The law regulating the economic situation of married couples in 1927 stated that where a family only had one income, one of the couple had to be considered economically dependent.[30]

It is clear, therefore, that from the middle of the nineteenth century until around the First World War, the principle of the male provider as the sole provider carried the day as the ideal of both lawmakers and politicians. Indeed, the years between 1935 and 1965 have been characterised as the heyday of the male provider system.

From the end of 1950s the male provider system increasingly gave way to the *two-wage system*. Married women's economic activity, as registered in the censuses, doubled between 1950 and 1960, and again between 1960 and 1970 (see p. 163). Other sources, which take into consideration part-time work, indicate that 42 per cent of all married women were economically active in 1970, but 57 per cent in 1980. Two-wage families comprised 56 per cent of all couples in 1972, and 70 per cent by 1979. The right to individual taxation, which married women lost in 1927, was reinstated in 1956.[31] Family survival strategies again relied on both the wife and husband providing for the family, and children now worked mostly to cover their own personal needs, which were viewed by some observers as being rather luxury-related.

The last two decades were also the period of other social and political upheavals, like the new and vigorous women's movement and an explosion in the number of women active in Norwegian politics. At first glance, the sexual division of labour in the family as well as in society as a whole may appear to have been shattered in a few decades. But is this really so – and how do we explain the transition from one system to the next?

The transition from the family economy system through the male provider system to the two-wage system

The first important change in the family economy system was the reduction in the number of servants in the household. The census of 1801 showed 12 per cent of servants in Norway's total population. A hundred years later this figure was down to 6 per cent. Added to this, male servants had by then almost disappeared, which further emphasises the degree to which production had now been removed from the household to society. The remaining servants were mostly house-servants,[32] but their numbers had also fallen significantly. Industrialisation and urbanisation at the end of the nineteenth century had drained the agrarian districts of young women. Although domestic service was the main occupation for young girls until 1930, the scarcity of female servants was already felt earlier in the century. The proportion of families with servants in the central parishes of Cristiania had been halved and even in the west-end parishes only 25 per cent of all families still employed servants between 1895 and 1918.[33] A reduction also took place in the eastern parts of the city, where households with servants had never been numerous. More work was therefore left to the wife, even if running water and electricity did help her to meet new expectations as to the quality and quantity of housework, particularly in the west-end parishes of the capital. However, many agrarian households were without such facilities until after the Second World War.

The reduction in the relative importance of children's work, combined with the increasing need for children to attend school and if possible to obtain a prolonged education, also added to the economic pressure on family incomes.[34] Although the cost of education was not a major factor, concern over the future of children, was an integral part of contemporary discussions on family planning. Girls, in particular, in addition to their educational needs, were also required to earn their own living in an acceptable way before marriage.

Family planning was one of the means adopted by bourgeois families to counteract economic strains from the end of the nineteenth century onwards. Thus changes in family production and family survival strategies led indirectly to changes in the structure of households and in family size. The falling birth-rate alarmed doctors and politicians alike, and measures to prevent a reduction in the population were found in re-educating women. Cleanliness, better house-keeping and better cooking were designed not only to provide protection against leprosy, but also became important in the fight to keep the fewer newborn infants alive. A number of schools for country girls, resulting from the 1864 investigation into the work of farmers' wives in western Norway, started out teaching mainly dairy work and a little cooking and house-cleaning. From the 1880s similar schools spread to urban areas, where cooking and cleaning became the main subjects. By 1920 a trend had started to convert agrarian schools into schools for housewives, with a fair amount of cooking, cleaning and childcare on the curriculum, even if instruction was still given in dairy work. The demand that schoolgirls all over the country should be taught how to clean and cook resulted in this subject becoming compulsory for girls, especially in towns, to the detriment of teaching in mathematics, physics and other theoretical subjects.[35] It is important to note that even the female emancipation movement at that time advocated and strongly promoted this trend. The class bias of these early feminist organisations was very clear in their support for the idea of educating working-class girls to become better servants, as well as in their more benevolent schemes for improving working-class homes by educating the mothers.[36]

From the beginning of the twentieth century doctors also ran a campaign stressing the importance of teaching mothers to breast feed their newborn infants for at least nine months. Bottle feeding and wet-nursing were condemned and so was the habit of leaving the infant with a servant. Although such advice had been given earlier in the nineteenth century, the scope and intensity of later propaganda campaigns from around the First World War onwards had a much broader effect.[37] Nursing and tending infants became a main occupation for bourgeois wives in the fight against infant mortality. Although this new knowledge was vital, the spirit of the medical campaign to educate mothers revealed a low opinion on the capacity of women to understand and take responsibility for even this part of their domestic work without the instruction and supervision of male doctors.[38]

Gradually psychological research added to the weight given to mothering as a decisive factor in forming children's future lives.[39]

Thus growing expectations as to the quality and quantity of women's home-making work, at a time when there were fewer helping hands in the household, became an integral part of the change from the family economy system to the male provider system.

Upper- and middle-class women complied more easily with the new situation and many seemed to thrive as guardians of the health and welfare of their children and husbands.[40] Although these women did not take part in providing for the family they stressed the social and economic importance of a well-ordered home. A presentable and hospitable wife was now an important asset to a bourgeois husband.[41]

However, recent research has shown that an unknown, but nevertheless significant, number of women registered in the censuses as dependent housewives could not or would not live up to the ideal of the male provider system. It is highly debatable if the principle ever applied in practice to the majority of Norwegian families. Even if census material registered most adult women as dependent housewives, many other sources reveal the hard work performed by women frequently hidden behind such statistics. Women in the agrarian districts by no means stopped outdoor work to concentrate on indoor domestic responsibilities. On the contrary, the changes in agrarian technology tended to augment rather than to reduce women's work. Cows were milked more often than before and milking machines were not to be found in an average farm household until the 1960s. Expectations as to the quality of the dairy products and cleanliness in the cowshed also grew. With no running water in the cowshed, and water-carrying traditionally considered women's work, dairy production continued to be at least as strenuous as before (table 6.4).[42] The system of central dairies and the daily collection of milk at the farm or its transportation from the farm to the dairy placed tighter time constraints on women's work. Investigations into working conditions in agrarian families in 1939 and 1949 revealed that most work on the farm was performed by family members. Women did more work there than men, who often had other sources of income, such as fishing, and sometimes combined farming with work in the local factory. An analysis of the correlation between women's work and number of births has confirmed that children, especially in agrarian districts, were still considered a labour resource until the 1930s.[43]

The home textile industry also flourished and expanded in some parts of the country – the Møre and Romsdal district – especially in the 1930s, mainly due to cheap female labour in the homes.[44] Married women's economic employment soared in some working-class districts of the capital, probably due to the periodic unemployment of husbands.[45] Thus in spite of the overall reduction in the registration of married women's paid work,

Table 6.4   *Percentage of Norwegian farms with running water in cowsheds and kitchens,*
1939, according to farm size (cultivated area in dekar)

Farm size	Running water in	
	Cowshed	Kitchen
5.1–10	10	21
10.1–20	19	22
20.1–35	35	27
35.1–50	51	35
50.1–75	66	45
75.1–100	79	56
100.1–200	89	71
200.1–500	96	89
500.1–1,000	98	94
Over 1,000	88	90

Source: *Census of Agriculture*, 1949, vol. 4, p. 235.

Table 6.5   *Percentage of Norwegian families with wife working in cowshed and fields, 1939,*
according to farm size (cultivated area in dekar)

Farm size	In cowshed	In fields
5.1–10	68	66
10.1–20	77	73
20.1–35	79	75
35.1–50	76	72
50.1–75	72	67
75.1–100	66	60
100.1–200	50	45
200.1–500	18	21
500.1–1,000	1	6
Total	71	68

Source: *Census of Agriculture*, 1949, vol. 4, p. 75.

some areas of Norway and some sectors of the economy saw an increase in
such work during the crisis years of the 1930s. The conflict between the
ideology of the male provider system and the reality of at least some
working-class families was clear.

If industrial production did reduce some of the traditional female
household chores, for instance by making the purchase of ready-made
clothes more common, it by no means witnessed an end to the home
production of clothing, especially of clothes for women and children. The
time needed to save additional expenditure by repairing and re-making
already worn clothes was still considerable.[46]

Traditional sources of economic history are in part responsible for the neglect by historians to take account of much of this kind of work performed by women. Statistics led researchers to conclude that most women were economically dependent housewives, whether they lived in the country or in towns. The narrow concept of economic activity, modelled on the typical male worker, has also hampered an effective analysis of women's work.[47] Work not rewarded in cash was not registered and thus most of the work performed by women in the agrarian family has been omitted. Estimates show that when married women's work on family-owned farms was included, the percentage of economically active married women more than trebled.[48] Moreover, work not performed on a full-time basis was often badly registered, thus concealing most of women's part-time activities, for instance, in fish- and vegetable-canning factories, seasonal fish-hanging and seasonal sewing, and so forth. Finally, work performed in the home was badly registered, even if paid in cash. Thus about 10,000 women who worked in the domestic textile industry around the First World War were only recorded in papers resulting from special investigations,[49] and not in the regular official statistics.

The reality for many families, therefore, did not correspond to the ideal of the male provider system. Married women, unable to comply with this ideal, often felt trapped between political ideology and the reality of family life. When a husband's income was adequate, families would often decide to go without money that might otherwise have been earned by the wife. The repeated justification for married women not working outside the home was the all-embracing responsibility they carried for the life and future of their children.

The recent change from the male provider system to the two-wage system was also related to the size and structure of the family. After the 1950s there was a further reduction in the number of births, a fall in the average age of women at marriage and a lower age at the birth of the first child, leaving married women with about half their adult lives independent of the responsibilities of childcare (tables 6.6, 6.7, 6.8).[50] This indicates a strong correlation between smaller families and married women's economic activity, an indication which is strengthened further by the observation that women with small children are somewhat less economically active than women with older children (table 6.9).[51] But the fact that most women are left with roughly another forty years to live after having finished their period of child care has emphasised the importance of preparing for other tasks than family caring activities. The growing number of women in higher education also indicates that women since the 1950s have staked more on preparing for an active professional life.

What may have been forgotten until the past ten to fifteen years is that the number of individuals needing care has not been reduced by the

Table 6.6   *Average number of children per married women in Norway, 1920–70*

		Municipalities	
	Whole country	Rural	Urban
1920	4.02	4.23	3.49
1930	3.45	3.70	2.82
1946	2.52	2.76	1.93
1950	2.40	2.68	1.84
1960	2.28	2.69	1.86
1970	2.24	2.63	1.95

Note: Because of the war no census was taken in 1940.
Source: Ståle Dyrvik, 'Marriages and number of children – an analysis of fertility trends in Norway 1920–1970', *Statistisk Sentralbyrå artikler*, 89 (1976), p. 13.

Table 6.7   *Average age at marriage in Norway, 1901–70 (selected five-year periods)*

	Men	Women
1901–05	29.52	26.52
1911–15	29.44	26.17
1921–25	29.39	26.12
1931–35	30.16	26.68
1941–45	30.15	26.85
1951–55	29.74	26.33
1961–65	27.84	24.48
1966–70	26.53	23.75

Source: Ståle Dyrvik, 'Marriages and number of children – an analysis of fertility trends in Norway 1920–1970', *Statistisk Sentralbyrå artikler*, 89 (1976), p. 15.

Table 6.8   *Timing of first births in Norwegian marriages contracted 1956–70 (percentage)*

	1956–60		1961–65		1966–70	
Age of mother at marriage	A	B	A	B	A	B
Under 18	43	49	43	51	44	
18–20	37	43	36	45	38	
21–24	25	40	24	37	23	
25–29	18	37	19	37	18	
30–34	16	32	17	32	17	
35–39	13	24	13	22	13	
Over 40	4	5	3	3	3	

Note: First birth within the year of marriage (A) and within 1 year from year of marriage (B) as a percentage of all marriages.
Source: Ståle Dyrvik, 'Marriages and number of children – an analysis of fertility trends in Norway 1920–1970', *Statistisk Sentralbyrå artikler*, 89 (1976), p. 21.

Table 6.9 *(a) Married women in Norway economically active according to number of children under 16, 1972 and 1983 (per 100 married women in each group)*

	1972	1983
1 child	44	73
4 or more children	32	48

(b) Married women in Norway economically active with children under 16, according to age of youngest child, 1972 and 1983 (per 100 married women in each group)

	1972	1983
0–2 years	28	54
11–15 years	55	81

Source: NOS, *Arbeidsmarkedstatistikk.*

reduction in the number of small children. The prolonged average life expectancy has doubled the proportion of old people in Norwegian society, more than compensating for the declining number of dependent children (table 6.10). At the same time the number of people traditionally responsible for the care of the elderly, i.e., women between the ages of 45 and 59 has declined sharply since 1940, from around 950 to 600 per 1,000 persons over 65 years of age.[52] The problem is most evident when public authorities have to take over caring responsibilities previously shouldered by unpaid women's work within the family.[53] The double responsibility of economic activity and caring work in the family is therefore still important in any discussion of women's work and family survival strategies. This also disproves the claim that the family no longer has any practical functions and is bound together by sentiment only.[54]

There is another sense in which the structure of the family today is important for women's work. With lower age at marriage and higher levels

Table 6.10 *Children and old age pensioners as a percentage of Norway's population, 1875–1975*

	0–14 years	*65 years and over*
1875	34	6
1900	35	7
1930	28	8
1960	26	10
1975	24	12

Note: Old age pensions start at age 67, which is the general age of retirement.
Sources: *Historical Statistics*, 1978, table 8.

of education of young women, grown-up daughters helping at home have almost completely disappeared. The wife who lost the helping hand of a maid-servant between the wars, now also has to do without the assistance of her daughters (table 6.11). The development and refinement of psychological research has increasingly stressed the importance of the emotional climate of childhood, and leaves no doubt that caring work is still very important in women's family responsibilities. But these continuing responsibilities are only to a minute extent alleviated by fathers taking part in child care.[55]

Table 6.11   *Housewives and daughters as a percentage of Norwegian women working at home without pay, 1875–1970*

	Housewives	Daughters	Total
1875 Whole country	79	21	100
1900 Rural municipalities Urban municipalities	80 81	20 19	100 100
1930 Rural municipalities Urban municipalities	71 78	29 22	100 100
1950 Rural municipalities Urban municipalities	84 94	16 6	100 100
1960 Rural municipalities Urban municipalities	91 97	9 3	100 100
1970 Whole country	97	3	100

Note: There are some problems in arriving at an accurate number of housewives and daughters due to changes in registration practices. This does not however affect the main trend of the figures.
Sources: NOS Census, respective years.

Family survival strategies in a changing society

It goes without saying that these fundamental changes in the nature of women's work and their importance to the family have not taken place only because of strategic deliberations between husbands and wives. Other important causal factors have been the labour-market and technological development. Industrial capitalism has needed cheap labour in the expanding tertiary sector, as well as in the more mechanised and technologically increasingly sophisticated production processes. The traditional artisan has been dispensed with in favour of either the unspecialised or highly specialised worker; theoretical knowledge has also been given priority over practical manual work. These trends went hand in hand with the feminisation of the workforce.

However, historians of women's work have shown that the pattern of women continuing in the factories, shops and offices the kind of production they used to perform in their individual households is insufficient explanation for the present-day sexual division of labour. Gender conflicts in the individual workplace and within individual trades, as well as the predominance of domestic ideology, have been stressed as important explanations for the tenacity of a seemingly traditional sex-differentiation in the labour-market.[56] The strategy of family survival on the male income has been seen as that of a patriarchal capitalist society, aimed at resolving the problem of female competition with male workers and at saving the costs of reproductive activities, without burdening either the employer or the national economy.[57] The strategy of the family depending on the male provider was, therefore, of central importance in the development of women's work outside the home, as it legitimised lower wages for women than for men, irrespective of the number of persons they provided for. If a lower age at marriage for women, and consequently an earlier timing of births were 'push-factors' within the family which influenced the nature of women's work, industrial capitalism's need for cheap labour must be considered an important external 'pull-factor'.

Even when studying women's work from a family perspective, the important consequences of the availability of cheap female labour to capitalist production should not be forgotten. The history of technological development and the conditions for male workers in the Norwegian dressmaking industry is a typical example of how knowledge gained from studying women's history changes our understanding of other fields of the past.[58] At the beginning of this century cheap female labour was especially abundant in the capital; in the 1930s it was found in Romsdal, part of agrarian eastern Norway. The regional switch in the location of dressmaking production enabled employers to overcome demands from male labour unions, and delayed the mechanisation of dressmaking by substituting centralised industrial plants by home-based production. Most of the families in the Romsdal area in the 1930s tried to weather the unemployment crisis by participating in dressmaking production. Cheap female labour clearly saved the family economy in a crisis situation, but at the same time it adversely influenced working conditions for men in the capital, at a time of technological change in the dressmaking industry.

The theory of the capitalist mode of production has been elaborated on the model of the male worker as the sole provider and therefore did not count the costs – born by women's work in the family – of reproducing the male worker's daily working capacity.[59] To have done so would have ruined the justification for the higher male family wage and for the systematically lower wages paid to women. This would have been against the interest of employers as well as of male workers; it would also have touched on the power relationship between spouses.

Internal power structures in the family

The quotation at the beginning of this chapter might lead the reader to assume that farmers' wives were powerful agents within the household. In a way this would be a correct assumption. As the saying goes, 'The key to the storehouse is the key to power.' Deciding the day-to-day disposition of household goods, planning and organising the female part of production, was an important base for power within a rural marriage and was sometimes viewed as the decisive factor in a family's survival chances.[60] Hence the tradition developed for less resourceful farmers and sometimes also for artisans to marry older women, who knew their business well and would not give birth to too many children.[61] Another saying, 'The hand that rocks the cradle rules the world', indicates another source of female power in the family; the bond between mother and children, tied primarily through caregiving work and through the wife's influence over the education of the young.

Needless to say, such sources of female power depended on the characters of the individual wife and husband and it should not be forgotten that the key to the storehouse did not necessarily fit the lock of the moneysafe or the drawer with the official documents. The official power relationship in Norwegian families, as expressed in laws and regulations during most of the nineteenth century, was strictly patriarchal.[62] Unmarried women had to be under the tutelage of either their father, brother or some other man.[63] A husband had the right to decide where the family should live, and divorce his wife if she refused to follow him. He could decide the education of the children and even lay down the guidelines for female household work. He could hire and fire servants, and they had to obey him if he gave orders that clashed with his wife's instructions. Legally, a wife was completely economically dependent on her husband, and she could not conclude economic agreements, or appear in court on her own. Even if the husband and wife each owned one-half of their common goods, he disposed of all of it, including that part which his wife had brought into their marriage. He also disposed of his wife's goods, and was subject to no official control, although this was the general rule for other persons exercising guardianship. The only legal way to control a spendthrift husband was to have him declared unable to manage his affairs.

Gradually, in 1845 and 1863, unmarried women were freed of this bondage and made legally majors on the same conditions as men. This paved the way for women to assume responsibility for the management of their own economic affairs without burdening their fathers and husbands, and at the same time released the cheap labour needed to build up the democratic school system and the developing health services of the welfare state.

In 1888 married women were given the right to dispose of the money they earned by their own work and certain restrictions were put on the husband's right to dispose of common goods. However, a paragraph of the bill stressing the continued duty of the wife to follow the husband where he decided to live and to gain his acceptance for any arrangements that might interfere with her duties as a housewife was only rejected by three votes in the Norwegian parliament.[64]

Not until 1927 did the law allow formal economic equality between spouses. Following this, any disposition of common goods could only be made by mutual consent. The work done by the wife in the home was to be valued as equivalent to the work done by the husband and paid for in cash outside the home. He was enjoined to give his wife money in 'convenient sums' to cover household expenses, as well as a sum for her personal needs.[65] This, however, did not hinder the husband who wanted to make his mastery of the family purse an efficient means of control over his wife. The only escape from this was for wives to earn their own money.

This meant that irrespective of whatever power the wife might possess in daily life and in decisions over the yearly work routines, until 1927 a husband had had the right to sell the family farm or the family business, should he so decide, without even asking his wife. If few husbands used this right, it was still legally theirs. The more the family depended on the husband's earning power, the more the wife would be dependent on him for anything she and the children might need. This actually placed urban bourgeois wives in a weaker position than working-class wives and some farmers' wives, and may help to explain why the women's movement in the 1880s was strongest in an urban bourgeois setting.

Legal and formal authority, however, was not the same as actual effective power. Some sources indicate that in spite of their legally weak position women had a strong influence upon husbands, and even upon fathers and brothers. At the abrogation of the union with Sweden in 1905, both socialist and bourgeois politicians appealed to the not yet enfranchised women to influence the male members of their families in order to carry the plebiscite in favour of abrogation.[66] One conservative politician, trying to prevent female suffrage in 1906, deplored the fact that his tired party-fellows, after a night with their wives, all came round in favour of female suffrage. Later, the same person – when he felt women's political power had become too strong – suggested abrogating the law of female suffrage and weighting male suffrage according to the number of children a man produced in his marriage. He was, however, a lonely swallow. Even if there were isolated examples of women with important political influence through male relatives,[67] these were channels of influence within the family difficult to research and quantify. Direct political influence by women was minimal until the last twenty-five years.[68]

A tentative conclusion to the question of power relations within the family as they related to women's work may be that women in everyday life must have had an important influence upon decisions in the household, especially as long as they lived under the family economy system. But throughout most of the nineteenth century formal legal authority was vested in the husband. When formal male authority weakened at the end of the century, the male provider system represented a more direct means of control by husbands over their wives, which was clearly strongest in urban bourgeois families.[69] All the time the most expedient means of gaining power within a family setting for wives was to earn and dispose of their own money, although this only became their legal right after 1888. As long as the number of children born remained fairly high and household chores were numerous and heavy, the attempt to gain a personal income might have demanded so much strength that it may have been a doubtful base for personal power. With the two-wage system, no legal hindrances, fewer children and modern household equipment, women clearly have a much more solid base for power within the family than their predecessors had.

Yet even within the two-wage system there were still important barriers to equality of power between spouses. According to some sociological theories, such barriers may be rooted in a sex-specific way of reasoning and in changes in the structure of patriarchal society. Both factors affected women's work in the family and how this related to work outside the family.

Sex-specific ways of reasoning and the transition from the patriarchal family to the patriarchal society

Even in the family economy where women could not give a high priority to care-giving work, it was mainly a female responsibility to take care of individuals who could not take care of themselves. At a minimum, the process of giving life to new individuals periodically restricted women from some of their other work, and obliged them to concentrate on the needs of another being. The way of thinking related to such work developed further during the period of the male provider system, when Norwegian society's political objectives were officially geared to educating and enabling women to fulfil their duties as wives and mothers.

Sociologists have produced a theory of sex-polarised prototypes of thinking. According to this theory, reproductive work − be it cooking or washing for the family, reproducing the daily labour of men or the next generation of workers, or taking care of small children – creates a specific female way of reasoning that may be characterised by the terms 'rationality of care' or 'rationality of responsibility'.[70] In this theory, acting according to the rationality of care and responsibility is determined by four characteristics: an identification with the well-being of others, an attention to the consequences of one's activities for others and the assumption of responsibility for such consequences, by appropriate changes in one's own behaviour. The fourth element is the acceptance of non-reciprocity, implying that women are also responsible for their own self-care, and do not expect others to reciprocate the care given to them by women.

Such a way of thinking and acting is indispensable for the effective care of other individuals, in the home as well as in public institutions. It is, however, in opposition to the rationality of ends and means resulting from the socialisation of boys to manhood, and to the process of domination in society, which rewards individual initiatives to obtain specific ends with little attention to the means involved. It is also a very dubious base for obtaining power. The rationality of care and responsibility is the *raison d'être* for women being provided for by their husbands, and disposes women to accept their work as mothers and wives within a patriarchal framework. Women who are economically active as nurses, teachers and secretaries may comply perfectly with this reasoning.[71] It leads them to accept the logic of a worker modelled on the male worker, banning factors pertaining to the privacy of family life from trade-union politics, as well as from the politics of government, and thus alienates the female worker and her special problems from public decision-making processes. This is all the more important, as the kind of work performed by women in the public sphere is dependent to a great extent on public investments in social institutions and in a growing bureaucracy.

With the growth of women's work outside the home and family many women have moved from a private economy within a domestic form of patriarchy to a public economy within a state dominated by male decision-makers, who harbour traditional patriarchal attitudes towards women's work and women's responsibilities.[72] The majority of economically active women perform the same kind of work in institutions – either in hospitals, schools, offices or factories – that women would earlier have performed in their homes: caring for others, or assisting men in their professional activities. Women, therefore, have not, according to this theory, escaped patriarchal bondage by becoming economically active.

However, other trends indicate that the sex-polarised way of reasoning is receding.[73] Women's work in the public sphere has become so important that joining forces in trade unions and other political organisations has given women wage-earners new resources. The first strike among nurses in the

1970s was met with utter disbelief. Today there is nothing surprising in such a show of strength, which has also been followed by strikes among kindergarten personnel. The modern women's movement, unlike the traditional emancipation organisations of the late nineteenth century, has focussed on the interaction of women's work in the family with their work in public production, and on the importance of understanding the problems this entails, not as individual, but as collective and structural problems. This change of perspective promises a better base for expanding the much needed rationality of care and responsibility to society as a whole, without accepting the fourth element of that rationality, non-reciprocity.

A change in the power structure of the family must be accompanied by equality of power in the public sphere in order to pave the way for a levelling out of the sex-specific way of reasoning. A female-headed government, since May 1986 comprising 40 per cent female ministers, appointed a commission in 1986 to look into the consequences such changes were bringing about for the male population. This seems a new step in the direction of equality and may permit women to regain the confidence found in the farmers' wives of western Norway in the 1860s, but this time on a collective and public scale.

Notes

1 H. O. Christophersen, 'Innledning', in Eilert Sundt (ed.), *Om renlighedsstellet i Norge*, 1st edn, 1869; reprinted Oslo, 1975, pp. XVII–XX.
2 K. L. Huus, *Om kvinden*, Bergen, 1872, pp. 4–5.
3 Louise A. Tilly and Joan W. Scott, *Women, Work and Family*, New York, 1978, use the terms family economy, family wage economy and family consumer economy. The first two terms are covered in this paper by the term 'the family economy system', the last by the term 'male provider system'.
4 Lennart Jørberg, 'The Nordic Countries 1850–1914', in Carlo M. Cipolla (ed.), *The Fontana Economic History of Europe*, vol. 4, section 7, 1970. *Historical Statistics* 1968, pp. 30, 36–37; Berge Fure, *Norsk historie 1905–1940*, Oslo, 1971, pp. 16–20. For more detailed statistical information on economic development in the period 1900–1950, see Economic Survey 1900–1950, *Samfunnsøkonomiskestudier*, no. 3, Oslo, 1955.
5 Hans Try, 'To kulturer – en stat. 1851–1884', in Knut Mykland, (ed.), *Norges historie*, vol. 11, Oslo, 1979, pp. 66–7.
6 Farms with an area of less than 5 cultivated *dekar* would leave the family income below subsistence level. On all such farms the male provider had additional income, from fishing, forestry, artisanal or factory work. The bigger farms were predominant in the eastern and middle parts of the country, the smaller farms along the southern, western and northern coasts and fiords.
7 Scott and Tilly, *Women, Work and Family*, pp. 124–5.
8 Ida Blom, 'Real excellent men do not grow on trees', paper for the Ruhrgas conference, Bonn, May 1987.
9 Ann Avdem and Kari Melby, *Oppe først og sist i seng*, Oslo–Bergen–Trondheim–Tromsø, 1985, pp. 9–50. Ingeborg Fløystad, *Kvinnekår i endring. Kvinnene sitt*

arbeid i Arna, Hordaland, 1870–1930, Oslo–Bergen–Trondheim–Tromsø, 1986. On a similar division of labour in Bavaria, see Robert Lee, 'Family and "modernisation": the peasant family and social change in nineteenth century Bavaria', in Richard J. Evans and W. R. Lee (eds.), *The German Family*, London, 1981, pp. 95–6. The special exploitation of female labour and wife-beating mentioned by Lee has not been documented in Norwegian sources.

10 Håvard Dahl Bratrein, 'Det tradisjonelle kjønnsrollemønster i Nord-Norge', in H. D. Bratren *et al.* (eds.), *Drivandes Kvinnfolk*, Tromsø–Bergen–Oslo, 1976; Britt Berggren, 'Kystens kvinner – kystens bønder', in Ingrid Semmingsen *et al.* (eds.), *Norges Kulturhistorie*, vol. 5, 1st edn, 1979, reprinted Oslo, 1984.

11 Ingrid Semmingsen, *Husmannsminner*, Oslo, 1960; Dagfinn Sletten, 'Barnearbeid i jordbruket', in Bjarne Hodne and Sølvi Sogner (eds.), *Barn av sin tid*, Oslo, 1984, pp. 65–75.

12 Ståle Dyrvik, unpublished manuscript. Dyrvik observes this change for the region of Rogaland. He explains it by the fact that young people were less eager to take over farms, emigration and work in towns providing a more tempting livelihood.

13 Sofie Aubert Lindbaek, *Hjemmet paa Faestningen. Af Aubertske Papirer*, Kristiania, 1912, p. 36; Gustava Kielland, *Erindringer fra mit liv*, 1st edn, 1882 reprinted 1889, pp. 25, 31, 64–5, 111–13, 143–5, 228–9, 254; Barbra Ring (ed.), *'Fra Hanna Winsnes' prestegaard'*, Kristiania, 1911, p. 78; Conradine B. Dunker, *Gamle dage. Erindringer og tidsbilleder*, Kristiania, 1909, pp. 231 and 287–8.

14 Sølvi Sogner, Hege Briit Randsborg and Eli Fure, *Fra stua full til tobarnskull*, Oslo–Bergen–Stavanger–Tromsø, 1984, pp. 128–30.

15 Ida Blom, 'Frauenarbeit und Familieneinkommen in der norwegischen Stadt 1875 bis 1930', *Jahrbuch für Wirtschaftsgeschichte*, no. 2 (1984), pp. 47–54. See also Liv Emma Thorsen, 'Kvinnene på Kampen', unpublished thesis in ethnography, University of Oslo, 1979, pp. 151–4 and 161–71, which draws mainly on oral sources from the working-class area of Kampen in Oslo. Thorsen provides evidence as to the paid, but not registered, work of working-class wives in this century, evidence confirmed by reports from benevolent societies and mothers' welfare centres, see Ida Blom, *Barnebegrensning – synd eller sunn fornuft*, Bergen, 1980, pp. 128 and 134–5.

16 Jeanne Boydson, 'To earn her daily bread: housework and antebellum working-class subsistence', *Radical History Review*, 35 (1986), pp. 7–25.

17 Anne-Lise Seip, *Sosialhjelpstaten blir til. Norsk sosialpolitikk 1740–1920*, Oslo, 1984, pp. 43–51.

18 Eiliert Sundt, 'Bygdeskikke', in *Folkevennen 1858*, p. 84.

19 Ståle Dyrvik, 'Den lange fredstiden 1720–1784', in Knut Mykland (ed.), *Norges historie*, vol. 8, Oslo, 1978, pp. 73–4 for reports from local officials criticising farmers for their lenient attitudes to children. A hundred years later the same criticism is still voiced by urban observers, see Ida Blom, 'Barneoppdragelse', in Bjarne Hodne and Sølvi Sogner (eds.), *Barn av sin tid. Fra norske barns historie*, Oslo–Bergen–Stavanger–Tromsø, 1984, pp. 37–51. The fact that hard work may have been an important factor explaining maternal and infant death-rates does not exclude emotional family ties; see Lee, 'Family and "modernisation",' p. 95.

20 Sogner *et al.*, *Fra stua full*, p. 127.

21 Blom, 'Real excellent men'.

22 Ida Blom, 'Nødvendig arbeid – skiftende definisjoner og praktiske konsekvenser', *Historisk Tidsskrift*, no. 2 (1985), pp. 117–41, and *idem*, 'Barselkvinnen mellom befolkningspolitikk, sosialpolitikk og kvinnepolitikk fra 1880 – årene til 1940', *Historisk Tidsskrift*, no. 2 (1982), pp. 141–61. A discussion in 1913 in Parliament of wages for teachers suggested the idea that wages should be regulated according to the number of individuals to be provided for. In 1916 the idea was accepted for college

teachers, to be implemented as an experiment following the principle of promoting larger families by raising wages with each new child. It was made perfectly clear that this system should not apply to female teachers. Married teachers with children were seen as a threat to the quality of work in the schools, as well as to the mother's work in the family in question. See Julie A. Matthaei, *An Economic History of Women in America: Women's Work, the Sexual Division of Labor and the Development of Capitalism*, New York, 1982, pp. 101–19, for a discussion of the impact of a capitalist economy on the sexual division of labour and on male and female identification, and Karin Hausen, 'Family and role division: the polarisation of sexual stereotypes in the nineteenth century – an aspect of the dissociation of work and family life', in Richard J. Evans and W. R. Lee (eds.), *The German Family*, pp. 51–83, for an analysis of the origins and functions of sexual role-division.

23 A discussion in parliament in 1913 gave married men the honour of producing healthy new individuals, and suggested rewarding them by a higher salary than that of unmarried men, and of course than that of any women. See Blom, 'Barselkvinnen', pp. 155–6.

24 Kirsten Flatøy, 'Utviklingslinjer innen Arbeiderpartiets Kvindeforbund fra 1901 till 1914', in Ida Blom and Gro Hagemann (eds.), *Kvinner selv ... Sju bidrag til norsk kvinnehistorie*, Oslo 1977, reprinted 1980, pp. 71–94.

25 Blom, 'Barselkvinnen', pp. 149–51. For a full account of this piece of social legislation, see Seip, *Sosialhjelpstaten*, pp. 185–216.

26 Ida Blom, 'Ingen mor må til tidsfordriv sitte med sit barn paa fanget. Konflikten mellom forsørgeransvar og omsorgsansvar blant ugifte mødre i Bergen 1916–1940', in Per Fuglum and Jarle Simensen (eds.), *Historie nedenfra. Festskrift til Edvard Bull på 70-årsdagen*, Oslo–Bergen–Stavanger–Tromsø, 1984, pp. 25–44.

27 Gro Hagemann, doctoral dissertation in progress, Department of History, University of Oslo.

28 Edvard Bull, 'Klassekamp og fellesskap 1920–1945', in Knut Mykland (ed.), *Norges historie*, vol. 13, Oslo, 1979, pp. 16–22.

29 Elisabeth Lønnå, 'LO, DNA og striden om gifte kvinner i arbeidslivet', in Ida Blom and Gro Hagemann (eds.), *Kvinner selv ... Sju bidrag til norsk kvinnehistorie*, Oslo, 1977, pp. 151–76.

30 Kari Skrede, 'Familieøkonomi og forsørgerlønn', unpublished manuscript, Institute for Applied Social Sciences, Oslo, 1982, pp. 7–8. See also Norges Offentlige Utredninger 12, *Familiebeskatningen*, Oslo, 1979, table 2.3.

31 Kirsten Bjøru and Annemette Sørensen, 'Fragment av norske kvinners livsløp', in Kari Skrede and Kristin Tornes (eds.), *Studier i kvinners livsløp*, Oslo–Bergen–Trondheim–Tromsø, 1983, pp. 70–104; Olav Ljones, *Female Labour in Norway*, Samfunnsøkonomiske studier 39, Oslo, 1979, table 2.3.

32 Sogner *et al.*, *Fra stua full*, pp. 127–8.

33 Blom, *Barnebegrensning*, table 9, p. 271. Other social indicators such as occupation of head of household, population density per room, infant mortality rates and frequency of new facilities, such as bathrooms, clearly indicate the class-specific character of the west-end parishes. *Ibid.*, tables 7, 8, 10 and 16, pp. 270 and 278.

34 The pressure on the family economy resulting from the need to educate children is evident in discussions in bourgeois women's periodicals between the 1880s and 1910. The introduction of a school system common to all social groups in 1889 was especially problematic for upper-class families, particularly for the schooling of daughters. Daughters, to a higher degree than sons, were sent to private schools, but the yearly costs involved were high, more than the yearly wages for a female servant. In 1930 13 per cent of children in Oslo still went to private schools, but two years later only

4 per cent were left in such schools. See Blom, *Barnebegrensning*, pp. 97–100, and tables 18, 19, and 20, pp. 280–1.

35 Gerd Fuglerud, *Husstellskolenes historie i Norge*, Oslo, 1979, pp. 68–77; Unni Berg Olsen, 'Framveksten av husmorskoler og skolepolitikken 1865–1908', unpublished thesis, University of Bergen, 1983, pp. 56–70, 108–43.

36 Kari Sletvåg, 'Vi husmødre slutter oss sammen. Fra Hjemmenes Vel til Norges Husmorforbund 1898–1915', unpublished thesis, University of Bergen, 1980.

37 See Ida Blom, ' '''Smaa barn som prøveklut for alskens gammeldags husraad''? Konflikt om ammerutiner i Bergen 1909–1940', in *Över gränser, Festskrift til Birgitta Oden*, Datafilm ab, Lund, 1987, pp. 41–64; Kari Martinsen, 'Legers interesse for svangerskapet – en del ar den perinatale omsorg. Tidsrummet ca. 1890–1940', *Historisk Tidskrift*, 3 (1987), pp. 373–90.

38 Ida Blom, *'Den haarde Dyste'. Fødsler og fødselshjelp gjennom 150 år*, Cappelen forlag, Oslo, 1988, pp. 104–8.

39 Elisabeth Badinter, *L'amour en plus. Histoire de l'amour maternel (XVIIe–XXe siècle)*, Paris, 1980; Monica Rudberg, *Dydige, sterke, lykkelige barn. Ideer om oppdragelse i borgerlig tradisjon*, Oslo–Bergen–Stavanger–Tromsø, 1983.

40 Avdem, *Oppe først*, pp. 127–50; Merete Wishman, 'Middelklasse husmødre i Trondheim 1900–1940. En Studie i den borgerlige familie', unpublished thesis, University of Trondheim, 1983. This development corresponds to what has been termed in American history the cult of domesticity. See Nancy Cott, *The Bonds of Womanhood: Women's Sphere in New England 1780–1835*, New Haven, 1977.

41 Blom, 'Real excellent men'.

42 Fløystad, *Kvinnekår*, pp. 53–4; Ellen Karin Brunvoll, 'Arbeidsdeling i jordbruksfamilien i etterkrigstida. Undersøoking frå Selbu', unpublished thesis, University of Trondheim, 1982; Ingunn Aagaard, 'Bondekvinner i Oppdal etter 2. verdenskrig. Ei analyse av bondekvinners arbeid og mulighet til makt og innflytelse', unpublished thesis, University of Trondheim, 1984; Lee, *'Family and ''modernisation''*,' pp. 85–96, points out a similar situation in Bavarian agrarian families in the beginning of the nineteenth century when land reforms led to more and harder work for women.

43 Sogner *et al.*, *Fra stua full*, pp. 130–3. Sogner shows that children were considered important labour well into the inter-war years. The reduction in marital fertility in agrarian areas between the wars started with families living on small farms combining farm work with income from other activities. The reduction is seen as an effect of changing aspirations within these families, who were involved in the modernisation of the agrarian areas to a greater extent than families living exclusively off the farm. The correlation between the reduction in marital fertility and women taking part in voting underlines the same point, as does the correlation between the amount of women's work on smaller farms and the reduction in marital fertility. See tables 6.8 and 6.9 for the correlation between number of children and age of youngest child and women's economic activity in 1972 and 1983.

44 Gro Hagemann, 'Teknologi, industrialisering og kjønnsdeling av arbeidet. Enkelte trekk fra klesproduksjonens historie', *Tidskrift for arbeiderbegevelsens historie*, 1985.

45 Liv Emma Thorsen, 'Kvinderne på Kampen 1890–1930', unpublished thesis, University of Oslo, 1978, pp. 161–9. In the 1910 census 5 per cent of married women in the Kampen area were registered as economically active, in 1930 they comprised 17 per cent. Although Thorsen cites the unemployment of husbands as one reason for this change, she also shows that these women were mainly mothers with no or few children.

46 Blom, 'Frauenarbeit', pp. 48–9.

47 Ljones, *Female Labour*, pp. 20–1.

48 *Ibid.*, pp. 33–4.

49 Innstilling fra hjemmeindustrikomiteen, 1916, printed in *Odelstingsproposition*, 38, 1917. The yearly reports of the Public Health Commission in Bergen for the period between 1926 and 1936 give an insight into the extremely difficult conditions of these women.

50 Dyrvik has shown clearly the fall in age at marriage and the tendency to have the first child earlier in married life. He concludes that 51 per cent of conceptions took place before marriage for women married between 1956 and 1970, with the proportion varying with age at marriage from 85–90 per cent in the case of brides under 18 years to 36 per cent for brides 30 years and over: Ståle Dyrvik, 'Marriages and number of children: an analysis of fertility trends in Norway, 1920–1970', *Statistisk Sentralbyrå artiklar*, 89 (1976), pp. 13, 15, 21.

51 NOS, *Arbeidsmarkedstatistikk*, cited in Likestillingsrådet, *Fakta om likestilling*, Oslo, 1984, p. 25.

52 Kari Waerness, *Kvinneperspektiv på sosialpolitikken*, Oslo–Stavanger–Bergen–Tromsø, 1982, pp. 39–44; Ivar Brevik, 'Flere gamle og aleneboende eldre krever økt innsats i eldreomsorgen', *Sosiologi idag*, 3–4 (1985), pp. 449–70; Susan Lingsom, 'Omsorg for ektefellen', *Tidsskrift for samfunnsforskning*, 3 (1984).

53 Waerness, *Kvinneperspektiv*, pp. 88–101, discusses the difficult economic situation for persons, mostly women, caring for elderly parents or other near relatives in their own homes. There were problems, especially important for elderly women, in obtaining additional pensions to provide adequate assistance in daily life, see *ibid.*, pp. 47–69.

54 Michael Anderson, *Approaches to the History of the Western Family 1500–1914*, London, 1980, pp. 39–64.

55 Susan Lingsom and Anne Lise Ellingsaeter, 'Arbeid, fritid og samvaer. Endringer i tidsbruk i 70-årene', *Statistiske analyser*, 49 (1983), pp. 37–9. This article is in a series edited by the Statistical Bureau.

56 Flatøy, 'Utviklingslinjer'; Gro Hagemann, 'Saervern av kvinner-arbeidervern eller diskriminering?'; Elisabeth Lønnå, 'LO, DNA og striden om gifte kvinner i arbeidslivet', all in Ida Blom and Gro Hagemann (eds.), *Kvinner selv … Sju bidrag til norsk kvinnehistorie*, Oslo, 1977, pp. 71–94, 95–121 and 122–55.

57 Heidi Hartmann, 'The unhappy marriage of Marxism and feminism: towards a more progressive union', *Capital and Class*, 8 (1979). See also Marit Hoel, 'The female working class', in Harriet Holter, (ed.), *Patriarchy in a Welfare Society*, Oslo–Bergen–Stavanger–Tromsø, 1984, pp. 106–18.

58 Hagemann, 'Teknologi', pp. 121–3.

59 Hartmann, 'Unhappy marriage'; Lydia Sargent (ed.), *Women and Revolution: A Discussion of the Unhappy Marriage of Marxism and Feminism*, Boston, 1981; Marit Hoel, 'The female working class' in Harriet Holter (ed.), *Patriarchy in a Welfare Society*, Olso–Bergen–Stavanger–Tromsø, 1984, pp. 106–18.

60 Avdem, *Oppe først*, pp. 48–50. See on this theme for France Martine Segalen, *Mari et femme dans la société paysanne*, Paris, 1980.

61 Eilert Sundt, *Folkevennen*, 1858, pp. 89–97; Conradine B. Dunker, *Gamle Dage*, Kristiania, 1909, pp. 329 and 403.

62 The term patriarchy has many definitions, see Harriet Holter, 'Women's research and social thoery', in Harriet Holter, (ed.), *Patriarchy in a Welfare Society*, Oslo, 1984, pp. 9–25. The term is used here broadly to denote the system of men's authority over women in the family as well as in society.

63 Ida Blom and Anna Tranberg (eds.), *Nordisk lovoversikt. Viktige lover for kvinner ca. 1810–1980*, Oslo, 1985, pp. 144–71 which gives a survey of important legislation in this field.

64 Anna Caspari Agerholt, *Den norske kvinnebevegelsens historie*, 1937, reprinted Oslo, 1973, pp. 135–9.

65 Agerholt, *Den norske*, p. 60.

66 Ida Blom, 'The struggle for women's suffrage in Norway, 1885–1913', *Scandinavian Journal of History*, 5 (1980), pp. 3–22.

67 Blom, 'The struggle'; *idem*, 'Barselkvinnen', pp. 152–3.

68 Torild Skard, *Utvalgt til stortinget*, Oslo, 1980, pp. 25, 43, 46 and 65.

69 Boydston, 'To earn her daily bread', maintains that the male provider system was a replacement for the legal right to decide on the work of wives and children and thus maintain male authority in the family. Hausen, 'Family and role-division', suggests seeing the polarisation of sexual stereotypes in the nineteenth century as a way of securing women's dependence on the family at a time when individualisation seemed to threaten the system of the patriarchal family.

70 Kari Waerness, 'The rationality of caring', *Economic and Industrial Democracy*, 5 (1984), pp. 185–211; Holter (ed.), *Patriarchy*, pp. 9–25; Bjørg Aase Sørensen, 'The organizational woman and the Trojan-horse effect', in Holter (ed.), *Patriarchy*, pp. 88–105; Hildur Ve, 'Women's mutual alliances: altruism as a premise for inter-action', in Harriet Holter (ed.), *Patriarchy in a Welfare Society*, Oslo, 1984, pp. 119–35.

71 Recent investigations into the perceptions of school leavers as to their future roles in society and family clearly demonstrate the difference between young women, reasoning in accordance with this theory, and young men, planning individually and without regard to the effects their personal decisions for the future may have on others. It is also interesting that the idea of the male breadwinner still dominates the thinking of men, while women aim at being able to combine family responsibility with economic activity. Hildur Ve, 'Kjønsroller – ''og som fedrene har kjempet – Mødrene har gredt''', unpublished manuscript, University of Bergen.

72 Helga Hernes, 'Women and the welfare state: the transition from private to public dependence', in Harriet Holter (ed.), *Patriarchy in a Welfare Society*, Oslo, 1984, pp. 26–45.

73 Matthaei, *An Economic History of Women*, pp. 278–320, traces the break-down of sex-typing of jobs and of the sexual division of labour in marriage in the USA, as well as the growth of the symmetrical family, as indicators of a more egalitarian, less competitive and more humane society.

PART THREE

Factory work and urban employment

Chapter Seven

Kinship, labour and enterprise: the Staffordshire pottery industry, 1890–1920

RICHARD WHIPP

The people of the Staffordshire Potteries[1] have not received widespread attention from social historians. The result has been the exclusion of relevant evidence from a number of major debates over, for example, the historical development of work, industrial communities and class and gender relations. This chapter demonstrates the cost of ignoring such industries by exploring the significance of women's work and the family in the pottery industry between 1890 and 1920. The potters' experience relates directly to many of the current concerns of social historians, feminist writers and economic historians. The chapter first reviews the key elements of the literatures which have built up around the issues of the role of women and the family in production; the remaining three sections reveal how the nature of women's labour and the family must be understood at a number of levels ranging from definitions of kin through to the construction of the family within the Potteries region. This understanding illustrates how the historical role of women and the family is not straightforward. In contrast to certain models of patriarchy and of the labour process this exploration of that role gives due weight to both structural determinants and the active ways in which men and women could refashion them. Through this process of making and re-making of gender relations in and around work the classic positions of dominance and subordination were modified.

The family and women's work

The family has remained the subject of historical contention throughout the attempts of different specialists to capture its form and function in the past. Social historians of work have focussed their attention on the family's changing connection with production during the process of industrialisation, its links with parallel transformations in community structures and

184

the family as a factor in skill or job succession and therefore in internal class division. The experience of the potter's family throws new light on all of these approaches.

Following the work of Anderson[2] on nineteenth-century Lancashire textile towns, a lively discussion ensued over the internal conduct of family members in growing industrial towns. In essence Anderson argues that kin in working-class families increasingly behaved in a calculative way so that each expected some return on their input into the family's activities. The family is likened to a joint-stock company. Subsequent work has indicated how the bases of this calculation have varied according to material endowment and personal disposition.[3] Writers on women and the family have set aside the notion of a calculative standard of behaviour and instead pointed to the patriarchal values which governed the working-class family throughout the various transitions from pre-industrial society to mature capitalism. Given the low status accorded to unpaid female domestic labour coupled with the exclusion of women from skilled wage labour, the family has been consistently cited as an institution which has accounted for a major part of the suppression of women.[4] The seminal account of women's work and the family by Tilly and Scott suggests that as industrialisation developed one manifestation of this suppression was the way married women were almost totally excluded from formal paid employment.[5]

In a similar way the values and codes by which eighteenth- and nineteenth-century industrial communities operated have been linked with the ideological oppression of women.[6] Berg reveals how the moral axioms which were central to the operation of, for example, the Yorkshire textile districts were also prejudicial to the interests of women. These textile trades drew on a cheap female labour supply which was 'cheaper by custom': such customary attitudes to women's work were generated within the family and sustained across the wider networks which made up the early industrial settlements.[7]

As the following sections show, the position of women in the potter's family was not one of simple subordination at work or at home. Women in the Potteries remained and indeed increased their numbers within the industry throughout the nineteenth century. Consequently the traditional bourgeois ideology of 'separate spheres' and women's domestic role did not have such application in the Potteries as it may have done elsewhere. Given this continuous and growing presence of the woman potter the moral codes of the 'Six Towns' which made up the region were not exclusively defined by men, nor was skill and job succession a male preserve. Our understanding of the suppressive nature of the family must be adjusted accordingly.

The considerable volume of feminist history has elaborated the secondary position of women in both the family and the workplace. In broad terms women's subordinate place in the labour process of capitalist economies is explained not just by reference to ideological considerations. Patriarchal social relations within paid employment developed for material reasons as well. In other words, male workers accepted the lower wage and status levels of women in so far as this segregation reinforced the dependence of women on male wage-earners. There appears to be a general agreement that 'industrial capitalism took shape in and was shaped by an already gendered world'.[8] In the nineteenth century, as employers tried to replace men with cheaper female labour, adult male workers sought to exclude such competitors as a means of securing jobs for themselves. The past decade of research has provided ample evidence of how the division of the labour force by gender has become entrenched in the social relations of industrial capitalism.[9]

However, a distinctive feature of recent sociological research has been the uncovering of wide variation in the way women workers experienced such social relations and above all the active fashion in which they sought to confront and cope with their secondary status. A shift in emphasis from researching not the passive but the active aspects of women workers in the past has occurred. This is most visible in the study of the ties among women and the creative aspect of women's organisation of domestic routines, work patterns and indeed family survival.

Anthropologists have long noted the importance of female networks across very different settings and have highlighted them as appropriate means of information exchange in, for example, migration. Further expressions of the ties between women appear in work on the matrilocal nature of working-class neighbourhoods in Britain and France and on the local networks which underpinned middle-class women's protest groups in nineteenth-century America.[10] Ross's work on the East End of London argues that such ties were central to the structuring of neighbourhood culture while Hewitt's review of 'friendship and support networks' among working-class women in the USA goes further: she regards them as potential 'crucibles in which collective acts of rebellion were formed'.[11] It is in this area that the women potters are of particular interest. Most of the existing literature on women's networks confines their operation to the neighbourhood. In the Potteries the ties among women penetrated the worlds of home, neighbourhood and workplace.

The third main area of historical research which has a bearing on the nature of the family and women's work concerns the management of industry. If the essence of patriarchal relations is to be understood by reference to its historical interdependence with the development of capitalism, then the operation of managerial control over female labour becomes of immediate interest. While students of management have stressed the means by which labour policies at the level of the firm reinforce the secondary position of women in the labour-market, there are further considerations which the Potteries and parallel cases can exemplify.[12] Management may have had a strong impact on the family by using it to provide adequate labour supply or by erecting an image of employment relations based on an idealised version of the family. Yet, this weapon of labour control could also be used against management, most especially by women workers because of their pivotal position in the link between neighbourhood, family and work.

The following sections explore each of these three areas of the family, women and work, and the relationship between women, family and management control in turn by reference to the Staffordshire pottery industry of the late nineteenth and early twentieth centuries. *Inter alia* this account suggests that if historians are to understand the full extent of women's subordinate position, they must accommodate those aspects of the women, family and work triangle where female dependency was not total and where women played an active part in the construction of influence and even authority.

Women and the family in the Potteries

It is possible to equate the Potteries with the pottery industry in a single breath primarily because of the region's complete domination by ceramic manufacturers. Of the country's pottery workers, 80 per cent lived within a 5-mile radius of Stoke Town Hall. Almost the entire Potteries population of a quarter of a million people was supported directly or indirectly by the staple industry in 1911.[13] The location of the industry in a compact, relatively isolated region led a succession of commentators to remark on this 'industrial island' separated from the rest of the country by 'tradition, heredity and a long-established special industry'. The Potteries have therefore been described as 'an isolatable case study which offers scope for intensive investigation'.[14]

Apart from constituting the 'world's greatest pottery industry', by 1900 the Potteries had two features of direct interest to contemporaries and subsequent historians alike: the extent of female labour and the especially close overlap of family, home and work. In 1901 there were just over 25,000 male and 21,000 female potters. By 1921 the industry contained 23,000 men and 29,000 women workers. As Collet's study of *Women in Industry* published in 1911 shows, the industry had run against the national trend which exhibited a general withdrawal of women from employment between 1851 and 1901. According to UK census data, in 1901 pottery manufacturing was the sixth largest industrial employer of female labour in Britain.[15] Two characteristics of the high female labour force are particularly noteworthy. First, as the 1891–1921 censuses (which under-recorded casual or part-time work) show, women pottery workers remained at work not only beyond

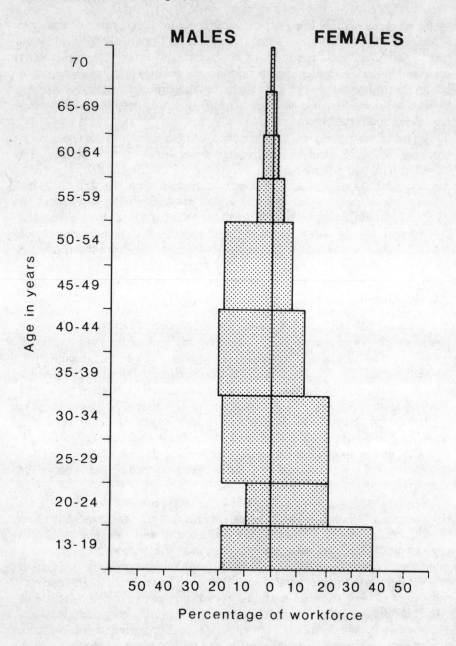

Figure 7.1 *Age and sex composition of the workforce in the Staffordshire pottery industry, 1921*

Source: Staffordshire Census, 1921, Table 18, pp. 93–6.

adolescence but more especially beyond their twenties. By 1921 nearly 20 per cent of the female workforce was aged between thirty-five and fifty-five. Secondly, the pottery industry had one of the highest proportions of married women workers in the country. The national average was just over 10 per cent of total female employment in each industry in 1921; for pottery the figure was 31 per cent.[16]

Given such heavy female presence in the industry the relationship between family and work received broad recognition at the time. For example, a general concern over the 'fertility of marriage' in the 1900s led to a reworking of the 1911 UK census to highlight family size in each industry. The results showed the potters to have one of the highest average family sizes at almost six.[17]

Great care is needed to convey the precise nature of so-called family employment in the Potteries at this time and attention must be given to the different possible meanings of the term 'family employment'. The high level of married women potters and working children (the Potteries were the second largest area of juvenile labour in the country after Lancashire) suggests the presence of others alongside male heads of families at work. Potters themselves were recorded as saying how family employment was as old as the industry and how an individual male skilled potter might 'employ his own family'. Clara Collet, a mathematician and fellow of University College London found in her study for the Royal Commission on Labour in 1892 how 'in many cases husband and wife or child work together' and The Royal Commission on the Poor Law in 1906 formed a similar conclusion.[18] Certainly, assertions by potters such as 'the men and women working in a (pottery) factory are often husbands and wives, brothers and sisters, fathers and daughters' can be verified but they mask the variety of family presences in the workplace.

The verification is relatively straightforward. Union records are especially useful since by 1921 union membership had reached almost 90 per cent. In the sample neighbourhood of Basford for the year 1920–21 the union register demonstrates the extent of family involvement even if the strictest definition of family is applied, i.e., co-residents with the same surname. Examples are given in Table 7.1. Out of the 400 recorded pottery workers 191, or 47 per cent, were in family groups where other members of the family household were potters. Within these family units the mean number of members per family working in a potbank was three. Comparable union surveys and the records of individual companies during the period confirm these findings.[19]

However, it would be entirely wrong to suppose that the meaning of family employment in the pottery industry related only to the immediate family workgroup working in the same potbank. The widespread existence of subcontracting in all the main stages or departments of production (see

Table 7.1   *Examples of family employment in the Staffordshire pottery industry, 1920–21*

Name	Place of work	Occupation	Union contribution rate (d)
Ducketts, 3 Helvetia Terrace			
Mr Ducketts	Wengers Ltd	Foreman	6
Mrs Ducketts	Wengers Ltd	Warehouse	3
Ethel Ducketts	Vickers Ltd	Presser	3
Ada Ducketts	Vickers Ltd	Presser	2
Munslow, 160 Shelton New Rd			
Mr J. H. Munslow	Twyfords	Pressman	6
Edith Munslow	Twyfords	Warehouse	3
Dorothy Munslow	Twyfords	Glazier	3
Hopkinson, 150 Shelton New Rd			
Mr John Hopkinson	Fieldings	Saggarmaker	6
Sara Hopkinson	Fieldings	Labourer	3
William Hopkinson	Fieldings	Saggarmaker	3
Nellie Hopkinson	Fieldings	–	3
Gordon, 146 Shelton New Rd			
C. Gordon	Cauldon	Transferrer	3
E. Gordon	Cauldon	Enameller	2
Eva Gordon	Twyfords	Warehouse	2
Phyllis Gordon	Cauldon	Gilder	2
Rabus, 54 Brick Kiln Lane			
Florence Rabus	Ridgeways	Warehouse	3
E. Rabus	Ridgeways	Warehouse	2
M. Rabus	Ridgeways	Dishmaker	2
Tinsley, 93 Victoria St			
William Tinsley	–	–	6
Ethel Tinsley	New Hall Works	Gilder	3
Annie Tinsley	New Hall Works	Gilder	3
Dolly Tinsley	New Hall Works	Gilder	3

Source: CATU COLL, William Broad's Collector's Book for July 1920–June 1921, covering the Basford area of Stoke.

Figure 7.2) meant that it was deemed entirely natural to employ other members of the family or relations. The unpredictable character of demand for pottery and the irregularity of employment alone meant that not all such family or kin groups could stay together. However, what is clear is that immediate and distant kin worked if not in the same workgroup or shop, then in the same department or potbank. The result was a pattern of immediate family and broader kin connections, involving both sexes, within individual potbanks and ultimately across the industry.[20]

The location of women in such patterns was a central one arising from both custom and necessity. The potters had not reached that point where a sharper division of labour in the household had resulted in women becoming only 'child care and consumer specialists'. Quite the reverse,

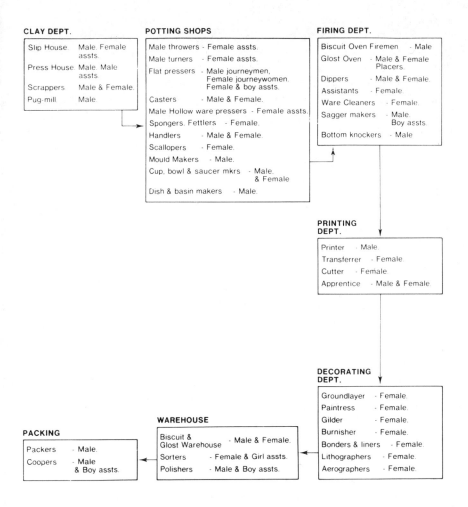

Figure 7.2 *The production process and the division of labour in Staffordshire pottery manufacture, 1890–1920*

Sources: C. J. Noke and H. J. Plant, *Common Commodities and Industries: Pottery*, London, 1924; C. Binns, *Manual of Practical Potting*, London, 1922; *The Times Engineering Supplement*, 2 April 1913, pp. 25–30; E. Sandman, *Notes on the Manufacture of Earthenware*, London, 1921.

as the first factory inspectresses noted, it was the conventional behaviour in the Potteries for a woman to be 'looked upon as lazy unles she takes her share in contributing to the family income'. The notion of the 'family wage' has always been a strong one in the industry, based on husband, wife and children's earnings. In the 1890s most of the potters' unions had rulebooks which set contribution and benefit rates according to a 'wife's earnings'. In the 1900s and 1920s alike the accepted code among the potters' families was 'that as parents they have not done their duty unless they have seen to it that *every girl as well as a boy* (emphasis added) is provided with a trade'.[21]

Women's prominent position in the pattern of family and wider kin involvement in work was also born of necessity. Not only was pottery employment unstable due to the vagaries of consumer demand, it was also the victim of a succession of downturns in the trade cycle during the period in 1900–02, 1904–05, 1908–09 and 1914. Custom apart, the precariousness of even the highest paid potters' (male or female) wages made it essential that as many members of a family or household worked as possible. The extent of this family reliance on mixed earnings power can be seen from the stream of criticism which it attracted from outsiders and visitors to the potteries. This extended from the Parliamentary Inquiry into the Employment of Children Act in 1907 to the comments of social reformers such as Bertram Wilson. He thought in 1900 that generations of girls 'know no better' than to work, as he put it, 'full escape seems impossible' and this could only lead to household neglect, thus 'victims in their ignorance of home, they become vehicles to perpetuate the system'. Stripped of his patronising moralising, Wilson was identifying the important contribution women made to family–household survival strategies.[22]

The male potter according to middle-class or outside commentators may have been given the title of head of household or 'bread-winner'. However, among the potters it was clearly recognised that the management of the family income *and* household budget was often a female preserve. The lot of a potter's wife was as one put it 'the most arduous and responsible to conceive, for upon her devolves the financing of the too-often uncertain income of the family'. The point to stress is that this responsibility, remarked on by some social historians was derived not from a woman's isolated domestic position but from her joint activities in the home and workplace. The generally accepted roles of male provider and female dependant were reversed quite naturally in the Potteries as men regularly were found at home due to ill-health and short-time working. The Physical Deterioration Committee of 1904 found in Longton that there were 'many cases in which the man stays at home while the woman goes out to work' and as a result it was apparently natural that 'men and boys willingly do their part in the domestic work of the house'.[23]

In patriarchal society the women potters (especially the single and widowed) were by no means in a position of equality with their male kin, yet by their joint activity in home and potbank the woman potter confronts the stereotypes of the time and those used by subsequent historians. The crudest such as that in Stearns' essay on 'Working class women in Britain 1890–1914' assert that such women 'were resigned to their lot'.[24] Most recently, Seccombe draws an equally extreme conclusion from the literature on women and the home:

> Working class men, as a rule, spent very little time at home beyond eating and sleeping ... This was not so much a patriarchal regime of direct on-site rule as it was, more often, a tyranny of abstention and neglect; predicated on the inescapable imperative for the wife to obtain as much of the main bread-winner's wage as she possibly could and to maintain, above all, his capacity to labour.[25]

The pottery industry's experience does not square with suppositions on the part of contemporary commentators and historians about gender relationships. This can be understood by examining the world of the potbank more closely.

Women, work and the potbank

Any discussion of work in the pottery industry must emphasise the intricacy of a production sequence composed of many inter-dependent phases. It was largely due to the fragmented, sub-contracted character of pottery work that women were able to exert their own influence. Just as male workers contested managerial authority so did female potters subvert or circumvent male power if necessary with the resources they could summon from inside and outside the potbank.

Because of the lack of a ceramic science or a unified mass demand for one type of china or earthenware, mechanisation in the pottery industry remained low until after 1945. The result was a production process broken down into thirty separate sequences in even the smallest firms. This made for a complex division of labour. A 1913 survey discovered eight-seven occupational groups within the earthenware trade alone. No single occupation was numerically dominant. In 1922 the three largest formed only 10 per cent of the labour force; most groups accounted for between 1 and 4 per cent. There was an immense range of skill from the juvenile clay carriers to the senior firemen who would often earn more than the small firm masters who employed them.[26]

In terms of skill, wages and social relations the women potters diverge from the generally accepted views on late-nineteenth- and early-twentieth-century women workers. As figure 7.2 shows women were well represented in every department. Similarly, they also were found at every level of

Factory work and urban employment

skill in the industry, as the following list indicates, and were not confined to unskilled low-paid jobs:

Skill hierarchy of pottery manufacture

Skilled men
Firemen
Turners
Throwers
Modellers
Mouldmakers
Stickers-up
Pressers
Dishmakers
Saggarmakers
Printers
Dippers
Gilders
Engravers
Packers
Placers
Head warehousemen
Casters

Skilled women
Paintress
Groundlayer
Liners
Gilders
Transferrers
Handlers
Jiggerers
Flat pressers
Casters
Placers

Unskilled men
Slip makers
Clay puggers
Emptiers
Scrappers
Pug mill men
Handle makers
Glaze makers
Dippers assistants

Bottom knockers
Saggarmaker assistants
Oddmen
Kilnmen

Unskilled women
Finishers
Aerographers
Handle makers
Enamellers
Dippers assistants
Fettlers
Spongers
Towers
Ware cleaners
Putters up and takers off
Sorters
Wrappers
Packers
Paperers
Stampers
Burnishers

Unskilled youths
Mould runners
Batters out
Clay carriers
Straw boys
Cutters
Ballers
Warehouse assistants

Source: C. J. Noke and H. J. Plant, *Common Commodities and Industries: Pottery*, London, 1924; M. Graham, *Cup and Saucer Land*, London, n.d. [1908?]; C. Binns, *Manual of Practical Potting*, London, 1922.

Certain jobs were almost exclusively done by women, and had been so since the eighteenth century. Yet these were not jobs which reduced women to the well-known secondary position in the labour-market. On the contrary, in the case of decorating, women dominated the department but at the same time exhibited high skill levels (with apprencticeships), enjoyed wage-rates which compared favourably with unskilled and even some skilled men and developed one of the strongest women's unions in the Printers and Trans-ferrers.[27] The range of skill and pay among the women potters, which included locally recognised women of high wage and craft levels, is well

195

documented by the contemporary research of Sylvia Pankhurst, or Malcolm Graham and appears naturally in the fiction of local author Arnold Bennett.[28]

This is not to argue that women potters did not have to face difficulties common to female labour elsewhere. In spite of the extent of female labour and skill some men, given the highly fragmented and therefore competitive nature of pottery work, attempted to marginalise women workers and minimise their labour when women competed directly with men in the potting or firing shops. Evidence of such behaviour is available throughout the nineteenth century and most especially in relation to women who could not call on family support.[29] The point being made here is that the image of the impermanent, young, unskilled, low paid and therefore marginal women worker does not fit the pottery industry. Instead, within the collaboration and competition among all pottery workers, women did not necessarily come out totally subservient or subordinate to men.

What were the means by which women potters survived the competition of the potbank? First, because certain women's labour was skilled and needed they could be more assertive. It was remarked in October 1891 how the woman potter 'lives an independent life and forms a circle of acquaintances of her own' and her husband treated her 'as a pillar of the household' conceding 'to her as her right the same indulgences and enjoyments as he takes himself'.[30] Secondly, from among her ties with other women, or men of her immediate family or distant kin, or simply her 'circle of acquaintances' women potters derived the knowledge whereby female job succession could operate alongside male versions. In an industry where subcontracting was so prevalent it was an entirely logical progression for children to follow their parents into specific trades. Evidence from Burslem town's union records for 1920 shows that daughters followed their mother's occupation to an even greater extent than boys did their fathers. Interviews with those who entered the industry in this period as girls suggest that not only parents but aunts and cousins could also provide information on job opportunities, means of job entry and informal training once in the workplace. As we see in the next section, employers sanctioned the operation of these mechanisms of sponsorship while women used them to defend themselves.[31]

Thirdly, family and neighbourhood networks were used extensively by women to support one another through the inevitable crises of unemployment, debt or ill-health. Women organised amongst themselves, often in their own department, subscription clothing clubs (known as maxims) and medical assistance schemes. It was the strength of these informal arrangements which so irritated the settlement workers in the 1890s and 1900s and the early women health visitors after 1911, as women potters refused to use the public and official apparatus. This was especially true of health questions. According to national figures, between 1906 and 1930 the potters were second only to miners in the numbers disabled from work by disease. Their afflictions derived from the lead, dust, heat and heavy weights involved in pottery manufacture. Medical considerations apart, the main problem for women was the fear of suspension from work if found to be ill. The attack rate per thousand for lead poisoning among females in 1908 was 26, for males it was only 12. Therefore women preferred to use their own information sources of how to counteract the disease rather than co-operate with new certifying surgeons. As one doctor complained: 'It is very hard to obtain reliable figures. The women working in the dangerous processes are very loath to give particulars, for they feel that if they make out the case to be as bad as it is they will lose their jobs.'[32]

The women potters are by no means unique in these three respects. As regards independent action and assertiveness they bear a striking resemblance to the female jute workers of Dundee during this period as described by Walker.[33] In the area of female ties and job information networks the strongest parallels are with the Lancashire and Yorkshire textile towns studied for different periods by Lambertz and Jackson. Similar sociological study of the Isle of Sheppey in Kent in the 1980s accords with both Roberts' celebrated account of Manchester and the evidence of the potters that women were able to, in Roberts' words, both store and redistribute information that could be important economically to themselves and to other women.[34]

Women, the family and enterprise

The study of the pottery owner or employer and his labour policies seems to corroborate the picture built up so far of the creative influence of women in the potbank. This comes through in the areas of management's recruitment needs especially. The reaction of women to employers' less-subtle attempts at control at workgroup or wider union level shows how the ties between women could be of significance beyond the immediate female network. Given the persistence of sub-contracting and the reliance of potbank owners on craft knowledge in the absence of scientific bases of production, managerial control of work was in essence simple. On the other hand, as foreign competition increased for the china trade especially and prices fell in the 1900–10 period, managers, supervisors and ceramic consultants were used increasingly. A mixture of traditional paternalism and more direct control resulted.[35]

Under the more indirect paternalist approach owners were happy to make use of the informal recruitment methods developed by men and women. The mechanism of a woman worker 'speaking for' someone not only saved time and money, it could also become a sanction against the sponsor should a new entrant misbehave. The transmission of skill within kin ties further reduced training costs. Owners were also quick to use the presence of relations in the same potbank to construct images of the company and potbank which could neutralise conflict. In 1919 the head of the Bullers Company spoke approvingly at a presentation to his employees of how 'when people had been with them through all their boyhood and manhood, girlhood and womanhood, that they had the desire to bring their children and their children's children there.' Other examples of the celebration of family events for workers and employers' families are legion across the industry.[36]

Yet there was a great risk involved in such paternalism. In spite of the benefits to management of the relative autonomy of men and women workers to recruit people of their choosing, the mechanism could be used by workers to their advantage. Managers' dependence on informal recruitment was often used against them by workers in disputes. This was especially true during the periods of high demand and labour shortage in 1899, 1910–13 and 1915–20. Further, potters were able to hand on knowledge of job controls and the means of thwarting supervision via kin ties. The grand statements of paternal concern by employers could face great obstacles in family-based workforces. A clear example is the case of the New Hall Porcelain Company which provided a day out for its workforce at Blackpool in September 1919. Much was made in the speeches that night of the length of service among generations of women employees and their loyalty. In December those same women struck successfully against the company's attempt to deduct stoppages from their wages.[37]

In the years of depressed trade and as management looked increasingly to methods of direct control involving conflict, family ties and female networks were arguably more useful to workers. In the 1890s the Women's Trade Union League (WTUL) made a sustained effort to broaden the base of female trade unionism in the industry by extending the principles already used by the Printers and Transferrers. Because employers very often refused full-time union officials access to their potbanks, union organisers naturally fell back on the family and neighbourhood ties of the potters. Marion Tuckwell, Mary McArthur and Doris Chew, organisers for the WTUL, built up branches of the League of necessity by basing their local organisation on house-to-house communication. Neighbourhood involvement was sufficiently strong to support a vacancy scheme and out-of-work benefit which used the informal models of the women potters' maxim and medical clubs.[38]

Nor was this an isolated or temporary phenomenon. By 1906 the twenty different unions in the industry had amalgamated to form the National Society of Male and Female Pottery Workers. Between 1911 and 1920, with rising consumer demand, membership grew spectacularly from just under 10,000 to 40,000. The rise in real earnings, the effect of the new union's combined strength plus a new generation of leaders including Sam Clowes and Jabez Booth helped to account for the numerical increase.[39] However, the means by which the union met the growth in local managerial control policies rested securely on the pre-existing linkages of home and work which was so much a part of potters' working lives. Inspection of the union's membership ledgers for 1916–20 reveals that in a 1 per cent sample of the union members, 30 per cent of the women and 45 per cent of the men were in the union as part of a male or female family group. As George Eardley, a collector for the union observed, the home-work link was vital. In his opinion people would not be persuaded to join the National Society 'unless the atmosphere of trade unionism prevails in the home or workshop'.[40]

The potters are an excellent example of Bornat's assertion that in industries with a high percentage of female labour 'the close link of home and work maintained through dependence on and exploitation of family ties provided the context for participation in trade unions'. Indeed, the family and neighbourhood basis of union organisation in the Potteries was an area where women made a telling contribution to trade unionism. Women potters' presence was especially strong in the collectors' ranks, where door-to-door collection of union dues and the processing of local grievances by female collectors developed naturally on the basis of neighbourhood networks.[41] In Fenton there were seven female and five male collectors. As the formal organisation of the union grew under new leaders the full-time organisers relied heavily on these local patterns of contact. This was especially true in Clowes' work in the Longton china district and Booth's campaign in the jet and rockingham trade. By 1915 there were several women on the newly created district or town committees of the union and men and women mixed freely in the lodges. Dora Mycock and Agnes Lawton were able as national organisers from 1908 to 1920, to use the rich pattern of workgroup and street-based union action to mount not only successful wage bargaining but also campaigns on broader issues such as protective legislation against the use of lead. Successes against the Henry Richards Company in 1907 and the notorious Grindley firm in 1911 were surpassed in the 1914–20 period of high demand by the winning of a series of equal pay agreements for men and women which became the basis of official union policy thereafter.[42]

Conclusion

The general argument of this chapter is that in the process of the making and re-making of gender relations in the home, neighbourhood and work-place, women such as the potters have not displayed the generally accepted female role of dependence and passivity. This is not to argue that there was a reversal of patriarchal relations in the Potteries, far from it. Instead we have been at pains to show how women did not overturn but modified important aspects of those relations by their role in the family, neighbourhood, workplace and union. Above all, the evidence from the Potteries shows how, in spite of the attention given to contemporary commentators and to subsequent writers' negative views of women, there existed a deep seam of creative women's activity. Like the women in Ross's or Yans-McGlaughlin's studies, the women in the Potteries were vital to the structuring of neighbourhood and workplace culture.[43] While the culture still accorded men a dominant position, that dominance was by no means absolute and in many respects was contradicted by the extent of female actions within the family at home and work.

The Potteries would seem to be an excellent example of the joint relevance of structural features, the level of female employment and the role of social values in the creation of family form. As Anderson notes, these factors have led to a pattern of family economy which 'involved subtle differences between groups and industries, only a few of which have so far been fully explored'.[44] Furthermore, it is by going beyond the model of the nuclear family that the interaction of women, family and work becomes more intelligible. By recognising the importance of both immediate and distant kin (as Hart's anthropological study of the Potteries in the 1980s does), it is possible to discover the continued relevance of family ties to work.[45] Just because the immediate family unit of parents and children did not always work together does not justify the conclusion that the family had disappeared from the workplace. Using the concept of kin reveals in contrast the range of ways family ties pervaded the world of work.

Lastly, recent research and debate among historians has identified the 'construction of masculinity' and 'the active role played by skilled male workers in creating gender segregation' as the areas deserving most attention in understanding patriarchy.[46] The experience of the potters together with parallel research by, for example, John on mining communities would suggest this to be only a partial answer.[47] The 'active role' of women in the creation of gender relations deserves equal attention. To ignore their role and therefore miss the subtle texture of the range of gender relations in the past would be as unjust as it would be historically inaccurate.

Notes

I am grateful for the helpful comments of Margaret Grieco, Pat Hudson, Robert Lee, Jane Lewis and Maxine Berg in the preparation of this paper. The Ceramic and Allied Trade Union kindly allowed me to quote from their archives in Hanley, hereafter referred to as CATU COll.

1 The Potteries is the collective name for the Six Towns of North Staffordshire made up of Tunstall, Burslam, Hanley, Stoke, Fenton and Longton.
2 M. Anderson, *Family Structure in Nineteenth-Century Lancashire*, Cambridge, 1971.
3 E. Ross, 'Survival networks: women's neighbourhood sharing in London before World War 1', *History Workshop*, 15 (1983), pp. 4 and 14; E. Roberts, *A Woman's Place: An Oral History of Working Class Women 1890–1940*, Oxford, 1984, p. 180.
4 M. Barrett and M. McIntosh, 'Towards a materialist feminism', *Feminist Review*, 1 (1979), pp. 95–106.
5 J. W. Scott and L. A. Tilly, 'Women's work and the family in nineteenth century Europe', *Comparative Studies in Society and History*, 1 (1975), pp. 26–64.
6 C. Calhoun, 'Community: towards a variable conceptualisation for comparative research', *Social History*, 5 (1980), p. 105; D. Gregory, *Regional Transformation and Industrial Revolution: A Geography of the Yorkshire Woollen Industry*, London, 1982, pp. 86 and 179.
7 M. Berg, *The Age of Manufactures, 1700–1820*, London, 1985, chapter 7.
8 For a commanding review of the literature see S. Rose, 'Gender at work: sex, class and industrial capitalism', *History Workshop*, 21 (1986), pp. 113–32.
9 Rose, 'Gender at work', pp. 117–20; S. Alexander, 'Women, class and sexual difference in the 1830s and 1840s: some reflections on the writing of a feminist history', *History Workshop*, 17 (1984), pp. 140 and 145.
10 M. Grieco, 'Family structure and industrial employment: the role of information and migration', *Journal of Marriage and the Family* (August 1982), pp. 701–7; M. Young and P. Willmott, *Family and Kinship in East London*, Harmondsworth, 1957; P. H. Chombart de Lauwe, *La Vie quotidienne des Familles Ouvrières*, Paris, 1956; J. Baker-Miller, 'Ties to others', in M. Evans (ed.), *The Woman Question*, London, 1982, pp. 95–106.
11 Ross, 'Survival networks', *passim*; N. A. Hewitt, 'Beyond the search for sisterhood: American women's history in the 1980's', *Social History*, 10 (1985), pp. 302, 309 and 315.
12 Rose, 'Gender at work', p. 114; R. Edwards, *Contested Terrain: The Transformation of the Workplace in the Twentieth Century*, London, 1979, p. 3.
13 *Census of England and Wales: County of Stafford*, London, 1911, County Borough of Stoke on Trent, Occupations, table 23, pp. 64–6.
14 *Morning Leader*, 11 December 1902; F. Thistlethwaite, 'The Atlantic migration of the pottery industry', *Economic History Review*, 11 (1958), p. 265.
15 *The Staffordshire Census*, 1901, p. 69, 1911, p. 65 and 1921, p. 54; C. Collet, *Women in Industry*, London, 1911.
16 *Staffordshire Census*, 1921, table 18, pp. 93–6.
17 CATU COLL, 1924 survey of union members; records of Johnson and Howsons sanitary workers, 1919; *Census of England and Wales*, vol. 13, London, 1923, Fertility of Marriage, part II, table XLVIII; B. H. Phelps-Brown, *The Growth of British Industrial Relations*, London, 1959, p. 6.
18 *Departmental Committee on the Employment of Children Act 1907*, cd 5229, London, 1910, pp. 101–3, Q. 2419; *The Census of England and Wales*, 1911, London, 1917, General Report, Diagram XXXIV; *The Daily News*, 2, 8, 9 January, 1904; *Royal Commission on Labour 1893*, vol. 3, Group C, C. Collet, The employment of women, the Staffordshire Potteries, fifth and final report, Appendix III. This wider kin-based pattern of family involvement in the industry contrasts with the interim findings of Paul Bellaby's research into work in a single pottery company in 1983–85 at the University of Keele.
19 The local term for a pottery factory was a potbank or 'bank': CATU COLL, 1924 survey; *Pottery Gazette (henceforth P. Gazette)*, 1 December 1893.
20 *Royal Commission on Labour*, Appendix III, p. 507; R. Whipp, 'Potbank and union:

a study of work and trade unionism in the pottery industry 1900–1924', unpublished Ph.D. thesis, University of Warwick, 1983, 112–14.

21 L. Tilly and J. W. Scott, *Women, Work and Family*, London, 1978, pp. 230–1; *P. Gazette*, 1 May, 1895, p. 360; Rulebooks of *The Amalgamated Society of Holloware Pressers and Clay Potters*, Hanley, 1890, p. 10 and *The China and Earthenware Gilders*, Burslem, 1890, section 2.

22 B. Wilson, *Young Oxford*, 2, Oxford, 1900, p. 52.

23 CATU COLL, 1924 Survey, Areas 7 and 24; H. Martindale in evidence to the *Inter-Departmental Committee on Physical Deterioration*, 1903, Appendix U, p. 127; *Daily Chronicle*, 19 July 1892, p. 6.

24 P. N. Stearns, 'Working class women in Britain 1890–1914', in M. Vicinus (ed.), *Suffer and Be Still: Women in the Victorian Age*, London, 1972, p. 105.

25 W. Seccombe, 'Patriarchy stabilised: the construction of the male bread winner wage norm in nineteenth century Britain', *Social History*, 11 (1986), pp. 53–76.

26 See Whipp, 'Potbank and union', pp. 58, 71.

27 *Royal Commission on Labour*, Group C, p. 71 and Collet, pp. 61–2; *Daily News*, 9 January 1904.

28 R. Pankhurst, *Sylvia Pankhurst: Artist and Crusader*, London, 1979, pp. 80–7; M. Graham, *Cup and Saucer Land*, London, n.d. (1908?); A. Bennett, *Anna of the Five Towns*, London, 1902, p. 120.

29 R. Whipp, '"The stamp of futility": the Staffordshire potters 1880–1905', in R. Harrison and J. Zeitlin (eds.), *Divisions of Labour: Skilled Workers and Technological Change in Nineteenth Century England*, Hassocks and Urbana, 1985, pp. 114–50.

30 *Report of the Departmental Committee on the Use of Lead in the Manufacture of Earthenware and China*, 1910, *passim*; *The Staffordshire Knot*, 30 October, 1891; *Workmans Times*, 10 October, 1890.

31 The National Amalgamated Society of Pottery Workers was formed in 1906. Whipp, 'Potbank and union', p. 114; Interview with B. Grocott.

32 R. Whipp and M. Grieco, 'Family and the workplace', *Warwick Economic Papers*, 1983.

33 W. M. Walker, *Juteopolis: Dundee and its Textile Workers 1885–1923*, Edinburgh, 1979.

34 Anderson, *Family Structure*, p. 35; Lambertz, 'Sexual harassment in the nineteenth century English cotton industry', *History Workshop*, 19, 1985, pp. 45–7; B. Jackson, *Working Class Community*, London, 1968; R. Pahl, *Divisions of Labour*, Oxford, 1984, pp. 198–232; R. Roberts, *The Classic Slum: Salford Life in the First Quarter of the Century*, Manchester, 1971, p. 43.

35 R. Whipp, '"The art of good management": managerial control of work in the British pottery industry, 1900–1925', *International Review of Social History*, 29 (1984), pp. 371–2 and 308.

36 *P. Gazette*, 1 October 1919, p. 1109 and 1 January 1911, p. 89, 1 August 1916, p. 849 and 1 July 1918, p. 562.

37 *P. Gazette*, 1 October 1919, p. 1109.

38 *Women's Trade Union League Quarterly Review*, October 1896, July and October 1895; *WTUL Annual Report*, 1898, pp. 10–11; *Justice*, 8 December 1897.

39 R. Whipp, '"Plenty of excuses. No money": the social bases of trade unionism', *Bulletin of the Society for the Study of Labour History*, 49 (1984), pp. 29–37.

40 Whipp, 'Potbank and union', p. 196.

41 *Staffordshire Sentinel*, 14 February 1901; *Staffordshire Advertiser*, 23 July 1898, p. 4; CATU COLL, S. Clowes scrapbook, 8 April 1907; Longton and Fenton Lodge registers.

42 *P. Gazette*, 1 March, 1908, 1 October 1911. *Staffordshire Sentinel*, 30 March 1907.

43 Ross, 'Survival networks'; V. Yans-McLaughlin, 'Patterns of work and family organisation', *Journal of Interdisciplinary History*, 2 (1971), pp. 299–314.

44 M. Anderson, *Approaches to the History of the Western Family 1500–1914*, London, 1980, pp. 65–80.

45 L. Hart, 'Family and kinship at work in the Potteries', mimeo, University of Birmingham, 1986.

46 Seccombe, 'Patriarchy stabilised', p. 62; Rose, 'Gender at work', p. 120.

47 A. John, *By the Sweat of their Brow*, London, 1980; M. Grieco and R. Whipp, 'Women and the workplace: gender and control in the labour process' in D. Knights and H. Willmott (eds.), *Gender and the Labour Process*, London, 1986, pp. 117–40.

Chapter Eight

Women in urban employment and the shaping of the Russian working class, 1880–1917

JANE McDERMID

The Russian working class of the late nineteenth and early twentieth centuries has been portrayed, by contemporaries as well as by historians, as a combination of an anarchic, rebellious mass of 'peasant-workers' with a minority of well-organised, politically conscious skilled workers, the organic intellectuals of their class. Women workers are generally seen as belonging to the first category. The cultural differences between the skilled and the unskilled workers were emphasised by the abyss between the male metal workers and the female textile workers drawn in the memoirs of one of the former.

> Metal workers felt themselves to be the aristocrats among the rest of the working class. Their profession demanded more training so that they looked down on weavers and such like, as though they were inferior country bumpkins, at the mill today, back to ploughing the land tomorrow ... I was struck by the oddness of the textile workers. Many of them still wore peasant clothes, looking as if they had wandered into the town by mistake, and as if tomorrow they would find their way back to their native village. Women predominated among them, and we never lost an opportunity to pour scorn on them.[1]

In her recent study of factory women in Russia in the period 1880–1914, Glickman has revealed the significance of gender in the development of the Russian working class. She highlights the peasant legacy of female subordination to men, as reflected in the continuing sexual divsion of labour at the factory.[2] However, as we shall see, this hierarchy of skill and gender is not so simple, while the peasant legacy is more complex than these views suggest.

Urban employment trends

Between the 1880s and the Russian Revolution of 1917 there was a gradual increase both in the numbers of women in the urban industrial labour force and in their percentage of the total. By the end of the 1880s there were around 200,000 female factory workers, accounting for one-quarter of the industrial labour force, and 40 per cent of the work-force in the textile industry.[3] According to Rashin, there was a tendency to increase the use of female labour wherever great physical strength was not required, although the impression is that women's work was nevertheless very physically demanding. Increasing mechanisation and low skill requirements meant that there was a multiplicity of openings for first generation urban migrants lacking industrial experience: the textile, chemical and tobacco industries were major employers of village girls from the 1890s. Above all, they were concentrated in the textile industry in which they constituted 58.6 per cent of the workforce by 1914. On the eve of the First World War, one in three factory workers was a woman.[4] Besides the textile, chemical and tobacco industries, women were also to be found in the lime, brick, glass, sugar-refining, distilling, food and rubber-processing industries.

Even though their increased employment, like that of men, was seen as a consequence of mechanisation, women tended to perform the least-skilled jobs with the lowest wages and lowest status. Indeed, the factory inspectorate in this period recognised that the burden of industrialisation in Russia fell especially heavily on women. Yet even as they noted the failure of the generally held belief in women as weaker beings to prevent the growth of the female industrial workforce, they accepted that it should not do so. They accepted, in effect, that women, or at least peasant women, should work. At the same time, they sought to 'improve' factory conditions so that women workers could still fulfil what was seen as their primary natural function, as well as their social duty, of maternity, so that they could meet their responsibilities for the health of future generations of workers.[5] Tsarist factory inspectors recorded that employers saw women as more industrious and abstemious than men and as less likely to organise in their own interests. Whenever possible, women were used to displace men, because of the former's cheapness and passivity, a trend that was reinforced after the 1905 Revolution, particularly in the cotton-weaving industry.[6]

Between 1906 and the eve of the First World War, peasant women in Russia were drawn into the urban labour force in increasing numbers. Indeed, their proportion of the labour force rose faster than that of males and the war quickened this process. The proportion of women in industry as a whole soared in Russia from 26.6 per cent in 1914 to 43.4 per cent in 1917; the numbers of factory women rose from 723,000 in 1914 to over one million in 1917.[7] During the war, the increase in the employment of women, and of children, was especially marked in those areas where large factories predominated. Thus, in the Moscow industrial region, the percentage of women workers rose from 39.4 in 1914 to 48.7 in 1917; in the cotton industry from 49.5 in 1914 to 60.6 in 1917; and in the metal industry from 7.4 in 1914 to 18.6 in 1917. The percentage of women employed in the Petrograd district was similar: it rose from 25.3 in 1913, to 33.3 in 1917. Before the war, men had constituted two-thirds of the Petrograd labour force. Towards the end of 1917, less than half the total of workers employed in Petrograd were men. Even in male-dominated sectors, such as the metal and chemical industries, the numbers of women and children employed towards the end of 1916 was at least one-third.[8] But urban working women were not typically found in the high-skill or high-status occupations. While women made up 37.5 per cent of the unskilled metal workers in the Moscow province in 1918, they constituted less than 1 per cent of the skilled toolworkers.[9] Besides the factories, there were thousands of women employed in the sweatshops and as domestic servants: by January 1917, around 130,000 women worked in Petrograd factories, while there were approximately 80,000 employed as domestic workers, 50,000 as office workers, and another 50,000 as shop workers.[10]

Alexandra Kollontai figures prominently in Western accounts of the position of women in Russia. In her view, the capitalist system of production plays the vital role in the emergence of the 'New Woman' by compelling an increasing number of women to participate in the economy. The working woman experienced at first hand the struggles of her class even though she did not perform the same kind of work as men. For Kollontai, the working-class woman's primary duty was to the collective of her class and not to her individual family.[11] Kollontai did not romanticise the lives of working women. She acknowledged the terrible working conditions, the unequal pay and continuing domination by men. The sometimes brutal attitude of proletarian men towards women she saw as their peasant heritage. Nevertheless, she firmly believed that the increasing numbers of proletarian women earning a living outside the home contributed to the creation of a new psyche for these women by giving them a new confidence and independence.[12]

Many contemporaries certainly feared that the development of an industrial capitalist economy in Russia, notably from the 1890s, would result in the break-up of the peasant community and in the liberation of individuals from community restraints following what they saw as the Western example. Russian society in the late nineteenth century became increasingly conscious of, and alarmed by, the rapidly growing size of the female proletariat. The fear was openly voiced, by revolutionaries as well as by conservatives, that industrialisation brought new, looser moral values and sexual relations. Urban factory life was recognised to be unsettling, insecure and potentially destructive of traditional norms. Despite the continuing predominance of agriculture in Russia into the twentieth century, the growth of industry brought increasing social diversification. Non-agricultural occupations became more and more important for the peasant household economy. In most areas, some form of seasonal migration had long been a necessity. At the same time, the conditions of urban factory life in Russia were not conducive to the setting up of nuclear families, let alone establishing the independent wage-earning woman. The stark reality was that working-class women in Russia often earned barely enough to survive, while the peasant belief in the inferiority of women proved tenacious.

The particularly harsh and difficult conditions of labour and life for women toiling in the factories of Moscow is described by Lyadov in a special pamphlet on women workers under capitalism written for study in the workers' circles of the 1890s. According to Lyadov, women were simply not paid enough in the factories and workshops for even basic subsistence. Yet they competed against each other in the labour-market for such meagre pay – about a third to a half of male wages. Lyadov noted how the lives of women had been profoundly affected by the introduction of machinery and the consequent demand for less skilled labour. He drew the links between the low pay of women workers, their semi-starvation diets, frequent periods of unemployment, the complete lack of minimum financial security, and such widespread social problems as prostitution and venereal disease. Indeed, prostitution seems to have been a major alternative to factory work for women, while it was often a necessary supplement to inadequate wages. Prostitution was officially recognised by tsarism, through the issue of government licences to women – the Yellow Card – which allowed them to act as prostitutes under police registration. As Lyadov pointed out, the 'choice' of prostitution was not an unusual one. Rather, it was a general situation, and in his view, the lot of women workers was deteriorating.[13]

The worker Vera Karelina also related that foremen forced female factory workers into prostitution. She wrote that women workers, many of whom were only thirteen years old, were sexually abused during searchings.[14] In her view, men could avoid the burdens of marriage and a family, and satisfy their sexual needs through recourse to prostitutes and illicit relationships. As for the resulting illegitimate children, they were left at the foundling homes which, if the children survived, would leave them vulnerable to recruitment as capitalism's wage slaves. Indeed, a number of leading women workers who were active in the study circles of the 1890s and in the revolutions of 1905 and 1917, including Vera Karelina, had been orphans from the foundling homes of St Petersburg. They had been recruited to work in the city's large textile mills which had special arrangements with the homes in order to get a steady supply of labour.[15] It seems, however, that the greatest number of prostitutes in pre-revolutionary Russia came not from factory workers but from the domestic servants who often fled want in the villages only to find economic insecurity, poor wages and appalling living conditions in the towns.[16] In his recent study of the Moscow working class in this period, Johnson points out that women who worked as domestic servants, day-labourers or seamstresses accounted for a disproportionately high share of the mothers of babies left at foundling homes, whereas the share of factory women was disproportionately low. He suggests that this fact does not preclude 'unwanted' pregnancies among factory women:

> the evidence of factory life suggests that sexual abuse and also voluntary liaisons were not uncommon. Unlike servants or artisans, however, factory women were part of a community that maintained many of the traditions and sanctions of village life. In such a setting, a father may have found it harder to shirk his obligations, and a pregnant girl less likely to be left to her own devices.[17]

In the 1890s, however, Lyadov had claimed that the unhealthy conditions of work adversely affected fertility among factory women. With such low wages and sexual abuse at work, it was not surprising to Lyadov that prostitution flourished among factory workers as well as others.[18]

The peasant inheritance

The Russian working class in the late nineteenth century did not yet reproduce itself. It was recruited overwhelmingly from the countryside, and was distinguished from most of the European working classes by the strength of its peasant traditions and values. There were regional differences in migration: thus, for example, peasants who migrated to Moscow came from the contiguous areas, whereas peasants who migrated to St Petersburg came from provinces more distant from the capital. In addition, Anderson has found that the general pattern of migration evidenced in the census year of 1897 was more similar by work status than by sex. While acknowledging that the work performed by female wage labour was different from that performed by men, Anderson believes that women may have been responding to the same kinds of motivations and inducements for migration as men. She suggests that women in late-nineteenth-century Russia may have exercised more independent decision-making in migrating than has generally been supposed.[19] Whether or not this was the case, peasants from the same locality – village or region – often lived at and worked together in the factories. This association was known as *zemlyachestvo* and it eased the transition into the urban, factory environment. Rooted in peasant life, regional networks provided a great feeling of strength and solidarity but given that much of the information on *zemlyachestvo* comes from memoirs of skilled male workers, it is difficult to assess the extent of its impact on women workers.[20] In general, and whatever the regional differences, the same demographic pattern can be traced: more men than women migrated, the majority of both were single and there was a tendency for children to be brought up in the countryside.[21]

Pavlov has described factory villages in the central industrial region in the late nineteenth century in which entire families found work in the mills, with the wives and daughters in relatively low-skilled occupations such as spinning and carding, while male workers were employed as machinists and fabric printers.[22] The textile industry grew enormously from the late 1870s, and according to Ivanov, there was a significant rise in the incidence of 'factory families' by the turn of the century, with husband and wife working in the same factory, while their children were a reserve labour force. Ivanov also noted that urban workers who married in the cities did so later than rural workers or peasants. Whereas the latter groups tended to marry before the age of 20, in Moscow in 1914, the median age of marriage was 22.6 years for women, 25.9 for men.[23] Men and women generally worked apart inside the factories, not in family work groups. Furthermore, married couples were not always allowed to live in the barracks accommodation provided by the employers. Thus only well-paid workers could afford to bring up their families in the towns: one reason why a hereditary working class grew first among the metal workers, a predominantly male trade.[24]

The existence of a second generation in the metal trades or at the textile factory was no proof that its members had severed ties with the village. Parents could force a son or daughter migrant worker to send money home by threatening to withdraw their internal passport. Male migrant workers could combine their earnings with their family's agricultural income to achieve a certain measure of economic security for the peasant household, which in turn enabled them to continue the rural pattern of early marriage and large families. In practice, the general trend seems to have been that female factory workers either remained single, or married and returned to raise their children in the countryside where the traditional patterns of family life had more chance of survival. Paradoxically, then, the abandonment of village traditions was most apparent among the skilled male workers and those female migrants who remained in the city.

Political consciousness

The working class in Russia thus developed through a peculiar interlacing of village customs and institutions with industrial change. The village's influence on factory life was subtle and complex. Women in the villages were the guardians of peasant culture and male workers, whether in country or town, continued to see women above all in their traditional, 'natural' role. In his memoirs, the skilled worker Kanatchikov expressed the belief that male workers looked on the woman worker as a 'creature of a lower order'. He claimed that she was seen as being uninterested in higher things, and incapable of fighting for ideals, a drag on the life of the conscious male worker. He recalled his own amazement at his first contact with two women workers who reasoned and argued just as men did. But in general, he observed, wives failed to understand their more conscious husbands' interests in politics and cultural matters. Indeed, according to Kanatchikov, women saw such preoccupations as a threat to the family, detracting from the male role as head of and provider for the family. Hence he concluded 'conscious workers have a negative attitude toward family and marriage, and even toward women. They look upon all contact with girls as a suffocation of personal freedom leading to the loss of their comrades from the revolutionary cause'.[25]

Reflecting on her experience of trying to involve women in the 1904–05 political upsurge, Karelina wrote that the mass of male workers felt that social activity was not a woman's affair; that her sphere for action was the machine in the factory and the stove at home; and that her task was to bring up the children. Karelina recalled that women workers were not considered worthy of mention; that even despite the fact of some industries, and specifically the textile industry, being predominantly female, male workers carried on as if they did not exist, except to be counted as appendages. It is not surprising that the women workers of Karelina's study circle refused to allow male workers to attend their meetings, fearing that the men would judge them wanting.[26] Nor was this attitude to women confined to men, as the Bolshevik underground organiser, Cecilia Bobrovskaya, revealed when she claimed that the only concerns of women workers lay in 'nursing the children and making their husbands' meals ... They were the most abject and ignorant creatures in the world.'[27] Certainly, Lyadov's pamphlet and Krupskaya's later booklet *The Woman Worker* (1900) focussed attention on this problem. Interestingly, Krupskaya included peasant women as well as factory workers in her study. But in general, female workers were seen as backward, their lives contained within the narrow orbit of home and mill, apart from society at large, isolated from the labour movement in particular. 'Exhausted, ill from unhealthy, unrelenting mill work, knowing no peace at home from morning to night, day in and day out, month after month, the worker-mother drudges and experiences only need, worry and grief.'[28]

Given their material insecurity and their sense of family responsibility, it was no wonder that women workers were the least conscious group in the working class. Efforts were made in the workers' circles of the 1890s to overcome the separation between male and female workers, but many of the latter rejected association with the godless intelligentsia.[29] Mandel insists that it was not sex but the level of skill and the social characteristics associated with it in Russia that were the primary determinants of political culture. Mandel has pointed out that in the Russian labour movement the term 'conscious worker' embraced an entire code of conduct for the skilled male that included relations with women.[30]

Unskilled men were very similar to unskilled women, for both were drawn heavily from the countryside. The main difference was that women tended to stay in unskilled work whereas men gradually moved into semi-skilled or skilled jobs. Besides the influence of an overarching gender division of labour the persistent lack of skills among women workers can be related to their literacy levels. Illiteracy was more widespread among women in Russia than among men. In 1897, it has been estimated that only 13 per cent of women in Russia were literate, although among factory women the percentage rose to 21.3, while the corresponding figures for men were 29.3 and 56.5 per cent.[31] Mass literacy, particularly writing, is a concomitant of industrialisation, whereas the peasant world depended more on ceremony than on the printed word. But literacy did not necessarily or immediately follow entry into factory work. In the early stages of industrialisation in Russia, and specifically in the textile industry in which women predominated, employers could rely on a vast pool of cheap, unskilled female labour rather than on sophisticated technology. Literacy was not a great need. Nevertheless, the late nineteenth century witnessed increasing literacy among the population in European Russia, including peasant women. But by 1918, when women workers constituted almost two-thirds of the textile industry, literacy in this labour force was only about 40 per cent, a situation repeated in the chemical, tobacco and food-processing plants. However, in the trades where there were skilled women, the female literacy rate was much higher, while the gap between male and female literacy narrowed in the younger age groups. In the needle trade, the only industry in which there was a significant proportion of skilled women workers, the overall literacy rate in 1918 was 68.2 per cent, compared to 37.2 per cent in the cotton industry in which unskilled female labour predominated.[32] In general, throughout this period, women remained associated with the peasant, pre-literate tradition.

Mandel conjectures that the inertia of the unskilled workers and their low level of participation in the labour movement in general, also had parallels in the peasants' fatalism and passivity.[33] But, as he acknowledges, this passivity did not preclude periodic outbursts of extremely militant collective action. Indeed, as an expression of collective suffering and demands, the bread riot, in which women played the largest part, was as significant in industrial regions as the strike. This is illustrated by the direct, spontaneous action taken by textile women workers in 1917 which proved to be the starting point of the Revolution. The Bolshevik Samoilova claimed that the First World War was an important catalyst for the development of the female proletariat, in political consciousness as well as in numbers.[34] The general historical view of the events in February 1917 is that they were above all characterised by 'elemental forces' set in motion by female spontaneity, and specifically by the textile workers, so long considered the archetype of the grey mass of unskilled and politically unconscious workers. In the Vyborg district of Petrograd, the women from several textile mills struck, went to the nearby metal works and called on the men to join them in their demands for bread and an end to war. Despite bloodshed and beatings by Cossacks, the women refused the military's call to disperse, and fraternised with soldiers from their own *zemlyachestvo*, trying to win them over, or at least to neutralise them.[35] They were successful.

Still, there were very few women in the first Petrograd Soviet – about ten – and it was mostly men who were elected to the factory committees. The majority of women continued to view trade unions as male bastions. Indeed, in the factories even after the February Revolution, female workers were often deliberately impeded in their attempts at organisation by men who continued to believe that women were not capable of organising or leading. Moreover, faced with growing unemployment, some factory committees tried to force women workers with male relatives working in the same plant to leave their jobs. Both the Bolsheviks and the metal workers' union condemned these efforts, but neither were thinking in terms of the women's rights as individual workers. The committees argued in terms of family interests whilst the Bolshevik concern was with class solidarity.[36] Certainly, there were attempts to attract female membership to unions; but the minority of politically conscious, organisationally experienced skilled male workers tended to monopolise positions of leadership and responsibility. A woman textile worker complained that while the predominantly male factory committee had done much to organise women workers, this male proletarian vanguard seemed to want to retain their monopoly of leadership. Yet in this particular cotton-spinning mill, women constituted over 90 per cent of the workforce.[37] Despite their lack of representation in the formal leadership of trade union and political movements it was precisely the 'backward' workers, and specifically the politically unconscious and unorganised women, who at each stage of the revolutionary process pushed the leadership into action by their militancy. Why was this so?

The role and influence of women in the peasant community

The key to understanding the position of women workers and the development of the working class in general in Russia seems to lie in the communal organisation of peasant life. Russian studies of the late nineteenth century recognised that Russia was a patriarchal society; but they also insisted that women had rights and that the husband's total authority was in practice balanced by customary law and the village tribunal.[38] In Russia, large and complex households predominated among the peasantry, while teenage marriage was common. The peasant family and village society were seen to interact at important moments of life, in the ceremonies surrounding birth, marriage and death. Life for the peasants had a fixed pattern, governed by innumerable traditions. Economic functions in peasant families were important, while marriage was an affair between families within the village community, involving an economic settlement of family property and usually entailing the movement of a woman from one family to another, from her father's to her husband's household. Contemporary observers noted that the members of a household perforce relied on each other, so that whatever the weight of male opinion, women could not be disregarded.[39] But although some believed that the patriarchal family was falling apart in the late nineteenth century, as individuals chafed against community controls, peasant values, including patriarchal attitudes towards women, proved to be tenacious, and the collective way of life with its sexual hierarchy retained its vitality.[40] Thus, despite the large-scale and rapid growth in factory industry in Russia in the late nineteenth century, and specifically in the size of the female labour force, it seems that many aspects of workers' lives, habits and attitudes remained much as before.

In peasant society, marriage was subordinated to the aim of main-taining the family, and practically everyone lived their lives within a family. The lot of a single person in Russia was usually economically unviable and socially deviant. Indeed, nineteenth-century observers, both foreign and native, agreed that in Russian society, 'neither in the home nor in the commune can a man be a complete workman unless he is married and can place at the community's service, together with his own hands, those of his wife'.[41]

Villagers in Russia did not distinguish the commune (*mir*) from the individual member. The *mir* was an ancient institution of local self-government, and its authority was increased in the nineteenth century. Towards the end of the century, Mackenzie Wallace, correspondent for *The Times*, noted that 'the Commune is, in fact, a living institution, whose spontaneous vitality enables it to dispense with the assistance and guidance of the written law, and its constitution is thoroughly democratic'.[42] Members of the complex type of household adhered to the strictest obser-vance of male superiority so that although women held positions of influ-ence and even authority within the family, and in certain circumstances could become heads of households (in the absence or death of their husbands), they were not thereby recognised as equal with men. Mackenzie Wallace noted that although the right of a female head of household to attend the village assembly was never questioned, in practice the women's views on matters affecting the general welfare of the community commanded little attention. He held that among the Russian peasantry 'woman as woman is not deserving of much consideration, but a particular woman, as Head of Household, is entitled to speak on all questions directly affecting the household under her care'.[43] Foreign observers saw the Russian family, and specifically the peasant household, as despotism in miniature. Yet often it seems that foreigners were scandalised less by the low esteem in which they believed women were held in Russia, than by the fact that peasant women worked alongside men in the fields. Thus, while Russian peasant women were responsible for housework and childcare, they were not restricted to such duties. Nor did they inhabit such a distinctly separate sphere of labour, since the whole peasant economy was based on the household. Certainly, however crucial the female role was in peasant Russia, however varied the tasks of peasant women, there was nevertheless a general division of labour in which women's work was seen as of less worth than men's. With the development of the economy from the 1880s, peasant women took on more of the responsibility for working the land so that the men might seek wage labour in industry, though this was not a new process: peasants had also migrated for work under serfdom. Moreover, agriculture remained important for female labour – the 1897 census showed that around one-quarter of all women wage-earners were hired field hands.[44]

Always there were the constraints of poverty as well as the tenacity of peasant culture. But the latter was not simply a consequence of the former. It is crucial to realise that this strength was not simply a result of Russia's backwardness, not merely part of the struggle for survival in a rapidly changing and insecure world. Rather, the peasant family was popularly valued as a proven structure. Indeed, peasant women saw the economic and political developments of the late nineteenth and early twentieth centuries as undermining their valued position.[45] Moreover, the Russian peasant community gave women a definite sense of purpose, if no choice. It allotted them an essential, pre-determined role within a limited, small world of intense solidarity and moral consensus. This is not to idealise the *mir*. It is to realise how all-embracing the community was. There were few uncertainties about the basic cognitive and moral framework of life within the Russian village. Personal identity was firmly integrated into the institutionalised order; the collective was set above the individual. There was, however, no simple antithesis between individual and community. Rather, women and men were considered as two complementary parts of the whole. This belief in the complementarity of the sexes had become integral not only in the imagery of culture, but to the structure of society itself. It persisted because Russia industrialised as a peasant society. There was thus no inevitability about the potentially liberating effects of industrialisation on women, in the sense of the liberaton of the individual, given the Russian stress on a social and cultural ideal of community.

Thus, even in the midst of the rapid growth of industry during the 1890s, the traditional social structure was able to adapt to the new environment. In his study of Petrograd workers in 1917, Smith shows that the position had not altered in the years of the First World War. The collectivist spirit of the rural community was maintained in the urban and factory environment.[46] It is significant that the 1917 Revolution took a conservative form in the villages. Often in a manner dictated by custom, the peasants divided up the landowners' estates among themselves, and even reversed the 1906 legislation that had encouraged some of the better-off peasants to turn their landholdings into individual property. The agrarian revolution of 1917 showed the enormous vitality of the peasant commune. Tradition and continuity seem to have outweighed disruption and innovation in the lives of the Russian working class which in this period was still essentially a migrant force. Migration itself was not a new phenomenon brought on by industrialisation in the late nineteenth century. Even before the emancipation of the serfs in 1861, peasants had migrated for work so that village family patterns had long been shaped by interaction with factories and cities. At the same time, this interaction gradually undermined the isolation of the village, eroded the patriarchal structure of family and commune, church and state. As Johnson has noted, village and factory in Russia were not opposites but were joined together in a symbiotic relationship.[47] In addition, peasant women had always contributed to the family economy. The legacy of work outside of domestic duties for the survival of the family went with them to the towns. So too did the legacy of sexual hierarchy, in which women were seen as inferior, though essential, members of the community.

Thus, the fact of increasing female employment outside the home and the important, indeed crucial, economic contribution of women to their families was not sufficient to reduce markedly the subordination of women. Peasant women, after all, had always contributed to the household economy. Indeed, such work had always been expected of them, had been seen as part of the domestic role. It was usually young and single women who left the villages for work in the towns and factories taking with them their family obligations. The peasant legacy also included hierarchies, specifically of age and sex, with a division of labour according to sex. This division of labour was not completely rigid as far as women were concerned, though they were always held primarily responsible for the housework and childcare. Peasant notions of gender and expectations of women which did not confine them to the home or to rigidly delineated tasks thus informed the development of the working class in Russia and the structure of the labour force.

The Russian working class

The Russian working class in the late nineteenth and early twentieth centuries has often been seen as an undifferentiated mass. Recent studies of Moscow and Petrograd in this period by Johnson and Koenker, Mandel and Smith have revealed that the Russian working class was in fact highly diversified:[48] between the skilled and the unskilled; between the urbanised and the recent migrants from the villages; between those working in huge plants and those employed in small workshops; between women and men. Women workers generally were closely associated with peasant traditions. The more they were integrated into the labour force through factory work, the stronger that association proved, with the women themselves acting as the major link between village and town. The town–village nexus was reinforced by patterns of migration so that even where peasants became year-round factory workers, their ties with the village persisted. Thus, in practice, traditional community forms and ties were preserved. The industrial system in Russia was permeated with the institutions, habits and customs of a recently enserfed peasantry and there was no great urge for the transformation of the traditional peasant structure. There was change; but migration to the cities did not automatically encourage the acquisition of 'modern' attitudes or the development of the nuclear family. The development of Russian industry and of a working class did not simply proceed along Western lines. Capitalist relations in industry developed before there were reforms in agriculture. The communal tradition retained its vitality. There was no sharp division between village and factory, peasant and worker.[49] Indeed, peasant hierarchies were now supplemented by urban divisions, in which women generally remained at the bottom. The hierarchies within the Russian working class were various and interlocking, so that however profound the class solidarity, subordination was implicit in the proletarian community. Given the sharp contrast between the minority of skilled workers and the mass of unskilled, the hierarchy of labour assumed a particular importance socially and politically. There was condescension and even scorn for the unskilled peasant-worker, and especially for women.[50] Such a craft hierarchy was diluted by the gradual influx of peasants and women into the growing number of semi-skilled jobs, so that as industry developed, the balance of forces within the Russian working class changed. But the increase in semi-skilled jobs also added to the complexity of hierarchical divisions and women, whether unskilled or semi-skilled, were still considered the 'dark mass' by the skilled male workers.[51] Smith has postulated that the material basis for craft consciousness did not exist in Russia to the same extent as in Western Europe, owing to the late industrialisation; and that the political context in which the Russian labour movement developed encouraged class rather than craft principles. There simply was not the chance of reforms under Tsarism to allow the growth of moderate, reformist craft trade unionism.[52]

Certainly, the revolutionary process in 1917 saw a radicalisation of the working class, while all the mass actions were initiated from below. Yet paradoxically, the Revolution strengthened the traditional village society. By 1917, the patriarchal authority of the male elder had been much diluted. Indeed, even in the late nineteenth century, the persistent patriarchal tradition was felt to be a restraint by the rural youth of both sexes, so that there was considerable tension between the generations in peasant families. Yet the traditional type of male authority persisted in the countryside.[53] Moreover, even after the tremendous upheaval of collectivisation in the 1930s, the peasant household remained the basic social and economic unit, in the collective farm as in the *mir*, since the former was ultimately allowed to correspond roughly to a village, and the collective farmers to retain a household plot. At least until Stalin's 'revolution from above' in the 1930s which forcibly transformed the economy, the development of the Russian working class was above all informed by a living, indeed a vital, peasant tradition. It was a tradition with a complex legacy for women workers in particular and the specifically communal notion of gender influenced fundamentally the structure and attitudes of the urban working class.

Notes

1 A. Buzinov, *Za nevskoy zastavoy: zapiski rabochego*, Moscow, 1930, pp. 20–1.
2 Rose L. Glickman, *Russian Factory Women: Workplace and Society 1880–1914*, California, 1984, p. 279.
3 A. G. Rashin, *Formirovanie rabochego klassa v Rossii istoriko-ekonomicheskie ocherki*, Moscow, 1958, pp. 214–217; A. Ryazanova, *Zhenskiy trud*, Moscow, 1923, pp. 33, 68.
4 Rashin, *Formirovanie*, pp. 185–95; S. Kingsbury, M. Fairchild, *Factory, Family and Women in the Soviet Union*, New York, 1935, pp. 7–8.
5 See, for example, I. I. Yanzhul, *Ocherki i issledovaniya*, Moscow, 1884, pp. 381–93.
6 Ryazanova, *Zhenskiy trud*, p. 34; Rashin, *Formirovanie*, pp. 235–6.
7 Rashin, *Formirovanie*, p. 43.
8 S. O. Zagorsky, *State Control of Industry in Russia during the War*, New Haven, 1928, pp. 54–5.
9 Rashin, *Formirovanie*, p. 541.
10 I. Gordienko, *Iz boevogo proshlogo, 1914–1918gg.*, Moscow, 1957, p. 34; see also Z. V. Stepanov, *Rabochie Petrograda v period podgotovki i provedeniya velikogo oktyabrskogo vooruzhennogo vosstaniya*, Moscow, 1956, pp. 33–6; N. D. Karpetskaya, *Rabotnitsy i velikiy oktyabr'*, Leningrad, 1974, p. 19; S. A. Smith, *Red Petrograd: Revolution in the Factories 1917–1918*, Cambridge, 1983, p. 23.
11 A. M. Kollontai, *Trud zhenshchin v evolyutsii khozyaystva*, Moscow, 1923, p. 97.
12 A. M. Kollontai, *Novaia moral' i rabochii klass*, Moscow, 1918, pp. 6–7, 35.
13 M. Lyadov, 'Koe-chto o zhenshchine rabotnitse', *Literatura Moskovskogo Rabochego Soyuza*, Moscow, 1930, pp. 163–70.
14 Vera Karelina in P. F. Kudelli (ed.), *Rabotnitsa v 1905g. v S-Peterburge. Sbornik statey*

i vospominaniy, Leningrad, 1926, p. 18. See also E. Bochkareva and S. Lyubimova, *Svetlyi put'*, Moscow, 1967, pp. 3–4.

15   See, for example, Vera Karelina, 'Vospominanii', *Krasnaya letopis'*, no. 4 (1922), p. 12.

16   Prof. V. Bronner, *La lutte contre la prostitution en URSS*, Moscow, 1936, pp. 5–14.

17   R. E. Johnson, *Peasant and Proletarian: The Working Class of Moscow in the late Nineteenth Century*, Leicester, 1979, p. 96. Diane Koenker's study *Moscow Workers and the 1917 Revolution*, Princeton, 1981, shows (p. 41) that domestic service accounted in 1912 for almost 100,000 wage earners, of whom 93 per cent were women. She agrees with Johnson that they had little family life of their own in the city.

18   *Literatura Moskovskogo*, p. 168.

19   Barbara Anderson, *Internal Migration during Modernisation in late Nineteenth-Century Russia*, New Jersey, 1980, p. 78.

20   See, for example, A. Buiko, *Put' rabochego*, Moscow, 1934, pp. 94–5; P. Timofeev, *Chem zhivet zavodskiy rabochiy*, St Petersburg, 1906, pp. 12–13.

21   See A. G. Rashin, *Naselenie Rossii za sto let*, Moscow, 1956; for local studies see Johnson, *Peasant and Proletarian* and Smith, *Red Petrograd*.

22   For Pavlov, see Victoria E. Bonnell (ed.), *The Russian Worker*, California, 1983, p. 18.

23   L. M. Ivanov, *Rabochiy klass i rabochee dvizhenie v Rossii 1861–1917*, Moscow, 1966, pp. 99, 100; Koenker, *Moscow Workers*, p. 57.

24   Rashin, *Formirovanie*, p. 541.

25   S. Kanatchikov, *Iz istorii moego bytiya*, Moscow, 1926, pp. 78–96.

26   Kudelli, *Rabotnitsa v 1905g.*, pp. 24–5.

27   C. Bobrovskaya, *Twenty Years in Underground Russia*, London, 1934, p. 109.

28   *Rabotnitsa*, 19 April 1914, p. 12.

29   *Literatura Moskovskogo*, p. 168; S. I. Mitskevich, *Na zare rabochego dvizheniya v Moskve*, Moscow, 1932, pp. 293, 305–6.

30   D. Mandel, *The Petrograd Workers and the Fall of the Old Regime*, London, 1983, pp. 16, 27.

31   Rashin, *Naselenie*, pp. 293, 305–6.

32   Rashin, *Formirovanie*, pp. 601–2; Stepanov, *Rabochie Petrograda*, p. 44.

33   Mandel, *The Petrograd Workers*, pp. 27–31.

34   K. Samoilova, *Rabotnitsa v rossisskoy revolyutsii*, Moscow, 1920, pp. 3–12.

35   E. N. Burdzhalov, *Vtoraya russkaya revolyutsiya: vosstanie v Petrograde*, Moscow, 1967, pp. 118–23; Gordienko, *Iz boevogo proshlogo*, pp. 56–67.

36   *Rabotnitsa*, 1 September 1917, p. 9.

37   *Rabotnitsa*, 18 October 1917, p. 15.

38   See, for example, S. S. Shashkov, *Sobranie sochineniy*, St Petersburg, 1898, vol. 1, p. 846; Ya. A. Kantorovich, *Zhenshchina v prave*, St Petersburg, 1896.

39   Baron von Haxthausen, *The Russian Empire*, London, 1856, vol. 1, p. 44, vol. 2, p. 230; M. N. Kovalevsky, *Modern Customs and Ancient Laws of Russia*, London, 1891, pp. 55, 61, 137.

40   See, for example, S. S. Shashkov, *Ocherk istorii russkoy zhenshchiny*, St Petersburg, 1872, pp. 121–3; L. Tikhomirov, *Russia, Political and Social*, London, 1888, vol. 1, p. 187; S. Stepniak, *The Russian Peasantry*, London, 1905, p. 155.

41   A. Leroy-Beaulieu, *The Empire of the Tsars and the Russians*, London, 1902, p. 495; see also Haxthausen, *The Russian Empire*, vol. 1, p. 44; M. N. Kovalevsky, *Tableau des origines et de l'évolution de la famille et de la propriété*, Stockholm, 1890, p. 142; Tikhomirov, *Russia, Political and Social*, vol. 1, p. 119.

42   D. Mackenzie Wallace, *Russia on the Eve of War and Revolution*, ed. and abridged from 1912 edn by C. E. Black, New York, 1961, pp. 185, 276.

43   *Ibid.*, p. 279.

44 Rashin, *Naselenie*, pp. 158–79.

45 Vera A. Bilshai, *Reshenie zhenskogo voprosa v SSSR*, Moscow, 1956, p. 65.

46 Smith, *Red Petrograd*.

47 Johnson, *Peasant and Proletarian*, p. 66.

48 Smith, *Red Petrograd*; Mandel, *The Petrograd Workers*; Johnson, *Peasant and Proletarian*; Koenker, *Moscow Workers*.

49 See for example M. N. Nechkina (ed.), *Iz istorii rabochego klassa i revolyutsionnogo dvizheniya*, Moscow, 1958, p. 282; I. I. Yanzhul, *Fabrychnyi byt moskovskoy gubernii*, Moscow, 1966, p. 155.

50 For example see Buzinov, *Za nevskoy zastavoy*, pp. 20–1.

51 Rashin, *Formirovanie*, pp. 225, 236; Gordienko, *Iz boevogo proshlogo*, p. 34; Stepanov, *Rabochie Petrograda*, pp. 33–6.

52 Steve Smith, 'Craft consciousness, class conciousness: Petrograd 1917', *History Workshop*, 11 (Spring 1981), pp. 33–56.

53 A. G. Kharchev, *Brak i semya v SSSR*, Moscow, 1964, p. 182. See also Dorothy Atkinson, *The End of the Russian Land Commune 1905–1930*, Stanford, 1983.

Chapter Nine

Women in a car town: Coventry, 1920–45

LINDA GRANT

This chapter is concerned with the effects on women's lives – on their consciousness, their politics, their work and their day-to-day experiences – of living in a town which owes its development, its politics and its character to an industry in which they are only marginally involved. More specifically, it looks at the consciousness generated amongst workers on the shop floor of Coventry car factories to examine the extent to which social processes specific to them have sustained a particular sexual division of labour and family form and contributed towards the *reproduction* of the opposing categories of the masculine and the feminine. It is based upon the recorded life histories of men and women connected with the Coventry car industry.[1] These are people born between the turn of the century and the early 1930s. All the men interviewed, and some of the women, have worked in the car industry, in a variety of trades and occupations. Some are the wives of car workers, women who have normally worked in other local industries.

It is the experience of places like Coventry which has encouraged an analysis of the inter-war years that denies that mass unemployment was its defining characteristic.[2] Some workers, it is argued, were not only producing but also consuming 'luxury' items like cars, vacuum-cleaners and fridges. This picture of a reasonable if not good standard of living amongst the working class in Britain, even when it is confined to certain geographical areas is, however, both superficial and inadequate. In the first place, it ignores the fact that many thousands of people had been forced to uproot themselves from friends, family and community and migrate in search of work. Like those who urge today's unemployed to go south, they view the working class simply as workers, not as people involved in relationships and communities which give their lives a meaning beyond the ability simply to survive. Indeed, the feelings of sadness and alienation expressed in the following, told by a man from Ireland who later spent

220

a great deal of his working life in car factories in Coventry, are still near the surface of the memory of many migrant workers:

> My father was already here and I hated the thought of coming to live here –
> I dreaded it. I'd say that was the most unhappy period of my life. I remember
> even on the boat I had to go away and hide and weep for a while and on the
> train coming down, kind of thing.I couldn't control the weeping. I'd have to
> go to the toilet or something. I remember I got off at Coventry station ... and
> I asked this fellow where the Holbrooks Hostels were. 'Oh', he says, 'I'm going
> by there, I'll give you a lift' ... So I looked at the place and I said, 'Oh no, it
> couldn't be there', I said, 'my father wouldn't stop there'. 'Well', he said, 'I'm
> sorry, this is the Holbrooks Hostel' ... I can remember feeling absolutely
> appalled by the conditions of the place. I thought, 'Oh God, I hope there's some
> mistake, we couldn't live here.'[3]

Secondly, the Coventry car industry did not provide a haven from depressed Britain for the working class. Whilst wages were relatively high, until the post-war period work was organised on a seasonal and short-time basis. Car factories often laid off the majority of workers in the summer months, prior to the annual Motor Show and families were forced to budget to cover indefinite periods of unemployment. Even those workers not completely laid off might experience long stretches of short-time working. Moreover, this insecurity was not confined to car workers. It affected whole sections of the Coventry working class. As a woman worker at the electrical firm British Thomson-Houston (BTH) in the 1930s explains:

> Well, you see, people were buying wirelesses and things in the winter and
> everything else. Well, they didn't want them in the summer and, you know,
> when there was no call for the work you just got laid off ... Soon as there was
> no work you were out. You'd probably start by going on three days a week and
> then as soon as the work dried up, before the new models came out, wirelesses
> and things, you were laid off completely ... Oh, it was seasonal, the work.[4]

Furthermore, within the car industry trade unionism was weak or almost non-existent in some plants. Thus car workers experienced a vulnerability which is often overlooked.[5] Also, with the introduction of new machinery and production methods workers were rapidly becoming deskilled and work was becoming routinised, heralding the soul-destroying pace and monotony of the post-war car plant.

In effect, the thesis that the 1930s have had an undeserved bad press fails to take into account the diversity of experience of different sections of the working class, even within the so-called prosperous areas. I hope this account points to the political significance of some of these divisions within the working class.

Coventry: the land fit for heroes?

Situated in the very heart of the sedate and opulent English countryside, Coventry became a key site in the restructuring of the British economy which took place in the inter-war years. Here were established the 'new' industries of the 1920s and 1930s – vehicle manufacture, electrical engineering and the weaving of artificial silk; a dynamic industrial development superimposed upon a small, medieval town. In these years the city was to experience social change on a phenomenal scale. For as communities based on the 'old', traditional industries of the British economy lay waste, so their unemployed workers flooded into Coventry in search of work. Between 1931 and 1951 the working population of the city grew from 84,000 to 127,000.[6]

Increasingly, from the turn of the century, it was the industries which employed predominantly men which gave the town its character and prosperity. Cycles, cars, aircraft and machine tools – a buoyant manufacturing base creating a fraternity of engineering workers. Above all it was the car industry which attracted the migrant labour force, defined the standard of living of the local working class and generated its political consciousness. Car manufacturers like Singer, Riley, Daimler, Morris, Jaguar, Rover, Hillman, Humber, Alvis, Standard and Armstrong Siddeley, all more or less household names in Britain, all had plants here. Men's work in the car industry had an importance in the town both objectively and in terms of its very culture. The motor car remains the enduring symbol of the town's identity, despite the savage results of redundancy, lay off and factory closure in the recent past.

The dominance in the town of the car and engineering industry, which employed around 37 per cent of occupied men over this period,[7] had very specific consequences for the lives of working-class women and it is this theme which is developed throughout this chapter. The local labour market was rigidly divided on the basis of sex. For although around 10 per cent of the total number of women workers over this period were employed in metal manufacturing trades, they tended to be concentrated in specific factories employing predominantly women, such as Renold Chain and Rudge Whitworth, with only a small number in factories employing both sexes. In these latter factories women were normally confined to routine machining jobs. In car factories, with the exception of the duration of the war, women workers on the shop floor were small in number and were largely concentrated in particular areas of work – in the trim shops as sewing machinists, or as car cleaners and canteen workers. Indeed, the figures reveal a great deal, for in 1931, for example, out of 25,303 workers in metalworking occupations living in the city women numbered only 2,426.[8] Of the 35,422 shop-floor workers in companies affiliated to the Engineering

Employers Federation in the city in 1935, which included electrical engineering companies such as the General Electric Company (GEC), only 5,727 were women.[9] In other words, women workers were only marginally involved in the town's major industry as table 9.1 shows. The car industry also differed from most of the other 'new' industries which expanded in the inter-war years, such as electrical engineering and food-processing, in that this expansion did not involve the recruitment of large numbers of women workers.

The proportion of women finding employment in the manufacturing industries as a whole declined markedly over these years, a development matched by a gradual increase in the numbers and proportion employed in the service industries. At the beginning of this period, in 1921, the percentage of women workers employed in manufacturing industries in Coventry was quite high (42 per cent) compared with that in England and Wales as a whole (30 per cent).[10] But that was the end of an era. The decline of the local ribbon-weaving industry is significant here. In 1921, 14 per cent of the female labour force was employed in the textile industry but by 1951 it was a mere 3 per cent, despite the presence of major Courtaulds plants in the town.[11] Apart from the metal-working industry the other important area of women's factory work locally has been the electrical engineering industry. GEC and BTH had large plants here, producing wirelesses, telephone equipment and electrical components for cars. But whilst an increase does occur in the number of women in the industry (from 280 in 1921 to 932 in 1951) this is a rise of only 0.8 per cent in the proportion of electrical engineering workers in the female labour force.[12]

If we set these changes against those in the service sector we can see just how dramatic was the transfer of women away from factory work. For example, in 1921 there were 2,542 women clerical workers in Coventry representing 16 per cent of the female labour force. By 1951 the figure was 9,169 or 25 per cent of local women workers.[13] Indeed, mirroring developments in many industrial areas, by 1951, 61 per cent of the local female labour force was employed in the service industries.[14]

We can thus see the inter-war years as a period which saw the consolidation of a particular form of the sexual division of labour in Coventry (and elsewhere) which has persisted into the 1980s. In this dynamic, increasingly clearer lines of demarcation were being drawn between the spheres of men's work and women's work, placing women solidly in the service sector. This shift in the location of women workers was significant for women's standard of living relative to men's. It also reflected and reinforced a particular view of the appropriate setting and role of the woman worker. In terms of standard of living women were increasingly placed in work which was, and is, notoriously badly paid and which has little dignity attached to it. It is work which is undervalued and, in turn, conceived of as

223

Table 9.1 *Composition of workforce by sex in selected Coventry engineering companies: 1930, 1935, 1939 (excluding office workers)*

Company	Section of industry	September 1930					October 1935					October 1939				
		Men		Women		Total	Men		Women		Total	Men		Women		Total
		No.	%	No.	%		No.	%	No.	%		No.	%	No.	%	
Humber Ltd	Cars	2,321	93.1	173	6.9	2,494	3,989	94.4	237	5.6	4,226	3,281	95.0	171	5.0	3,452
Armstrong Siddeley	Cars	2,637	100	–	–	2,637	3,749	98.9	41	1.1	3,790	4,591	100	–	–	4,591
Daimler Co. Ltd	Cars	2,240	97.5	58	2.5	2,298	3,376	99.0	32	1.0	3,408	2,933	99.0	28	1.0	2,961
Standard Motor Co.	Cars	1,351	92.7	106	7.3	1,457	3,013	93.5	210	6.5	3,223	1,512	95.0	78	5.0	1,590
Morris Motors	Cars	2,485	100	–	–	2,485	2,854	100	–	–	2,854	2,524	100	–	–	2,524
Rover Co. Ltd	Cars	967	95.8	42	4.2	1,009	1,311	84.7	237	15.3	1,548	1,068	86.0	175	14.0	1,243
General Electric Co.	Electrical engineering	714	37.2	1,205	62.8	1,919	1,751	36.6	3,037	63.4	4,788	2,358	45.6	2,815	54.4	5,173
British Thomson Houston	Electrical engineering	816	53.0	723	47.0	1,539	1,124	58.8	787	41.2	1,911	1,857	67.7	887	32.3	2,744
Rudge Whitworth	Cycles	517	60.6	336	39.4	853	369	63.3	214	36.7	583	NA	NA	NA	NA	NA
Alfred Herbert	Machine tools	2,229	97.8	49	2.2	2,278	3,029	97.0	95	3.0	3,124	3,628	95.5	172	4.5	3,800
Total of all companies in Coventry affiliated to EEF		23,211	84.4	4,289	15.6	27,500	26,695	83.8	5,727	16.2	35,422	39,806	87.4	5,723	12.6	45,529

Notes: – indicates no women employed.
 NA indicates no figures available.
Source: Calculated from statistics collected in 1930 and 1935 by the Engineering and Allied Employers National Federation held at Modern Records Centre,
 University of Warwick, MSS 237/13/3/20; MSS 237/13/3/36.

peripheral to the working of the economy. Indeed, we might almost describe it as invisible when we compare it to that of the car worker. For the worker in the car factory may have little identification with the finished car but in the production of a tangible product his labour's contribution is identifiable and concrete. There is no lasting evidence of the work of the woman who, for example, types the foreman's work schedules, cooks the meal in the works canteen or cleans the office floor.

Men at work

It is important to see this contrast in the location of men and women in the labour market in the context of the pre-war car factory where tens of thousands of local men earned their livelihood. That is, it is important to view the car factory not simply as a place for making cars but also as one significant arena within which men's consciousness and male identity was shaped. In turn, we need to explore the extent to which this consciousness was effective beyond the factory gates and thus part of the social processes by which gender division at work, within the family and in the wider community was reproduced and sustained.

Many of the workers in the car factories of these years retained the complex and traditional skills of the turner, sheet-metal worker, pattern-maker, coach builder and trimmer and so forth. Furthermore, despite the gradual deskilling of the workforce which has so characterised the industry and which now confronts many car workers with boredom and monotony, pre-war workers maintained an intense pride in their work and the product of their labour. Indeed, it is this consciousness which epitomised a significant section of the local male working class. The processes involved in making a car are lovingly described. The cars produced and the companies which made them are remembered with pride. To some extent the city had not entirely shaken off nineteenth-century expectations concerning the appropriate relationship between master craftsman and worker. For there has emerged in the course of the interviews the expression of a powerful consciousness of the importance of maintaining a hierarchy of workers within the factory, a hierarchy based on skill and competence. But it is a consciousness which often contradicts the reality of an increasingly deskilled labour process. As a result, objective criteria which might define the skilled worker within the factory hierarchy, such as apprenticeship or training, existed side by side with more subjective assessments. For example, many semi-skilled workers of this period were recruited into workshops dominated by apprenticed workers and acquired not only some of their expertise and working practices, but assumed, also, aspects of their consciousness. Similarly, semi-skilled workers became 'skilled' at their work, viewed themselves as such and had conferred upon them the status of skilled workers. Thus the stress on skill and competence at work was not confined to the craftsman; it permeated all layers of the workforce. The ethos created on the shop floor had implications beyond the factory and, in terms of our interest here, implications for the lives of women in Coventry.

In the first place, many workers placed themselves within the historical traditions of Coventry itself, a history which, from the point of view of labour, has emphasised and institutionalised the distinction between apprenticed craftsman and worker, whereby the craftsman earned the political rights of freeman of the city.[15] As a toolmaker, born in 1922, argued, 'It was very much the thing that was thought about in the Coventry area, the fact that you served your time and you came out of your time and you became a good person of the City. I think all that was part of the training.'[16] Universal suffrage has not wholly eliminated the significance of the tradition. A time-served worker retained a certain status into the twentieth century which went beyond his ability to get a job and do it well. It opened the door to a world of citizenship, a world of adult men with something to say and a dignity with which to say it – the opportunity to be a 'good person of the city'. It was almost totally a male preserve and there occurred a huge furore when a woman, Lily Stevenson, tried to acquire the status of freeman (*sic*) in the 1930s.[17]

But it is not simply that women were excluded from pursuing engineering apprenticeships, or attaining the freedom of the City, and the status and dignity assumed with both. They were also excluded from the culture of the city's primary industry and as a result were almost outsiders in their own town. The car industry was so dominant in the city's economy and women were so noticeably absent from it that they had no place in the factory hierarchy, no place in its political debates and thus virtually no place in what made the city tick. Women occupied another and almost wholly distinct political and cultural arena.

Men's political consciousness, then, was shaped in the car factory. Within it they clung to the distinctions surrounding skill. People knew their place and the place of those around them. A toolmaker starting work in the 1930s explained that:

> Going from one toolroom to another, when you talk to toolmakers ... you talk the same language. And it all stems from the sort of training in your earlier years, as an apprentice ... I think in teaching your craft you become associated to the people that are doing the teaching and I think they also pass on their knowledge of other things as well ... and that's no slight on people that work in production shops, because you've got some people that produce. But I think you can tell the training.[18]

If the toolroom was one of the most exclusive of 'clubs', there were other 'clubs' a man could join. Male workers who were not time-served apprentices might view toolroom workers, for example, as an elite but would neverthe-less, consider themselves distinct and superior to other less-trained and experienced workers. This was the case even in situations where changes in the labour process had made a skill redundant. What was important for self-esteem was knowing that you *could* hand-paint a car body or work from a blueprint, despite the fact that automatic machinery was eliminating the need for such proficiency.

> In a paint shop now they're not skilled. It's just repetition, you see. Most of these people that work in paint shops these days, such as the Jag, if I was in business I wouldn't give them a job ... Before I was 21 I was capable of doing a job right through the paint shop.[19]

A grinder, born in 1911, who had not served an apprenticeship, agreed in conversation that his expertise had been increasingly irrelevant to the work he was required to do. But at the same time he argued,

> I always considered myself a universal grinder, which in relation to being a machinist is highly skilled. Course, myself I would go where I'm sent – external, internal, surface grinding, gear grinding. I was capable of setting any of them machines up.[20]

Few of the men I have talked to who have defined themselves as 'skilled' would concur with the sentiments behind the following comment made by a woman sewing machinist who worked for forty years in a car factory:

> How did pride show itself in the factory? Well, it was just prestige, you know, I'm a tinsmith, I'm a little better than you because you're only a so and so ... There was always that element of snobbery in a factory. Your job is that little bit better than that person's or whatever. But when it all comes down to it all factory work is the same.[21]

Of course, the ability to perform a skilled job, or indeed any job, well is appropriately a matter for pride. The skills and abilities of car workers are rarely recognised or adequately acknowledged, especially in the popular myths about them. When new machinery threatens to make a skill redundant it can be politically crucial to endorse its value. But at the same time this strong attachment to hierarchy stood in the way of organisational unity. It looked to the past, to a period when, for example, one man could build a car body from beginning to end and it turned its back on the new recruits of a changing industry. The politics of difference, pay differentials and union rivalry – the politics of compe-tition were paramount.

The effects on union organisation of division amongst the workforce have been documented elsewhere.[22] The members of the Transport and General Workers Union were viewed by the Amalgamated Engineering Union, the union most threatened by their recruitment drive in the late

1930s, as upstarts with no place in the engineering industry – trouble-makers, 'a bloody nuisance', as one man argued. They were transforming the practices and traditions of the 'real' union for engineering workers by recruiting any Tom, Dick or Harry. They even recruited the odd Jane!

> We was resentful of them (TGWU) trying to negotiate a skilled man's terms because we didn't trust them as a skilled engineering union ... We used to joke amongst ourselves about working our way up to the labourer. Because they was getting just as much money.[23]

Pervading some of the skilled shops was an atmosphere which almost implied that the day-to-day practice of trade unionism was something of a sordid affair, beneath the dignity of the skilled man. The strike, for example, was the weapon of the common man. The artisan won his reward slowly, with reasoned, sober argument. As a toolmaker remembers,

> I was only a young lad, they had an election for the shop steward and it was quite noticeable that all the skilled men from the toolroom – never heard a word from them. All the chatting was done by the unskilled people, the ones with the loudest – the ones that could talk ... You see [in] the toolroom they didn't want to be bothered with that. You got the impression they considered it beneath them to sort of get up on a bench and start haranguing the crowd ... The staid, skilled man's attitude. Not, specifically saying, 'I'm better than you', but virtually implying it.[24]

There was another area in which division between workers existed – the relationship between the Coventry-born and the migrant. The extent of this is difficult to assess and the responses to questions concerning the relationship between the two groups are very varied. Nevertheless, under-lying many comments on this question, particularly for the skilled Coventry-born worker, there is a patronising reluctance to accept the migrant as a genuine engineer.

> There was a good degree of skill in Coventry, in engineering, although I say it myself ... Because they did heavy engineering up North, shipbuilding, heavy engineering and all that. This fine work down here, aero work and car work, they weren't accustomed to that up North. When they came down here they didn't get it straight away, you see. They'd make it eventually if they were skilled men. But the type of work we did down here was more skilled than the work they did. It was smaller and finer, you see.[25]

The migrant, it was conceded, could grasp the job eventually but it took time and he never quite made the grade. It is possible that the migrant was viewed as embodying all that was changing in the industry – the breakdown of skills and traditions, new methods, new machinery. He was a new type of man and he was kept at a distance as a result. But to be on the receiving end of hostility, condescension or even indifference at a time of upheaval from friends, community and a culture which was familiar made for a miserable life at times. It was an atmosphere which always hovered around the outsider. 'They would never turn round and call me an Irish bastard to my face. But it was there. It was there all the time.'[26]

Even where relationships were not openly hostile, the method of recruitment in the car factories at this time very definitely militated against the migrant worker. The foreman played a key role since the new recruits were generally 'spoken for' by friends, family or other workers. It meant that those jobs considered 'good' jobs, either in terms of pay, prospects, security or training were more difficult to secure by a migrant than by someone whose father or brother was already an employee. Foremen had a great deal of power, as one man testifies:

> I mean, I can remember the time in the toolroom when there wasn't a Catholic. My gaffer who took us all on wouldn't have a Catholic in the place ... This foreman didn't like the Irish, he certainly didn't like the Welsh, he tolerated the Scots. In fact, if you were born outside Coventry he wouldn't have you in if he could help it.[27]

This practice did not die in the 1930s. As a result very few black workers have been recruited into the car factories in Coventry since the war. Those that have tend to be foundry workers or labourers. It has not been a priority for the trade unions to challenge this racism and the racial division of labour within the Coventry economy.

The migrant worker might, therefore, experience a particularly precarious relationship with the labour market, compounded by the seasonal nature of work in the industry. Many workers were laid off in the summer months and security of employment depended, to a large extent, on the arbitrary decisions of the foreman. 'There was a lot of people kept on. The foreman liked them and kept them on and the others got the sack. I mean, they could sack anybody they liked. The fellers they didn't like had the sack.'[28] Once in the factory the 'out of towner' might find co-operation from his work-mates conditional on his 'credentials'. One man, who described how his colleagues refused to assist and train new recruits, argued, 'I couldn't see a bloke floundering and struggling, not if he was a bona fide craftsman.'[29] But permanent workers often viewed and referred to new workers as 'tinkers, tailors, candlestick makers'; 'they'd have *anyone* in the production shops!' In a sense Coventry itself and its male workers in particular are conceived of as embodying craftsmanship by tradition rather than training. The Coventry car worker is born not bred and one senses the hard-earned struggle of the migrant worker to gain acceptance in the industry.

> There was a resentment of people coming in and going to the motor industry who hadn't got that background, the training and so on ... And lots of Welsh

miners came to Coventry and also the Irish ... and they hadn't the training and the background ... If you came as a craftsman, like I did, you were accepted as such.[30]

All this does not mean, of course, that solidarity between workers in a car plant did not occur or that some men did not strongly reject an emphasis on division. But almost overwhelmingly men working in this period stressed their own abilities in a competitive manner. 'I could do every operation on the section', was a commonly expressed assertion. Or, 'these people today aren't car workers'. Contained within this consciousness are notions of appropriate masculine achievement. These men had followed their fathers into a world of work, a man's world where an importance was attached to proving skill, intelligence and competence over and above the next man.

There was scope for your skill then because you wasn't spoonfed or feather-bedded like they are now, with jigs and tools. You could go in your best things and do the job. But you'd have to improvise ... you were an individual worker.[31]

Craftsman v. semi-skilled, semi-skilled v. unskilled represents a rivalry in men's relationships with other men and it is a rivalry within which women had no place. For although women have always worked in the car industry they rarely feature in men's comments about divisions within the workforce. Women's place inside and outside the factory was wholly separate and distinct and it was seen as such. This consciousness of hierarchy is thus not about skill alone, it is also about men and masculinity. It is a consciousness which arranges the behaviour, priorities and places for men and which subjectively puts women in a different terrain with distinct ground rules. When women have strayed into this male sphere, as I argue later, they were immediately reminded they were out of bounds. The differences existing between men became institutionalised divisions within the factory which in turn were significant in the shaping of male consciousness and male identity; in producing and reproducing a model of masculinity which implicitly constructs a model of feminity. These divisions between men are important to them. They are about the dignity men seek from work but they fashion a man's behaviour in a context much wider than the factory. The car factory is a place where men assert their value as workers confronting capital but it is also an arena within which men create their identity as men.

Women at work

If what I have described constitutes part of the culture of work for men, it stands in sharp contrast to the culture of work for women. As I have indicated, there was a rigid sexual division of labour within the local economy. Just as sons traced the footsteps of fathers, so daughters followed mothers and sisters. People knew the boundaries of the labour-market and, whatever their aspirations, few were encouraged to cross them. Recruitment for girls depended, as it did for boys, on being 'spoken for':

> When I left school? Oh dear ... well, I didn't know what I wanted to be. I didn't want to be this, that and the other and they [my parents] got me in this weaving place. Yes, Dalton and Barton.[32]

> I went to work at Peel Connor with my eldest sister ... My sister got a job there and she spoke for me and I got a job there.[33]

When I asked people where women worked in Coventry in this period they normally responded by giving a very precise list of factories which was always the same.

> Most of them went into Courtaulds or Cash's or the London Laundry. And one or two of them left these places and went to the GEC, because it began to be noted for starting girls, and the BTH. And the Chain [Renold Chain] the girls used to work there.[34]

The limited occupational spread of female workers in Coventry is illustrated in table 9.2. In these female occupations wages and conditions of work were very poor compared to those in the car and engineering industry. Indeed, those few women who did secure jobs in the car trade commanded considerably higher wages than the vast majority of women workers in the city. For example, a woman who worked in the trim shop of the Standard Motor Company, gluing fabric to car interiors, remembers that when she was aged twenty-one in 1938:

> I was earning, on a full week, £3 a week. Well, that was a good wage ... And I remember being several months on three days a week and I went down to the labour, because you signed on for those days, and they sent us to GEC ... and it was thirty bob a week – for a full week. So, I thought, well, I'm better off where I am on thirty bob for three days.[35]

Outside of the car industry women workers were subject to low pay and often harsh work routines. A woman starting work in the late 1920s at the London Laundry in Coventry, a laundry which employed several hundred women, recalls:

> The first week I was there ... I started at 8 o'clock in the morning, from eight til one, you had an hour for dinner, worked til 8 o'clock at night. That was Monday, Tuesday, Wednesday, Thursday, Friday, Saturday til 1 o'clock. But you had your wages on a Friday night and I got 8s 9d, eight shillings and ninepence! Nearly always through the winter I worked til 8 o'clock and I've known the time when I've done sixty eight hours ... It was 10s a week when you were fourteen and then you had 1s 6d rise every twelve months, something

Table 9.2 *Summary of female occupational structure in Coventry, 1921–51*

Occupational group	1921[a]		1931[b]		1951[c]	
	No.	%	No.	%	No.	%
Personal service	3,189	20.0	4,544	19.6	7,018	19.1
Clerks, typists, etc.	2,542	16.0	3,833	16.5	9,169	25.0
Textile workers	2,210	13.9	3,320	14.3	1,263	3.5
Metal workers, inc. vehicles	2,002	12.5	2,426	10.5	3,350	9.1
Commercial, inc. shop assistants	1,812	11.4	2,619	11.3	4,268	11.6
Clothing	932	5.9	870	3.8	800	2.2
Professional	887	5.5	1,155	5.0	2,626	7.2
Paper and printing	392	2.5	414	1.8	278	0.8
Watchmaking	284	1.8	105	0.5	d	
Electrical apparatus	280	1.7	1,129	4.9	932	2.5
Unskilled workers NES	138	0.8	1,007	4.3	4,049	11.0
Other manufacturing workers	506	3.2	1,010	4.3	971	2.7
Other service workers	755	4.7	751	3.2	1,938	5.3
Total women occupied	15,929	100	23,183	100	36,662	100

Notes: [a] Aged 12 years and over
[b] Aged 14 years and over
[c] Aged 15 years and over
[d] Figures not available

Source: Calculated from occupational tables, Census of England and Wales, 1921, 1931, 1951

like that ... In the summer it was very hot because all the steam pipes were under the floor ... It was really hard work but I coped with it and I got used to it. We used to iron thirty three shirts an hour.[36]

This was at a time when a male car worker of the same age would be earning around 50s a week.

Many women remember their first years of work as a demoralising and frightening experience. Edna, for example, who left school aged fifteen, in 1931, and worked at Bushills, a box-making company, says:

It was making these boxes. I got 8s 3d a week. But the bosses there were tartars. I used to have nightmares, it frightened me ... The money was very, very poor. But eventually Mum and Dad says it wasn't right to be worried stiff with the job. Because you daren't lift your eyes up.[37]

Whilst it was relatively easy for women to move from job to job at this time, the work available was low paid and intensively supervised. Typical is the experience of a young office worker at White and Poppe's in the early 1920s:

Really and truly, it was nothing but work. I often say now that if you went to the toilet you were lucky...(there was) a whole pile of work that they put on one side for you to type ... and the minute you were getting low there'd be another pile. I remember getting severely reprimanded for laughing, 'You're not here to laugh Miss Worsley'. I can't think what it was that managed to tickle me.[38]

Although women tended to work in factories or offices employing mostly women, they were usually supervised and controlled by men. This meant that the problem of getting a job was informed by criteria which applied exclusively to their sex. Take the experience of a woman attempting to get a job at Courtaulds in the 1930s:

> I always remember it. We stood in this yard and there were crowds of girls round ... and I stood there and the boss was always after the blondes and one thing and another. Anyway, all of a sudden he said, 'Hey you, the blonde there, start on Monday.'[39]

Of course, this incident is about much more than hair colour. Getting a job and keeping it often relied on succumbing to the sexual advances of supervisors and others. A sexual favour granted allowed a woman to get on. Women workers became, in many instances, the victims of men's definition of their sexuality in a way which materially affected their wages and standard of living. Thus for many women the factory could become not an arena within which to develop a dignity and pride in their work but a minefield to be negotiated. Women were constantly reminded by men that they were women and as such they were viewed primarily as sexual beings. Time and again women have spontaneously recounted incidents in which their sexuality had intruded on their ability to earn a living. A woman who worked at GEC in the 1930s recalls:

> There was women, big powerful women doing little jobs sitting down. [The foreman] said, 'That's the job she should be on'. And, of course, this fella that put me on the job, he put me on it to get his own back on my sister, because my sister wouldn't go out with him. She wouldn't go out with him and he said, 'I'll make you go out with me', and that's what he did ... As I got older I got the same as my sister. They'd give me a decent job if I'd go out with them. I used to tell them where to put their jobs![40]

This sexual abuse of women did not stop on the factory floor, or with the foreman. A woman office worker in a car factory in the 1930s was asked:

> Did you see the top manager at Holbrooks Bodies much?

> Captain Stowbanks? Yes. Used to dread going in his office because he wanted to get hold of you and kiss you, you know. He was one of those sort of men. I used to dread it, used to try and leave the door open but he'd get behind you and push the door to.[41]

Sexual harassment in some factories was only matched by the paternal attitude taken by supervision in others. 'He treated you as if you were his own daughter, he spoke to you like a father.' 'They used to call us little girls, even when I'd been there fourteen years they'd say, "What do you want little girl, yes little girl?"'[42]

This emphasis on women's sexuality by men was not the only means by which the day-to-day relationships between men and women at work reproduced accepted models of the two sexes in a way which had material repercussions for women's lives. The stress on gender difference, which refuses to accept women as genuine wage-earners was brought into sharp relief in Coventry factories during the Second World War. Coventry was a centre for the munitions industry and this initiated a temporary breakdown of the sexual division of labour. Thousands of women were drafted into Coventry from all over Britain and many found themselves on the shop floor of the engineering factories, working alongside men, for the first time. Some men still remembered the migrant women workers of the First World War, who had also come to work in Coventry munitions factories. But for others this influx of women was a new and startling experience. A toolmaker was asked,

> What was it like working with mainly women?
>
> Shocking! Pretty embarassing! It's a pity these have come in now ... We were fairly innocent. I mean, you'd never come across women in industry at that time and what they got up to, quite frankly, was, you know, what you would expect anyway when it was all women ... They needed them during the war but they got rid of them. Other factories are full of women.[43]

Although women were theoretically filling the places of absent men for the duration it was almost impossible for women to attain the status of equal replacement. Those men remaining on the shop floor were still able to exercise control over the women, not simply by taking a derisory attitude towards them and their abilities, but by virtue of the very organisation of work. Work routines could be structured in such a way as to favour men, male earnings and male control over the job. For example, the following series of events were recalled by one woman who worked in the general section at the Rootes Shadow factory at Ryton, Coventry during the Second World War. The women recruits at Rootes had a number of grievances. First, the rate of pay:

> 'A' job was the top rate money. 'B' job was the middle one. 'D' job the women were supposed to do. Well, I've known men to be doing 'D' jobs, little washers and that and we've been doing 'A' jobs, but we got our jobs knocked down to 'B'. I said, 'We do 'A' jobs and get them knocked down to 'B' and he's on a 'D' job and gets is plussed up to 'A'.[44]

Secondly, women were often allocated the worst jobs on the section, those jobs which earned the least money and were also considered the most boring. Men were allowed a choice in the jobs they did and as a result frequently chose the best jobs. Thirdly, experienced men knew the tricks of the trade but it was knowledge which they were reluctant to share with the women.

They knew, for example, that they could set their machines on 'slow motion' when the rate-fixer came to time the job and then speed up to carry out the work and, as a result, increase their earnings:

> I could never understand it. I never left my machine and Jim W— was on the same job and he could come up and stand and talk to me and go to the toilet and spend no end of time and yet he was earning double my money. 'How come?', I said. Well a man will never give away on another man and he just grinned.

Over a period of time the women at the Rootes factory had had several arguments over their grievances. They took them up with the foreman and the chargehand and achieved nothing. They complained to the convenor who prevaricated over the issue. Eventually the women decided to go over the head of the convenor and take up the matter with Jack Jones, local organiser of the Transport and General Workers' Union (TGWU). Jones immediately called a factory meeting, which infuriated the convenor, but persuaded the Company to pay the higher rates to the women. The women were determined to ensure that all women entitled to the rate for the job got it:

> Mr. Payne was the Superintendent and we were coming out [of the meeting] and he says to us, 'Now listen, you're going out there on that machine and keep that shut.' 'Oh no', we said, 'every girl in the shop that's doing an 'A' job, we'll tell her she's entitled to the rate for it.' And we came out and we told them all. Some of them was on capstans, doing facing up, big jobs and that, and, of course, they all put in for it and we put in for it and we got it!

By this time the women had learned how to speed up their machines and they were also insisting that everyone took a share of the good and bad jobs coming onto the section.

> I said [to the setter], 'It's the same with that cage and the jobs that's in them. I have to do any job that you bring out to me ... yet the men can have a choice and pick whatever job they want.' And all the donkey work was left for the women. I said, 'From this on they can all take their share of the bad jobs ... I'm not refusing to do any job in that cage provided everybody else in the section, including all the men, takes their turn on it. But we're not going to be the lackey any more on this section for the men.'

Victory for the women, but it had its price. The woman who related this story reflected that its effect lingered on in the relationships between men and women on the section. The men resented the women securing the rate for the job and withdrew co-operation from them. She gave examples of the occasions when she had to replace her grinding wheel at the stores. It was extremely heavy to lift, 'the men would see you do it but they wouldn't help you. But you got the rate ... Some of the men could be really cattish.'

235

This dispute also points to other, more general aspects of women's position within the local labour market and trade-union movement. Clearly, in crossing the boundaries of the accepted division of labour, women had come up against the indifference to their grievances of the plant representatives of the TGWU. They were forced to go beyond the accepted procedures of the union and contact Jack Jones personally. As other studies have shown, 'dilution' and the introduction of women into the engineering industry was a consuming issue for the trade-union movement during the Second World War, in Britain generally and in Coventry.[45] Women workers were viewed as the 'dilutees' *par excellence* – they were not only 'unskilled', they were also women. Whilst some men recalling this period in Coventry's history conceded that amongst the dilutees, 'there were some good workers', this generosity does not extend to women. Thus the fear of the implications of dilution may well have been part of the dynamic of the Rootes incident. But on the other hand, we have to look hard to find an example of the trade-union movement taking a spontaneously positive attitude towards women workers in this period. In theory, the TGWU was committed to the organisation of women. But, as Steve Tolliday has argued, 'the T & G only recruited in large numbers when the situation was virtually thrust upon it' and this was particularly the case where women workers were concerned.[46] He cites several examples in Coventry where it was only the strike action taken by women over wages which encouraged their recruitment into the union. This was the case at GEC in 1935 and at Courtaulds in 1937.[47] Women had to go out of their way to gain the attention of the trade unions and once they acquired it it could mean little or nothing in terms of the union's future concern with their interests. This is clearly supported by all the historical and contemporary studies of women's role in the union movement.[48] In effect, women have been pushed to the sidelines of these organisations.

In fact, at times of industrial action in the car industry women's vulnerability as workers and as women, within the context of a predominantly male workforce, was starkly revealed. For example, in 1930 an attempt was made to introduce the Bedaux System into the trim shop at the Rover. The Bedaux System, named after its founder Charles Bedaux, was a work-study scheme, the crucial effect of which was to increase the intensity and speed at which people worked.[49] Unsurprisingly, it was the un-unionised women sewing machinists, rather than the National Union of Vehicle Builders (NUVB) members amongst the male trimmers, who were initially approached by management to work the system. Most of the women were determined not to work it but ambiguous and dilatory support from both the NUVB and the TGWU left the women prey to insidious management persuasion. As one woman remembers:

So Searle came up, the Managing Director, and he went round and he came up to my friend and I and he picked on me and he picked on another girl. She'd got red hair, she was rather an attractive girl ... And he said, 'Would we work', and he would take us and buy us any dress we'd like – the most expensive dress – if we would persuade the others to try it. 'Just try it', he said ... [We] more or less told him to get lost, you see.[50]

In September the women, still largely unorganised, took strike action when the company began to introduce Bedaux working. But, as Steve Tolliday has shown in his account of the strike, official union negotiation over its settlement went ahead without any consultation with the women involved and largely disregarded their interests.[51] Ultimately, the Bedaux System was not put into practice at the plant. But the indifference of the trade unions to the women and their demands allowed demeaning management practices to continue unhindered and left the women as isolated from the union movement as they were prior to the strike.

The events at Rover highlight the low regard with which women car workers were generally held by their male work-mates and the trade unions in particular. Thus within the consciousness which celebrates the achievements of the industry's workers, women are not located. Women's work in the car factory, and certainly their work outside of it, was typically seen by men as peripheral and unskilled and was often totally overlooked. As one man commented, 'Factory work was men's work. There weren't any women in factories before the war. Not in this town anyway.'[52] Such a view was certainly a factor in the degradation of women's skill as sewing machinists. There is no doubt that many machining jobs took years of training and experience to perfect. Largely made of leather in this period, a difficult fabric to work, car seats had to be sewn with a high degree of accuracy and neatness in order to achieve the perfect results required in the luxury models of the time. Women sewing machinists regarded themselves as skilled workers, as they continue to do today. But it is difficult to find a male car worker who unambiguously conferred upon women the status and dignity normally accorded to the skilled worker.

They were skilled jobs. Although, there again, it was only an acquired skill. I mean, basically anybody could press their foot on a treadle and let the stuff go through, can't they? It was just how quick you could do it, how quickly you could turn it round and so on.[53]

Even in 1986 some men have forcefully indicated their opposition to the relatively recent introduction of women workers onto track jobs, describing the work as either too heavy or too difficult and articulating the view that 'a woman's place is in the home'. In the 1930s, the confinement of women to the trim shops could be viewed as an immutable law of nature:

> Well [the women] used to cover all trim pads and linings ... arm rests, squabs and all sorts of things like that. The women could – they were adaptable to that sort of work and if it was very important sort of work they'd have men on it, you see. But the women did the lesser side of it.[54]

The widespread absence of recognition of women's skill inevitably bred resentment in some trim shops. Significantly it had implications for women's wage packets:

> I think, basically, there was X amount allowed for the whole completed work. They'd allow the men trimmers so much, and the men that cut out and did that sort of thing, and the sewing machinists. And there was a certain amount of money allotted ... We always felt that [the men] had the best of the deal and we had what was left over. I don't know, I mean, it might have been sour grapes but we always felt we were a little cheated. Because we, again, always felt that we were the skilled – mind, men trimmers are skilled workers, there's no doubt about that ... but then we were too. Because there's no-one could just sit down and do the work we did. So we always felt ... a little bit cheated.[55]

It is important to remember that the whole tenor of the 1920s and 1930s was one in which women's right to earn a living, particularly that of married women, was being challenged very forcefully by the state. Its main vehicle for these ideas was the legislation passed at the time concerning the unemployed and unemployment. The administration of the 'genuinely seeking work' clause attached to the payment of unemployment benefit and the introduction of the Anomalies Act in 1931 were the most blatant expressions of a refusal to accept that married women were genuine claimants of the Unemployment Insurance Fund.[56] But all the discussions in Parliament, within the many and various Commissions appointed to investigate the working of the Unemployment Insurance Fund in the 1920s and 1930s, and in the press reveal a growing and powerful body of opinion which regarded the woman claimant as an 'evil' intruder in the system, as Margaret Bondfield, Minister of Labour in the 1929 Labour Government, described her.[57] By implication the 'illegal claimant' was also the non-genuine worker. One woman in Coventry explained that when she was put on short-time in the 1930s from a small engineering factory, she attempted to claim unemployment benefit but was told at the union office where she signed on that she could not return to her job and her insurance cards would be withheld. Her job, it was argued, was needed by a single woman or man. In this case the woman fought and won her right to return to her job. But up and down the country married women were harassed out of their jobs and off the dole. And as non-registered unemployed they became the hidden unemployed of the decade. The arguments put forward to justify the introduction of these laws, which were in fact aimed at reducing public expenditure on the unemployed, served to bolster and support the ideology which proposes that a woman's place is in the home. This ideology had a resonance within the trade-union movement, as the popular demand for a 'family wage' paid to the male breadwinner bears witness.[58] It certainly survived into the war period, despite Government efforts to backtrack and encourage married women to join the war effort.

Women were further marginalised in the local economy by the operation of a marriage bar, widely enforced in both public and private industry. Those who attempted to challenge this can recall the hostility they encountered from their work-mates. For example, one woman who married in the mid 1930s found that her fellow workers refused to buy her a wedding gift, which was traditionally given, when she announced her intention to remain at work after marriage. The reason she had decided to stay on at work was because her future husband was unemployed. It was an uncomfortable situation, however, and she soon left her job.[59] Invariably, women who came up against the marriage bar argue that they accepted it – 'it was the way things were.' The effect of the bar was reflected in the low numbers of married women in Coventry industries indicated in table 9.3

Factory work a as men's work

Whilst a marriage bar was rooted in the culture of the town, it was a tradition sustained within the private arena of the home and any contradictions it posed for women were fought out there. Men took a pride in their ability to provide for a dependent wife. The role of breadwinner emerged as a central aspect of men's identity. Many of the men interviewed exercised a veto against the waged labour of their wives:

> When I married my wife she wanted to carry on nursing. I said, 'No', I said, 'if I marry you I provide for you … I want you here when I come home.' Well, I was very dogmatic on that. Ooh, she played hell up, she played hell up. I said, 'Look, I don't care, you're going to be at home when I come home. You can do what you like during the day but when I come home I want you home.' I used to leave at quarter past seven in the morning, on my pushbike, and when we was working over I'd never get home until eight o'clock at night. She was on her own pretty much until the lad was born. Then she was alright. She'd got the lad to look after.[60]

But buried within this conflict between men and women is men's assertion of their own sexuality and their definitions of female sexuality. For within the debates which took place within many households on this issue men tended to emphasise what they viewed as the 'sexual dangers' of the workplace. For example, a woman keen to get a job whose husband did not approve of this was asked why he objected:

Table 9.3 Marital status and age structure of female workers in selected local industries in Coventry, 1921

Occupation group		Single	Married	Widowed and divorced	Total	Aged 12–19	Aged 20–24	Aged 25–34	Aged 35–44	Aged over 45
Metal workers	No.	1,791	113	98	2,002	733	736	378	110	45
	%	89.5	5.5	5.0	100	36.6	36.8	18.9	5.5	2.2
Textile workers	No.	1,876	225	109	2,210	1,116	440	307	132	215
	%	85.0	10.1	4.9	100	50.5	20.0	13.8	6.0	9.7
Clothing workers	No.	785	97	50	932	319	195	201	103	114
	%	84.2	10.4	5.4	100	34.2	21.0	21.6	11.0	12.2
Commercial	No.	1,096	542	174	1,812	380	314	344	350	424
	%	60.4	30.0	9.6	100	21.0	17.3	19.0	19.3	23.3
Personal service	No.	1,869	703	617	3,189	1,013	614	514	461	587
	%	58.6	22.0	19.4	100	31.8	19.3	16.1	14.4	18.4
Clerks	No.	2,466	49	27	2,542	1,157	803	417	127	38
	%	97.0	1.9	1.1	100	45.5	31.6	16.4	5.0	1.5

This selected list represents 80 per cent of the total female workforce.
Source: Calculated from Occupation Tables, Census of England and Wales, covering Coventry CB 1921.

I think he was a bit jealous of people like me ... He was more moral, if I could say that about him. You know, he used to think of who you was going to mix with in factories. He knew what factories were like and I think it was probably that. Anyway, I went anyway.[61]

Women were clear that their husbands sought to exercise a control over their sexuality. In stepping into the 'outside world', the world outside the home, women undermined that power. In so doing they revealed that the equation work/men struck the very heart of their relationships with men. For men, a woman's femininty was sustained only in the home, untainted by the threat of a sexual rival. A woman whose children were evacuated during the war and was 'shattered by the separation', felt that she 'couldn't stay at home and do nothing'. She took a job and recalls her husband's response:

But, of course, my husband was such a jealous man that he loathed me going. I mean, I earned £2 a week and I had to pay three six shillings for each evacuated child. I paid it out of my own money, because he wouldn't because I'd got this job. So I think I earned about 2d by the time I'd paid my bus fares to go.

What was he jealous about?

Well, in case I went off with somebody else, I suppose ... Oh yes, it was terrible. It spoiled our lives really. But he was alright when we got older. I guess he realised those days had gone. I think it spoiled his life, being as he was. I mean, it was most unfounded. I mean, I never cared for anybody else, only him.[62]

Thus although the war encouraged the greater acceptance of the married woman's presence in the labour force, the issue remained one of bitter contention between married couples. Male car workers carried with them into their intimate relationships an image of the workplace and its culture within which women had no place.

Within the home the division of labour was often as rigid as that in the economy generally. Women were invariably responsible for housework, child care and for managing the family budget, with minimal assistance from their husbands:

She did everything. She paid the mortgage, the rates. She saved for the holidays. She did all the holiday booking. The only thing I did was sorted out me horses and done me work. She did everything and she wanted to. I never had to worry about a thing ... Always kept a decent table and she was ever so careful. But with me she was ever so soft.[63]

In fact, the fluctuating income of the car worker, resulting from frequent periods of lay off, short time and unemployment, tended very clearly to delineate women's identity as housekeepers. Thus a woman's success in organising the family budget and stretching scarce resources shaped her view of herself:

> I never knew what he earned, but I knew people who had more than I did and I also knew people who had less. And never once in my married life did I ever ask for any more. I sort of had an obsession on managing on what I'd got.[64]

Equally, the management of money established a woman's standing as a wife and, by implication as a woman. Good wives, good women were careful wives. 'She was very careful. I mean, she could spend a pound and make it go a lot further than I could. So I was lucky that I'd got a good housewife.'[65]

Whilst these private domestic arrangements were rooted in the tradition of the time, they were clearly reinforced in Coventry on the shop floor of the car factory. The day-to-day events and exchanges which took place there continuously reproduced concepts of appropriate roles and behaviour in the home. As a male car worker remembers:

> I remember several instances. One where a man, in his lunchbag, there had to be twenty Woodbines every morning. And this particular man didn't come to work one day and so everybody wondered why. And it was, 'Oh, the missus hadn't put my fags up.' And so he didn't lose anything. She lost the pay. He said, 'She'll not do that again' ... They were commonplace things ... That was the sort of thing that went on.[66]

The young recruit in the car factory acquired not only his skills as a worker but was also welcomed into a man's world, within which his definitions of men and women were consolidated.

In a town dominated by a single industry the culture of the workplace inevitably spreads beyond the factory gate into the very life of the city, its politics and its people. Shop-floor culture within the car factory applauded the car worker's skill and competence. A hierarchy of men was created within which women had no place. This consciousness relating to status at work was permeated with concepts of appropriate masculine achievement and behaviour, effective both within and beyond the factory. But if the culture of the workplace defined part of what it was to be a man implicitly, and at times explicitly, it generated ideas of a woman's place and role. Day to day, week to week, this culture and consciousness confirmed and reinforced distinctions between men and women. The events, exchanges and hierarchy within the factory were part of the mechanisms by which sexual division was continuously recreated.

But life in the factory meshed with processes and activities taking place outside. Thus the woman at work could find her value as a worker degraded by sexual harassment, low pay and unequal opportunity with men. Marginalised within the trade-union movement, she found no voice adequately to express her dignity and value as a worker. The expression of the dignity of labour, so central a feature of the male worker's consciousness, was for women a battle against all the odds. The culture of the local working class accentuated the supremacy of the male breadwinner over the female, consolidating time-honoured divisions within the economy and within the home. The apparently private decision for a wife to stay at home was in fact a public statement, an assertion of masculine achievement, part of the definition of masculinity. Equally, it defined femininity as something to be sustained within the home, protected from the moral dangers of the factory. Such a view was to have real material effects on all women who sought to earn their living in Coventry.

In examining the emphasis placed on division within the pre-war car factories of Coventry it is not my intention to deny that those who owned and controlled the factories fostered such divisions; capital has a crucial role here as a major beneficiary of them. An analysis of this role would, however, require a separate study. Moreover, in focussing on a particular locale there is no necessary implication that social processes occurring in Coventry are unique to the city or the car industry.

For many women at work, both then and now, in Coventry and elsewhere, the daily routine involves a recognition of the significance of gender-consciousness to their life chances, their standard of living and their dignity. It is however constantly challenged. Today both men and women shop stewards in Coventry car factories have begun to put the question of sexual division on the agenda – as an issue to be fought around. Men's refusal to accept women in particular areas of the factory is being broken down, for example. On the other hand, the absence of recognition of women's skills remains a bitter bone of contention in some workplaces, where women feel they lack crucial support from the men. Solidarity between men and women at Ford in Dagenham brought the victory of equal pay to the women sewing machinists. But in Coventry old ideas die hard. The fabric of the community remains infused with its identity as a place of craftsmanship; the craftswoman is an oddity, a contradiction in terms. In the inter-war years the tenacity of this ideology was remarkable. For whilst Coventry could absorb thousands upon thousands of migrant workers into its factories, a traditional model of gender division was so firmly rooted as to resist any suggestion that the new recruits could be the wives, daughters or sisters of the established male workforce, despite the existence of poverty in many households. If the *bona fide* craftsman from Newcastle or London was placed on the sidelines in the celebration of Coventry's accomplishments, what chance for the woman?

Notes

1 The interviews have been carried out in the process of research for the project: Car Workers in 20th Century Britain and Italy, which is based at the University of Essex, Colchester, and funded in England by the Leverhulme Trust. In Italy the project is based

at the Istituto Antonio Gramsci in Turin. In Coventry we have recorded 100 in-depth, life-history interviews with car workers and their families, drawn from four generations born between 1890 and 1960. Some of the Coventry interviews were recorded by Peter Lynam, who has kindly allowed me to use his material. Other interviews have been conducted by myself over the past three years. I would like to thank all the people who have agreed to be interviewed for the project and who have patiently listened to our questions and talked openly and honestly about many aspects of their lives in Coventry.

2 J. Stevenson and C. Cook, *The Slump: Society and Politics During the Depression*, London, 1977.

3 Interview No. 16. Male, paint sprayer, worked at Standard, Chrysler, Rover, born Dublin, 1932.

4 Interview No. 6. Female, worked at GEC, BTH, Courtaulds, Rover, later shop assistant, born Coventry, 1912.

5 F. Carr, 'Engineering workers and the rise of labour in Coventry 1914–1939', unpublished Ph.D. thesis, University of Warwick, 1979; Andrew L. Friedman, *Industry and Labour*, London, 1977; A. Exell, 'Morris motors in the 1930s', *History Workshop Journal*, 6 and 7 (1978–79).

6 Census of England and Wales, *Occupation Tables*, Coventry CB, 1931, 1951.

7 Census of England and Wales, *Occupation Tables*, Coventry CB, 1921, 1931, 1951.

8 The percentages and numbers of women within the occupational structure cited here are drawn from figures given in the Census of England and Wales, *Occupation Tables*, Coventry CB, 1921, 1931, 1951. See table 9.2.

9 Engineering and Allied Employers National Federation, *Work Statistics*, MSS 237/13/3/36, Modern Records Centre, University of Warwick. See table 9.1.

10 Census of England and Wales, *Occupation Tables*, 1921, 1931, 1951.

11 *Ibid.*

12 *Ibid.*

13 *Ibid.*

14 *Ibid.*

15 J. Prest, *The Industrial Revolution in Coventry*, Oxford, 1960; K. Richardson, *Twentieth Century Coventry*, City of Coventry, 1972.

16 Interview No. 11. Male, apprenticed toolmaker, worked at BTH, Standard, born Worcestershire, 1922, moved to Coventry 1925.

17 *Midland Daily Telegraph*, 22 March 1937.

18 Interview No. 11.

19 Interview No. 32. Male, paint sprayer, worked at Midland Light Bodies, Riley, Jaguar, born Coventry, 1909.

20 Interview No. 8. Male, universal grinder, worked at Humber, Alfred Herbert, Morris, Massey Ferguson, born Coventry, 1911.

21 Interview No. 9. Female, sewing machinist, worked at Standard, born Coventry, 1927.

22 J. Zeitlin, 'The emergence of shop steward organisation and job control in the British car industry', *History Workshop Journal*, 10 (1982); Carr, 'Engineering workers'; S. Tolliday, 'Trade unions and collective bargaining in the British motor industry', unpublished paper presented at the International Conference on Automobile Workers: Past, Present and Future, Lanchester Polytechnic, Coventry, 1984.

23 Interview No. 8.

24 Interview No. 48. Male, apprenticed toolmaker, later manager, worked at Standard, Courtaulds, Rootes/Chrysler, born Coventry, 1924.

25 Interview No. 1. Male, turner, worked at Daimler, Riley, Armstrong Siddeley, born Warwick, 1899.

26 Interview No. 16.

27 Interview No. 10. Male, apprenticed toolmaker, worked at Standard, born Yorkshire 1928.
28 Interview No. 26. Male, carpenter, worked at Riley, Alvis, born Coventry, 1910.
29 Interview No. 1.
30 Interview No. 6.
31 Interview No. 1.
32 Interview No. 6.
33 Interview No. 15. Female, worked at Peel Connor/GEC, Dunlop, born Coventry, 1913.
34 Interview No. 40. Female, worked at London Laundry, Coventry until marriage, born Coventry, 1913.
35 Interview No. 45. Female, sewing machinist, Standard Motor Company 1933–45, born Coventry, 1917.
36 Interview No. 40.
37 Interview No. 34. Female, sewing machinist, Standard Motor Company, born Coventry, 1916.
38 Interview No. 33. Female, office worker, worked at Patterson and Holborn, White and Poppe, Brico, born Coventry, 1907.
39 Interview No. 6.
40 Interview No. 15.
41 Interview No. 2. Female, office worker until marriage, worked at Holbrook Motor Bodies, Riley, born Coventry, 1914.
42 Interview No. 39. Female, weaver at Britannia Mills until marriage, born Coventry 1892. See also S. Tolliday, 'Militancy and organisation: women workers and trade unions in the motor trades in the 1930s', *Oral History*, 11 (1983). Steve Tolliday describes the paternalism extended by Captain Black, Managing Director of the Standard Motor Company, to the sewing machinists in the factory. Black provided tea parties and Christmas dances for 'his girls' and other workers referred to them as 'Captain Black's pets'.
43 Interview No. 10.
44 Interview No. 21. Female, spinner Belfast flax mill, munitions worker First World War, Lancaster and Coventry, machine operator, Rootes, born Belfast, 1898, moved to Coventry, 1916.
45 P. Summerfield, 'Women workers in the Second World War, *Capital and Class* 1 (1977); J. Hinton, 'Coventry communism: a study in factory politics in the Second World War', *History Workshop Journal*, 10 (1980).
46 Tolliday, 'Militancy in the motor trades'.
47 *Ibid.*; F. Carr, 'Engineering workers'.
48 S. Boston, *Women Workers and the Trade Unions*, London, 1980; S. Lewenhak, *Women and Trade Unions*, London, 1977; N. Soldon, *Women in British Trade Unions 1874–1976*, Dublin, 1978; A. Coote and P. Kellner, *Hear this Brother*, London, 1981; J. Hunt and A. Adams, *Women, Work and Trade Union Organisation*, London, 1980.
49 See C. R. Littler, *The Development of the Labour Process in Capitalist Societies*, London, 1982, pp. 105–16.
50 Interview No. 72. Female, worked at GEC, Rover, born Southport, 1908, moved to Coventry, 1911.
51 Tolliday, 'Militancy in the motor trades'; *Midland Daily Telegraph*, 11 September 1930, 13 September 1930.
52 Interview No. 10.
53 Interview No. 37. Male, apprenticed patternmaker, worked at Singer, Armstrong Whitworth, Morris, Standard, born Coventry, 1915.
54 Interview No. 56. Male, apprenticed coach builder, worked at Holbrook Bodies, Morris

Bodies, Riley, Daimler, Rootes, Standard, born Buckinghamshire 1906, moved to Coventry, 1927.

55 Interview No. 9.

56 See A. Deacon, 'Concession and coercion: the politics of unemployment insurance in the 1920s', in A. Bridge and J. Saville (eds.), *Essays in Labour History 1911–1939*, London, 1978; A. Deacon, *In Search of the Scrounger: The Administration of Unemployment Insurance in Britain 1920–1931*, London, 1976 (for the Social Administration Research Trust: Occasional papers on Social Administration, No. 60); See also Linda Grant, 'Women workers and the sexual division of labour: Liverpool, 1890–1939', unpublished Ph.D. thesis, University of Liverpool, 1987.

57 See, for example, Ministry of Labour, *Royal Commission on Unemployment Insurance* (Gregory), 1931, Minutes of Evidence; *Hansard, Commons Debates*, November 1927 and the debates in the Commons surrounding the Report of the Blanesburgh Committee. Margaret Bondfield's comment on unemployed married women claimants, 'I have definitely come to the conclusion that there is an evil here that ought to be cured', *Hansard, Commons Debates*, 8 July 1931.

58 M. Barrett and M. McIntosh, 'The family wage: some problems for socialists and feminists', *Capital and Class*, 11 (1980); H. Land, 'The family wage', *Feminist Review*, 11 (1980).

59 Interview No. 70. Female, office worker at Lea and Francis, Triumph Engineering, Coventry Eagle, born Coventry, 1917.

60 Interview No. 12. Male, apprenticed coach builder, worked at Daimler, Standard, born Coventry, 1905.

61 Interview No. 36. Female, worked at London Laundry, Quinton Hosiery, GEC, BTH, born Coventry, 1913.

62 Interview No. 33.

63 Interview No. 32.

64 Interview No. 33.

65 Interview No. 26.

66 Interview No. 47. Male, grinder, worked at Rootes, born Coventry, 1923.

PART FOUR

Unemployment and casual labour

Chapter Ten

Unemployment and the making of the feminine during the Lancashire cotton famine

CLARE EVANS

The outbreak of the American Civil War reversed a long period of expansion in the cotton textile trades. Lancashire's 2,300 cotton factories were heavily dependent for 80 per cent of their raw material supplies on the southern states of the USA. The prolonged cessation of these supplies, and the delays in establishing a viable alternative, provoked a severe crisis for the region. By November 1862, over a quarter of a million people were being relieved by the Boards of Guardians.[1] As mills began to close or work part-time, the number of operatives forced to claim relief from Boards of Guardians or relief committees rose alarmingly. In February 1863, around 25 to 30 per cent of the population of the major manufacturing centres were in receipt of relief: 29.9 per cent in Manchester, 38.8 per cent in Preston and 37.3 per cent in Ashton-under-Lyne.[2] The long-term effect of the American Civil War in Lancashire was to be a legacy of approximately 330 permanent mill closures.[3]

Discussions on how to deal with the large numbers of unemployed operatives included the options of emigration, public works schemes at home and the establishment of educational – training schools such as sewing schools for women. In this chapter it is argued that these discussions were noticeably dominated by assumptions about gender and reveal differing conceptions of men's and women's rights of access to both paid labour and the disposal of their labour power on international markets. Through studying a group of workers in a period when their paid work was temporarily withdrawn, this chapter explores the prevailing definitions of male and female work and offers an insight into the active construction of masculinity and femininity in the mid Victorian period.

Our analysis of policy regarding unemployed male and female factory operatives during the cotton famine must begin with a brief survey of employment and wages in the cotton sector at this time. The middle years

248

of the nineteenth century saw the expansion and consolidation of the cotton textile sector within the Victorian economy. The steady advance of large-scale production in the cotton districts brought with it increases in both manpower and capital. The spread of power-loom weaving from the 1830s saw the expansion of women's participation in the cotton textile industry such that there were 272,000 females to the 255,000 males employed in cotton manufacture in 1851.[4] Many women entering the factories at this stage had inherited a training in the domestic sector through being daughters within handloom weaver households. The earning power of the young women in the mechanised sector was a vital supplement to the depressed wages existing in the handloom sector in the 1830s and 1840s, and was part of a tandem operation of 'dual technologies' which was to persist in the textiles districts well into mid-century.[5]

Factory systems introduced a complex hierarchy of operational procedures which were shifted and redefined as mechanisation affected the various processes. Nevertheless, women were predominantly engaged in the subsidiary and preliminary procedures of the whole operation such as carding, where women prepared the yarn for spinning. Women were debarred from mule spinning which was seen as requiring too great a degree of strength and skill and they were thereby isolated from a relatively rich section of the trade. Women were also absent from positions of managerial authority such as overseers, a product of the patriarchal ordering of the genders both within and beyond the factory walls.[6]

As a result of a series of legislative measures from the 1830s onwards, textile workers at mid-century worked a ten-hour day with no night working for women. Approximately 28 per cent of women workers were married, with the highest percentage of married women occurring in the weaving towns of northern Lancashire.[7] But the bulk of cotton textile workers were young unmarried women and this was increasingly the case. During the period 1834–78 there was a general decline in the numbers of male workers, particularly among the age group 13–18, which declined from 12.5 per cent in 1834 to 7.2 per cent in 1878. Across the period as a whole, child labour averaged around 8 per cent of the total workforce but there was a rise in the deployment of children in the increasingly competitive years of the 1870s (see table 10.1).

The earnings of textile workers were highly volatile and subject to trade fluctuations and differences not only between the genders but between production sectors, regions and manufacturers. Wages in the cotton sector were amongst the highest in the textile trades. The rate of female child wages was slightly higher than male but those of adult women were considerably lower than those of male workers. Women were likely to earn their maximum at around 25 years old but thereafter they were not offered the same routes of salary increases due to promotions through the factory

Table 10.1   *Age and sex distribution of cotton workers in England, 1834–78 (%)*

	Children	Males 13–18	Females 13+	Males 18+
1834	13.3	12.5	47.8	26.4
1839	4.7	16.6	53.8	24.9
1847	5.8	11.8	55.5	26.9
1850	4.6	11.2	55.5	28.7
1856	6.5	10.3	55.8	27.4
1861	8.8	9.1	55.7	26.4
1867	10.4	8.6	55.0	26.0
1870	9.6	8.5	55.9	26.0
1874	14.0	8.0	53.9	24.1
1878	12.8	7.2	54.7	25.3

Source: Mark Blaug, 'The productivity of capital in the Lancashire cotton industry during the 19th century', *Economic History Review*, 13 (1961), p. 368.

hierarchy that male workers enjoyed. On average, women earned less than 50 per cent of the male rate with the greatest disparity in wage-rates occurring in the age range 31–36 when it was around 40 per cent (see table 10.2). Although women did not rise through the factory hierarchy (to become overseers for example) women did move between departments, and were anxious to move from the dirtier and lowest paid sections, such as carding, to the weaving departments.

The highly sex-segregated work structure makes it virtually impossible to compare directly the wage structure of male and female workers. Even in weaving where there was a greater equality of work performed, earnings were rarely if ever equal because men wove different qualities of cloth and, on average, more pieces than women. Power-loom weavers' wages were highly dependent upon the sort of cloth being woven, the number of looms weavers were in charge of, and the quality of their training. Women, who were dependent on the skills of male mechanics and male overseers to ensure that their machines were in full working order, were in a less advantageous position than some male workers in terms of their earnings. Weavers of four looms who were assisted by a young helper would need to deduct that person's wages of around 3s from their own earnings. A Stockport weaver in the 1830s was earning from 13s to 15s a week, another in the same survey only 8s to 9s, whilst a Manchester weaver of four looms was earning 16s a week. In the 1840s some women's earnings were reported as high as 16s 8d a week after deductions.[8] In the card room women earned an average of 9s in the 1830s and 1840s in Manchester whilst throstle spinners in the lowlier form of spinning could earn around 7s 6d on average per week in Wigan or 9s to 11s a week in Manchester.[9] In 1859 in a survey of one cotton mill where women and girls accounted for 74 per cent of the workforce, the average weekly wage for men was 18s 6d, for women,

Table 10.2 *Wages of operatives, by age and sex, in selected Lancashire cotton mills, 1834*

Age	Males		Females	
	Number	*Av. weekly wage*	*Number*	*Av. weekly wage*
Below 11	246	2s 3½d	155	2s 4½d
11–16	1,169	4s 1½d	1,123	4s 3d
16–21	736	10s 2½d	1,240	7s 3½d
21–26	612	17s 2½d	780	8s 5d
26–31	355	20s 4½d	295	8s 7½d
31–36	215	22s 8½d	100	8s 9½d
36–41	168	21s 7¾d	81	9s 8¾d
41–46	98	20s 3½d	38	9s 3½d
46–51	83	16s 7¼d	23	8s 10d
51–56	41	16s 4d	4	8s 4¼d
56–61	28	13s 6½d	3	6s 4d
61–66	8	13s 7d	1	6s 0d
66–71	4	10s 10d	1	6s 0d
71–76	1	18s 0d	–	–
76–81	1	8s 8d	–	–
Total	3,770		3,844	

Source: Edward Baines, *History of the Cotton Manufacture in Great Britain*, London, 1835, p. 436.

10s 2d, for boys 7s and for girls 5s. The highest paid sector of male workers, the spinning aristocrats, were earning 29s a week at this time.[10] Against the background of the gender division of labour, of labour hierarchies and of differential wage payments in the cotton sector, the effects of the cotton famine on attitudes to female labour can begin to be unravelled.

The emigration question

As the numbers of unemployed continued to rise through the winter of 1862 there were renewed debates about the value of emigration. Operatives, through their trade-union spokesmen stressed the right for the free movement of factors of production to gain a fair price for labour elsewhere when denied it at home. Their approach was guided by the wage-fund theory of value, that labour's value would rise if labour became more scarce. As Augar has said: 'During the Cotton Famine, arguments in favour of emigration were underpinned by the beneficial effects it would have on those remaining, these being the very reasons why most manufacturers opposed any shift of population out of the cotton districts'.[11]

Emigration, he argues, represented for the operatives a 'rejection of the place offered to the operatives in the Lancashire textile industry', and was part of a general battle of interests between employers and workers whereby emigrants recognised that their 'best interests were not being served by bowing to the masters' interests'.[12] The emigration question thus reveals differences of interest between capital and labour, but it also reveals differing conceptions of men's and women's labour and the disposal of labour power on international markets.

The major problem governing the exportation of large numbers of operatives it was argued, was that they were trained in such a way that in structural terms they were unsuitable for adaption to alternative labour-markets. The demand for male labour in Australia and America revolved around the need to plough, reap, tend cattle or act as general labourers, for which the cotton factory operatives could claim no experience. Yet they were seen as suitable material for general labouring under the conditions of the Labour Test. Logically, there existed the same structural problems for female as for male labourers; the majority of women labourers required abroad, particularly in Australia, were trained servants who were also very much in demand at home. It was argued that a movement of women to the colonies could redress the unsatisfactory sex ratios there. Indeed, it was said that women had a socio-moral role there. They 'would be the humanizing and refining of a society which deteriorates very much by their absence'.[13]

However, contemporaries' concern with the way in which women should or should not emigrate to the colonies brought out their underlying dissatisfaction with the movement of women on international labour-markets. The relationship of women to the emigration process was debated in quite different terms to that of men. It was as *women* rather than as unemployed workers that their case was considered. Gender was ultimately the base-line to which all other arguments finally referred.

The cessation of paid labour and the fall off in demand for female operatives provoked a 'peculiarly embarassing' situation according to one contemporary account.[14] The issue of how to deal with unmarried women operatives had to be governed, it was argued, by the question of 'What is best for them, and best in this case, *for the general community.*'[15] Women were considered in these terms because they were all assumed to be 'destined to the honours of maternity'.[16] They were perceived in their dual role as labourers and potential mothers with an elision from the first to the second. Women were seen to engage in productive labour only in accordance with and shaped by their reproductive labour through the life cycle. Married women workers who accounted for approximately 28 per cent of the female cotton textile workforce[17] were not considered as equally 'unemployed', and disappeared safely back into the home in an assumed relationship of dependency on a male. The case of single women workers was dictated by *future* life-cycle events, as *potential* married women. They were assumed by implication, to possess only a transitory work commitment.

In their dual capacity as labourers as well as women, protective measures were thought necessary which militated against their movement in wider spheres. Women were defined in terms of societal needs and perceived as existing within familial structures. This can be seen in the official guidelines on emigration. 'Single women cannot be taken without their parents, unless they go under the immediate care of some near relatives. Single women with illegitimate children can in no case be taken.'[18] Women, when seen as bearers of the commodity of labour power, were ideally only to work within regulated conditions under the auspices of familial bonds. Indeed, the argument was essentially circular since women themselves would be unwilling to emigrate because they recognised that they remained rooted within the family environment: 'But the better class of these girls would not make willing emigrants. Women of worth are ever the most loath of any persons to leave their homes, unless accompanied by their friends.'[19]

The clear division of the terms of debate for emigration along gender lines can also be traced in the language of the male operatives discussing emigration. At a meeting of factory operatives in Preston in February 1863 it was argued that: 'the working classes of this town, conscious of being looked upon as paupers, because dependent on public charity for support, feel themselves degraded in their own estimation, and are desirous of occupying a *more manly and independent position by honourable labour*'.[20] Here we see the association of the right to work, of '*honourable labour*' and *manliness*. The removal of such work was seen not only to reduce the labourers to paupers (conflating the distinctions between honourable labourers and the poor) but to upset the 'natural' order of things: 'to see an army of workers, with all the mental and bodily capacities for labour, made suddenly powerless for self-help, is so contrary to the established order of nature as to exercise emotions which defy expression in words, and which will only be satisfied by prompt and vigorous action'.[21]

That men were seen as the generators of labour power and the natural productive labourers in society can be seen from Factory Inspector Red-grave's comments on the mens' attendance at educational classes: 'it was impossible not to feel that the time spent there was, compared with their former labour, unproductive; and I was therefore the more impressed with the attention of the men in these classes, and the anxiety of so many to improve themselves, especially in arithmetic'.[22] The association of productive labour with men meant that in general the conception of an industrial labour force was masculine. Work done by women, on the other hand, was referred to in terms of the benefits for themselves as women and for their families. Womanhood then, was being constructed throughout this period as residing in *sexuality*, in production related to *being* not economic generation.[23] Men were the ones with the freely disposable commodity of labour power; it was men therefore who could engage freely with the transferral of their labour on international markets. Women were seen always in terms of social beings to whom tasks had to be fitted. It was this conception of their role which led to the establishment of the sewing schools for them, since as Redgrave argued: 'the employment of females in sewing and knitting was a proper and congenial occupation for them'.[24]

The idea that the sewing schools for the female textile operatives were particularly valuable was in sharp contrast to the idea that men's attendance in educational classes was essentially 'unproductive'. The attendance of the women at sewing schools was not discussed in terms of their former employment but in terms of the benefits of domestic training for them as *women*: 'and though the attendance at classes might have been somewhat irksome, yet upon the whole they were all doing something which had a practical result'[25] so that, 'if the work of women be not equally beneficial, it may be made highly advantageous to themselves as a means of instruction in domestic requirements and otherwise, which is so urgently needed by many of the female mill hands'.[26] Where men attended the equivalent of the sewing schools, their work was overlaid with notions of skilled, masculine trades (shoemaking and carpentry); in one school it was taken further with instruction in military drilling.[27]

The gender-specific differentiation in the right to labour and the disposal of labour-power was accentuated during the cotton famine. When these rights became fused with political rights which could potentially accrue to labour through emigration to America, conceptions of manhood, of labour and of dignity became inexorably linked in the eyes of the male operatives. 'In every sense of the word you have been treated as an inferior order of men, when you get into the United States, you are invested with the full rights of man in every respect.'[28] The priority given to the right of males to work over that of females was of course also shot through by a more complex hierarchy of race whereby white, male labour was further privileged over the four million black slaves in America.

Both official and unofficial conceptions of an emigrant labour force were primarily male, so that far fewer single women than single men emigrated. Women were not able to enter the debates concerning emigration equally since the right to labour became increasingly bound up with masculinity. Women were defined in a relation of dependency on men and familial structures which meant that men as breadwinners had priority claims to labour.

There were sustained efforts on the part of philanthropic bodies and individual operatives to encourage emigration. The Emigrants' Aid Society helped approximately 1,000 to emigrate.[29] The colonies offered substantial sums to assist passages: in 1863 the Australian states of Victoria and Queensland both donated £50,000 each.[30] Half the sums donated by the province of Canterbury, New Zealand, were placed at the disposal of the Government Emigration Board for the immediate dispatch of a ship.

The operatives showed a great deal of interest in these offers of help, with the Blackburn Power-Loom Weavers' Emigration Society seeking a grant of £5,000 from the relief committee to aid emigration. In September 1862, 245 were granted aid for their removal to Queensland and in May, 1862, 1,000 left for Canterbury.[31]

However, the principle of 'assistance' with removal costs rather than payment of total emigration costs, when coupled with official discrimination against women's movement, was especially burdensome for women. It was estimated that one-third of the costs would be met by the emigrant, one-third by colonial governments and one-third by public sources. Yet for the unemployed women in Manchester petitioning the Manchester and Salford District Provident Society (MSDPS) relief offices, the money for the cost of clothes necessary for the journey was beyond their reach. When one woman sought help with the cost of her outfit for her passage to Australia she was turned down.[32] Nor did the Society seem willing to help female operatives move by taking up the offer of a free passage to Western Australia for the women of their sewing schools.

In the movement to Australia there may also have been resistance on the part of the women themselves. When James Chaunt, the Commissioner for Perth, toured Manchester, Stockport, Stalybridge and Preston early in 1864 seeking women to train as domestic servants, there was reported to be a general lack of interest owing to, 'the evil reports which have lately emanated from female emigrant ships'.[33] Although transportation to New South Wales had ceased in 1836 it continued to Western Australia until 1867, so there may well have still been the taint of association with convict ships. The discomfort of the two-and-a-half to four-month long journey was notorious and required, in the words of Miss Rye, founder member of the Female Middle Class Emigrant Society, women of 'a certain stamp'.[34]

It was not only the larger scale problem of emigration that caused difficulties for women trying to move into work. Migration within Britain was seen as more problematic for young women than for young men, but it was a more acceptable option as a short-term solution. As many as 4,000 operatives moved across to Yorkshire where there was a commensurate boom in the woollen and worsted trades.[35] In September 1862, the MSDPS did agree to aid 18 women to move to Kent to take up offers of work.[36] However, this individual offer of help in transferring to work elsewhere seems to have been balanced by refusals on more than one occasion. Requests for assistance to respond to work offers in Taunton, in a Dundee flax mill and as silk doublers in Yorkshire were all turned down.[37] Some efforts were made to provide help with badly needed clothing but there was a reluctance to invest any sums of money in the movement of the women away from their home environment.

The independent response of the women themselves was dictated by the state of local labour-markets. In Wigan, for instance, Arthur Munby encountered 39 mill women who had moved across to 'unwomanly' work as pit-brow lasses,[38] that is, in precisely the opposite direction to that aimed at in the sewing schools. Some women utilised agencies aiding their transfer into positions as domestic servants.[39] Many more must have moved into the haphazard livelihood to be gained in the informal economy; singing, scavenging, begging, selling steeped peas and oatcakes and haunting the soup kitchens and special 'mothers' ' kitchens.[40] In so doing, they were forced to compete actively with the hidden army of women workers directly dependent on the mill workers for their own livelihood such as the tea-women, washer-women, and childminders.

The emigration question highlighted the perceived differences between male and female relationships to labour. Women were projected primarily in terms of life-cycle events, their needs to be met within the contexts of familial demands. Labour became increasingly an essential element of man's worth and dignity, and as a provider, he had priority claims to movements to gain such labour. This notion of men as producers of labour power and of value production, governed primarily by work or life-course events, and women as potential reproducers of labour power and producers of use-value, governed by life-cycle events can also be traced in discussions about the labour test imposed by the Board of Guardians with varying degrees of success throughout the cotton famine.

The labour test

Under the regulations of the 1852 Out-door Relief Regulation Order: 'able-bodied men shall, if allowed out-relief, be set to work by the Guardians, and ... the relief afforded to them shall be given half in kind'.[41] The application of the labour test during the cotton famine was greatly resented by male operatives, and became a focus of struggle with local Guardians. Despite pressure for implementation by the Poor Law Board there was considerable resistance from many poor law unions, particularly Preston, Burnley and Bury.

In Preston the labour test was introduced under the belief that:

> if there was no test established by which it could be seen whether the operative was really engaged in some other work for which he got wages, imposition and demoralization might be carried on to a large extent. The advisability of keeping up even in a time when there was no work to do, at least a certain amount of energy; and preventing the operatives from yielding to the too powerful feelings of enervation and idleness; these amongst others, were reasons which led to the conception of the scheme.[42]

Initially the men were engaged upon a range of labouring tasks, such as quarrying and stone-breaking. Local landowners engaged labourers to break up and drain land, and to build new embankments. Under the provisions of the Public Works Act of 1863, large amounts of labour were directed towards schemes of municipal improvement, such as the laying-out of parks, road-making and paving, the laying of water pipes and the digging of sewers.[43]

In organising the labour test the underlying rationale was one of a necessary distinction between wages and relief. Wages were seen as payments in return for work in a voluntary contract entered into by labour and capital; relief was a charitable payment related to family size and graduated accordingly. Throughout these programmes the relief committees were not merely concerned with social control and keeping the operatives occupied in order to head off any potential confrontation with the authorities. The programmes were also governed by the need to reproduce and maintain the differences not just between *work* and *pauperism* but the rights of *men* as men to work for payment. There was every effort made to carry over into non-work time the cultural connotations of the work form.

If the labour test is looked at in the light of ideologies concerning men's relation to labour, another facet of the debate concerning its use is revealed. Augar is right to redress the balance of received opinion on the conduct of the operatives during the cotton famine arguing that: 'the "quiet, patient and honourable conduct" of the operatives was disturbed on many occasions'.[44] This was particularly the case in Preston where the Guardians were 'unusual in continuing to enforce the letter of the law', with regards to the labour test.[45] Already by the winter of 1862 there was real discontent among the men working at the quarries. The overlooker, Henry Jackson told the Board of Guardians: 'the work is all performed by the well disposed portion and others do not work at all'.[46] It was not merely the nature of the work which the operatives objected to; there were only 300 shovels for the 1,500 men at work. In these circumstances there was no sense in which the scheme was operating as anything other than a palliative measure. Leaders such as Thomas Banks of the Spinners and Minders Association and the labourers themselves began to organise and agitate for the removal of the labour test. The hostility to the labour test is clearly visible in a meeting of the operatives as early as August 1862, where it was recorded:

> That this meeting is of the opinion that applying the labour test to industrial operatives is both cruel and insulting, and believes the serfs of Russia and the slaves of America are better treated than the factory operatives either on the Moor or in the Stoneyard'.[47]

There were then, clear objections to the labour test, but what is immediately apparent is that what the operatives are in fact objecting to is not a labour as such but the particular form applied. The labour test they are talking about was in fact for male industrial operatives. The women's labour test, producing particular goods within sewing schools, is never alluded to as a labour test. This is because the schemes for women were bound up with notions of relief since they were seen as dependants. Despite the fact that in work they were all distinctly graded by occupation, unemployed women were not seen as industrial labourers. Therefore, the need to continue the work – wage relation was not deemed of any importance. Their scale of payments was not related to the amount of garments produced but based on daily attendances.

In the series of meetings held across many towns one of the most serious objections raised against the labour test was its relation to principles governing the levels of relief. At a meeting at Oldham, for example, 'Resolutions declaring the scale of relief to be inadequate and establishing an organisation to bring pressure to bear on the Relief Committees were passed.'[48] This meeting was addressed by Kinder Smith, the leader of the Preston lock-out of 1853–54, and he was specifically addressing the men as heads of families. Throughout the meetings attended by male operatives such as those at Ashton and Stalybridge, a condemnation was invariably made of applying a 'test to men that it never was intended for who have neither been idle nor improvident'.[49]

The concern about the scale of relief and the focus on male heads of families must be set against previous decades of debates giving priority to the adult male wage as the key wage. From the 1840s onwards there was an increased emphasis on the idea of a 'family wage' amongst skilled male workers which helped to aggravate distinctions between the importance of men's and women's work. The idea that a man should earn enough to keep his wife and children without them having recourse to the labour-markets became an increasingly important element of 'respectability' in the mid Victorian period.[50]

Policies concerning unemployment during the cotton famine not only reveal differences between capital and labour but highlight the perceived differences between male and female labour. The notion of suitable work differed for men and for women and consequently there were different meanings attached to the terms 'productive' and 'unproductive' labour. Men were increasingly associated with 'production' and women with 'reproduction', thereby emphasising the increased spatial segregation of production under industrial capitalism from family life. It was above all, a concern with female reproductive activity which precipitated the establishment of sewing schools for women from 1862 onwards.

The establishment of the sewing schools

The establishment of the sewing schools was one of the priorities of the Central Relief Committee. Hitherto this type of provision had been the work of philanthropic bodies such as the Manchester Domestic Mission Society, but now they became codified as official relief policy.[51] The principal aim of the sewing school was to overcome what was thought to be a lamentable degree of ignorance in basic domestic accomplishments. As Factory Inspector Redgrave commented:

> In many of the sewing schools, I was told that one-third of the females knew nothing of sewing upon their first attending the classes ... that when they first took a needle in their hand, they pushed it through their work by pressing it upon the table; and that many had no idea of mending or patching clothes.[52]

The schools were to be aimed primarily at young women working directly in the cotton industry, or dependent for work upon it, who were not supported by their families. They were to work five or six hours daily for up to five days a week and be paid in the region of ¾d to 1d an hour. The schools were to be run by 'competent paid supervisors' and attended by unpaid lady visitors who assisted in the execution of the classes.[53]

As a result of concerted efforts on the part of local dignitaries, relief committees and the Board of Guardians, the Central Executive Committee in Manchester could report by February 1863 when over 40,000 women were covered by such schemes that there was: 'scarcely a Relief District, however sparsely inhabited, without this excellent means of protecting by daily occupation the otherwise unemployed females of the Cotton Districts'.[54]

The sewing schools drew upon a combination of sources to cover their expenses including local philanthropic bodies, subscriptions, capitation grants from the Central Relief Committee and help from London funds such as the Mansion'House Fund.[55] In an effort to ensure that only those women who were eligible for entry into the sewing schools were in fact admitted, a policy of careful home visiting was initiated in Manchester in June 1863 to assess the genuine need of every woman in the schools that received funds from the Committee. The women were interviewed to check the accuracy of their statements as to their financial and familial position. On the whole, the average acceptance rate was only 32 per cent after home visitation.[56] As a further economy measure the districts were reorganised and stream-lined in July 1863.[57]

Undoubtedly the major cost of the sewing schools was the provision of materials for the garments to be made up by the women. The need to ensure a steady supply became the subject of great anxiety for many a committee since: 'For every third part of the money expended in wages, two thirds are locked up in materials.'[58] To overcome this problem a policy was adopted aimed at stimulating supplies at local level from resident manufacturers and encouraging any interested party to transport materials to Manchester. The Central Executive Committee urged the provision of depots as local collecting points to be organised throughout the country. In Manchester the main depot was established at Commercial Street as the central collection point.[59]

As a response to this demand, Ladies Committees sprang up throughout the country with those at Leeds and Warwick co-operating closely with Manchester.[60] Local advertisements in papers throughout the country brought a considerable response. In order to co-ordinate nationally, applications were received from the larger railway companies such as the Great Western, offering free carriage of parcels and clothing.[61] Much of the goods transported to Manchester was however sold rather than directly distributed as it was often felt to be inappropriate for the operatives' needs.

In deciding the sort of sewing work the women were to produce the local committees followed a number of practices. In the Preston Union it was resolved that: 'materials for clothing be provided by the Board to be made into under clothing for the female paupers, the actual cost of the sample to be repaid as relief by way of a loan'.[62] The committees were particularly concerned that any garments produced in the sewing schools would be those 'which would not interfere with trade'.[63] In Manchester the women worked up simple garments such as shirts which were supplied cut out ready for sewing.[64] In Wigan, the women worked from great rolls of coarse grey cloth and linen check which were cut up for their daily work.[65]

The end products of the women's work were orientated towards the needs of the women or their families. The women were encouraged to take pride and interest in their work and at Bolton the women running the sewing schools 'encouraged the girls to purchase necessary articles of wearing apparel made in the schools and often by themselves'.[66] In Wigan, the women bought the goods by a stoppage of a shilling food ticket a month.[67] This helped solve the problem of competing with trade and flooding the market with goods whilst also, it was hoped, discouraging the women from redeeming their 'fancy finery' from the pawnshop.

The women's efforts were also linked to servicing the men working on the outdoor labour programmes who were desperately short of clothing. Those at Wigan were offered goods at cut-price, by-passing the cost of the labour involved in their production.[68] Where possible though, the Ladies Committee also accepted orders tendered by outside agencies, which, strictly speaking, were competing with trade. The Preston sewing schools completed an order of shirts for the Third Royal Lancashire Militia and knitted stockings at 4d a pair for the local asylum.[69] These orders were especially useful as they not only generated an income but did not cause the Committee any problems with the disposal of the finished goods.

From their original inception as a small-scale, philanthropic scheme, the sewing schools spread rapidly throughout the whole of the textile districts. Through a combination of central funding and local paternalistic charitable efforts the schools became one of the most successfully organised relief measures of the cotton famine.

The women of the Manchester sewing schools

The women textile operatives in Manchester attended the nearest sewing school in their residential district within the umbrella framework of the Manchester and Salford District Provident Society's (MSDPS) nine organisational areas. Through the peak months of the cotton famine over 4,200 women attended the schools. One of the original sewing schools under the auspices of the MSDPS was at Garden Lane. Here from 31 July 1862 to 25 September 1862 there were 2,634 applications for admittance and 841 admitted. At any one time, the school registered a regular attendance of approximately one-sixth of the female intake. The women, on average, stayed in the school for two-and-a-half to three months with around 11 women leaving each week to take up employment or through changed economic circumstances.[70] The women, then, moved quickly through the schools, utilising them as a resource to tide them over until their economic circumstances had changed.

The women in the sewing school were broadly categorised by the MSDPS under nine headings: weavers, winders, throstle-spinners, cardroom hands, warpers, drawers-in, piecers, fustian cutters and miscellaneous. Weavers, winders and throstle-spinners formed by far the majority of the intake in the school, comprising 85 per cent of the total. Over 75 per cent of the women came from a group of eight firms with around 35 per cent of all women in the school drawn from either Messrs Stirling or Messrs Birley. Both of these manufacturers were active in the organisation of relief operations for the MSDPS. For the women attending the schools there was a continuity of workplace relations during the period of unemployment, either in the overarching sense of organisation or sometimes in a more literal sense when sewing schools were held on mill premises. More importantly, there was a continuity of workplace relations in that a percentage of their work-mates from the mill would be attending the same sewing school, thereby sustaining the networks of friendship so important for avoiding demoralisation and loss of self-esteem in a period of unemployment.

The movement out of the schools across a six-month period varied dramatically according to the original occupation of the women involved. Weavers, winders and throstle-spinners were disproportionately able to move on to new work or to leave the schools, thereby implying a greater degree of security and control over their life-courses. Weavers, whilst comprising around half of the total sewing school numbers at the start of the period fell to only 25 per cent of the intake by the end of six months. Whilst over 40 per cent of the weavers stayed one month, just over 1 per cent are recorded as having stayed six months. By comparison, piecers who were less than 1 per cent of the total intake at the start of the six-month period, formed 10 per cent by the end.

A similar pattern of differential re-absorption of the workers into the economy is noticeable when a study is made of 805 women who left the school (see the list below).

Re-employment breakdown of 805 women who left Garden Lane sewing school, Manchester across a six-month period in 1863

Re-employed in textile industry

Weavers	349
Winders	142
Throstle-spinners	117
Card-room hands	26
Warpers	2
Piecers	6
Fustian cutters	8
Miscellaneous	4
Total	654

Not re-employed in textile industry

Married	15
Engaged	30
Domestic service	64
Family able to support them	8
Left through illness	14
Died	2
Dismissed	18
Total	151

Source: MCR M294/1/1/6 1863.

In all, 650 of the women (81 per cent) who left the school were re-employed in textile firms. In terms of their re-employment, Messrs Stirling provided the most significant single firm, accounting for 16 per cent of the intake. These women then, organised within sewing schools supported by such manufacturers, were moving back into direct employment with their former employer. The schools were a useful means of retaining labour in the area until supplies of cotton were renewed. Whereas card-room hands formed 8 per cent of the total number of workers admitted to the school, they formed only 4 per cent of those re-employed at their former jobs. Weavers on the other hand, accounted for 48 per cent of the total numbers at the school and 53 per cent of those re-employed at their former jobs.

Even where work was gained other than by working in their former employment, there were significant variations by occupational categorisation. This again suggests that the ability of weavers, winders and throstlespinners in particular to gain some degree of control over their working patterns, was greater than for other women workers at the school. In all, 64 of the women (42 per cent) who left gained employment as domestic servants and were noted as having migrated. This suggests two possibilities. First, that there may have been a consensus of opinion between workingclass women and middle-class commentators on the validity of domestic service as the ideal form of alternative employment. However, the mention of migration suggests that the pressure of gaining renumerative work was uppermost in the motives of the working-class women. Secondly, it could be cited as evidence of 'deskilling' amongst the textile women which has been noted as a common consequence of unemployment for working-class women workers.[71] Domestic servants received lower pay and possibly less attractive working conditions than most textile workers, and this was reflected in a general preference for textile work over domestic service where the local labour-market ensured its availability.

The women who were able to utilise this option the most were precisely those categories of worker who could be most easily re-absorbed into the textile economy, winders and weavers in particular. For example, well over half the winders (58 per cent) who left the Garden Lane sewing school entered domestic service. For this reason, it is argued here that these women had a far greater sense of themselves as *workers* and were as willing as the men to transfer their labour power to seek renumerative work.

The construction of femininity

A central facet of the sewing schools was the personal supervision of middleclass ladies. Attendance by these ladies who were used to supervising working-class women in their households cut across the polarisation between factory operatives and domestic servants as opposites of the working woman paradigm. By utilising the structure of unpaid lady visitors, with paid superintendents and the unemployed women as underlings, the schools drew upon the image of the hierarchical, well-ordered moral environment of the Victorian household as a replacement for the polluted atmosphere of the mill.[72] Through both the work to be performed and the social and moral environment in which the women were to be trained, the sewing schools reveal the construction of femininity and womanhood among the textile workers and offer a vital insight into how ideologies 'transform sentiment into significance and so make it socially available'.[73]

After the initial success of schemes introducing basic sewing and knitting techniques for the women, it was argued that this work had to be built upon by a more thorough grounding in 'domestic management'. At a meeting of the Manchester Statistical Society it was suggested that:

> As the demand for that kind of sewing on which so many thousands are exclusively employed may every month be growing less, would it not be well to economise it, by introducing fresh varieties of sedentary work, but especially by intermixing with the labours of the needle, on a larger scale than has yet been done, the operation of domestic management and household service?[74]

The image of the domestic servant was once again introduced and reinforced by the suggestion of inculcating greater domestic management skills. This could be achieved, it was argued, by the ladies taking, 'some of the well-behaved' into their own homes to transmit their knowledge on these matters directly to them. In this way, the ladies could wean the women from their reliance on pre-cooked foods, just as they had attempted to curb their expenditure on expensive clothes. This would enable the women to be economical in their expenditure patterns and thereby overcome the way 'the hard-won earnings of men are largely absorbed in a diet which is at once expensive and indigestible'.[75]

These schemes encapsulated the essential facets of women's relief policy: economy, domesticity and servicing the household. One such scheme for teaching women cooking techniques did operate briefly in Blackburn as an appendage to a sewing school. It was privately funded and the women were taught the rudiments of 'plain cooking' for a fortnight, a few women at a time in a relay system. The dishes were then distributed to the sick and destitute.[76]

The imagery of the schools therefore was permeated by the notion of lower-class women as domestic servants. Their social subordination in the schools was reflected in their being addressed as 'girls'. This operated at several levels. On the one hand it operated at the level of class, distinguishing the women from their supervisors, who were all, in this context, termed ladies. Through utilising a hierarchy of class distinction the women were drawn into a relationship of dependency on the philanthropic goodwill of the ladies. This in turn helped reinforce the textile women's position as receivers of public relief and generosity. This was further emphasised by the spatial ordering of the women within the physical environment of the school. The textile women sat on long benches arranged in rows whilst the lady supervisors and visitors circulated amongst them. Respect was enforced through fining systems and the disciplined regulation of the work-day routines. In this way, the time-keeping discipline of the factory was re-negotiated within the new context of the closely supervised 'household'. Furthermore, something of the 'culture of the factory' was re-created with paternalistic employers' symbolic rituals of celebration, such as collective dinners being introduced by the organisers in an effort to incorporate the women into the new 'family' of the school.[77]

The interaction of middle-class women with working-class women did not only operate at the level of class. It also worked through the medium of their sexuality and addressed the women as women through a particular notion of femininity and of motherhood. The middle-class women related to the working-class women through a common bond of projected life-cycle events. The women were not seen primarily in terms of their youth as the usage of 'girls' suggests, but as imminent mothers and managers of households. The distinction between girlhood and womanhood was transient and became telescoped so that motherhood enveloped the current status of the women.[78]

Whilst it was suggested by some opponents of the men's labour test that: 'the employment of cotton mill hands on any laborious occupation would unfit them when trade revives from performing their usual work',[79] the work of the women in the schools was always expressed in terms of it being a 'proper and congenial occupation'.[80] The argument rested on a belief that domestic skills were *naturally* innate in women. Yet the gathering together of women in practical, small-scale and above all *sedentary* work was as different from their industrial labouring as stone-breaking was for the men. It was a social construction of feminine labour predicated on the fact of their being born women.

The fact that it was not recognised as such resulted from their being seen as women first and industrial operatives second. That the women in the schools felt the strain of adjustment to this new form of labour can be seen from the perceptive comments of a middle-class visitor from London, Ellen Barlee: 'What troubled them most was their sitting still so long at needlework; being accustomed to stand all day at the mill, it was as hard a task to them to sit as it would be to others to be on their legs.'[81]

The sewing schools also reveal a preoccupation with one area of tension between working-class women's labour and working-class women's femininity, that is, their relationship to technology which only became apparent when they were no longer working in a technological environment. Sewing schools removed women from an association with machinery, noise, dirt, and an 'unfeminine' spatial context. This was then reinforced by a stress upon personal interaction with middle-class ladies to reinforce a microcosmic relationship between women and social space. The school environment replaced bodily agility, involving stretching across machinery within the sweating heat of the factory, with contained body movements and restricted manual dexterity. They removed the women from a close relationship with advanced technology in favour of one emphasising a traditional technique. Expensive capital equipment was substituted by an individual needle, trans-historical in its connotations of womanhood.[82]

The element of instruction in domestic skills through the sewing schools reveals a central paradox of the construction of womanhood. That is, whilst the skills and attributes deemed essential for feminine behaviour were on the one hand 'naturally' present in the women, they had to be constantly worked at and moulded. Women's femininity is constantly being re-negotiated and reinforced whereas masculinity as a norm is felt in less need of definition.

For the women involved in the schools they offered a number of opportunities. For the middle-class women they offered scope for the development of considerable managerial and financial skills and potentially a first opportunity for many to become directly engaged in public activities. The schools were undoubtedly popular amongst the textile operatives, with far more applications for admittance than places. Their appeal lay in a variety of reasons. Attendance at the schools guaranteed a payment of relief, however small, which would be particularly vital for the poorest categories of women textile worker, such as the fustian cutter. For the mill women, used to daily contact with large numbers of other women workers, the sewing schools could be utilised as a resource to sustain the culture and friendships of working time in a period of unemployment. This was aided by the likelihood of attending the same sewing school as other women from a particular mill. The actual conditions within the sewing schools meant talking and communication with other women were made easier than at the mill and offered opportunities for striking up new friendships. The links between manufacturers and sewing schools meant the women still moved within the orbit of their employer which may have eased the transition back to paid employment with them. In all, over 10,000 items were made at the schools revealing the competent sewing skills of the textile women.[83] In well-supported schools, such as those of the MSDPS, the women also had the opportunity to learn reading and literacy skills. Within the schools, recourse to the withdrawal of dinner tickets and threats of fines suggest that the operatives were well able and willing to make their own feelings known and that the schools were not experienced without resentment.

The sewing schools were run down and streamlined through the summer and winter of 1863 as running costs became especially burdensome and confidence grew in the possibilities of the resumption of normal mill working within the near future. The main schools in Manchester and Preston closed at Easter 1864 and the women were referred to the Relief Board to receive relief in the ordinary way.[84]

The women attending the schools, it was argued, had not only received training for 'the performance of important home duties and thus enabled them to render home attractive to their future husbands', but the 'inspiring presence' of ladies, 'their genteel manners and their insensible moral influence saved thousands from irretrievable ruin'.[85] For those running the schools and no doubt the manufacturers supporting them, it was the conditions under which the training was performed that was of vital importance. So that, 'in addition to the girls having been taught the use of the needle, the lessons of cleanliness, order and thrift which have been impressed upon their minds, will bear abundant fruit in the increased comfort of their homes and their own moral improvement for many years to come'.[86]

Philanthropic initiatives continued in this area throughout the late nineteenth century, but the teaching of domestic accomplishments became increasingly institutionalised within the framework of expanding educational provisions.[87] The emphasis shifted towards a stress on learning from trained instructors and domestic economy became imbued with the language of science and of management. It was felt that it was as domestic managers, rather than comforters that future mothers must be trained.

Conclusion

The cotton famine years were a period of crisis for the Lancashire cotton textile districts after a decade of expansion within the industry. This period also witnessed a more rigorous emphaiss on ideologies of masculinity and femininity which must be considered, together with the ameliorative responses of employers and the state, as a stabilising influence socially and economically. This process can be traced through policies concerning the treatment of the unemployed textile operatives which reveal the perceived differences between male and female rights of access to waged labour. Women were not primarily perceived as unemployed industrial labourers. They were projected primarily in terms of life-cycle events and were therefore provided with 'proper and congenial' employment, orientated towards use-production and reproductive needs. Debates concerning emigration and the labour test reveal that labour was expressed as an essential element of men's worth and dignity. Schemes for women, on the other hand, were bound up with notions of relief, with women placed within structures of heterosexual dependency. It was men who were seen as the bearers of labour power and therefore the real unemployed cotton operatives in the years 1861–65.

Notes

I wish to thank the editors for all their help and numerous improvements and the following for their ideas and suggestions: Dr M. E. Rose, Dr P. Joyce, Dr S. H. Rigby, the Manchester Women's History Group, R. S. Crouch.

1 W. O. Henderson, *The Lancashire Cotton Famine, 1861–5*, Manchester, 1969 edn, p. 1.
2 N. Longmate, *The Hungry Mills*, London, 1978, p. 103.
3 Henderson, *Cotton Famine*, p. 26.
4 P. Mathias, *The First Industrial Nation*, London, 1983 edn, p. 239.
5 M. Berg, *The Age of Manufactures, 1700–1820*, London, 1985, Introduction; J. S. Lyons, 'The Lancashire Cotton Industry and the Introduction of the Power Loom, 1815–1850', unpublished Ph.D. thesis, University of California, Berkeley, 1977.
6 See Judy Lown, 'Not so much a factory, more a form of patriarchy: gender and class during industrialisation', in Eva Gamarnikow *et al.* (eds.), *Gender, Class and Work*, London, 1983, pp. 28–45.
7 M. Hewitt, *Wives and Mothers in Victorian Industry*, London, 1983 edn., p. 13.
8 Parliamentary Papers (henceforth PP) 1833 (XX) pp. Di, 84; 34–5. Factory Inspector's Report 1842, XXII, pp. 85, 87.
9 Factory Inspector's Report 1842, XXII, pp. 85, 97.
10 Longmate, *Hungry Mills*, p. 44.
11 P. J. Augar, 'The cotton famine: a study of the principal cotton towns during the American Civil War', unpublished Ph.D. thesis, University of Cambridge, 1979, p. 190.
12 *Ibid.*, p. 200.
13 R. A. Arnold, *The History of the Cotton Famine*, London, 1864, p. 507.
14 *Ibid.*, p. 505.
15 Rev. Alexander Munro, 'Our unemployed females and what may best be done for them', *Transactions of the Manchester Statistical Society*, read 18 March 1863, p. 26, emphasis added (Manchester Central Reference Library (henceforth MCR) MS 310.6 M1, 1858–72).
16 Arnold, *The History of the Cotton Famine*, p. 505.
17 Hewitt, *Wives and Mothers*, 1958 edn., p. 13.
18 PP 1852 (XXIII) 1, pp. 32–5.
19 Arnold, *The History of the Cotton Famine*, p. 505.
20 *Preston Guardian*, 12 February, 1863, emphasis added.
21 J. Watts, *The Facts of the Cotton Famine*, London, 1866, p. 152.
22 PP 1864 (XXII), 3 November 1863, p. 69.
23 Sally Alexander, 'Women, class and sexual differences in the 1830s and 1840s: some reflections on the writing of a feminist history', *History Workshop Journal*, 17 (1984), pp. 138–9; Joan Scott, ' ''L'Ouvrière! Mot impie, sordide ...''': women workers in the discourse of French political economy, 1840–60', paper presented at the City as Social Crucible Conference, University of Texas, Austin, 9–11 May 1986.
24 PP 1864 (XXII), 31 October, 1863, p. 68.
25 *Ibid.*
26 PP 1863 (XXII), Pt 1. Appendix No. 7, p. 42.
27 Ellen Barlee, *A Visit to Lancashire in December 1862*, London, 1863, p. 111.
28 *Blackburn Times*, 31 January 1863. For black male workers' use of 'manhood rights' at this time see James Oliver Horton, 'Freedom's yoke: gender conventions among antebellum free blacks', *Feminist Studies*, 12, 1 (Spring 1986), pp. 51–76.
29 Henderson, *The Lancashire Cotton Famine*, p. 118.
30 *Ibid.*, p. 117.
31 Augar, 'The cotton famine', pp. 171, 174–5.
32 MCR M294/1/1/6, 4 September 1862.
33 *Preston Guardian*, 24 February 1864, 2 March 1864.
34 Una Monk, *New Horizons: A Hundred Years of Women's Migration*, London, 1963, p. 4.
35 Henderson, *The Lancashire Cotton Famine*, p. 115; Watts, *The Facts of the Cotton Famine*, p. 226.
36 MCR M294/1/1/6, 11 September 1862.

37 MCR M294/1/1/6, 2 January 1863; 3 September 1863; see also 30 October 1862.
38 Angela V. John, *By the Sweat of their Brow: Women Workers at Victorian Coalmines*, London, 1980, p. 177.
39 For example, a scheme run at Blackburn by Mrs Potter reported in *The Times*, 31 July 1862; 12 August 1862; 30 August 1862; 29 September 1862.
40 Barlee, *A Visit to Lancashire in December 1862*, pp. 27–9; Watts, *The Facts of The Cotton Famine*, pp. 124, 137, 139, 145, 149. On the informal economy see John Benson, *The Penny Capitalists: A Study in Nineteenth Century Working-class Entrepreneurs*, Dublin, 1983; R. E. Pahl, *Divisions of Labour*, Oxford, 1984.
41 PP 1861 (XXVIII), 13th Annual Report of the Poor Law Board, p. 16.
42 4th Report of the Proceedings of the Preston Relief Committee, p. 7, cited in Augar, 'The cotton famine', p. 86.
43 For full details see Henderson, *The Lancashire Cotton Famine* pp. 61–8; Augar, 'The cotton famine', pp. 162–3; PP 1866 (LXI) Report of Robert Rawlinson, Government Engineer to C. P. Villiers, 12 January 1866.
44 Augar, 'The Cotton Famine', p. 131.
45 *Ibid.*, p. 134.
46 Lancashire Record Office (henceforth LRO) PUT/1/27, 30 December 1862.
47 *Preston Herald*, 2 August 1862.
48 *Oldham Times*, 25 October 1862.
49 *Ashton and Stalybridge Reporter*, 2 August 1862.
50 See material cited in Wally Seccombe, 'Patriarchy stabilized: the construction of the male breadwinner wage norm in nineteenth-century Britain', *Social History*, 11 (1986), pp. 53–76; Sonya O. Rose, 'Gender at work: sex, class and industrial capitalism', *History Workshop Journal*, 21 (1986), pp. 113–31.
51 Herbert E. Perry, *A Century of Liberal Religion and Philanthropy in Manchester: A History of the Manchester Domestic Mission Society, 1833–1933*, Manchester, 1933, p. 13.
52 PP 1864 (XXII), 31 October 1864, 68.
53 MCR M294/1/1/6, 24 July 1862; Central Executive Committee Manual for the Guidance of Local Relief, Appendix in Arnold, *The History of the Cotton Famine*, p. 551; LRO PUT/1/26, 5 August 1862.
54 Central Executive Committee Report for Cotton Famine Relief, MCR P3339, Appendix, 23 February 1863; Watts, *The Facts of the Cotton Famine*, p. 211.
55 Central Executive Committee Manual, Appendix in Arnold, *The History of the Cotton Famine*, p. 551.
56 MCR Misc. 331, 15 June 1863.
57 MCR M294/1/1/6, 30 July 1863.
58 *The Times*, 5 August 1862.
59 Central Executive Committee Report, 30 September 1862, p. 3.
60 *Ibid.*
61 *Ibid.*
62 LRO PUT/1/26, 5 August 1862.
63 MCR M294/1/1/6, 16 April 1863.
64 MCR M294/1/1/6, 14 August 1862.
65 Edwin Waugh, *Home Life of the Lancashire Factory Folk During the Cotton Famine*, London, 1867, p. 139.
66 PP 1864 (XXII), 31 October 1863.
67 *The Times*, 10 September 1863.
68 *Ibid.*
69 LRO PUT/1/27, 9 December 1862; PUT/1/28, 21 April 1863; PUT/1/27, 30 September 1862.

70   The following section is all drawn from an analysis of material contained in tabular form at the end of MCR M294/1/1/6. For full details see Clare Evans, 'The separation of work and home? The case of the Lancashire textile industry, c1830–1865', Ph.D. thesis, University of Manchester, in progress.

71   Angela Coyle, *Redundant Women*, London, 1984; Jenny Popay, 'Women, the family and unemployment', in Paul Close and Rosemary Collins (eds.), *Family and Economy in Modern Society*, London, 1985, pp. 174–91.

72   See Anne Summers, 'Pride and prejudice: ladies and nurses in the Crimean War', *History Workshop Journal*, 16 (1983), pp. 33–56.

73   Clifford Geertz, *The Interpretation of Cultures*, London, 1975, p. 207.

74   Munro, 'Our unemployed females', p. 30.

75   *Ibid.*, p. 31.

76   Barlee, *A Visit to Lancashire*, pp. 141–2.

77   Patrick Joyce, *Work, Society and Politics: The Culture of the Factory in Later Victorian England*, Brighton, 1980; MCR M294/1/1/6, 26 February 1863; 3 December 1863.

78   Mica Nava, 'Youth service provision, social order and the question of girls', in Angela McRobbie and Mica Nava (eds.), *Gender and Generation*, London, 1984, pp. 14–15.

79   LRO PUH/1/7, 17 January 1862.

80   Redgrave, PP 1864 (XXII), 31 October 1863, p. 68.

81   Barlee, *A Visit to Lancashire*, p. 25.

82   R. Parker, *The Subversive Stitch: Embroidery and the Making of the Feminine*, London, 1984.

83   PP 1864 (XXII), 31 October 1863, p. 129.

84   MCR M294/1/1/6, 21 July 1864; 31 March 1864; 15 May 1864, Garden Lane school closes; PUT/1/28, 3 May 1864; 26 April 1864.

85   Watts, *The Facts of the Cotton Famine*, pp. 351, 205.

86   PP 1864 (XXII), 31 October 1863, p. 129.

87   Perry, *A Century of Liberal Religion and Philanthropy in Manchester*, p. 48; E. Roberts, *A Woman's Place: An Oral History of Working-class Women, 1890–1940*, Oxford, 1984, pp. 30–1.

Chapter Eleven

The hidden economy of dockland families: Liverpool in the 1930s

PAT AYERS

The related issues of working-class income and standards of living have stimulated considerable interest and debate. Among economic historians, discussion has largely centred around the effects of industrialisation on living standards. Quantitative judgements by historians generally begin with time series of rates of normal or full-time pay and then use cost-of-living indices to deflate the earning series, thus revealing real wage trends.[1] Some studies of the quantitative kind do try to allow for such things as women's earnings and unemployment rates.[2] Other studies deal, in a descriptive way, with the qualitative aspects of life which might well have augmented or offset changes in real wages.[3] What both leave out is the interface between the formal economy and the web of interpersonal community and familial relationships which comprises an important dimension of how people earned, spent and stretched out what were often highly irregular and insubstantial incomes, to cover the day-to-day needs of living. They omit also the efforts of the 'sub-penny capitalists'[4] to earn extra income in the unrecorded economy.

What all the studies by contemporaries[5] and historians have in common is that they take the wage-rate of adult males as their starting-point. This approach is inadequate: first, because it assumes that what is earned is what is available for family expenditure and secondly, because it fails to take account of other sources of family income which were often more important in determining whether or not a family was in poverty. We know from the work of Ross, Roberts and Tebbutt,[6] the crucial importance to many working-class families of women's networks and survival strategies and access to credit. Their findings have shown that analyses of working-class living standards and the family economy which are based only on formal, measurable income and expenditure can be misleading. It has become increasingly clear that there is a lot more to the hidden economy of working-class families than is sometimes indicated by traditional approaches and assumptions: a salutary lesson at a time when model-building and testing of the formal economy only is so fashionable in economic analyses. For the inter-war period, for example, Benjamin and Kochin have asserted that the rate of unemployment in England was positively correlated with real increases in unemployment benefit.[7] Apart from the various technical criticisms which their work has invoked (and especially their failure to consider regional as opposed to what may be quite spurious relationships at national level)[8] the whole approach totally ignores supplementary incomes, which may have been important enough to iron out more formally measured movements of wages and unemployment benefits.

This 'evening out' of income was made up of a highly complex set of variables which differed across time, between geographical locations, within the dockland communities themselves, and according to the relationship of individuals to the local labour-market. Recent attempts to measure economic activity in the so-called 'black economy' have concluded that many people who are recorded as being unemployed are in reality working.[9] This would seem to substantiate the findings of Benjamin and Kochin. Clearly the accuracy of assertions of this sort has crucial implications for the development of political strategies directed towards those registered as unemployed and to the distribution of welfare benefits. If, as I argue, supplementary income is a very important element in working-class household economy, then it is equally important to identify just who has access to it.

Size and security of income are the main economic concerns of families. Income provides the boundaries within which a family can maintain itself and by which economic status is measured. To state this is to state the obvious. Often, though, considerations of family income place a central emphasis on actual cash brought into a household, be this from wages or state benefits. Even more frequently, the emphasis is on the earnings of the head of the family, who is generally assumed to be a man. Definitions of what comprises income do sometimes include non-monetary contributions and job 'perks', for example, cheap coal for miners or, especially in rural communities, produce grown for a family's own use. But usually, when income is discussed, it is the money income of the family which is the main concern. Although the single most important element in family income might well be the wage, or in the absence of this, dole or poor relief, for the purpose of this chapter, the definition of family income is much wider. It includes all sources of money that are contributed to the family housekeeping purse over and above the main source and all those goods and services which would have to be paid for from the family purse, if not available from other sources.

For the inter-war period quite detailed wage series do exist and, in addition contemporary local information about rates of pay is available.[10] However, knowledge of rates of pay does not necessarily tell us a lot about what earned income actually was, particularly within a port economy such as Liverpool. The Merseyside Social Survey showed, in 1932, that almost 60 per cent of the insured population were working in notoriously unreliable employment sectors which were particularly subject to casual and seasonal unemployment.[11] Earnings could be erratic and unpredictable and casual labour, mainly associated with the docks, brought particular problems. Dock workers and their families were forced to develop strategies for counterbalancing irregularity of income, as shown below.

Access to supplementary money income is dependent on a number of factors: most important among these are the ability of the chief wage-earner to earn money from sources outside his or her regular employment; the availability of formal and informal paid work for women and children; the type of paid work regarded as 'suitable' for married women, and the stage in the life cycle the family has reached.

Men and supplementary income

Perhaps the best documented and most immediately identifiable way in which men involved in dock work supplemented and regularised their wages was by use of the 'three on the hook, three on the book' system. There was an increasing outcry about this system throughout the 1930s, most visibly in the editorial and letters columns of newspapers, where charges against 'professional wranglers' who used the continuity rules to 'rob the insurance fund' were rife. In 1920, because of the difficulties of dock employment associated with such events as ships being delayed by bad weather, the Ministry of Labour had introduced a scheme whereby the men who could not get work on the first or second half of each day could sign for unemployment benefit. In order to qualify for benefit from the first day, however, a man had to be unemployed for three days in any consecutive six days. Thus, because a man was seldom guaranteed a complete week's work the following week, even when work was available for a full week, he was unlikely to work for more than three days so that his continuity qualification did not run out. Clearly, for those men able to gain employment reasonably regularly this was a way of regularising their income. The system did lend itself to abuse as many commentators were quick to point out. However, this 'working the system' was a perfectly rational strategy for regularising income on the part of those able to participate. It is important to point out also, that the continuity rules could and frequently did work in the opposite direction, for example, for those at the bottom end of the casual ladder, a man obtaining half-day jobs on four separate days each week and earning very little would not be entitled to unemployment benefit.[12] This desire to regularise incomes is an important feature of supplementary income and other survival strategies of working-class families, as we shall see.

Other men, though, found ways of actually earning extra cash. One man, a builder's labourer, told me that in the 1920s, when his children were young:

> I had a barrow, not a proper one you understand, more a box on wheels, but I could load it up with brushes and lime and a tub and I'd push it up to Old Swan or Tuebrook or Walton and whitewash back yards for 2/6 all told. As the lad got bigger I'd take him with me to help.[13]

Another man, a warehouseman, worked on Sundays and summer bank holidays selling ice-cream. The ice-cream manufacturer had push-bikes with boxes on the front which were lined with blocks of ice and filled with boxes of ice-cream. Then the casual workers employed by him would peddle them to places where people would go to walk or picnic, on the outskirts of the city;

> I generally made for what's now the other end of Townsend Lane, although I do know of a feller who used to go all the way up to Halewood where the charas used to park up. The main problem was selling it before it got too soft, although the containers were well insulated. You were paid for what you *ought* to have sold, you see, regardless of any slops.[14]

However, the chance of underemployed dock workers obtaining paid work in any of the other casual trades was severely limited by the need to sign on twice daily.

Most domestic property was rented so work might well be obtained by undertaking minor repairs. Landlords generally were reluctant to go to the expense of employing a regular firm to maintain houses and often wanted 'patching' rather than full-scale repair. It is worth noting that 'foreigners' of this sort did not always involve an exchange of cash, sometimes they were undertaken on a 'job-for-job' basis.[15]

Almost every street in dockland Liverpool had a bookie's runner:

> There were a couple of street bookmakers ... one of the local ones had runners all over the place. These were fellows who were on the dole and trying to make a few bob to keep their family going. We had one in our street ... he operated in the back entry because it was all illegal in those days ... What the runner used to do was to take all the bets up to the bookie before the race had started ... and then collect the pay-list from the bookmakers, once he had the results in at the end of the day and see to the pay-out.[16]

It was largely unemployed men who acted as street runners, but equally important to the bookmaker were the men who worked in the factories, stables and warehouses and on the docks, who acted as his representatives.

One man, employed in a local gas works just prior to the Second World War, described how he took 'trade' from the existing runner because he never accepted a share of the winnings from those he paid out: 'I wouldn't take a back hander. I said "No, I get commission that will do me fine" ...I used to take fifty to sixty pound a day.'[17] His commission on this was 1s 6d (7½p) in the pound. Workplace runners had the advantage also of being able to accept bets on credit because they were on site on pay-day to receive settlement of debts. For the same reason, men who made a business of lending money to work-mates, were also very well placed to ensure repayment.

Supplementary income was seldom as regular as in the above cases, however. Many families did receive additional money income, but it is important to point out that these types of 'supplements' were seldom integral parts of the household economy. Usually 'foreigners' would be taken on when available, although perhaps more eagerly sought in times of particular hardship. Income of this sort was always highly irregular and unreliable. The main problem with access to work of this kind was that it became relatively more important to individuals when competition for additional sources of family income was most intense.

Any attempt to assess the value to the family economy of supplementary income earned by husbands is problematic, primarily because it is by no means clear that this money was put 'in the kitty'. As noted above, the destiny of the male wage is one of the difficulties to be taken into account when using it as a criterion by which to measure family income. In Liverpool, on the face of it, husbands seem to have been quite generous with their household contributions. Most of the people interviewed say that, in their house, the man gave his wage to his wife and was given a certain amount back as pocket money. As one woman told me: 'The wages always went to mother to sort out. She'd see to father's cigarettes and then he'd have some money back for a drink and a bet.'[18] Closer questioning, however, reveals that overtime, tips or any extras earned were considered to be the husband's.

A man, then in this twenties, got a job as a cab driver in 1928:

> I worked for him for about nine years but the business was then going rapidly downhill, although we had cars by then but not very reliable ones like today. I think of that as a wasted period of my life. It was every bit as bad then as it is now, in fact, in many ways it was worse. Still at least I was earning and I could make tips.[19]

I asked him if he was able to keep his tips for himself. He said he could and that this meant he could go for a drink or play a game of cards with the other drivers.

Those men who did not give up their whole wage to their wives

275

generally set aside a set amount each week as housekeeping. One man was proud of his marital record as regards money:

> In all the years we were married, we never had an argument over money. If I had a good week or if I had a bad week, it was all the same to her. She always got her money *and* I never asked her what she did with it. I often went short but her money was always on the table.[20]

This man was a bricklayer. His work was subject to seasonal fluctuations but he was mainly employed by one contracting firm. In winter he might be lucky to get two days work, but in summer he worked reasonably regularly and often from early morning until late evening. His earnings varied between 15s (75p) and £3.00. Housekeeping money was 22s (£1.10) when he earned that much, less when he did not.

A woman, whose husband was unemployed in 1932, explained to me the difficulties of managing on the dole, '... like a tunnel with no light at the end.' Her husband was able to earn some money as a casual worker at the fruit market but most of what he was able to make was kept for himself. She explained:

> Father needed to get out of the house but he'd never touch mine or the children's money. The coppers he made on the side meant he could go out for a drink or have a little bet – he'd always share if he had a win – plus there was the club and that.[21]

Here we have an indication of the complexity of the whole subject. Invariably, 'extras' were regarded as the man's to spend as he wished. Even money earned by the unemployed did not necessarily go to the family purse and, where at all possible, men retained some part of dole or poor relief for their own use. On the surface it might seem that these Liverpool men had a very narrow view of their responsibilities; they accepted the role of 'provider', but in most instances this was not at the expense of their pleasures. However, scratch the surface and it is possible to uncover an intricate web of needs, motivations and priorities. For the casual worker, access through social life to information about ships due in or (in the case of building workers) tenders just won or sites or firms taking men on, was crucial. In addition, friendships and contacts had to be maintained to increase the chance of 'someone speaking for you' if jobs came up, be these formal or informal. Dockland labour-markets were very tight and entry from 'outside' was extremely difficult. Access to employment invariably came via family or neighbourhood networks. Also, the occasional drink bought for foremen, gangers and such like might well stand a man in good stead when he was at a stand or work-gate seeking employment. This would seem to reinforce Medick's point that where reciprocity was important in the informal economy, drinking and socialising in the community was a way of consolidating relationships.[22]

In addition, many men paid into Christmas or holiday clubs or tontines. Often these clubs were organised by pub landlords and, even when not, weekly contributions were usually collected and pay-outs made, at the 'local'. These sorts of payments generally came out of the man's pocket money. Many of the people interviewed recalled husbands 'helping out', when asked, with particular items of capital expenditure not affordable from the housekeeping, for example, children's shoes. One man who could earn, on top of his basic wage, significant amounts of commission, which were his to do with as he liked, bought several items of furniture out of it paid for on hire purchase.[23] It was not unusual for men to help out with 'extras', for example, a doctor's bill. However, in general, all items of household expenditure were considered to be the responsibility of the woman. It is clear that in Liverpool during this period, supplementary money income earned by men was not normally available for household expenditure and so was not as directly important to the family perhaps as 'extra' money earned by other members. It was not necessarily profligate to dispose of income in socialising and gambling, but it does make it very hard to assess the real value of money supplements earned by men or even to assess the real value to family living standards of the male 'breadwinner's' formal earnings.

Married women and family income

During the inter-war period availability of full-time work for women was increasing, most particularly in food-processing, electrical manufacture and for pools firms. But women invariably left full-time paid employment upon marriage.[24] This does not mean that women did no paid work within marriage, only that it became less visible. Where there was room, families would frequently take in lodgers. These might well be strangers but more often were relatives. Arrangements of this sort varied both in organisation and the amount of money they actually brought in. Lodgers would not necessarily have rooms to themselves but shared with members of the family, extra privacy being afforded by means of a curtain strung across a bedroom. The Merseyside Social Survey noted the presence of lodgers in Liverpool homes.[25] The difficulties of obtaining employment during this period meant that few young couples wanting to marry were able to set up house on their own and many, at least initially, lived with one or other sets of parents. It is difficult to generalise about the benefits to the family purse of taking in lodgers. In the case of outsiders, it could be quite profitable, especially if the house were big enough to allow the family to sub-let a whole room. Making room for kin might well have been at exploitative rates:

> Her mother did well out of us. There was us two and the brother-in-law and his wife and we were paying enough almost to cover the rent and you couldn't so much as boil a kettle without putting in a penny for the gas.[26]

But this would seem to have been exceptional:

> Living at the aunty's helped us to get on our feet, like. She was very good to
> us, Uncle Alb never knew the half. She used to say, 'If he ever asks, tell him
> you pay 25/-.' We didn't, but he never asked. When the baby came along she
> wouldn't take any more even with the extra it cost to boil the nappies and such
> like.[27]

It is clean though that any money earned or cost incurred was regarded as
the woman's.

Women could also earn money by cleaning, either for other women
who could pay for help, or in the offices of the shipping companies, insurance
agents and other city businesses. Then, as now, many large companies sub-
contracted cleaning, so even in larger organisations, workers could be casual.
Work of this sort was very hard and usually at exploitative rates of pay but
the margin between 'managing' and 'not managing' a household budget was
often so fine that women would readily take it on. One woman spoken to,
worked in a shipping office about 2½ miles from where she lived:

> Sometimes I'd get a tram but I generally saved that for coming back if I could
> afford it. I had to be in by five-thirty [a.m.]. I carried my own bucket, mop and
> scrubber and cloth and a cloth mat to kneel on. My job was to brush and scrub
> the steps inside and the ones leading into the building, and the entrance hall.
> There was no hot water or anything and we had to use soda. It was murder
> on your hands, especially in winter.[28]

At this time the woman had five children aged between four and twelve.
She would return home for eight a.m., prepare breakfast for her family, see
children out to school, do her housework, prepare her husband's meal, settle
the children to bed and then go out to another cleaning job from eight p.m.
until ten p.m. She did this six days a week and her income from both jobs
was 12s (60p).

Some women took in laundry or minded the children of women who
did go out to work.

> Half-a-crown a bundle she would charge and there'd be all sorts in it, sheets,
> shirts, all sorts. I'd collect it and carry it back when it was done and whoever
> it was would usually give me something to eat or something.[29]

This and most paid work for women outside the home mirrored the unpaid
work women were expected to do inside the home, that is production of use
values − caring, cleaning, working, sewing and so on. One woman, whose
mother did sewing both as a private dressmaker and as an outworker for a
ladies outfitters, recalled:

> She never actually went out to work as regards a nine-to-five job. I don't think
> my father would have allowed that … [But] I remember one time, she used

to mind an old lady all night ... because the old lady used to be too old to look after herself – had help during the day – she used to sit up night after night and never go to bed. Never went to bed during the day when she came in. She used to get on with everything. She did that for a year.[30]

Women also engaged in all manner of homeworking which might be quite a personal task but could involve the labour of the whole family. Sewing was perhaps the most universally utilised form of employment. Many of the tailoring and dressmaking firms of Liverpool employed out-workers. Often these workers were recruited from the ranks of former employees who had married:

> When I got married I took in work. I am a skilled tailoress. I used to make vests at home. I used to collect them from where I worked before I got married. They were already cut out. I'd make them up, line them, buttonhole and press and I used to get 2/6 for each one I finished. I had to supply my own cotton.[31]

Another woman took in sewing for a high-quality dress shop;

> Most of the work was alterations but I made full dresses as well. Sometimes I would go in to collect the work and Mrs. R. would say, 'Well Frances, what about this?' And she'd show me a picture from a magazine that one of her customers had brought in. She'd supply the material and I'd cut out the pattern and make up the dress.[32]

A man described his wife's work:

> I've seen her sit up all night sewing to finish a wedding dress or man's suit because she couldn't work with the children around during the day.[33]

The daughter of another woman recalled:

> My mother would buy, for instance, a coat from a jumble sale. She'd unpick it, wash it, turn it and make a smaller coat from it. And then she'd say 'Go and ask so and so does she want a coat for their Mary for 2/-?' Of course, if they had the money, they'd jump at it, you couldn't tell her re-makes from new.[34]

Other forms of homeworking included box-making, painting tin-soldiers, embroidery, putting hooks on Christmas tree globes and packing them in boxes (which also had to be made up), and making Christmas crackers. If a family owned a sewing machine, less-skilled sewing work could be taken in, such as hemming linen. Making chamois leathers could be done on an outwork basis but might also be an entrepreneurial enterprise of the family. Pieces would be bought by the sack, made up by the family and then sold door-to-door. As in previous centuries, 'putting-out' and 'petty production' remained alternative forms of family enterprise.

Hawking, street selling door-to-door, was quite common although some people undertook it more readily than others. A tradition of flower or fruit selling grew up in some families mainly carried on by women and perpetuated through daughters and other female kin. Money earned might be supplementary income, but in the case of widowed, deserted or un-married women it might well have been the main source of family income – a point I will return to later. Others were less open about their money-raising activities:

> I had a little job, my sister got it me, cleaning these sisters' house in Sefton Park. They were elderly and I went each day for a couple of hours to do out and get messages and things and make them a bit of dinner ... I could do it because it was quite a bit away and I didn't know anyone up there.[35]

I asked her why it was so secret. She said that people roundabout 'knew enough of your business' and her husband would have been angry at the thought of his wife working:

> J. would have gone berserk but I needed it. And you know, the kids knew but, cute enough, they never mentioned it – they knew that they'd be the ones who'd feel it if I had to give it up.

This comment indicates a further complexity when considering the work undertaken by women; certain economic activities were more acceptable than others. Taking in washing was 'respectable', but taking in washing from ships in port was not something many women would readily undertake.[36] The source and amount of supplementary income a wife was able to earn was dependent not only on the burden of her other respon-sibilities or circumstances (for example whether she was a pregnant or a nursing mother or whether she had young children to look after) but also on the desire to maintain pride and respect in her own eyes as well as those of her husband and the members of the wider community within which she lived. Ideas of respectability and maintaining self-respect in terms of being seen as a 'good' wife (primarily synonymous with being a good financial manager) were very important.[37] Despite the reality of everyday life, what comes through most forcibly in discussions with women who ran homes in the period, was the necessity of maintaining a façade of respectability and avoiding the appearance of acute need, wherever possible. But no matter how good a manager a woman might pride herself on being, she could live in permanent dread of potential misfortune. The sickness of a child necessitating a doctor's visit could involve expenditure totally beyond her means, as might the expense associated with confinement. Even if a paid midwife was not called, the loss of earnings from homeworking or other work, even for a short time, could prove disastrous.

Of course, not all families had a male breadwinner. The Merseyside Social Survey found in 1931 that in parts of inner Liverpool nearly one-quarter of families were without an adult male wage-earner.[38] For women

with dependants the situation could be desperate. Employment opportunities were limited and even if work was obtained, women were paid at
a lower level than men. What was supplementary income for one family
was subsistence for another.

> I worked because he'd gone off and so I had to. I took summonses out on him
> but he didn't always turn it up even then, so I had to go out to work.[39]

For seafarer's wives access to some money of their own was crucial.
With men away at sea for long intervals, allotments were often inadequate.
However, the situation of the women might well worsen when her husband
arrived home. Local convention meant that he was expected to 'treat' his
friends and male members of the family. In addition men 'backed out' from
time to time. They would jump ship abroad and come into another port and
not travel back to Liverpool. Usually the first a woman knew of this was
when she went to the shipping office to collect her allotment, to find there
was nothing there for her. The plight of such wives could be desperate.[40]

Even where there was a male wage-earner, cumulatively the income
of other family members might be equally or even more important to family
survival than his individual wage. Additionally in situations where men
were not so generous, women's income, low though it might well have been,
became the family's main support. The woman mentioned above who took
in washing was married to a man who was a ship-breaker. When work was
limited locally he would travel up to Scotland to work, sometimes staying
there for months at a time. His children do not recall him as being a generous
man but he must also have had personal living expenses while working
away. Nevertheless, his son recalls:

> I've seen her waiting for the last post, one o'clock of a Saturday and she'd get
> a registered letter with a pound in it. My sister was working, she was bring-
> ing a few bob in and when the banana boats came in we [he and other local
> children] used to go down and say 'Do you want your bag carrying?' Used to
> carry it to the car and get a tanner or ninepence. And I always used to go home
> and give it to my Mam.[41]

This also illustrates how relevant children's income is in any assessment
of household economy during this period, a point I return to later.

There were other less visible, but nonetheless important, ways
that some women could earn extra cash. Pawn runners were common in
working-class districts,[42] and collecting and selling used clothing was most
frequently done by women, who took still wearable items to the markets
and sold them from heaps piled high on the floor. Money lending was an
activity men engaged in (it was known on the docks), but informal money-
lenders in working-class communities themselves were generally women.
Some made a proper business of it, others combined money-lending with

hawking, others lent small sums to 'oblige' neighbours. There was a huge outcry during this period about the exploitative practices and profiteering of money-lenders.[43] But they seem to have been viewed with ambivalence by the women who used them. Whatever the nature of their business, they were providing a service that many women saw as crucial.

A woman I have spoken to, who prided herself on her ability to manage without incurring debt, made quite a good business of getting 'cheques' in her own name and passing them on to her neighbours for a 'small commission'.[44] These were used to buy goods for personal use, to pawn or to resell. Similarly women could organise numbers clubs within their streets or neighbourhoods to earn some money or goods.[45] Other ventures were illegal, sometimes landing women in court, for instance organising raffles. Tickets were sold up and down the street for new items bought with cheques or on credit from the 'tally man'.[46]

Examples are selective and clearly give only snapshot views of individual circumstances at a particular moment in time. Nevertheless, they are representative of the resourcefulness of Liverpool women during the period. A woman who brought up a young family in the Dingle area during the 1920s and 1930s told me:

> There weren't many who didn't do something on the side, you couldn't have managed without. My husband was good – he never laid a finger on me – but you still couldn't rely on the money always, you had to have that bit of your own to fall back on.[47]

Another woman said:

> I used to be ashamed of having to do some of the things I did – even now I wouldn't like my family to know – but there was nothing else for it, everyone was in the same boat, I know I couldn't have managed without.[48]

Family income and children

As we have seen above, in terms of 'making ends meet' even quite young children were able to help out. Most of the people interviewed spoke of the small amounts of money that children could earn and its destiny: 'If you run a message for someone in the street you'd usually get a penny, but you knew when you went that it was for the gas and not to spend.'[49]

Another recalled:

> Saturday mornings, we'd go round the street and knock to see if anyone wanted us to take their accumulators to be charged. We'd put them in the pram and wheel them up to the shop where the man would do them … when we took them back, we'd get a penny for each one.

I suggested that this might have been quite profitable:

Not really, most people who weren't on the Parish had a wireless but then all the kids knew about Saturday mornings and so they'd all want to go. So, usually, we'd end up doing it between us, a whole group of us, helping to push the pram and lift it out, you know. [laughing] So, unless it was raining, we'd be lucky to get 2d each.[50]

Other sorts of child labour mentioned include helping at stables, being a look-out for games of pitch and toss or for the bookies, taking things to the pawn shop, scrubbing steps and fronts and child-minding. Invariably, though, what children earned ended up in the communal purse. It seems to have been universally recognised that pennies went into the gas and anything more to mother, although in return children might, if lucky, get enough jam jars to get them into the Saturday matinees at the local picture house. Much of this sort of income was spontaneous but some children, such as cleaners, shop assistants, delivery boys and girls, newspaper seller, and so on, could bring in regular sums of money. Either way it was relevent in terms of family income, as little seems to have been held back. It is particularly interesting in the case of children's income that it was not usually regarded as their own to spend. The same is true of adolescents who left school and found employment. A woman, whose brothers worked for their father, remembered that they received no actual wages at all. Their father was a building contractor and was paid in lump sums on completion of the job:

They never received any wages for working. Mother used to hand out money for extras ... they didn't go drinking in those days and they didn't smoke to the extent that they did now and if they did, it was only 2d or 3d. for a packet of cigarettes. But they never grumbled at the fact that they didn't have any wages ... It was all just coming into the household.[51]

Clearly this extreme was exceptional, but it was usual for money earned, even in formal work situations, to be handed to the mother, the worker being given some back as pocket-money. The woman who spoke of her brothers' situation, herself worked in a small dress shop. She earned 7s 6d a week and was given 6d back to pay off the bike she needed to travel to work on and for delivering orders.[52] This perhaps calls into question some of the assumptions drawn from the work done on the nineteenth century, which notes the earlier earning potential of working-class children and concludes this meant that they could achieve emancipation from parental control at an earlier age than children of previous periods. As late as the 1930s in Liverpool young people were still handing their income over to be pooled. It seems that it was only when children became engaged or in the case of boys, went into the army (and not *always* then), that children were given some autonomy in deciding how to spend or save their money.

The importance of income earned by children and young adults is closely linked to the stage in the family life cycle that a particular family had reached. As noted above, the expense associated with having and rearing children, created pressures on household income, when for those same reasons access to supplementary women's income was most limited.

Less-visible income

More unpredictable than the income discussed above and markedly less visible were other family supplements. Windfall gains might come from a variety of sources from a lucky find to a win on the horses. Small gifts of money frequently changed hands, most often within extended family networks, but the practice was not uncommon between friends and close neighbours: 'His mother would slip me a shilling or so when she could. I think she knew what it was like with having had a big family herself.'[53]

A wife of a dock worker told me:

> If he had a good week in, then I'd be able to let Lily (her close friend who lived in the same street) have a couple of bob.

I asked her if this was a loan, she said:

> Oh no, she'd do the same if she could, we helped each other out. Like when her eldest started work ... and I had the baby, she'd sometimes buy a vest or something, when she could.[54]

At times of particular need someone would organise a street collection for a family. This was usual when there was a death and sometimes if the breadwinner had an accident which prevented him or her from working. As in less industrialised societies, reciprocity, redistribution, exchange and mutual aid were integral parts of kin and community relationships during this period. Kin and community networks were not necessarily separate entities existing in isolation from each other. They frequently merged and overlapped in situations where young couples set up homes in the same streets and districts as parents, sisters and aunts. Because of the way in which information about vacant houses was passed on and the desire on the part of the landlords to get reliable references for potential tenants, existing tenants would 'speak' for relatives. Neighbours were often related by blood or by marriage.

Supplementary family income was not always actual cash; the family economy could be bolstered by getting free goods or services which would otherwise need to be bought. Food is perhaps the most readily identifiable necessity that falls into this category. Although 'growing your own' is more usually seen as a rural occupation, many city dwellers prided themselves on their allotments, the work and produce of which might be shared by more than one family. Some families kept chickens but this was not normally very popular with neighbours. More common was pigeon-keeping. Many of the tiny yards in the dockland areas contained a pigeon loft and, although most of the women who were married to pigeon fanciers begrudged the time given to the birds, they did find some compensation in the pigeon pies they were able to make, from time to time.

Summer excursions to the countryside to pick blackberries could ensure jam for the winter. Poaching is usually associated with rural economies, but Lord Sefton's estates seem to have been regarded as fair game by Liverpool people. Fishing and collecting shellfish, like mussels, are frequently spoken of. Family clothing was made at home by those able to sew, seldom using new materials but re-making clothes bought at jumble sales or clothing worn out by other members of the family:

> We were comparatively well-off to other families living roundabout, as regards shoes and clothing. With my mother sewing we looked nice, she even used to make the trousers ... We seldom went to a shop to buy anything; jumble sales, coats turned inside out, all the pieces washed, re-sewn, re-made and very, very seldom bought *anything* new from the shops.[55]

One man and his wife spent many hours making toys (his of wood and her's sewn) to give to their children at Christmas.[56] Shoes were cobbled at home: 'He used to get the last on the floor and sole and heel them. And when we got new shoes, he used to stick rubber soles on the top [laughing] which made it impossible to walk.'[57]

Some children qualified for police clothes. Local policemen could recommend certain families in particular need, and the children would be given corduroy jackets and pants and boots. This clothing is remembered as having a very strong smell and being marked so that it could not be pawned. Even within areas where poverty was endemic, the wearing of this clothing carried a stigma. It was accepted very reluctantly and only by the desperate.[58]

Rag rugs were made from scraps of material that were no use for anything else. But perhaps the clearest evidence to support the phrase, 'nothing was wasted', was most dramatically seen in the Garston area of the city. Here, people would deposit urine, from overnight use of chamber pots, in containers outside their back doors each morning. The 'lint' man from the copper works would collect it each day and at the weekend he would distribute payment, in the form of a packet of tea. The urine was used in the processing of the copper.

Fuel was a major item of expenditure and relatively more expensive when it was only possible to buy small amounts at a time, so it is not surprising that little, in this respect, was wasted. Anything that could be burnt was burnt; old shoes, bones, potato peelings, anything considered rubbish: 'All the bin men ever emptied from our bin, was cinders.'[59] Fuel collecting was a chore most children were familiar with: 'She'd say, ''get out from under my feet and get some boxes'', we'd go up to Greaty and get the empty boxes that were round, to chop up for wood.'[60] Another person said: 'Every night after school it was the same – putting your head in the shops to ask if they had any empty boxes.'[61] Children in the Athol Street area of the city had access to their own coke supplies, which they would steal from the backs of the stream of wagons which daily left the gas works.

Most streets had a woman who 'did' for them. As in previous centuries, women did sub-professional work, the professional side of which had been taken over, from the seventeenth century or so, by men. These were generally older women, who advised and sometimes treated when people were ill, assisted at births, laid out the dead and were available to help at other times of crisis. Using the services of women in this way could save a family quite a lot of money.

> Grandma Peg did for our street. She delivered all the babies, *all* of them – she even delivered me! ... She'd wash the bodies as well, if anyone died, and lend the sheets [to partition off a corner of the room behind which the corpse would lie] ... If one of the kids had a rash or something the mother would bring in Grandma to have a look and she'd tell them what it was.[62]

Theft, of course, is one of the more obvious ways of getting things without paying for them. Few families would, it seems, refuse to buy or receive as gifts something that, sometimes quite literally, 'fell off the back of a lorry'.[63] As kids we'd run behind the wagons, climb up and split the bags. Then, as it went along, we'd be running behind, collecting the sugar, or whatever, in our skirts' [laughing].[64]

In the case of theft by adults, those fortunate to be in work had a distinct advantage over those who were unemployed. Theft from workplaces was largely regarded as a justifiable entitlement.[65] Pilferage and even large-scale theft from work was not regarded as something to be ashamed of. Almost everyone interviewed had his or her own tale of particularly notable events of this sort. Even local policemen generally recognised the validity of workers' claims to a limited share of what they produced or were handling. Dock police, in particular, would 'look the other way' for a share of the goods or, out of sympathy, 'not see' things that were taken from the docks. As one ex-policeman remembers:

> If, say, a docker had back-heeled a tin of salmon or something into his pocket, you'd let him through because you knew it was for the family to eat. If he had ten tins of salmon, then they would probably end up being sold and you'd pull him up.[66]

Certain dock workers, though, were not adverse to taking advantage of such attitudes. One woman remembers how her mother, a dock canteen worker, brought home numerous tins of paint by telling the dock police that the tins contained soup 'for the children'.[67] Like so many elements of family income, it is not possible to measure the regularity, extent or monetary value of such supplements. However, lack of measurability alone is insufficient reason for ignoring such vital elements of family subsistence.

The implications of this investigation are immense, not just in terms of extending the standard-of-living debate, but also in helping to build a critique of current neo-classical methods in economics. As noted above, the starting point in attempts to quantify trends in working-class standards of life has been the wage-rates of adult men. There are problems with this because, even when known (and this itself is problematic within a port economy) such knowledge tells us nothing about its distribution. None of the families interviewed depended wholly on adult male monetary income for survival during the inter-war period and few depended totally on the formal income of the family group. Furthermore, formal and informal income should not be viewed in isolation, as working-class patterns of expenditure are equally complex. The working-class family economy consisted of monetary and non-monetary, personal and impersonal, formal and informal, legal and illegal elements.

In Liverpool, in the time between the wars, the difficulties associated with unemployment and casual labour meant that the need to earn a 'bit on the side' often became crucial at a time when more people were in competition to do so. However, there is little evidence to indicate that the strategies described were born out of the severities of the depression. It is suggested that they were, and are, permanently embedded in a port economy but become more visible and necessary at times of particular hardship, such as in the 1920s and 1930s (and indeed today). However, because of the greater opportunity afforded by contact with other paid workers, access to information, the potential to 'top up' income by theft, bonus or tips, it is the fully employed rather than the underemployed or unemployed, who have the greatest possibility to supplement their incomes.[68] Of course the distribution of these 'extras' is another question and one for which there is no space here to follow through. Some proportion of the supplementary income of the employed undoubtedly found its way into the wider community and to those without work. As I said at the beginning, the whole area of family income and expenditure is extremely complex.

Karl Polanyi and others have attested that the formalist assumptions of neo-classical economics can provide little assistance in explaining behaviour in pre-industrial economies, but are relevant to an understanding of advanced market economies.[69] It is argued here that the interrelatedness of economic and 'non-economic' variables remained a crucial part of life well after industrialisation, although undeniably this is more visible at times of economic crisis, such as depression in the formal economy, or when we look at existing evidence using a different perspective. At best, it is inadequate to assume that real income is merely the purchasing power of the money wage. With the limited data available estimates of true family income and its purchasing power must cover a wide range of factors. This conclusion has important implications for economic historians and economists who take formalist, neo-classical assumptions as their starting-point. Perhaps the reason that models of the current British economy have such a poor prediction record is that they are far too removed from people.

Notes

Taped interviews have been conducted between 1981 and 1987 for an on-going study of the income and expenditure of working-class families, in dockland Liverpool, between the wars. References marked Docklands History Project (DHP) relate to interviews conducted in 1987–88 while working as a research assistant at the University of Liverpool.

1 See, for example, M. W. Flinn, 'Trends in real wages', *Economic History Review*, 3 (1974), pp. 395–413; T. S. Ashton, 'The standard life of the workers in England', in A. J. Taylor (ed.), *The Standard of Living in Britain in the Industrial Revolution*, London, 1975.

2 P. H. Lindert and J. G. Williamson, 'English workers' living standards during the Industrial Revolution: a new look', *Economic History Review*, 1 (1983), pp. 1–25.

3 E. P. Thompson, *The Making of the English Working Class*, Harmondsworth, 1968: F. Engels, *The Condition of the Working Class in England*, St Albans, 1974 edn.

4 John Benson, *The Penny Capitalists: A Study of Nineteenth Century Working-Class Entrepreneurs*, London, 1983.

5 See, for example, C. Booth, *Life and Labour*, London, 1892; S. Rowntree, *Poverty: A Study of Town Life*, London, 1902; D. Caradog Jones (ed.), *Social Survey of Merseyside*, Liverpool, 1934.

6 E. Roberts, 'Working-class standards of living in Barrow and Lancaster 1890–1914', *Economic History Review*, 30 (1977), pp. 306–14; E. Ross, 'Survival networks: women's neighbourhood sharing in London before World War I', *History Workshop Journal* 15 (1983), pp. 4–27; M. Tebbutt, *Making Ends Meet: Pawnbroking and Working-Class Credit*, Leicester, 1983.

7 D. K. Benjamin and L. A. Kochin, 'Searching for an explanation of unemployment in inter-war Britain', *Journal of Political Economy*, 3 (1979), pp. 441–78.

8 For critiques of the Benjamin and Kochin thesis, see papers by P. Ormerod and D. Worswick; D. Metcalf, S. Nickell and N. Floros; M. Collins; R. Cross, in *Journal of Political Economy*, 2 (1982), pp. 369–409.

9 K. G. P. Matthews, 'National income and the black economy', *Economic Affairs*, 3 (1983), pp. 261–7. K. G. P. Matthews and A. Rastogi, 'Little Mo and the moon-lighters: another look at the black economy', *Quarterly Economic Bulletin*, 6 (1985), pp. 21–4.

10 Jones (ed.), *Social Survey*, II, pp. 25–207; Ministry of Labour, *Standard Time Rates of Wages and Hours of Labour of Great Britain and Northern Ireland at 31 August 1929*, HMSO, London, 1929; F. G. Hanham, *Report of Enquiry into Casual Labour in the Merseyside Area*, Liverpool, 1930.

11 Almost half the insured population were involved in shipping and 9 per cent in building: Jones (ed.), *Social Survey*, II, p. 2.

12 Hanham, *Report*, pp. 88–9.

13 Interview No. 6. Male, born 1901. These districts were between one and three miles from where he lived.

14 Interview No. 33. Male, born 1898. Townsend Lane was about 2 miles from the ice-cream factory, Halewood about 6.

15 For instance, a painter and decorator might well undertake to decorate a house in return for the repair of his roof. This exchange of skills was, and remains, common in working-class districts.

16 Oral evidence, J. Kinsella, July 1986.

17 DHP Interview, G001, April, 1988.

18 Interview No. 11. Female, born 1922.

19 Interview No. 18. Male, born 1909.

20 Interview No. 39. Male, born 1906. In conversation Liverpool men frequently make a virtue of having handed over all financial responsibility to their wives. They present this as a magnanimous act which gives the women power, whilst maintaining the image of men as 'breadwinners'. At the same time, of course, it is the woman's responsibility as a 'good' wife to manage on the money she is given, no matter how unrealistic this might prove to be. See Pat Ayers and Jan Lambertz, 'Marriage relationships, money and domestic violence in working-class Liverpool, 1919–1939'; Jane Lewis, *Labour and Love*, Oxford, 1986. This view conflicts dramatically with the analysis of Carl Chinn, 'Wife beating and women fighting back – oral testimony in Birmingham', paper given to Oral History Society Conference, Bradford, April 1988.

21 Interview No. 27. Female, born 1900.

22 H. Medick, 'Plebian culture and the transition to capitalism' in R. Samuel and G. Stedman Jones (eds.), *Culture, Ideology and Politics*, London, 1982, pp. 84–113.

23 Interview No. 30. Male, born 1905.

24 Women were generally required by employers to leave work upon marriage.

25 Jones (ed.), *Social Survey* II, pp. 193–7.

26 Interview No. 32. Male, born 1907.

27 Interview No. 30. Male, born 1905.

28 Interview No. 7. Female, born 1900. This woman continued cleaning various offices morning and evening until the ill-health of her husband forced her to give the work up in 1979. As a result of the damage done by cold water and washing soda when she was younger, her hands, even now, open into gaping cuts each winter.

29 DHP Interview G003, May 1988.

30 Interview No. 1. Female, born 1922. The woman being 'minded' had a paid domestic help/nurse during the day but was without assistance through the night.

31 Interview No. 41. Female, born 1908. 'Vests' were men's waistcoats.

32 Interview No. 14. Female, born 1896.

33 Interview No. 6. This indicates the fallacy of the common myth that women do homeworking because it 'fits in with the children'!

34 Interview No. 35. Female, born 1920.

35 Interview No. 42. Female, born 1898.

36 This is because to go on board ship was to risk being equated with 'ship women' or prostitutes. Ideas about what was 'respectable' varied from district to district, street to street and even from family to family. Women who *did* do ship's washing or who worked as cleaners on ships often did so in family or street 'gangs'. See Second Chance to Learn, *Women Dockworkers*, Liverpool, September 1987.

37 This created great pressures on relationships between husbands and wives. For a discussion of this see Ayers and Lambertz, 'Marriage relationships'.

38 Jones (ed.), *Social Survey*.

39 Interview No. 2. Female, born 1893.

40 See P. Ayers, *The Liverpool Docklands: Life and Work in Athol Street*, Liverpool, 1987.

41 DHP G003.

42 Not all women would feel comfortable about being seen to pawn their belongings. Pawn runners would take bundles to the pawn shop on behalf of other women. They would make a charge for taking them and another for redeeming them.

43 Tebbutt, *Making Ends Meet*, pp. 55–6.

44 Interview No. 41. Female, born 1908.

45 Local shops would encourage women to organise numbers clubs around the sorts of goods they sold, crockery, linen etc. One woman would recruit the members, usually 12 or 24, and the women would agree to pay a certain amount into the club each week (usually sixpence or a shilling). The women would then draw numbers; as each of their turns came up they would receive a voucher for the total value of the money subscribed to spend in the shop. The shopkeeper would allow so much in the pound commission to the organiser which she could spend in the shop, or sometimes collect as cash, when all the women had had their turn.

46 Tally men sold goods, door-to-door, on credit, generally at inflated prices.

47 Interview No. 9. Female, born 1908.

48 Interview No. 42.

49 Interview No. 49. Male, born 1927. In certain very poor parts of dockland Liverpool, however, children would have been severely disciplined if they had accepted money for running an errand. They were regarded very much as common property and were expected to do such chores for neighbours for nothing. If they were lucky they might receive a piece of bread or perhaps even cake but were not 'allowed' to accept money even if offered it. This illustrates vividly the difficulty of generalising even within relatively small localities.

50 Interview No. 11.

51 Interview No. 1.

52 Interview No. 1.

53 Interview No. 27. Female, born 1900.

54 Interview No. 15. Female, born 1903.

55 Interview No. 1.

56 Interview No. 11.

57 Interview No. 11.

58 Ayers, *Liverpool Docklands*, p. 22.

59 Interview No. 49.

60 Interview No. 35. 'Greaty' refers to Great Homer Street market.

61 Interview No. 57. Female, born 1908.

62 DHP Interview A062, January 1987. The respondent was not related to the woman. 'Grandma' and 'Granda' were courtesy titles given to most elderly people.

63 Ayers, *Liverpool Docklands*, pp. 13–14.

64 Oral evidence, Peggy Holden (neé Furlong), born 1912.

65 Ayers, *Liverpool Docklands*, pp. 64–6.

66 DHP Interview number A089, September 1987.

67 DHP Interview number A078, June 1987.

68 This conclusion supports the analysis of J. Gershuny who argues that 'households without formal employment' are limited in their ability to engage in 'informal production activities': J. Gershuny, *Social Innovation and the Division of Labour*, Oxford, 1983. R. E. Pahl, in his study of work and community on the Isle of Sheppey, concludes that it is households with money (those, generally speaking, who have paid employment) that are best equipped to participate in work of all sorts. R. E. Pahl, *Divisions of Labour*, Oxford, 1984.

69 K. Polanyi, *The Great Transformation*, Boston, 1957; Marcel Mauss, *The Gift: Forms and Functions of Exchange in Archaic Societies*, London, 1969.

INDEX